NAZIMOVA

NAZIMOVA

A Biography

GAVIN LAMBERT

UNIVERSITY PRESS OF KENTUCKY

Paperback edition published by The University Press of Kentucky

Scholarly publisher for the Commonwealth,
serving Bellarmine University, Berea College, CentreCollege of Kentucky,
Eastern Kentucky University, The Filson Historical Society, Georgetown College,
Kentucky Historical Society, Kentucky State University, Morehead State University,
Murray State University, Northern Kentucky University, Spalding University,
Transylvania University, University of Kentucky, University of Louisville,
and Western Kentucky University.
All rights reserved.

Editorial and Sales Offices: The University Press of Kentucky
663 South Limestone Street, Lexington, Kentucky 40508-4008
www.kentuckypress.com

Reprinted by arrangement with Alfred A. Knopf, an imprint of The Knopf Doubleday Publishing
Group, a division of Penguin Random House LLC

Frontispiece: Photo courtesy of mptvimages.com

Grateful acknowledgment is made to the following for permission to reprint previously published material:

Harcourt Brace & Company: Excerpts from *Shadow and Light: The Life, Friends, and Opinions of Maurice
Sterne,* edited by Charlotte Leon Mayerson, copyright © 1965
by the Estate of Vera Segal Sterne and renewed1993 by Michael Biddle, Charlotte L. Mayerson, and
Harcourt Brace & Company. Reprinted by permission of Harcourt Brace & Company.

Philip Langner: Excerpts from *The Magic Curtain* by Lawrence Langner (New York: Dutton, 1951).
Reprinted by permission of Philip Langner.

Magiclmage Filmbooks: Excerpts from *My Hollywood, When Both of Us Were Young* by Patsy Ruth Miller
and Philip J. Riley, copyright © 1988 by Patsy Ruth Miller. Reprinted by permission of Magiclmage
Filmbooks, Absecon, New Jersey.

Library of Congress Cataloging-in-Publication Data
Lambert, Gavin.
Nazimova : a biography / by Gavin Lambert. — 1st ed.
p.   cm.
Includes bibliographical references and index.
ISBN 0-679-40721-9
I. Nazimova, 1879–1945. 2. Actors—United States—Biography.   I. Title.
PN2287.N29L36   1997 792'.028'092—dc20
[B]   96-36441 CIP

ISBN 978-0-8131-5342-1 (pbk: alk. paper)

This book is printed on acid-free paper meeting
the requirements of the American National Standard
for Permanence in Paper for Printed Library Materials.

∞

Manufactured in the United States of America

Member of the Association
of University Presses

ASSOCIATION
of UNIVERSITY
PRESSES

to Mart Crowley

What happened to Alla Nazimova as a woman, as an actress, as a thinking person who had felt too long and too little valued her own certitude, is matter for biography.

—Djuna Barnes

CONTENTS

NAZIMOVA

I

"She Was Not I"

> I carry about with me a role I am going to play in
> the future, and even when I do not think about it,
> it is with me. It comes before my eyes at all sorts of
> moments, on trains, on my way to the theatre, at
> table, while I'm talking with people, and I cannot
> get it out of my mind. . . . The great joy is not in
> playing a character, but in creating it.
>
> —NAZIMOVA

TO HAVE BEEN FAMOUS FOR FORTY YEARS, then forgotten for fifty, is better than simply being famous for fifteen minutes; but fame as intense and prolonged as Alla Nazimova's is rarely followed by almost total eclipse. Acclaimed as "the new Duse" and the first truly "modern" actress in the American theatre, she became merely "the last of the old world giants" for theatre historians after her death. But as Nazimova herself remarked not long before she died in 1945, "People do not change, but styles and attitudes change," and when books about so-called Broadway and Hollywood lesbians began to appear in the 1990s, styles and attitudes changed again. Nazimova made a minor comeback in the supporting role of godmother of them all—Katharine Cornell, Lynn Fontanne, Eva, Tallulah, Garbo, Marlene—and was also alleged to have seduced sixteen-year-old Mildred Harris, Chaplin's first wife, married off two of her lovers to Rudolph Valentino, paid homage to Oscar Wilde by producing a silent movie of *Salome* with an "all-gay" cast . . . fictions less strange, and less compelling, than the truth of her life in the theatre and the theatre of life.

ON NOVEMBER 12, 1906, when a Russian actress made her first entrance for her first appearance on Broadway in *Hedda Gabler*, the audience saw a small, slight, pale woman of twenty-seven with pitch-black hair and tragic eyes. Nazimova had learned English in five months, and when she spoke the audience heard a lightly accented, finely expressive voice that sometimes faltered over a word. But the actress never lost her hold on the violent, disturbing reality of Ibsen's play. A young man later to become the first major American playwright saw her performance ten times, and it gave Eugene O'Neill, as he said later, "my first conception of a modern theatre."

Equally successful in *A Doll's House* and *The Master Builder* the following year, Nazimova went on tour with her repertory of all three Ibsen plays until 1910 and made a profit of over $5 million for her manager Lee Shubert, who named one of his theatres "Nazimova's 39th Street Theatre" in her honor. No other foreign actress would make such an impact on the American public until Garbo appeared in her first Hollywood movie. But Nazimova was not only a powerfully original dramatic presence. "My ambition is not to make my audience laugh or cry," she remarked soon after the opening of *Hedda Gabler*. "I want to feel that when they go away, I have made them *think*." A subversive idea for the New York theatre of the time, but even more subversive was what Nazimova made her audience think about.

Ibsen's New Woman, hell-bent on independence, protesting the hypocrisy of "respectable" middle-class society and refusing to settle for being "a doll-wife," had come to town. Meanwhile, the Broadway stage was a doll's house for Maude Adams, asking audiences to believe in the sexless Never-Never-Land of *Peter Pan*, and assuring them *What Every Woman Knows:* "Charm is the bloom upon a woman. If you have it, you don't have to have anything else." For Anna Held the theatre was Ziegfeld-Land, where she fluttered her eyelashes and sang "Won't You Come and Play Wiz Me?"; for Ethel Barrymore, a drawing room where she could display her line in majestic flirtation; and for overweight divas like Mrs. Leslie Carter and Olga Nethersole, a pretext to declaim and pose operatically in *Du Barry* and *Mary Magdalene*.

All these stars were personalities first and actresses second. The one exception was Minnie Maddern Fiske, an actress first partly because she lacked personality. Thirteen years older than Nazimova, she married a wealthy newspaper owner, Harrison Grey Fiske, who acquired a New York theatre for her and directed many of her productions. In *Becky Sharp* and *Tess of the D'Urbervilles* Fiske was applauded for her energy, versatility, and brilliant technique, but when she gave the American premiere of *Hedda Gabler* in 1893, she puzzled audiences and critics with a repressed, low-key performance in a high-key drama, and by costuming herself throughout in the kind of long white frilly gown favored by ingénues. Fiske was a "dedicated" actress who seems to have aroused more admiration than excitement. Comparing her style with Nazimova's, one critic neatly summed up the difference: "If the actress you're seeing knows what she's saying but you don't, it's Mrs. Fiske. But if the actress doesn't know what she is saying and you do, it's Alla Nazimova."

No play by Ibsen had lasted more than a month in New York before an actress who was herself a New Woman made Hedda's offstage pistol shot and Nora's slammed door echo across the country for more than three years. But after succeeding on her own terms, Nazimova changed managers and was persuaded to trade Ibsen for a series of kitschy lust-and-revenge melodramas. More sophisticated and exotic than the plays of David Belasco (the Cecil B. De Mille of the 1900s) or Clyde Fitch (specialist in vehicles for an actress to commit suicide, take drugs, discover she's married her half-brother), they earned Nazimova a great deal of money but eroded her prestige. In 1918, she signed a contract with Metro Pictures that made her the highest-paid actress in silent movies. Although she fascinated a new public in Arab, Chinese, and dual roles, she aspired to more independence than Metro was prepared to grant, and in 1922 formed her own company to produce and star in *A Doll's House* and *Salome.*

Both were drastic commercial failures that left Nazimova almost broke, and "The Star Without a Rival," as Metro had originally billed her, was eclipsed by younger rivals—Garbo, Pola Negri, Gloria Swanson. She made a few potboilers at a greatly reduced salary, then sold her house in Hollywood; and in 1928, at the age of forty-nine, reconquered critics and audiences on the New York stage in *The Cherry Orchard.*

The first actress to make Ibsen popular in America now did the same for Chekhov. Nazimova won further acclaim in *A Month in the Country* and *Mourning Becomes Electra* before starring in her own production of *Ghosts* in 1935, by general agreement the finest performance of her career. On tour in St. Louis, it was seen by a young man later to become the second major American playwright. "The first time I wanted to become a playwright," Tennessee Williams remembered years later, "was when I saw Alla Nazimova in *Ghosts*. . . . She was so shatteringly powerful that I couldn't stay in my seat."

By this time other playwrights—Thornton Wilder, Noël Coward, and Clifford Odets—had become passionate followers; and Don Marquis, the New York columnist and author of *archy and mehitabel*, had written a play that he asked his agent to submit to Nazimova. When she refused it, he withdrew the play, because "I can think of no one else to whom, on consideration, I would trust it":

> It needs that quality of *strangeness* which she knows how to give to a thing—which is, indeed, one of the most effective weapons in the armory of her genius. . . . There is never anything commonplace about Nazimova; she can take you with her into the fourth dimension by some inexplicable magic of her own. She has given me moments unequalled in the theatre, and I remember Modjeska and Sarah Bernhardt, too.

The Lunts and Laurette Taylor felt the same way. Rather than risk unfavorable comparison with other actresses, Laurette refused to play classic roles until she created one in the last year of her life, and *The Glass Menagerie* made her a legend. But even though Ibsen's plays shocked her, Laurette was thrilled by Nazimova as Hedda and Nora, and envied her nerve in playing them. Alfred Lunt and Lynn Fontanne, although commercially most successful in light comedy, played more classic roles (in Shakespeare, Chekhov, O'Neill, Dürrenmatt) than is generally remembered. "The great joy of creating a character" that Nazimova had learned as an apprentice at the Moscow Art Theatre, the Lunts learned from Nazimova and applied with equal care to *The Guardsman* and *The Seagull*. They also followed Nazimova in living with their roles "at all sorts of moments," most notably when they began trying out a new approach to a scene on a crowded Boston street, oblivious to the audience they attracted. As the first actress in America to apply Stanislavsky's technique of supervising every detail of a production, casting and directing actors, working closely with set and costume designers, Nazimova passed on another lesson to Lunt and Fontanne. And the tremendous appetite for rehearsal that she acquired from Stanislavsky was a particular inspiration to Lunt as director. Once again, he followed her example so enthusiastically that, on the morning before the final performance of *The Taming of the Shrew*, he called a final rehearsal to correct a few moments that had seemed sloppy the previous night.

A line, not straight but unbroken, runs from Stanislavsky to Nazimova to the Lunts to the Group Theatre to the Actors Studio, which was founded two years after Nazimova died. Although she approved the Group (and was one of its early financial supporters), Nazimova would have applauded her friend Robert Lewis' resignation from the Studio. During the 1930s, she had heard enough about Lee Strasberg's acting classes to know that he distorted Stanislavsky's intentions when he insisted on actors finding the "truth" of a scene by relating it to personal experience; and she had seen enough of Strasberg's productions to note the result: technique and humor in equally short supply.

For Nazimova there could be no work without joy, and no joy without humor. (Sixty years after seeing her last revival of *Hedda,* Ned Rorem still remembered a moment of unexpected comedy, the way Hedda rolled her eyes at her husband's announcement of the subject of his latest book: "Agriculture in medieval Brabant.") But soon after *Ghosts* ended its tour, Nazimova fell seriously ill and feared she might never be strong enough to work in the theatre again. Emerging from a long depression, and broke once more, she moved back to California in 1938, hoping to find work in the movies. No longer a star in Hollywood, she had to test for supporting roles. She landed only a few, none of them substantial, and her final appearance was the briefest of all. As a Polish refugee in *Since You Went Away,* Nazimova had only six minutes onscreen, but they were enough to create an indelible coda to an extraordinary career.

WHEN SHE died, there were many people still living who remembered Nazimova's great performances in the theatre, but the obituary writers were apparently not among them. She took a posthumous curtain call as an early costar of Valentino's, as a featured player in *The Song of Bernadette,* a movie in which she did not appear, and as the actress whose house on Sunset Boulevard became a hotel called The Garden of Allah.

It would not have surprised her. Even before Nazimova became famous she wrote in her diary: "I am vain, and afraid that I'll leave nothing of myself behind when I die, nothing to be remembered by. . . . An actress is dead when the last person to remember her dies! And that's not enough for me!"

Fortunately, when I began researching her life in 1991, quite a few people who remembered Nazimova were still alive. She also survives through impressions left by friends and colleagues among the dead—and, of

course, by the camera. Almost half of her twenty-two movies escaped the
scrap heap, and hundreds of photographs still exist. But the camera preserved Nazimova only in black and white, and although several artists
painted her, the portraits were always of an actress in disguise, made up
and costumed for one of her roles in the theatre.

Unlike the movie actor who plays for the camera, the stage performer
has no continuous present. So visible from first to last night, his art then
becomes invisible forever. No filmed or televised record, and least of all
a portrait or photograph, can convey the special relationship he establishes with a live audience, the signals exchanged in a silent entrance or
exit, the dramatic space opened up by a sudden pause. They can only be
witnessed and experienced at the moment they occur. In her 1906 diary
Nazimova anticipated this too: "Where is Rachel? Adelaida Ristori? Nobody now can make us see them as they really were!"

When I asked people who witnessed *The Cherry Orchard* and *Ghosts*
to tell me how they "saw" Nazimova, and to describe a particular moment or scene, they all agreed that her first entrance as Mrs. Alving was
so drab and subdued that they failed to recognize the elegant Madame
Ranevskaya until they heard her voice. She seems to have made a point
of disappearing physically into a role, and often told the story of a
woman who came to see her in *A Doll's House* on tour, refused to believe
it was the same actress who had played the previous week in *Hedda
Gabler,* and demanded a refund at the box office. Nazimova also described herself as "neither tall nor short, fat or thin, ugly or beautiful. . . .
I am what the part demands of me." And because she transformed her
looks just as often and as radically in life, no photograph ever captured a
definitive likeness, just as no one appears to have seen the same person in
the flesh.

Patsy Ruth Miller, who appeared with her in *Camille* (1921): "Those
incredibly blue eyes! I'll never forget them!"

Irene Sharaff, who began her career as assistant to Aline Bernstein,
costume designer for the 1928 production of *The Cherry Orchard:* "I don't
remember anything special about her eyes, but she had a wonderful nose,
a nose of great character."

Djuna Barnes, who interviewed Nazimova in 1930: "Gorgeous eyes,
winged nostrils and an upper lip to match, made doubly dangerous by a
lower, which for a brief inch in its middle, ran as straight as any Puritan
praying for rain."

Alexander Kirkland, who appeared with her in the 1930 Theatre Guild
production of *A Month in the Country:* "Her face, pale, alert and obser-

vant, had an intellectual cast. . . . Despite her bookish, rehearsal grayness, she was outlined by an aura of enchantment."

Vincent Sherman, who was twenty-six when he acted onstage with Nazimova in *The Good Earth* (1932): "She was in her early fifties by then, but with a girlish body, and sexually very attractive. I could have gone for her."

Mercedes de Acosta, playwright and woman about town, who first met Nazimova in 1916: "In the photographs of *Hedda Gabler* and *Bella Donna* she had worn a long train and I had imagined her as tall. . . . Here before me in flat Russian boots she seemed tiny and more like a naughty little boy."

Frances Dee, who was introduced to Nazimova on the Paramount lot in 1938: "Are you sure she wasn't tall? I know I looked up at her. I suppose it was awe. . . ."

Stanislavsky, who saw Nazimova again after many years when he brought the Moscow Art Theatre to New York in 1923: "She has grown old, but is very sweet."

D. W. Griffith, who first met her in 1907 and saw her again in 1925: "Nazimova is no longer a young woman, but she preserves the appearance. She has taken care to do so. It is her bread and butter, and she must."

On the inner Nazimova, I found far more agreement among her friends, who remembered her as intensely emotional but with a keen sense of humor, proud, generous, and, in a recurrent phrase, "the most intelligent actress I've ever known." The only unsympathetic verdict came from her sole surviving relative, Lucy Olga Lewton, the daughter of Nazimova's elder sister Nina. Ninety years old, a former research chemist living in a retirement home in Ventura, California, Lucy Olga was crippled by arthritis but mentally athletic. She began by warning me to expect trouble "if you write anything about Nazimova of which I don't approve."

I asked Lucy Olga if she had anything specific in mind.

"You told me you'd been through her private papers—which you had no right to do without my permission, because I'm her legal heir." She wasn't, but I let it go. "What she wrote about being sexually abused by her father is *completely untrue*," Lucy Olga said, and gave me no time to ask what made her so sure. She changed the subject by pointing her cane toward an alcove in the living room where a fuzzily painted portrait of Nazimova in a blond wig hung on the wall. "I don't know who the artist was. But he painted it when she was appearing on Broadway in a play called *The Comet*." Below the portrait stood a Chinese-red dressing table. "One of my aunt's favorite pieces, she always took it with her on tour. Most of her furniture she didn't keep very long. She was always changing her decor." Lucy Olga gave a thin smile. "And her friends."

Now the first pause in her monologue occurred, and I asked if she'd ever known Nazimova's father. Lucy Olga shook her head. "But remember, my mother was his daughter too, and she told me that *everything* Nazimova said about him was *completely untrue*." Then she changed the subject again. "I suppose you know that we came to this country at Nazimova's invitation?"

I did, and I knew that "we" referred to Nina Lewton, Lucy Olga, and her brother, Val.

"In 1909, after my father, Maximilien Lewton, died. He was an officer in the British Navy."

He was a research chemist, born in Yalta, and his name was Hofschneider, but I let that go too.

"Nazimova prepaid our tickets—second-class—and we were all very grateful, of course. We stayed ten years at her house in the country outside New York. But I have to say she wasn't easy to live with. . . . So full of promises that she didn't keep, and such an Indian giver, making us presents of furniture and so on, then asking for them back. . . . My mother always forgave Nazimova her faults—in spite of everything, she remained fond of her—but one day my aunt criticized both of us so unfairly that I got angry and wrote her a letter accusing her of being a terrible *intrigante*, a troublemaker. We never spoke again," Lucy Olga said with no apparent surprise or regret. "And did you know that, although Nazimova was Jewish, she tried to cover it up by making anti-Semitic remarks? But it's *not* true she was a lesbian!"

"Really?" was all I said, and all Lucy Olga gave me time to say.

"You know how that rumor started?" she went on, another statement framed as a question to which only Lucy Olga knew the answer. "My aunt became friends with Eva Le Gallienne—who *was* a lesbian, because *she'd* been sexually abused by her father and it turned her against men. . . . But later Le Gallienne accused Nazimova of having designs on her girlfriend—*completely untrue, of course*—and they had a falling out. . . . Although Nazimova had quite a few women friends, they were just a coterie of hangers-on, and she used them to run errands that she was too lazy to do herself. . . . Many famous and wealthy men were interested in her, but she kept almost all of them at arm's length. Isn't that strange? . . . And when Eugene O'Neill offered her *Anna Christie*, she turned him down, saying it wasn't 'exotic' enough for her. . . ."

Then, having apparently forgotten her complaints about Nazimova as an "Indian giver," Lucy Olga mentioned that the Fabergé silver-and-topaz bracelet on her wrist, the Fabergé spoons displayed on a table, and the chair in which I was sitting were all gifts from her aunt. So, of course, were the dressing table and the portrait. And when much of the rest of her information turned out to be inaccurate, I understood Nazimova's comment, in a letter to Nina after a particularly disagreeable scene with sister and niece: "I don't believe in family any more."

ALWAYS AFRAID of being forgotten, Nazimova kept a store of things by which she could be remembered, scrapbooks, diaries, letters, photographs, and playbills. She also left an unfinished autobiography, begun in 1941. Although these documents provide extensive coverage of her childhood and adolescence in Russia and Switzerland, her apprenticeship at the Moscow Art Theatre, her career in New York and Hollywood, the material relating to her personal life after the age of twenty is as elusive (and sometimes as contradictory) as the physical impression she left behind.

Nazimova had a unique range of friends and acquaintances, from Chekhov to Rudolph Valentino, Ellen Terry to Stanislavsky, Eugene O'Neill to Noël Coward, Laurette Taylor to Marlene Dietrich, D. W. Griffith to George Cukor, Emma Goldman to Nancy Reagan, but her letters and diaries refer only briefly to some of them. Between the lines they shed occasional light on her affairs with Eva Le Gallienne, Hollywood cameraman Paul Ivano, actress Jean Acker, and former actress Glesca Marshall, with whom Nazimova lived from 1929 until her death. They also help to unravel her mysterious relationship with Charles Bryant, whom she passed off as her husband from 1912 to 1925; but the autobiography dismisses in a couple of baffling paragraphs the man Nazimova actually married, and left almost immediately, when she was a summer-stock actress in Russia.

All this material Nazimova willed to her longtime companion, Glesca Marshall. A hopeful young actress when they first met, Glesca gave up her career for the woman she loved. Soon after Nazimova's death she began an affair with Emily Woodruff, formerly married to Hume Cronyn and unhappy with her second husband, whom she gave up for Glesca. They rented an apartment in Hollywood for a few years, then moved to Columbus, Georgia, hometown of the Woodruff family, major shareholders in the Coca-Cola Company since the early 1920s. One of the city's finest antebellum buildings is the Springer Opera House, where many stars of the American stage appeared on tour and Oscar Wilde lectured on "The House Beautiful." By 1950, the theatre had fallen into serious neglect, and Glesca persuaded Emily to underwrite not only the work of restoration but the Glesca Marshall Library of Theatre Arts, which now occupies most of the second-floor office space. In spite of its name, the library contains only a few shelves of theatre and movie books. Its heart is the Nazimova room, in which all her papers are faithfully preserved.

The collection includes Nazimova's unfinished autobiography in typescript, a sizable but tantalizing fragment of seven hundred pages. Less a stream than a Niagara Falls of consciousness, it breaks off when she's only seventeen. Glesca took on what she called "the awesome task" of completing it, with the help of scattered notes and drafts of later chapters that she found after Nazimova's death. Wisely, she made no attempt to imitate Nazimova's style, aiming instead to combine "an accurate account" of the rest of her life with a personal memoir. But although Glesca had seen every play and film in which Nazimova appeared from *The Cherry Orchard* to *Since You Went Away,* her own impressions are of the devotional "magnificent, as always" kind. She interviewed only two of Nazimova's colleagues—Harry Ellerbe, who played Oswald in *Ghosts,* and Abe Feder, who lit the production. Many others were alive at the time—Rouben Mamoulian, who directed Nazimova on stage and screen; Vincent Sherman, who worked with her as both actor and director; admiring contemporaries from Lillian Gish to the Lunts—but she never contacted any of them, preferring to fall back on quotes from newspaper and magazine articles.

Most people whom I talked to about Glesca detected shyness behind her emphatically hearty exterior, and felt that her love for Nazimova was always tinged with awe. This may explain her diffident approach to the actress, but not the tone of her personal recollections. After confessing a deep need "to seek to hold a hand no longer there," she keeps the woman at arm's length as well. Shyness and awe are not the problem here. Fueled by an uneasy mixture of devotion and denial, Glesca has decided to play keeper of the flame. In her elected role of trusty confidante and "assistant," she not only dismisses the rumors of Nazimova's affairs with women but alludes to her own "flings on the side," without specifying names or gender. The gesture is too naïve and awkward to conceal the intention behind it.

Since Nazimova never had any children, it was superficially plausible for Glesca to portray herself as a surrogate daughter. If shyness prevented her from approaching Mamoulian or the Lunts, it was the need to sustain a case that made her avoid several friends and former lovers of Nazimova whom she knew fairly well. Interviews with George Cukor and Robert Lewis, or with Mercedes de Acosta, Ivano, and Eva Le Gallienne, posed an obvious risk, and Glesca gave them all a wide berth. Not surprisingly, no publisher expressed interest in her completed task, which she submitted with a rather formidable covering note: "I await your reaction on Nazimova's behalf."

BUT WAS Glesca acting on Nazimova's behalf or her own when she locked them both in the closet? Although the autobiography breaks off too early to provide a definite clue, other evidence suggests that Nazimova never intended to write openly about her sexual identity. Like Glesca, she had strong reasons for covering her tracks, and I suspect they agreed on a conspiracy of silence. In the flamboyant early days of her stardom in silent movies, Nazimova enjoyed dropping hints about her bisexuality, which became one of Hollywood's best unkept secrets; but she later regretted this and did her best to set the record straight.

"Dealing in emotions," she wrote in her autobiography, "seemed to be my destiny," and Nazimova not only made theatre her life but made theatre out of her life. Again perhaps because she was so conscious of posterity, she gave an enormous number of interviews, often mesmerizing for the way she boldly contradicted herself and blurred the line between fact and fiction. When the truth was inconvenient, she denied it. When it lacked drama, she supplied it. But although some of the legends that sprang up about Nazimova were self-created, there were many that she neither invented nor liked. Something like this has happened to many artists, of course, for the self they project is the self they are constantly reshaping and reinventing through their work. And in the case of performing artists, the more completely they assume another self in the characters they play, the greater the risk of being taken over by it. At the Moscow Art Theatre, Stanislavsky taught his students to "lose themselves" in their roles, but he never addressed the problem of how to find themselves again.

Looking back on her life, Nazimova recognized that her talent for self-dramatization was also a curse. "My unableness to keep emotion in control," she wrote in her sometimes scrambled English, "created havoc in my work." Sometimes, she explained, the skill with which she could dominate an audience led her to settle for exhibitionism, the gloriously false effect, and the result was "a constant and exhausting exercise in self-discipline."

The same is true of her unfinished autobiography. Starved for work as an actress when she began it, Nazimova compensated by writing a major role for herself, a long and subjective monologue about her early years, which turned into a one-woman show when she read scenes from it aloud to friends. She never planned to publish it during her lifetime, for she dreaded the explosions of denial that the truth about her family would provoke from her sister and niece, and she always expected (rightly, as it turned out) to die before they did. But the emotional temperature of the text, unrelentingly and exhaustingly high, reflects a need for more than performance. Nazimova was setting out on the road to self-examination, unburdening herself of the secrets she had kept from almost everyone for so long, and in spite of the repetitions, and a tendency to go way over the top, many brave and painful insights emerge. Most of these concern her feelings as an abused and terrorized child, but there are equally startling pages that recall her gradual discovery of a vocation, the almost out-of-body experience of recognizing a second self in Nazimova the actress, the "she who was not I." This figure stalks the wounded child like a shadow of the future, and when it finally catches up with her, plump and gawky Adelaida Leventon is transformed into slim, determined Alla Nazimova, face heavily made up and hair dyed flaming red.

At this point in the story, the storyteller's time begins to run out. She will live to complete only a few sketches of the still-obscure actress at nineteen, one of which describes how she left a rich lover in Moscow to join a provincial repertory company, excited by an offer to play the wounded heroines of *Hedda Gabler, The Seagull,* and Strindberg's *Miss Julie.* When she gets on the train, her lover and the friends left behind suddenly cease to exist, blotted out by characters on a stage where she's already living in her imagination.

Imagination, for as long as Nazimova could remember, had been her surest defense against the real world. Severely beaten when she tried to rebel against her father and the almost grotesque reign of terror that he imposed on his family, Adelaida Leventon withdrew into fantasies of escape. But when escape finally became possible, she could see only two ways of earning her living, in the theatre or on the streets. At that time in Russia no other professions were open to someone of her gender and racial background. Imagination rescued her again by ruling out the streets. Only the theatre could satisfy her ferocious drive for creative release.

When she read *The Brothers Karamazov* at the age of fourteen, Adelaida Leventon felt that her own childhood might have been invented by Dostoevsky. And when Nazimova wrote about it almost fifty years later, she reached a Dostoevskyan conclusion. Outrage at her father's deranged cruelty gives way to forgiveness, and she even thanks him for teaching her to find liberation through despair. Convinced that she could only have risen to the heights after being forced to the depths, Nazimova ends by embracing her father as demon and savior, the "familiar spirit" who haunted her life and created its recurring pattern of abysmal lows and ecstatic peaks.

THIS COMMENT on her father is a rare example of Nazimova stepping back to take the long view. Her autobiography is mainly an up-close account not only of Yakov's brutality but of everything, vital or inconsequential, that she remembered about her early life. A work of total recall is often wearisome to read, yet in this case the lack of selectiveness adds to its value. Nothing has been precensored in these seven hundred pages, the only source material for a past that Nazimova's sister and niece later tried to obscure.

In its frequent digressions, the autobiography may take a few lines to describe every store window on the street in Yalta where Adelaida Leventon lived, or twenty pages to recount the Leventon family's diaspora after its expulsion from medieval Spain. Often occurring out of continuity, they suggest that Nazimova set down thoughts, sensations, and memories as they entered her head. And for the most part they were concerned with her immediate surroundings. She wrote almost nothing about tsarist Russia, the dictatorship beyond the family dictator's home.

Apart from (severely) pruning the material presented by Nazimova, and sometimes reorganizing the narrative to make it more coherent, I have added some historical information about late-nineteenth-century Russia. Much of this deals with anti-Semitism, and clarifies why Yakov took his family into exile in Switzerland for a while, and why Nazimova as a drama student in Moscow was fearful of exposure as a Jew. And occasionally I had to decide when Nazimova's self-confessed habit of self-dramatization veered into fantasy.

Among her posthumous papers is an account of an episode that supposedly occurred soon after she arrived in Moscow to study at the Philharmonic drama school. Two policemen demanded her identity papers, saw the name Leventon, accused her of being a Jew, and ordered her to leave the city at once. But they relented when she promised to renounce her faith and undergo public baptism in the Orthodox church, which involved ducking her head in a font of filthy water. This struck me as improbable when I read it, for Nazimova's passport allowed her as a Jew to travel freely in Russia, and later to leave for Europe and the U.S.A.

A few months later, Patsy Ruth Miller told me an alternative version of the same story, as told to her by Nazimova in 1920. This time renunciation and unpleasant public baptism were done in the name of love, when a Russian aristocrat wanted to marry Nazimova, and his family insisted on a religious conversion so that the wedding could take place in an Orthodox church. Then her lover changed his mind and married someone else. This version struck me as no less unlikely, for, when the aristocrat whom Nazimova actually married insisted on a wedding in an Orthodox chapel, he was able to arrange it with no questions asked.

The autobiography contains a few more anecdotes that read like fantasies of humiliation; but from someone who discovered a source of creativity in suffering, their existence is not really surprising. Like the wife who never gives up hope for a sign of love from her abusive husband, Adelaida persistently imagined a day when Yakov would no longer beat her for being stupid or ugly. She was just as persistently disappointed, and years later Nazimova's fantasies became metaphors for early sorrow. Notably dramatic, as might be expected from an actress, they were also lies that, like art, told the truth.

2

The Deep Shadow
1844–1896

My heart was born in a deep shadow. . . .
—NAZIMOVA

T HE SHADOW WAS CAST BY YAKOV LEVENTON,
of course, and Nazimova's autobiography begins with an account of her
father's early life. Born in 1844, Yakov grew up in the Pale of Settlement,
the southern part of the Ukraine, to which Jews were confined by Russian law. Merchants, artisans, and university graduates could apply for
passports to live elsewhere, but Yakov's father was a miller who never
learned to read or write. He sent his five children to an elementary synagogue school in the nearby small town of Berdery, fifty miles north of
Odessa, then put them to work in the cornfields. They returned every
evening to an unchanging ritual in the dark, airless family hut, cornmeal
mush from the communal bowl and a recitation from the Talmud. Then
their father locked the door and everyone went to sleep among the chickens on an earthen floor covered with straw.

At the age of sixteen, the eldest son suddenly announced that he was
leaving home. For two years Lyev supported himself by tutoring the children of local landowners, studied at night, and saved enough money to

complete his education by graduating in medicine at the University of Kiev. After he became a surgeon at the Imperial Hospital of St. Petersburg, Lyev began putting his brothers and his sister through college. Isaac established himself as a lawyer, Ilya as a farmer; Lysenka finished her medical studies in Geneva, where she too became a surgeon; and finally Yakov, the youngest, graduated in chemistry at the University of Kiev.

Unlike his siblings, Yakov failed to get ahead. He hoped to become a research chemist, but found no openings in Kiev and had to settle for a miserably paid job as a pharmacist's assistant. Early in 1872, he moved to the town of Berdichev, a hundred miles away, to work for a pharmacist who offered slightly less miserable pay and free sleeping quarters in the cellar. Yakov went down there almost every evening after closing time, lit a tallow candle, and worked on his formulas for artificial ice, medicated soap, and a tablet containing enough concentrated food to supply essential nourishment for twenty-four hours.

Obscure and poor at twenty-eight, Yakov was the only person he knew who believed in his future. Convinced that his "inventions" would lead to more than fame and fortune, he dreamed of recognition throughout posterity as one of the great benefactors of the world.

AFTER SEVERAL months in Berdichev, Yakov had found no one who took his ideas seriously, and he carried the additional burden of being a poor Jew. In 1872, pogroms had not yet begun but anti-Semitism was widespread, fomented by church and state. God's representatives in the Orthodox church denounced Jews as heretics, and a nationalist wing of the government, believing that racial impurity threatened to undermine Russia's greatness, denounced them as undesirable aliens. Although wealth protected the middle-class banker and industrialist whatever his ethnic background, the Jew in the street had little hope of making his way up in the world, and was often the target of stones or gobs of spit. But Yakov was lucky in two respects. His university degree allowed him freedom of movement, and he didn't look stereotypical. Pale, with sandy hair and light-blue eyes, he always tried to cut a prosperous figure in public. Two used suits and shirts handed down from his brother in St. Petersburg formed Yakov's basic wardrobe, and he took great care of them. He waxed his mustache, carried gloves, swung his cane like a dandy, and perfumed himself with attar of roses stolen from the pharmacy.

One evening in the late summer of 1872, Yakov dressed with particular care for an evening at the City Club. He would never have been accepted as a member, of course, but the club's charity functions were open to anyone who could afford a ticket. Yakov bought the cheapest available ticket, because he liked the idea of mingling with the rich and successful and imagining himself one of them. It was one of his rare indulgences, for he didn't smoke or drink, and only very occasionally treated himself to a bargain-basement whore.

Lyev Horowitz, the most prominent Jew in Berdichev, was a respected member of the club. A banker, and the owner of a sugar refinery, he bought seven of the most expensive tickets and made an impressive entrance with his entire family, his wife, three sons, and two daughters. Yakov happened to be standing close by and was immediately fascinated by the appetizing plumpness, long black hair, and dark, dreamy, innocent eyes of the younger girl, Sonya. He kept staring at her, and when Sonya finally noticed her admirer, she smiled. Then she pointed him out to her brother Osip, who found something touching about Yakov, so thin and eager in a suit that didn't fit too well. The evening began with an amateur performance of a passion-and-poison melodrama by Schiller; then the buffet opened, and an amateur orchestra struck up music for dancing. Osip went over to Yakov and invited him to join the family for supper. Sonya found him immediately charming and was delighted when he asked her to dance. Only fifteen years old, she had practiced the mazurka with other girls at boarding school, but this was her first dance with a man. Yakov danced well, which made him even more attractive; he spoke fluent French and German, which established him as a man of culture; and when he stopped dancing for a moment, looked deep into her eyes, and quoted lines from a romantic poem by Heinrich Heine, Sonya knew that she loved him too.

A few days later, they managed to meet in secret, and Yakov proposed marriage. Sonya accepted on the spot, but it took several weeks to gain her father's consent. Horowitz suspected Yakov of being a fortune hunter and dismissed, like everyone else, his ideas about artificial ice and medicated soap. He made inquiries in the town and was not pleased to discover that Yakov went with whores. But Sonya's tearful, moonstruck appeals finally wore her father down. Relieved to learn that Yakov, like himself, was a freethinker who never went to the synagogue, Horowitz invited *le tout Berdichev* to a grand, traditionally Russian wedding, with celebrations that lasted three days and nights.

ALL THIS, Nazimova wrote, she learned many years later from Sonya's brother Osip, who was already living in New York when

Nazimova first arrived there in 1905. "Your father was so very shy at first," he said. "But later he loosened up. His ideas for inventions seemed a bit crazy, although now, of course . . . But you know how fascinating he could be when he was feeling happy."

"No," Nazimova said quietly. "That I would not know."

"Such an intelligent fellow, an intellectual . . . He nicknamed your mother Babotchka, butterfly, and he was right. All youth and flutter, and nothing up there . . ."

ON THEIR first night together, Sonya found Yakov a tender and passionate lover. A month later, after he had struck and insulted her several times, she was bewildered but still adoring. Although financially secure on account of the dowry that marriage had brought him, and socially acceptable everywhere for the first time in his life, Yakov had been warped by years of disappointment and failure. Living with Sonya in her parents' house, he felt painfully inferior. He imagined sly allusions to the fact that he was sponging on Sonya's family, and began to humiliate her to compensate for his own humiliations in the past. Whenever Horowitz gave a dinner party, Yakov managed to convince himself that he had seen Sonya flirt with a guest, and in the privacy of their bedroom he called her a whore and slapped her face.

Eventually she confided in Osip, who summoned the family to a conference and suggested a divorce. But Horowitz wouldn't hear of it. He warned Sonya that as a divorced woman she would become a social outcast and embarrass her family. To Osip's astonishment, Sonya not only agreed that divorce was out of the question, but accused her brother of being a troublemaker. "Yakov is just high-strung," she said, then threw herself in her father's arms and with tears in her eyes announced that she was pregnant.

Their first child was a boy, named Vladimir by his father and fondly called Volodya by his sixteen-year-old mother, whose black hair, dark eyes, and gentle nature he inherited. For a while Yakov seemed calmer and happier, but he exploded again when Sonya decided that she was ready to return to the world of parties and dances. A wife's place, he insisted, was in the home. When Sonya pleaded, Yakov called her a bird-brain. When she protested, he called her a whore and slapped her face. When she burst into tears, he left the house.

Later he apologized so touchingly that Sonya forgave him, and their reconciliation produced a second child, Nina. Yakov adored his daughter, who inherited his blond hair and blue eyes, and domestic peace continued its run. Early in 1876, during the third winter of their marriage, Yakov developed a bad cough. The family doctor diagnosed weak lungs and warned him to beware of tuberculosis. Yakov was elated. Illness provided a double alibi, an excuse for his treatment of Sonya in the past, and a reason for them to leave her parents' house and settle somewhere farther south, where the climate was milder.

"A fresh start," he told Sonya. "I'll set myself up in a small pharmacy somewhere and work on my inventions." Still in love and eager to forgive, Sonya thought it a wonderful idea. Horowitz did not. He had a low opinion of Yakov's business sense and foresaw Sonya's dowry thrown away on an enterprise doomed to failure. Undeterred, Yakov wrote for advice to a distant cousin, director of the Imperial Botanical Gardens near Yalta, on the Crimean peninsula. "Even though Yalta is accessible only twice monthly by boat via Odessa," Yakov's cousin wrote back, "its attractions as a health resort are unequalled." The climate was semitropical, like the French Riviera, with occasional rain and fog in winter; Tsar Alexander II had a palace nearby; various grand dukes owned grand estates in the region. . . . It was enough to send Yakov on his way by carriage and boat to look the place over.

He found a sun-dazzled small town on the Black Sea, with a backdrop of mountains, snow on their upper ranges, orchards and vineyards on the lower slopes, mimosa perfuming the air. Clusters of white stucco houses faced the bay, where a breakwater pier stood midway between the beach and the port. Yakov was so overwhelmed that he had to sit down for a while in the park near the center of town. Then he walked along the main street to explore Yalta's business section. Only two blocks long, it contained a fleabag hotel, a bakery, a grocery store, an elementary school, a post office, a pawnshop—but no pharmacy, a stroke of luck that Yakov was hardly able to believe.

In June 1876, he moved his wife and children to a two-story house on an unpaved street behind the post office in Yalta. Stairs led up to the flat roof, which had a view of the whole bay. Yakov converted the first-floor premises into a pharmacy, and lived with his family in three rooms upstairs. The house had no kitchen, bathroom, or toilet, but a patch of land in back contained a privy; and Yakov installed a kitchen and laundry room in a shed occupying one corner of the entrance courtyard, and a steambath in another corner shed. Sonya's dowry also paid for a cook, a maid, a nurse for the children, and a barn just outside the town that became Yakov's laboratory.

Within a few weeks, Sonya decided that Yalta was boring. Her social life was restricted to weekly dinners with Yakov's cousin and his wife, at which the main topic of conversation was either botany or Yakov's latest "inventions," soil analysis and weather bureaus to help farmers. The elite of Yalta—the judge, the chief of police, and a few well-heeled families whose elegant villas Sonya envied, never mixed with the ordinary middle class. The Oriental Bazaar, a holdover from the Tatar and Turkish occupations of the Crimea, was "picturesque," but Sonya fled from its stench of goat cheese and unwashed bodies.

With no City Club to organize dances and amateur theatricals, her fashionable clothes from Paris and Vienna hung unworn in a wardrobe. At first Sonya's only entertainment was to watch life in the street from her second-floor balcony, but one day a funeral procession, with the dead man in an open coffin, passed right outside the house. The idea of death terrified her. She ran inside, closed the shutters, turned to romantic French novelettes, and for a while, like Madame Bovary, consoled herself with dreams of a lover. Then she ran away to Odessa, where she had relatives, but Yakov followed, brought her back, and gave her a savage beating. A few weeks later, Sonya escaped again, got as far as Berdichev, and begged her father to let her come home. But Horowitz feared that Yakov would create a scandal and shipped his daughter back to Yalta, where Yakov gave her another beating.

Her only chance of happiness, Sonya now decided, was to realize her dream of a lover. Yakov spent almost every day in his laboratory, leaving an assistant in charge of the pharmacy. Sonya liked the young man's looks and decided to confide in him. He proved more than sympathetic to her unhappy story of submitting to Yakov's lovemaking to avoid being beaten, then being beaten all the same when she tried to run away. After the first excited weeks of their affair, she wrote the assistant a letter: "You are my one, my first and only love. . . . We have to leave this dreadful place together!" The assistant was willing, but then Sonya discovered that she was pregnant again.

Without telling her husband or lover, she tried all the peasant formulas for miscarriage: steambaths, bitter and nauseous herbal concoctions, jumping up and down the stairs to the roof. When none of them worked, Sonya decided to make a noble sacrifice, just like the heroine of a French novelette. She told her lover that it was all over between them, told Yakov that he would soon be a father again, and pretended to be happy about it. On June 4, 1879, she gave birth to a plump, healthy daughter, with hair as black as her own and eyes a deeper shade of blue than Yakov's.

They named her Mariam Edez Adelaida, and called her Adel for short until Sonya decided that "Alla" was prettier.

ALL THIS, and the story of her mother's life over the next two years, Nazimova wrote that she learned in 1895, a few months before she finally escaped to Moscow. The old Mongol nurse, long retired, came to pay the Leventon family a visit, and the two of them talked in the outhouse kitchen. "How your mother loved you! Wouldn't let Nina sleep with her no more, wouldn't even let the master sleep in bed with her no more, just you. . . . Well, Nina was always snooty. Never liked the girl, she wasn't like that angel Volodya, or you. . . . You two were just like your sweet mama. . . . But the master, one day he'd beat your mama black and blue, and the next—nothing was too good for her! He'd send abroad for fineries for his Babotchka, but then he'd lick the life out of her again."

"My poor Mama," Nazimova said.

The old nurse gave a long sigh as she poured tea from the samovar. "Well, that's how it is, that's life. . . ."

SONYA ADORED her second daughter partly, of course, out of guilt for having tried to stop her from being born. And when Nina exclaimed, "It's red and ugly!" and begged her mother "to get rid of it," Sonya became doubly protective of this child who seemed doubly unwanted.

A few weeks after Alla was born, Yakov's assistant paid a visit to Sonya in the hope of resuming their affair. Although she refused, because he aggravated her guilt over the attempted miscarriage, Sonya was still eager for adventure. Yakov had bought a fine carriage and pair, which he seldom used, but in the fall of 1879 it began to appear frequently on the streets of Yalta. Beside Sonya in one of her Paris dresses sat the nurse with a gaudy kerchief over her head, happily bribed to secrecy.

Their destination was the park where Yakov had sat on a bench during his first visit to Yalta. It was the haunt of troopers as eager as Sonya for adventure, and a group of them spotted the carriage as soon as it appeared. While little Alla slept on the nurse's lap, the troopers paraded alongside on their horses and bowed to her mother. Although Sonya seemed satisfied with some mildly flirtatious conversation, the troopers had more ambitious plans. They discovered where Sonya lived and began parading outside her house. The click of spurs lured

Sonya back to her balcony, where she sat pretending to do needlework.

By a fortunate coincidence, she soon found it possible to play her balcony scene even when Yakov was in attendance at the pharmacy down-
stairs. Tsar Alexander II arrived for a stay at his palace, came to the
pharmacy for a headache remedy, and happened to find the owner himself behind the counter. Yakov engaged His Imperial Majesty in a discussion of scientific ideas, which the tsar found so interesting that he
returned several times to hear more about medicated soap and concentrated food tablets. Each of his visits cued Sonya to the balcony and the
troopers to increasingly eloquent body language. One of them became a
favored admirer, and when they met in the park Sonya began taking
walks with him while the nurse remained with little Alla in the carriage.

By an unfortunate coincidence, little Nina overheard Sonya and the
nurse discussing their jaunts to the park. She told her father. "*Ookh!* Did
the master beat her and beat her and beat her?" the nurse remembered.
"I thought he must have broken every bone in her body. . . . She just lay
there on the bed, poor dove, wouldn't eat, wouldn't sleep, wouldn't speak
to nobody. . . . Just give you her breast and rock and rock you. *Ookh!*"

"My poor mama," Nazimova said, and between noisy gulps of tea the
nurse told her that worse was to come. When Yakov's assistant heard
what had happened, he gave the nurse a letter for Sonya. Hurrying upstairs to deliver it, she met Yakov on his way down. He snatched it from
her hand and read a declaration of undying love. "*Ookh!*" Before kicking
the assistant out, Yakov searched his room, found Sonya's own declaration of undying love, gave her another beating, and forbade her to use
his carriage or sit out on the balcony any more. "*Everything* forbidden,"
the nurse remembered. "Now the backyard was as far she got!"

Sonya was still a prisoner in the house when, on March 1, 1881, a ter-
rorist bomb killed the tsar in St. Petersburg. A moderate progressive,
Alexander II had been unable to prevent Russia's corrupt bureaucracy
and the secret police from undermining many of his reforms. He succeeded in relaxing censorship of books and newspapers, and reducing the
military draft from twenty to five years. But although he liberated the
serfs by permitting them to buy land of their own, the bureaucrats sent
land taxes soaring; technically free, the majority of serfs found it impossible to make a living from the amount of land they could afford to buy,
and continued to work for their masters. The bureaucrats often sabotaged the new local governments that Alexander set up to improve public health and education, going slow on the paperwork necessary to make
them official. Alexander II had also instituted a system of open trial by

jury for the first time in Russia, but the secret police convinced him to exclude political trials from the new courts. This was a major grievance of the terrorists who plotted Alexander's assassination. They hoped to provoke a revolution, but only succeeded in making the old regime close ranks. His father's death turned the new tsar, Alexander III, into an implacable enemy of reform. He strengthened the secret police, outlawed trade unions, and made censorship more rigid than ever. And because one Jewish woman had played a minor role in the assassination plot, the tsar launched a propaganda campaign depicting Jews as murderers, dangerous revolutionaries, and moneylenders who exploited the poor. So the pogroms began, over two hundred of them in the first six months of Alexander III's reign.

Although thousands of Jews left Russia during this time, Yakov remained for over a year, believing himself safe in a backwater like Yalta with a small Jewish population. But he became alarmed when the pogroms swept from Kiev to Odessa in the spring of 1882. Because he felt they were still too young to understand the situation, Yakov never told the children he was Jewish, only that he'd decided to resume his chemistry studies in Switzerland. Then he asked his cousin's advice on what to do about the pharmacy. The director of the botanical gardens, officially protected as a state employee who had converted to the Orthodox church, felt certain the pogroms would soon burn themselves out. He saw no reason for Yakov to fear permanent exile, urged him not to sell his flourishing business, and offered to find a chemist who could take temporary charge of it.

In June 1882, a few days after Alla's third birthday, the Leventon family arrived in Montreux, where they stayed at a lakeside hotel. Yakov did in fact plan to take a postgraduate course in chemistry, and when his sister, Lysenka, came up from Geneva for a visit, she recommended the Polytechnic in Zurich. Lysenka also recommended suppositories for Alla, who had developed severe constipation during the journey. They proved painfully effective, but Yakov administered a more damaging shock.

In the room that she shared with her parents, Alla woke up one morning to see her mother pinioned beneath a grunting, thrusting Yakov in the opposite bed. When Sonya called out that their daughter was watching, Yakov sat up and beckoned to Alla, smiling in a way that reminded her of a dog showing its teeth. "Then he grabs me, tosses me up like a ball, pinches me, scratches my face with the hair on his mouth, bites my cheeks, my neck, my arms, my legs, and I cry '*Chien! Chien!...*' " An-

gered, Yakov pushed her away. Sonya took Alla in her arms, and "I cry
and cry. . . ."

Later, to comfort her, Sonya suggested a trip on the lake. She rented a
boat, rowed for a while, then dived over the side. As Alla sat watching her
swim toward the horizon, turning back to laugh and wave, she felt a rush
of intense, unforgettable happiness. Sixty years later, Nazimova wrote
from Hollywood: "Whenever I go abroad—no matter what my destination, who my companion—I stop for a few days at a Montreux hotel.
Was it Hôtel du Lac, des Bains, Splendide, du Golf? I have not found it,
not as yet. But always, at the clear blue lake, on the small jetty with a few
rowboats under the willow trees, I find—indelible and precious—my
laughing, luscious Mama as she was then."

WHEN ALLA began to talk, her first language was French.
Like many educated Russians, her parents preferred it to their own. But
when Yakov rented a small house with a garden in Zurich, he enrolled
himself at the Polytechnic and his children at German-speaking schools.
During the seven years that Alla spent in Switzerland, German became
her first language; and unlike Nina and Volodya, who were more advanced in Russian, she gradually forgot the few words she'd learned of her
native tongue.

Five days a week, the plump child in a sailor suit, her dark hair cut
short in bangs, walked by herself to the kindergarten across the street.
For music and gymnastics Alla displayed a precocious talent. She had an
extraordinarily pure singing voice, and the gym instructor considered her
"as good as the boys" when she swung on the trapeze. But at the Polytechnic, Yakov distinguished himself only as an eccentric. The professors
dismissed his "inventions." His exiled compatriots among the students
were obsessed with politics. When Yakov invited a group of them back
to the house, they smoked a great deal and talked revolution. Nothing
else seemed to interest them, and after they left Yakov took out his frustration on Sonya. Lying in bed, Alla heard him shouting in Russian, and
her mother starting to cry.

In the Leventon household, tears, slaps, screams, and beatings soon
began to measure time as regularly as the nearby church clock that struck
the hour. Increasingly jealous of Alla as their mother's favorite, Nina gave
her sister a mean pinch on the buttocks whenever she saw Sonya kiss
her—and when Alla screamed, Sonya slapped Nina. Yakov, who had ordered Volodya to take piano lessons, beat him in front of the rest of the

*The Leventon family in Montreux, Switzerland,
1882. Center: Sonya and Yakov; left to right: Nina,
three-year-old Alla, and Volodya*

family whenever he discovered that his son had missed a practice. And once, after slapping Alla, he offered her a chocolate bar by way of apology—but demanded a kiss first. When she refused, he slapped her again.

Looking back on the fear and loathing that her father inspired, Nazimova recreated Alla's thoughts as a child: "I don't love papa. My mama does not love papa. Volodya does not love papa. . . . *Why must we have him?*" Only Nina continued to love Papa, who never beat *her*—and if he beat the others, she said, it must be their fault.

Shortly before their third Christmas in Zurich, Sonya began slipping out of the house after Yakov left for the Polytechnic. She managed to do this without Nina or Volodya ever noticing, but one day Alla found her mother standing in front of the bedroom mirror, wearing one of her dresses from Paris and a hat with a veil. Sonya told Alla never to say anything to anybody—it was their secret—and hurried out.

The next night, Alla was woken by Yakov snoring in bed. Sonya stood nearby, wrapped in a cloak. She put a finger to her lips, helped Alla to dress, then carried her through the garden to a gate at the back. Beyond the gate a fair-haired man waited in a sleigh, blowing smoke rings from a cigarette in yellow paper. He kissed Sonya, then Alla; the little girl was surprised but pleased, because he kissed very gently, unlike Yakov, and had no mustache. As they drove to the station, it began to snow heavily. They took a train to the nearby town of Winterthur, and another sleigh carried them to a wooden Alpine house with a sloping roof, the kind Alla had seen in picture books. For the rest of that night, in the apartment upstairs, she slept between Sonya and her new lover.

At her mother's suggestion, Alla called him *Mononcle*, "My Uncle," but she thought of him as The Prince. When it was very cold, he wrapped her in his greatcoat. She loved to watch him blow smoke rings, especially when he lay in bed with Sonya's head resting on his shoulder. And *Mononcle* loved to hear her sing, with Sonya at the piano. When she finished, he gave her a kiss and a sip of red wine.

Within a few days, Yakov turned up. After an angry scene in Russian, *Mononcle* threw him out of the house. He came back next day and gave *Mononcle* a letter to read. Sonya recognized the handwriting and cried "*Nyet-nyet!*" but her lover read it anyway. A long silence followed, during which he refused to look at Sonya. When she came over and tried to kiss him, *Mononcle* pushed her away. Yakov gave his dangerous smile and told Sonya he was going to take Alla for a walk. Outside, snow lay thick on the street. Yakov bought his daughter some candy, and they walked together in silence until Alla began to feel cold and asked to go back to the house. He didn't reply. When they reached a streetcar route, Yakov flopped down on the rails and began poking the snow with his cane. He looked so desperate that Alla felt a twinge of pity and decided to cheer him up with a folk song. Then she started to dance, and fell flat on her face in the snow. Yakov picked her up, carried her back to the house, and walked off without a word.

Her mother lay crumpled and alone on the bed. When Alla asked where *Mononcle* had gone, Sonya wailed like an animal. Finally she calmed down, held Alla tight, and said they both had to forget him.

Mononcle would never come back, and in any case he wasn't Alla's uncle. She never learned his real name, or anything more about him, but many years later, in New York, her real uncle Osip explained that the fatal letter was Sonya's declaration to the assistant pharmacist in Yalta: "You are my one, my first and only love. . . ."

ON CHRISTMAS EVE, Sonya and Alla moved to a hotel in Berne, where Osip was studying at the university. He joined them for a Christmas dinner, and had a long discussion with Sonya in Russian. She began to cry and was still in tears when they went up to bed. Alla sang lullabies to her, then dropped off to sleep herself. Next day Sonya announced that they were leaving for Yakov's house in Zurich.

In the living room, Yakov sat at a table with Lysenka and a bearded stranger. Nina and Volodya huddled together on the couch, looking puzzled and frightened as Sonya took Alla on her lap. As Yakov began to speak in Russian, the bearded stranger took notes. Alla had no idea why she was there or what was happening, but saw Sonya shake her head when Yakov finished his speech. Yakov shouted at her, banging the table with his fist, and Sonya burst into tears. Her father suddenly grabbed Alla and handed her to Lysenka, who tried to drag her out of the room. She finally broke away, but found Sonya had vanished. And when she asked where her mother had gone, nobody answered. Only the scratch of the lawyer's pen, as he continued to make notes, disturbed the silence.

Realizing at last that he couldn't beat Sonya into loving or pretending to love him any more, Yakov had decided to divorce her. And the day after he turned Sonya out of the house, a letter arrived from his cousin in Yalta. Almost three years had gone by since the pogroms began, the director of the botanical gardens wrote; the town had been spared; and since few Jews remained, he felt certain the danger was over. The pharmacy was still doing excellent business, so why didn't Yakov come and see for himself that he could safely remake his life if he wished?

Yakov said nothing of this to his children, nor did he explain why their mother had gone away. He simply announced that he was returning to Russia, would drop off Alla to stay with his brother Ilya in Yedintsy, and would leave Nina and Volodya in care of their aunt Lysenka in Geneva. Nina and Volodya asked no questions, but although Alla had no idea where Yedintsy was, and didn't care, she very much wanted to know what had happened to Sonya. The only answer she got was a slap in the face.

As the train pulled out of the station, she asked the same question again and got the same answer. On the first night of the journey, Alla had a beautiful dream about her mother swimming in the lake, laughing and waving; on the second, a nightmare about her father, who turned into a wolf and bit her. At Odessa they got off the train and took a carriage across the plains of Bessarabia, a province on the western border of the Ukraine. It rained heavily as they passed through villages where the men wore tall fur caps and carried whips, barefoot children walked among pigs rolling in the mud, smoke drifted from the narrow windows of cottages with straw roofs. Yedintsy was a village like all the others, but Ilya Leventon and his wife lived just beyond it, in a farmhouse surrounded by cornfields. Yakov kept the carriage waiting while he presented Alla to her uncle and aunt, then set off back to Odessa.

At first Alla was afraid of Ilya, because of his strong resemblance to her father, and began to cry. But he comforted her so tenderly that she decided it would be all right to ask for news of Sonya.

"Dyadya Ilya," she began, then switched to German, "is my mama in Winterthur?"

He shook his head sadly. "I don't know, Allyotchka."

"Then she must be in Montreux. Yes?"

"We don't know, Allyotchka," her aunt said. "You mustn't upset yourself."

Although this was disappointing, their kindness reassured her.

"Tyotya Sofya, may I sit in your lap?"

A few minutes later, she had such a violent attack of stomach cramps that they sent for a doctor. He diagnosed typhus.

A few weeks later, while she was convalescent, she came down with chicken pox. Although warned by the doctor not to scratch her scabs, Alla sometimes couldn't help it, and they left a few shallow pockmarks on her face. By the end of May 1885, she was convalescent again; then a rash appeared on her forehead. The doctor diagnosed measles, and Alla spent her sixth birthday in a darkened room.

When she was finally well again, Yakov reappeared. He arrived unexpectedly at night, looking tired and ravaged as Ilya and Sofya brought him to sit on Alla's bed. "I'm the unluckiest man in the world," he said in French, then spoke with her uncle and aunt for a long while in Russian. Next morning they explained what had happened. After a long delay, the authorities in Yalta had finally granted Yakov permission to take charge of his pharmacy again. Only a few days later, a fire broke out in the house next door, spreading to Yakov's property and burning it to the ground. He planned to build a new house and pharmacy, but in the meantime Alla would have to stay in a new home.

"With my mama?" Alla asked immediately.

"He's taking you to Zurich. That's all we know."

Alla ran to look for her father and risk his anger by asking whether Sonya was in Zurich. She found him slumped in an armchair, head bowed, shoulders twitching convulsively, and was so astonished that she left the room without a word.

But when they got on the train, Yakov seemed in better spirits. "Is my mama in Zurich?" she finally asked. No slap, but no answer either, just a blank stare before he turned to look out the window. Secretly interpreting this as *Yes, but I don't want to talk about her,* Alla didn't bring up the subject again.

When the train arrived in Zurich, she looked for her mother on the platform, then in the street outside the station. As Yakov lifted her into a carriage, she said nothing, but felt certain that Sonya would be waiting at the house. They drove out of the city, up a winding mountain road, and Alla supposed that her mother must have moved to the country. Finally the carriage stopped at a row of four white houses facing a patch of land where goats and cattle grazed. As Yakov led Alla to the first house, the front door opened and Volodya ran out, followed by Nina, who jumped into her father's arms. Then two strangers appeared, a man with a long white beard who smiled, and a woman who did not. "Your new family," Yakov told Alla, who toppled to the ground in a faint.

She revived to find herself on a hard bed in a cell-like room, with the woman standing over her and Nina crying because Yakov had gone away. When Volodya smiled at her, Alla asked him in German, "Where's mama?" But the woman answered, also in German, "Forget her. No more mama. Never."

THE GROELICHS were small farmers who sold milk from their cows and goats, fruit from their orchards, honey from their beehives, and grew their own vegetables. Alla shared a bedroom with their eight-year-old daughter; four sons lived in the house next door; an ancient, toothless, fanatically religious grandmother shared the next house with the Groelichs' unmarried aunt, who taught at the village school. Herr Groelich belonged to an anarchist group in Zurich, edited their newspaper, and told Alla that all European monarchs, including the tsar, would soon be kicked from their thrones in the name of justice and equality. Frau Groelich told Alla that she was expected to help with the housework, polish the men's shoes, and milk the goats.

Although Frau Groelich rarely smiled, she could be gruffly affectionate. She put an end to Alla's persistent questions about her mother with a smack on the head, then held the child on her lap and said, "I am The Mother here." In a letter to Yakov she reported that Alla had an unusually sweet nature and boundless energy, and was growing so fat that they nicknamed her Little Ball. Frau Groelich added that, when her eldest son, Albert, practiced the violin and played a wrong note, Alla always corrected him. Since she also sang beautifully, it seemed that she had "musical ears." Yakov wrote back that he had no wish for his daughter to become a singer, but would like her to start violin lessons at once.

Alla protested that she would rather learn to play the piano, but *Die Mutter*, as all Yakov's children soon called The Mother, said that a father must be obeyed. By this time she had increased Alla's regular chores by putting her to work in the vegetable garden, delegating her to feed the chickens as well as milk the goats, and teaching her to sew, so that the six-year-old child could lend an extra hand at mending the boys' shirts. Now, as well as attending kindergarten Monday to Friday, Alla took violin lessons twice a week.

Die Mutter found only one serious fault with Alla, her tendency to fantasies and daydreams. The first time the child saw a black goat, she looked appalled and asked if it gave black milk. One day she wandered into the last house on the row, where the farm workers lived, and found a deaf-mute couple weaving cloth in the cellar. The rhythmic clack of the loom convinced Alla that they were playing a new kind of musical instrument, and she began to dance. Then *Die Mutter* arrived and jolted her back to reality with a disapproving "*Phantasien!*"

As Alla later discovered, the reason for Frau Groelich's disapproval was her second son, Otto, whose delusions were far more extreme. But for a while they became soulmates. Volodya and Nina—who went to the local school, where the unmarried Groelich aunt taught—were too preoccupied to pay much attention to their fat little sibling. Volodya was studious, preferring books to company; Nina often retreated to the summerhouse, where she cried because she missed her father, and refused to let Alla comfort her. Eager for companionship when Otto invited her to join what he called his Bund, Alla accepted at once.

At fifteen, Otto was large for his age, rather ugly, and suffered from headaches and epileptic fits. Until Alla joined the Bund, of which Otto had elected himself The Leader, its only other members were the two younger Groelich sons and the son of a neighboring farmer. They held meetings at a clearing in the forest high in the mountains, and on her first trip there Otto showed Alla the knife he always carried in his pocket.

For protection from his enemies, he said, and began talking wild revolutionary politics, obviously influenced by his father. After confiding his plan to assassinate Tsar Alexander III, he called a halt and gave Alla the Tests of Pain and Silence. Pointing his knife between her eyes, he warned her not to cry out or even flinch as he moved the blade gradually closer, until it touched her skin. Then he seized Alla's thumb and bent it so far backward that she feared it would break. After she passed both tests, Otto told her to prepare for the last and most difficult. Swearing her to silence again, he hung her from the branch of a tree by her feet, which were tied together.

Alla passed this test as well, and The Leader rewarded her with a demonstration of his own strength. He took out his knife, slashed his arms and legs several times, never winced, and stared with a blank expression as blood streamed down his body. Finally he shouted a command. The others stood to attention and saluted. Then they chanted "*Unser Fuehrer ist der Fuehrer unter Fuehrers,*" "Our Leader is a leader among leaders," and Otto wiped his knife on his pants before disappearing into the forest.

By now Alla was no stranger to strangeness. She had been terrorized by her father, taken on unexplained journeys, and left with alien families in remote Bessarabian and Alpine villages. She had been carried off by her mother in the middle of the night, then snatched from her arms and told never to speak of her again. Now, apart from Yakov, only thunderstorms truly scared her. Perhaps they reminded her of Yakov's violent rages, for she never got over a fear of ominous rumbles in the sky, which made the adult Nazimova hide in a closet. But Otto's weird games in the forest merely excited Alla's imagination. When he announced at supper one evening that he had formed a new World Revolutionary Party, with a network of spies and assassins, she was the only one to take him seriously. Frau Groelich wondered why she hadn't sent Otto to a sanitarium long ago, but Otto gave Alla an almost beatific smile and promised to protect her forever.

Next day he took her to the forest without the others, and when they reached the clearing told her to prepare for the ultimate Test of Pain and Silence. However much it hurt, he said, she mustn't scream or ever tell anyone about it. He ordered her to lie down and close her eyes, then removed her skirt, pushed her legs farther apart, and clambered on top of her. His weight was oppressive, and she felt even more uncomfortable when it began to rain. And then came the Ultimate Pain, as if Otto had started to jab her crotch with his knife. Alla was about to scream when he rolled away with an agonized sob, apparently unable to bear the Ultimate Pain himself.

Opening her eyes, Alla sat up and saw Otto twitching and shuddering as he lay on his back, his features contorted in an epileptic fit. She ran to a nearby stream, scooped up water in her hands and splashed it over Otto's face. Eventually he quieted down and fell asleep. Although Alla's own pain had lessened by now, the skin between her legs felt tender when she touched it, and she saw a few drops of blood there. Sitting under a tree that dripped rain, she stared at The Leader who had promised to protect her. When it began to grow dark, she woke him and suggested going home. Otto said he had a terrible headache, apologized for his behavior, begged rather than ordered Alla not to tell anyone what had happened, and proposed exchanging Oaths of Fidelity for Life. Ready to swear to anything if he would let her go, Alla agreed. Then Otto said he would be away a long time on a mission for his party. Muttering that he had only to whistle for his "ambassadors" to kill his enemies, he wandered off into the forest.

Alla kept her promise not to tell anyone what Otto had done, but for the next few nights woke Gretl, the Groelichs' daughter, with whom she shared a room, by crying "Help! Help!" in her sleep.

IN THE SUMMER of 1887, after Alla had been living with the Groelichs for a year, a large package from Yakov arrived in the mail. Addressed to his three children, it contained boxes of Turkish delight and Russian nougat. Yakov also enclosed a photograph of a woman with large, dark, mournful eyes and a long nose. In a letter attached to it, he asked the children if they would like her for a new mama. Nina and Volodya refused to tell Alla what they wrote in reply, so she kept her own letter a secret. Only half a page long, it announced that she definitely didn't want a sad long-nosed woman for a new mother, and still longed for her real mama.

The next letter from Yakov was addressed to Frau Groelich. It said nothing about a new mama, but contained immediate marching orders for Volodya and Nina. His son was to leave for the military academy in Riga, his elder daughter for a boarding school in Moelis, two hours away from Zurich. Alla would remain with the Groelichs until he made up his mind about her future, and since Yakov failed to explain this, yet another of his abrupt directives, Frau Groelich could only say that a father must be obeyed.

Although Nina told Alla that she looked forward to going away because she had never been happy with the Groelichs, she burst into tears when the time came to say goodbye. "I'll miss my little sister so much, when will I ever see you again?" she said to the little sister she'd cold-shouldered for months, kissing her again and again. Volodya, stunned into silence at the prospect of a life he was obviously unsuited for, held back his tears and gave Alla a quick handshake before setting out on a fifteen-hundred-mile journey to the Baltic coast.

After they left, Alla hid in the Groelichs' primitive latrine and cried. And in the months that followed, with Otto still away on his imaginary mission, she bonded with his sister, Gretl. Although they shared a room, Gretl had always kept a superior distance. "That's not interesting!" was her invariable response whenever Alla attempted to make conversation. Not even Alla crying "Help! Help!" in her sleep interested Gretl, who only complained about being woken up. Then she suddenly wanted to talk, and what she wanted to talk about, the only subject that Gretl seemed to find truly interesting, was sex.

At night in their room she began telling bedtime stories almost as deluded in their way as Otto's accounts of his spy ring, and Alla was ignorant enough to believe them. If a man kissed her, Gretl warned, a baby bastard would grow in her belly, and girls with bastards were known as whores. Although a whore from a poor country family usually killed her baby bastard and drowned herself in the nearest lake, a city whore was often clever enough to marry the rich man who had kissed her. You could tell a city whore, Gretl added, by her fancy clothes and especially her hats, which always had feathers in them. Alla felt relieved that Otto had never kissed her until Gretl hinted that men had other, more mysterious ways of creating a bastard in a girl's belly. She couldn't describe them exactly, but the hints were graphic enough for Alla to understand what Otto had almost done, and how his epileptic fit had saved her from becoming a country whore. Although she hated him now, she stuck to her promise, never told Gretl about the Ultimate Pain, and only remarked, "Now, *that's* interesting!"

After almost a year had passed with no further word from Yakov, Alla saw a sleigh drive up to the Groelichs' house as she walked home from school one day. A man and two women stepped out, then went inside. A moment later, the front door opened again and Gretl called to Alla that *Die Mutter* wanted to see her at once. When she entered the living room, one of the women ran over and handed her an envelope. "From your mama," she said. "It's her photograph. . . ."

But to Alla the woman in the photograph didn't look like Sonya at all. She was rather fat and wore a hat with a feather in it, like a city whore. When one of the visitors asked Alla if she had any message for her mama, she shook her head. As soon as they left, she stared at the photograph again and felt a whiff of perfume in the air, but it wasn't the perfume she associated with Sonya. Then Frau Groelich snatched the photograph from her hand. "Never speak to anybody about this," she said angrily, "and never speak of *her*."

Six months later, on a hot midsummer morning in 1889, Frau Groelich announced, "Your father's arriving from Paris today!" She washed and cut Alla's hair, told her to put on her best dress, then go to the living room, stand by the window, and watch for a carriage. When she saw it approach, Alla hoped that her father was just passing through on his way back to Russia and wouldn't stay long.

He got out of the carriage, looking important and prosperous in a gray silk suit, carrying gloves and a cane in one hand, a small package in the other. "He's a very rich man now," Frau Groelich said. At the sight of Alla, Yakov bared his teeth, picked her up as if she were a baby, and kissed her several times on the mouth. Sweating and flustered, Frau Groelich admired his suit. Yakov told her that he'd bought an entire new wardrobe in Paris, then opened the package and presented Alla with a beret. It was bright red, her favorite color, and had the Eiffel Tower embroidered in gold thread across the front. When she tried it on, Yakov frowned. "Why is everything else you're wearing so old and shabby? I can't have you going around like that in Yalta."

Alla stared at him. "Yalta!" he said again, raising his voice: "My home! I'm taking you back to my home!"

Her instinct was to run away and hide, but Yakov grabbed her arm and ordered her to pack. Then the old grandmother pressed a New Testament into Alla's hand and said, "Remember this. When you pray, always cross yourself. Crossing yourself is a sign to God that you're willing to be crucified for your faith in Him." Later, Yakov told her to wait in the carriage. When Alla went outside, she saw Otto standing under a tree, and his sudden return seemed like a miracle. Forgetting that she hated him, she had a wild thought that perhaps his secret network really existed and could come to her rescue. But when she explained that Yakov was taking her to Russia and begged for help, Otto shrugged. "We're soulmates for life, so it doesn't matter if you go away," he said. "I can always find you if I want." Then he walked away.

During the drive to Zurich, her father never said a word until he ordered the driver to stop at a clothing store, where he bought Alla a new traveling outfit and a red ribbon for her hair. But when she asked for a handkerchief as well, Yakov refused angrily: "You think I'm a millionaire?" In the train to Vienna he broke a long silence to tell Alla that he wanted her to learn Russian; later, he broke another by showing her a gold medal with his name engraved on it. As a reward for his invention of medicated soap, Yakov said, the government had made him an honorary citizen of Yalta. He spent the rest of the journey reading medical journals.

They stayed a day and a night in Vienna, where Yakov played the man of the world. Viennese women, he informed Alla, were less chic but more beautiful than Parisian women. He showed her the Prater and the Burgtheater. The finest theatre in Europe, Yakov said as they stood looking up at the famous flight of steps that led to the entrance. Molière, Shakespeare, Schiller, he recited gravely, and other names that Alla had never heard before, Sarah Bernhardt, Eleonora Duse, Adelaide Ristori, great actresses whom he promised to take Alla to see when they came to Russia. As he spoke of them, Yakov seemed to become a different person, almost humble, and Alla began to wonder if life with him would be so bad after all.

She soon changed her mind. When Yakov decided to buy her more new clothes, she made the mistake of objecting to one of the dresses he picked out, all white lace, ruffles, and bows. Yakov gave his dangerous smile, then told the saleslady it was too expensive. He said nothing to Alla until they got back to their hotel room, where he flew into a rage. "I'm only taking you back to Yalta because nobody else wants you! I don't want you either, and wish I never had to see you again, but they won't take you at Nina's boarding school because you're too young!"

On the train to Odessa next morning, Nazimova wrote, Yakov refused to speak to Alla, or even look at her. Still wounded by his outburst at the hotel, she had no wish to break the silence. It lasted until nightfall, when she began to feel hungry. Rather than say anything to Yakov, she tried to sleep. After a few minutes, the train stopped at a station, an old man with a hooked nose and red hair sat down opposite her father, and they began talking in a strange language. When the old man saw her looking puzzled, he smiled and told her they were speaking Yiddish. The word meant nothing to her. He smiled again and said, "I am a Jew." The little that Alla knew about Jews she had learned from Otto. A peddler sometimes passed through the village with a rucksack, and one day Otto pointed him out. "A dirty thief, like all Jews," he said. "They murder babies, and he's probably carrying a dead one in his rucksack." Remembering this, Alla noticed a rucksack on the seat next to the old man, backed away in panic, and screamed at her father, "Take me away, I don't want to stay here with a dirty Jew!"

Yakov struck her hard across the mouth. "I'm a Jew myself, and so are you," he said. It was like a second, equally painful blow. "You can't be," she almost whispered. "You don't look like one." Yakov turned away, and the Jew said nothing. Finally Yakov fell asleep and the old man opened his rucksack. Instead of a dead baby, he took out a loaf of black bread, broke off a piece, poured a little wine into a tin cup, and offered Alla the cup and the bread.

Thoroughly confused by now, Alla hesitated. Although ugly, this Jew seemed very kind, and she decided that Otto was a liar as well as a madman. "Thank you," she said. The Jew looked pleased as Alla ate and drank. Seeing how hungry she was, he gave her another piece of bread. Then he asked, "Would you like to sleep now?" Alla nodded, he tucked her in a blanket, and when she woke up the train had stopped at another station. The old man smiled as he got out, and Alla waved goodbye. Later she was sorry not to have thanked him.

At the Russian frontier, everyone was ordered off the train to pass through customs. Alla looked around at the other passengers, most of them Russian, sullen, and ragged. The officials had brutal faces, and two of them roughed up an old man as they dragged him away. Like everyone else, Yakov looked scared. "Police," he said quietly. "Keep your mouth shut."

The train to Odessa was much dirtier than the European trains, and when it stopped at a station, hordes of tattered children beat desperately on the windows, begging for food. To Alla, the face of Russia seemed even more alien than its language until she followed her father into the lobby of their clean, modestly comfortable hotel in Odessa, where the maid smiled as she showed them to their room. Yakov ordered supper, but when it arrived he complained that the food was terrible and Russia a barbarous country. Then he went to the bathroom. Alla noticed that her violin case had fallen open, and found the envelope containing her mother's photograph wedged beside the bow. Frau Groelich, she supposed, must have relented and hidden it there. As she took out the photograph and stared at it, Yakov returned. She expected him to be angry, but he took the photograph from her hands quite gently and stared at it himself.

Finally he asked, "Who gave you this?"

Alla explained.

Yakov looked very thoughtful for a moment. Then he said quietly, "Did you know she lives in Odessa? Just a few streets from here?"

Alla was too astonished to answer.

Yakov put a hand on her shoulder. "Would you like to see her?"

"Yes," she said, thinking it might be possible to love her father after all. "Can we go now?"

Then Yakov showed his teeth like a dog and Alla realized that he had tricked her. "No, I don't want to see her," she said, trying not to sound frightened. "I've forgotten her."

But the lie came too late. "Then why are you crying?" her father asked, moving closer. Alla backed away and ducked under the table. "Why are you crying?" she heard him ask again. He swept the cloth away; plates and dishes crashed to the floor, and cabbage splattered her face. Alla ran for the door, but Yakov got there first. After punching her in the face, knocking her down, and kicking her, he left the room.

A few minutes later, two servants came in and found Alla lying dazed on the floor. The maid carried her to the bed and put a wet towel over her eyes while the waiter gathered up the broken dishes. After they left, Alla lay completely numb for a while, then tried to make sense of what had happened. "When he struck me across the mouth in the train, it served me right. I shouldn't have said that about Jews. But why did he beat me here, in this room? He wanted to talk about mama, he asked if I wanted to see her, but when I said Yes, he scared me so much that I lied. . . . But he didn't beat me because I lied, he beat me for telling the truth. . . . He hates the truth and he hates mama and he hates me for loving mama. He beat her too, and she was right to run away. . . . Now I'd like to run away myself, but where could I go?"

Too tired to think any more, Alla fell asleep and was woken by a hand lifting the towel from her eyes. Yakov stood over the bed, carrying a doll and a bar of chocolate. He laid them beside her, then knelt down and started to sob. In the past, when she saw her father desperately unhappy, Alla had felt a twinge of pity, but this time she felt nothing at all. Yakov was just "a dead man crying, a nobody, a thing."

On the boat to Yalta next day, Alla's eyes were still swollen and her body ached. As she stood on deck, a high wind blew the beret off her head, and it whirled away into the air, past screaming gulls. "The only thing from papa I ever loved," she thought. "And now it's lost."

Yakov, who had avoided her eyes all morning, stood nearby. As the beret disappeared over the Black Sea, she heard him say quietly, "There's a woman in my new house in Yalta."

"With a long nose?" Alla asked.

"A man can't live alone all his life." Yakov seemed to be talking to himself. "He needs a woman in the house."

"Somebody's got to do the housework, I suppose."

"We have servants. . . . She used to teach music at a school in Moscow, until she got sick and came to Yalta for her health. I married her a few months ago." Then Yakov's voice struck a familiar domineering note. "Now she's my wife and you'll have to obey her!"

Alla didn't answer. A moment later, as the boat rounded a promontory, Yalta came into view. In the seven years since she had left it, the place had faded from memory. Now she couldn't decide whether to love it for looking so beautiful, or to hate it because she knew what a horrible life awaited her there. But finally she decided, "It doesn't matter." Living in Yakov's house would be another Test of Pain and Silence. Even when Yakov beat her, she would pretend that she felt nothing, like Otto when he slashed his arms with a knife.

Above all, Nazimova wrote, Yakov must never know what Alla was thinking. "I'm taking you home," he'd said, but she knew that her real home, although she had no idea where to look for it, was somewhere else.

3

"Dealing in Emotions"

She was Russian—*completely.*
—DAGMAR GODOWSKY

WHILE ALLA WAS IN SWITZERLAND, AN exclusive settlement had sprung up on the edge of town. In "New Yalta," Nazimova wrote, an unpaved dead-end street ran for four blocks, past the Hotel Russiya ("for millionaires and aristocrats only," according to her father), past various stores to a residential section: Italianate villas with high walls, wrought-iron gates, and entrance courtyards. In the hallway of the last and most recently built villa, a large, elaborately framed portrait of Yakov dominated one wall. Ordered to wait in the salon while he went upstairs, Alla sat in a room that felt uninhabited, stiff and formal like a display window in a furniture store, with chocolate-brown lace curtains blurring a view of the Black Sea.

"*Komm,*" Yakov said as he reappeared, and led Alla to a bedroom, where the woman with a long thin nose lay back in an armchair. She wore a white lace dress and held a bundle of white lace on her lap.

"This is my wife," Yakov said in German. "You may call her Aunt Dasha."

The woman frowned and offered Alla a flushed, blotchy cheek. "I am your mama. You may kiss me."

Alla shook her head. "My mama's in Odessa. And my papa told me he married you because he wanted a woman in the house."

The woman laughed, then had a coughing spell, and held a handkerchief smelling of creosote to her mouth. Finally she said, "Call me Aunt Dasha if you like." The bundle of lace on her lap gave a sudden twitch, and she picked it up. "His name is Valentin, but we call him Valya."

As she began to breast-feed the baby, Yakov grabbed Alla's arm and led her out of the room. Halfway down the stairs, he stopped. "Never slide down these banisters. And never go into our bedroom without permission. My wife doesn't like to be disturbed. Is that understood?"

"That's understood," Alla said, and followed him to a door at the end of the hallway. He unlocked it, and walked to another door at the end of a dark passage. "This is my private entrance. You're not allowed to use it." Yakov pushed her into a room beyond the second door, and she found herself in Yakov's new pharmacy. Much larger and grander than the old one, it had a crystal chandelier, glass-fronted mahogany cases with rows of colored bottles and jars, and a portrait of Tsar Alexander III on the wall. Yakov pointed to a door at the opposite end, open to the courtyard. "Customers' entrance. You're not allowed to use it either. Is that understood?"

A young man in a white coat hurried forward, kissed Alla on the cheek, and introduced himself as Yakov's nephew Victor. "My assistant manager," Yakov explained with a self-important air. "His father's the famous surgeon, Lyev Leventon." Two other young employees in white coats stood behind the counter, and Victor introduced Alla to each in turn: carroty-haired Mezhuk, the head chemist; and Tayzi, the clerk, a Greek with a mischievous grin. Then Yakov grabbed Alla's arm again and took her aside. "Never come in here without special permission," he said, "and never talk to anyone except Victor."

He took Alla back to the hallway, locking both doors, and unlocked another. It led to the garden in back, with a tall, skeletal pine tree in the center of a lawn. A ladder rested against the trunk, and at the top several large thermometers protruded from a tin bucket. "The first meteorological station in the Crimea," Yakov said proudly. "You're not allowed to climb that ladder. Is that understood?"

"That's understood," Alla said. "But is there somewhere I'm allowed to piss?"

He led her to the back porch, opened a door to a small windowless room, and lit a candle in a niche on the wall. Yakov was equally proud of his flush toilet, something that Alla had never seen before, but didn't warn her to stand clear when she pulled the chain. A cascade like a waterfall drenched her with spray.

That night Alla joined her father, her stepmother, and Cousin Victor for a "family" dinner. As Dasha poured glasses of tea from a samovar, a young maidservant with dark eyes and a flat round face served the first course, blubbery objects with a strong fishy smell.

Alla turned to her cousin. "What are they?"

"Oysters," Victor said. "From the sea."

She had never heard of them and didn't like the way they slithered around her plate. "Are they alive?" she asked.

"Don't talk at the table," Yakov said. "Eat!"

It was like putting slime in her mouth, and she got rid of her first oyster by spitting it back on the plate. Victor laughed, but Dasha gave a scream of horror and left the room. Yakov smacked Alla's head, then ordered her to eat all six of her oysters, beginning with the one she'd expectorated.

Alla passed the test in silence. Before the next course arrived, Dasha returned to the table. Her left eye had developed an unnerving squint, which Alla soon came to recognize as a sign of anger. "Your father never told me he was bringing you here," Dasha said. "It's really most inconvenient. The house has only one spare bedroom, and Valya sleeps there with his nurse." With a sharp nod to Yakov, she got up from the table again. Yakov seized Alla's arm, and they followed Dasha to the salon.

At the far end, heavy plush curtains were drawn across an archway. Dasha flung them open to reveal an alcove with books lining the back wall, a tall chest, a writing desk and chair. "From now on," she told Alla, squinting again, "this is your corner. You'll sleep here, and you can use the salon if you like, because I never go there. But when you're in the alcove, close the curtains, and when you're in the salon, close the door. I want you to keep out of my sight, and never speak to me or my baby again."

Yakov ordered Alla to keep the windows closed as well, because they faced the sea and salt air made Dasha feel ill. He closed the alcove curtains, leaving Alla in darkness. Hungry as well as abandoned, she determined to pass another Test of Pain and Silence.

Eventually the curtains parted again and an old, lame servant appeared. He carried an iron cot, which he placed against one wall of the alcove. The young servant girl followed with a small washstand. She set it down, smiled at Alla, put her finger to her lips, and hurried out. A few minutes later, she reappeared with a tray of bread, salami, and cheese, and a candle in a brass holder. Alla ran to kiss her three times on the cheek. Although the girl spoke nothing but Russian, they quickly learned to communicate with kisses, smiles, and sign language.

Sitting beside Alla on the cot, the servant pointed to herself and said "Melanya," then pointed to the bread and cheese and spoke the Russian words for them. By the time she finished eating, Alla had learned the Russian words for "desk," "chair," "bed," and "candle" as well. Signaling that she'd be back shortly, Melanya went out. She came back with Alla's violin case, sheets, and blankets. Alla opened the case and took out the photograph of Sonya. "Mama," she whispered, then clapped a hand over her mouth. Melanya understood at once, kissed the photograph, put it away in the desk drawer. Then she indicated that it was time for Alla to go to sleep, helped her undress, tucked her in bed, and closed the curtains.

Next morning, when Alla woke up, the house was very silent. She got dressed, went looking for Melanya, and found her in the kitchen. A moment later there was a whiff of creosote in the air and Dasha appeared, handkerchief to mouth. The sight of Alla produced another scream of horror, then an urgent call to Yakov, who dragged his daughter back to the alcove. "This is your corner! How dare you upset my wife by going into the kitchen?" He threw her on the cot and beat her so violently Alla had to break her vow. Her yells of pain brought Dasha to the archway, distracted and squinting. "That child is giving me a migraine," she said.

A FEW WEEKS later, when Yakov beat Alla again because her fingernails were dirty, she couldn't help yelling again. After he went upstairs, Melanya hurried to the alcove and bathed Alla's face. "*Nitchevo!*" she said; although by now Alla had started Russian lessons and mastered the basics of the language, this was an expression she didn't know. When Melanya explained how many different things it could mean—"Don't let it get you down," and "It's nothing," and "Who cares?" and "Things could be worse"—*nitchevo* became Alla's mantra. Repeating it under her breath the next time Yakov beat her, she was able to keep herself from crying out.

Sometimes, at night, war broke out between Yakov and his wife. Screams from Dasha at the top of the stairs brought Alla and Melanya to the hallway, where they huddled in their nightgowns and heard the same dialogue so often that they soon knew it by heart. Dasha: "Don't you dare come to my bedroom again!" Yakov: "I am the master of this house!" Scuffling sounds, and a final scream as Yakov dragged Dasha back to the bedroom. "*Nitchevo!*" Alla and Melanya said to each other, stifling their laughter.

If Yakov and Dasha had any friends, Alla never saw them, for the couple never entertained. And for several years Alla had no friends of her own age. Yakov refused to send her to the local elementary school. Too common, he said, for the daughter of an honorary citizen and distinguished inventor. Instead, following the example of "the best families," he employed private tutors to continue her education. Sometimes he stood in the salon doorway during Alla's lessons, and once he fired a Russian teacher on the spot for translating a passage from the New Testament. Denouncing all religions as a fool's game, he ordered the astonished woman out of the house. Secretly, Alla for once agreed with her father. Unlike the fairy tales by Hans Christian Andersen that she found on the bookshelves in the alcove, God failed to excite her imagination. But to hedge her bets she knelt in prayer at night, and implored Him to kill Yakov as soon as possible.

On Fridays, Yakov left the house immediately after lunch to spend the rest of the afternoon at the steambaths. Released from solitary confinement, Alla ran to the pharmacy, where she knew Mezhuk, Tayzi, and Cousin Victor would be celebrating the boss's absence by smoking cigarettes. They hung a Closed sign above the pharmacy entrance and took her to the garden in back. There, under the tall spindly pine, they joked about Yakov's Ladder and encouraged Alla to climb it; at the top of the meteorological tree, she took a bow.

After Melanya served tea, Alla entertained the company with impersonations of Yakov, brandishing an imaginary cane and scratching an imaginary mustache, baring her teeth like a dog. Encouraged by cries of "Bravo!" she began to expand her repertoire of characters: Mezhuk cringing when Yakov bawled him out, a sick old woman hobbling up to the pharmacy counter, a fat rich one wiggling her hips. And when Victor called out, "Bravo, Sarah Bernhardtochka!" she took another bow, this time as an actress.

Although Alla found nothing more enjoyable than pretending to be somebody else, the idea of becoming an actress did not occur to her for several years. At the time she had another plan of escape in mind. Determined to develop Alla's "musical ears," Yakov insisted that she continue her violin lessons. The teacher he engaged was a pale, emaciated young man called Ephraim Savelson, who had managed to get a permit to live beyond the Pale and study at the St. Petersburg conservatory under the famous Leopold Auer, to whom Tchaikovsky dedicated his violin concerto. But tuberculosis destroyed Savelson's hope of a career. Like Dasha and so many others, he moved to Yalta, where he lived in a tiny one-room apartment, taught violin and piano, and founded a symphony orchestra. All its members were tubercular, and under Savelson's baton gave summer concerts in the park.

Stooped, hollow-eyed, with a beaked nose and thin, bitter mouth, he made an alarming first impression. Sometimes while Alla played, he coughed blood into a handkerchief and stared at it with a remote expression, but a wrong note affected him like an electric shock. He seized the bow, struck her across the fingers, then played the piece himself and produced the most beautiful sounds Alla had ever heard. Listening in the doorway, Yakov grew misty-eyed, but raised hell when Alla tried the piece again and played another wrong note. "You'll tour the world with your damn violin if I have to break your damn neck!" This threat made Alla decide to practice very hard, become as proficient as Savelson, then escape to perform all over Europe while Yakov stayed home to mind the pharmacy.

EVERY YEAR Savelson's students gave a Christmas Day concert at the Hotel Russiya, and a few weeks before Christmas 1889 he asked Yakov's permission to include Alla on the program. At first Yakov refused, then changed his mind on one condition. "She mustn't call herself Adelaida Leventon. Everyone will know she's my daughter and I can't have her bringing disgrace on the family." Then he gave Alla another twist of the knife. "If and when you're good enough, and become famous, you can use my name. But not before."

Alla had recently read a Russian novel called *Children of the Streets* and liked the sound of the heroine's name, Nadyezhda Nazimova. Savelson objected. He found "Nazimova" much too ordinary, almost as common as "Petrovna," and pointed out that everyone would think her incredibly naïve if she called herself Nadyezhda, which was the Russian word for "hope." Ordinary or not, Alla told him, "Nazimova" was music to her ears. But she agreed to use her original first name when Savelson suggested it might bring her luck: there was a famous Italian actress called Adelaide Ristori.

When Adelaida Nazimova arrived at the Hotel Russiya on Christmas

Day, she discovered that Savelson's other students were all boys, several years older than herself, lined up with their violins in a room adjoining the concert hall. "You're the smallest and you come on last," Savelson said, "and I want you to be the best." Like hell, she thought as the concert began and she heard how expertly each boy played; I'd better get out of here before everyone discovers that the smallest and last is also the worst. When Savelson finally called "Adelaida Nazimova!" she was so nervous that he had to call several times before she remembered her new name and made her reluctant first entrance on a stage.

Peering over the kerosene footlights, she saw Yakov sitting in the front row with Dasha. The way they smiled and applauded along with the audience struck her as horribly false. "Liars!" she thought with a flash of anger. "Smiling at me as if they knew I'd be good . . . How I hate them, and all the others out there as well. . . ." But suddenly it no longer seemed to matter whether they liked her or not. "What do they know? Maybe I'll be rotten. . . ."

She performed two popular sentimental pieces, *Regrets* and *Légende,* by two famous virtuosos of the time, Vieuxtemps and Wieniawski, and the audience not only responded with cries of "Bravo, Nazimova!" but demanded an encore. Not having prepared anything else, she gave them *Légende* again. More applause, a woman rushed onstage to present her with a box of chocolates, Savelson surprised her with a kiss and led her to the banquet room. Its glittering Christmas tree brought back sudden memories of Christmas with the Groelichs, then of a Christmas Day with Sonya, at the hotel in Berne, just before she went away forever.

A plump, beautiful woman with red roses in her black hair was standing by the tree. "Mama! Mamotchka!" Alla called, ran forward, and held out her arms. It wasn't Sonya, only a woman who resembled her from a distance. She laughed, kissed Alla anyway, and praised her performance on the violin. As other members of the audience came up and added their congratulations, Yakov approached. He grasped her arm impatiently, said her stepmother wasn't feeling well and they had to leave. On the way home, neither of them said a word about the concert. Dasha went straight upstairs to bed; Yakov followed Alla into the salon and closed the door. She saw the cane in his hand begin to twitch and, knowing it was impossible to escape, stood her ground and waited. "Just because a few provincial fools applaud you, don't imagine you're Paganini," Yakov said, then grabbed the box of chocolates she was clutching and threw it out the window.

As he aimed a blow at her with the cane, Alla managed to sidestep. It smashed a table lamp instead. Yakov grunted with rage, deliberately smashed another lamp, then lurched toward Alla as she was about to flee to the hallway. He gave her a whack on the arm that knocked her to the floor, called her stupid, ugly, untalented, the black sheep of the family, and left the room.

Alla crawled to the alcove and lay down on her cot. When the pain in her arm lessened, she fell asleep. But she woke up early the next morning, tried to lift her arm, and gave a shriek as the pain returned, more intense than before. Melanya hurried in, then went to fetch Yakov. Exactly as he had done after beating his daughter in the Odessa hotel, Yakov dropped to his knees. But instead of sobbing he muttered, "Sonya, Sonya," then hugged her so fiercely that the pain in her arm became unbearable. "Stay away from me, leave me alone!" she begged, but Yakov held on and began kissing her on the mouth.

"Now I understand," Alla heard a woman's voice say. Yakov suddenly let her go, and she looked up to see Dasha standing over the cot.

"Yes, now I understand," Dasha repeated. "An apple never falls far from the tree. Like mother, like daughter . . . *Shlyukha!*" This Russian word that Alla had never heard before brought Yakov to his feet. He threw his wife against the wall and punched her on the nose. Dasha screamed "Yid!" and kicked him in the stomach. They both toppled to the floor. Then Dasha had a coughing fit, and spat blood and another "Yid!" in Yakov's face before she collapsed.

Yakov sent for the family doctor, who prescribed several days of rest in bed for Dasha and put Alla's broken arm in a splint. That night, after hearing the front door slam when her father left the house, Alla went to Melanya's room. "What is *shlyukha?*" she asked. Melanya, in bed with Mezhuk, seemed too embarrassed to answer. But the head chemist laughed. "She might as well know," he said, and told Alla it was slang for a girl who slept around with men. "Then are you a *shlyukha?*" she asked Melanya. The servant admitted it, then crossed herself. "But I'm sure God will forgive me for a sin as sweet as Mezhuk."

A YEAR LATER, before Adelaida Nazimova performed again at the Christmas concert, she had a series of nightmares in which she lost her violin, was unable to tune it, or fell flat on her face as she made her entrance. On Christmas Day she walked onstage sick to her stomach with nerves and saw Yakov sitting in the front row. This time he was alone, for Dasha felt unwell, and somehow his falsely genial smile had a calming effect. "You can't fool me any more," Alla thought. "I know you'll beat me for something or other afterward, but while I'm here this isn't your black sheep, this is Adelaida Nazimova and you can't touch her!" Then, as she tuned her violin: "Stop thinking of yourself or you won't play well. You're somebody else now, let her do it." And finally, acknowledging applause: "Isn't Nazimova good today? I'm so happy for her!"

But in the banquet room, when people came up to congratulate Alla, she felt cheated and empty. Changing her name had failed to change her life; she was still a nobody desperately pretending to be somebody. In her autobiography Nazimova added that she suffered from postperformance depression as well as stage fright all her life, and wondered whether to attribute both to the senseless beating Yakov gave her after that first concert. "Even after the thirty-eight recorded curtain calls for being Mrs Alving and for directing Ibsen's *Ghosts* at the Empire Theatre, New York, December 12, 1935 . . . I felt like biting everybody and wishing I could hide somewhere or vanish out of sight."

IN JUNE 1891, when Alla turned twelve, she was old enough to be enrolled at the Imperial Gymnasium, the only school that Yakov considered exclusive enough for a daughter of "the most important man in Yalta," as he now saw himself. Formerly a palatial health resort for the rich, the Gymnasium now educated their children in rooms with crystal chandeliers, bay windows, and balustraded terraces. School began at ten in the morning and ended at eight in the evening, but Alla was so eager to get out of Yakov's house that these hours seemed hardly long enough. As well as studying French, German, history, geography, religion, and math, she took extra classes in drawing and sewing. Hopeless at math, which earned her a series of bad report cards and beatings by her father, Alla excelled at drawing and, especially, sewing. From Frau Groelich she had learned only to darn and patch, but "there isn't a thing in planning, cutting, fitting, sewing, trimming, embroidering, which [the sewing instructor] did not teach us. We even learned to make our own uniforms, yes, everything from head to foot except shoes. This is the reason why I was able to design and sew the costumes for twenty-two people—Orlenev's company in New York, 1906—when our star had suddenly decided to play *Tsar Fyodor.*"

The first time Alla came to sewing class, the instructor glanced at her feet and remarked that it was absurd for a rich father to send his daugh-

ter to school in a pair of dilapidated shoes. He took her to see the principal, who shook her head in disbelief at the holes in Alla's shoes, wrote
a note to Yakov, and told Alla to take it home at once. She found Yakov
in the pharmacy. After reading the note, he led Alla to the garden in back
and thrashed her for entering the pharmacy without permission. But at
least, after complaining about the expense, he bought her new shoes.

A few days later, the history teacher noticed that Alla screwed up her
eyes when she read from the blackboard, and had large dark cavities in
her teeth. This time the principal went to see Yakov, who sent Alla to a
dentist, and to an optometrist, who prescribed glasses for nearsightedness. She thought they made her look ugly, and hated to use them. But
without them she would never have seen His Imperial Majesty sharp and
clear. To celebrate the arrival of Tsar Alexander III and his family for their
annual visit to Yalta in August 1891, flags hung outside the windows of
houses and stores, two-headed eagles decorated the street lamps, and
mounted police paraded the length of the town. The entire school,
alongside local dignitaries, assembled at the pier to greet the royal yacht,
but when the Romanovs walked down the gangway, Alla was deeply disappointed. They weren't wearing crowns.

FOR MORE than two years, Dasha had refused to speak to
Alla, and even ignored her presence at mealtimes. Since giving birth to a
second child, she often remained in bed all day, but as Alla got home
from school one evening, she heard someone playing a Chopin prelude
on the piano in the salon. Tiptoeing to the doorway, she saw Dasha at
the keyboard, wearing a white lace dress. When her stepmother finished
the piece, she gave Alla an alarming squint. "Schubert, Schumann . . ."
she said. "And I used to dance too, I loved dancing. But I caught a cold
after I went to a ball in Moscow, and they sent me here." A long sigh;
then she got up and walked out slowly to the hallway.

Another two years would pass before she spoke to Alla again.

UNTIL SHE went to school, Alla lived in almost complete
isolation from the world. An exile within her own home, she was allowed
no visitors apart from her private tutors, and forbidden to speak to anyone except Yakov himself and her cousin Victor, who stayed amiably
aloof and saw his own friends outside pharmacy hours. At home she
made one true friend, Melanya, but they could meet only in secret. At

school she made another, Nastya Popandopoulos, whose father was a rich Greek merchant and banned everyone except Greeks from his house. And since Yakov refused to let Alla bring Nastya home, their friendship had to be kept secret as well. During the school lunch break, the two girls sneaked off to a patch of wasteland behind the Hotel Russiya, hid in the bushes, and discussed their mutual admiration for George Sand. Nastya was particularly impressed by Sand's scandalous affair with Chopin, Alla by her gesture of wearing men's clothes and carrying a sword stick in the cause of equal rights for women.

In June 1892, at the start of Alla's summer vacation, Volodya returned to the wasteland of Yakov's house after graduating from the military academy in Riga. During their years together at the Groelichs' farm, Alla had fantasized Volodya as the ideal elder brother, someone to confide in, someone who would understand. She made no move to turn the fantasy into reality, only kept hoping, because Volodya had an air of emotional privacy that warned her off. But it warned everybody off, so she didn't feel personally rejected and continued to believe that an unspoken sympathy existed between them. When they met again after five years, Alla thought she detected something else unspoken. A hint of conspiracy in Volodya's smile, and the way he pressed her hand, implied that he was finally ready to drop his guard.

But from the first, Yakov made it impossible for them to be alone together. The family had just finished lunch when Volodya arrived, and Yakov lost no time in ordering Alla back to the salon. She didn't see her brother again until supper, when Yakov announced that Volodya would start work in the pharmacy next morning. For a month, she only saw him at mealtimes. Immediately after lunch Yakov ordered Volodya back to work, immediately after supper dismissed him to his sleeping quarters in a room behind the pharmacy. Then the master of the house locked every entrance to the premises and pocketed the keys.

On a hot, humid day in July, Alla, Volodya, and Dasha had just sat down to another lunch when Yakov hurried into the room brandishing Alla's report card from school. He called her an idiot for failing her math examination again, and dealt her a blow on the head that knocked her to the floor. Volodya intervened as Yakov prepared to kick Alla in the stomach. A fight broke out between father and son, and Yakov suddenly staggered back, lost his balance, and blacked out.

The scene apparently made no impression at all on Dasha. As her husband lay crumpled and still, she poured herself a glass of tea from the samovar. Between the time Volodya ran to get the family doctor and when he returned with him, Dasha ate the meal Melanya had served. She poured herself more tea as they carried Yakov upstairs, was still calmly sipping it when they came back to the room. The doctor, aware of Dasha's precarious condition and beyond surprise at anything that occurred in the house, told her not to worry. Yakov had suffered nothing more serious than an attack of sunstroke. Dasha merely nodded, coughed, and said she needed to lie down for a while.

As soon as the doctor left, Volodya told Alla that Yakov's stroke had nothing to do with the sun. The medical details she understood only vaguely; the important thing was that Yakov would have to stay in bed for several weeks, and she ran to the pharmacy to break the good news. But Mezhuk and Tayzi knew everything already, for the doctor had given them several prescriptions to make up, and they were jubilantly smoking cigarettes. One prescription, Tayzi announced with a wink, was for a disease called syphilis. Alla had never heard of it, and he explained with another wink that it was the price men paid for a good time in Paris. Incurable, he added hopefully.

Next morning, while Alla and Volodya were at breakfast, Dasha appeared in her nightgown. Ignoring Alla as usual, and directing her remarks to Volodya, she claimed to be feeling so weak and confused by a migraine attack that she could hardly stand up. But she seemed to be thinking remarkably straight. Nina, she said, was expected home from finishing school in Dresden at the end of the week, and it was out of the question for Dasha to have three stepchildren living in the house without a father to keep them in order. The only solution was for Volodya and Alla to leave as soon as possible for their uncle Ilya's place in Yedintsy, where Nina would join them directly from Dresden. "I've already written letters to arrange everything," Dasha added, as impatient to clean house as Alla and Volodya were delighted at the prospect of escape.

But they were shocked by their father's appearance when they said goodbye. Dasha had allowed no one except the doctor to see him since his collapse, had only shrugged when Volodya asked after him. They found Yakov lying in bed, one side of his face weirdly distorted, one eye closed and the other glaring. After they left the room, Alla reported what Tayzi had told her about the French disease, and hoped it was true.

Now that they could talk freely, brother and sister happily discussed their mutual unhappiness. If Volodya had been so hard to know in the past, Alla discovered, it was because he didn't know himself. But at military school he reacted so strongly against the military code that he underwent a spiritual crisis. He began reading the works of Tolstoy, secretly converted to pacifism, and decided that he wanted to be a writer. Although desperate to get out of Russia and breathe uncensored air, Volodya managed to carry out his father's wishes by graduating. Then he asked Yakov to let him take a course in journalism at the University of Berlin. "Too expensive," Yakov wrote back, insisted that Volodya had no literary talent, and ordered him home. With no money and no alternative except to enlist in the army, which was unthinkable, Volodya obeyed. Only a few minutes after arriving at the house, he learned that Yakov expected him to work in the pharmacy without pay.

By the time they left for Yedintsy, Alla and Volodya had puzzled for hours over Yakov's determination to humiliate almost every member of his family. Only Nina had been spared so far, but when she finally came home, would Yakov give her the same treatment, or decide that he needed one person to love him? They failed to solve any part of the puzzle, except that Yakov's love, as Sonya had found, could be even harder to bear than his hatred.

On the boat to Odessa, Volodya told Alla that he still hoped to go to Berlin, where everyone could read and write freely, and make a living as a journalist there. "What do you want to write about?" Alla asked, and a look came over Volodya's face that she found very beautiful and pure. "Universal brotherhood," he said. "It could happen, if everyone in the world followed the teachings of Christ."

Although this impressed her, the idea of escape was never far from Alla's mind. "Why don't you run away now?" she asked.

"I don't have the money. And until I come of age, I can only get a passport if papa writes a letter to the authorities. But he'll never do it," Volodya said. "When I asked him again to send me to Berlin, he hit me in the face."

"Why didn't you kill him?"

"It's against my faith."

Their futures, it seemed, depended on that French disease. In the meantime, as soon as they arrived in Odessa, Alla suggested they try to find their mother. She remembered the name of the hotel near which Yakov had said that Sonya lived, and they knocked at the doors of houses in neighboring streets. After two hours, they gave up and sat in a café opposite the City Theatre. "I used to go to the theatre quite often in Riga," Volodya said. "Apart from books," he added solemnly, "there's nothing in the world so instructive."

Sitting in the train the next day, they discussed Nina, whom neither of them had seen since she went away to her first boarding school.

Volodya knew that Yakov wanted her to become an opera singer. For the last two years she'd studied at the Conservatory of Music in Dresden, while boarding at a nearby "finishing school for young ladies of good family." Then her singing teacher wrote Yakov that Nina's voice would never be good enough. "And now that papa's decided to bring her home," Volodya said, "I suppose she'll have to live there too, like you and me, until he dies. Unless she finds a husband."

Although they had grown very close in the last few days, Alla couldn't bring herself to talk to her ideal elder brother about sex. She felt sure it would embarrass him. ("We never quarreled, but nor did we ever kiss," Nazimova wrote in her autobiography. "He was so timid in a way that I got timid too.") Since the birth of Dasha's second child, Alla had started wondering again exactly how babies came into the world. Melanya, she felt sure, would know a lot more about it than Gretl. But at first Melanya only blushed and giggled at Alla's questions. Finally she said that husbands had a trick of doing something to their wives without the wives' realizing it; nine months later babies emerged from their bellies; and "that's why there are so many screaming brats in Russia!" For the next few weeks Alla had a recurring nightmare in which howling babies erupted without warning from her navel. And at the age of thirteen she decided that marriage was no less risky than prostitution.

"THIS CHILD has the memory of an old elephant," Uncle Ilya said when Alla found that she remembered everything about the farmhouse at Yedintsy, everything that had happened during her first stay, even the name of the family dog. Many years later, Nazimova supposed that she couldn't bear to forget anything connected with her only experience of a real home and loving family. Although Frau Groelich had been kind in her stern, grudging way, the shadow of Otto fell across that house. Ilya, Sofya, and their two sons worked just as hard as the Groelichs, but were never grimly dutiful about it. They loved music, and encouraged Alla to sing folk songs after supper. Then Volodya, who accompanied her, took turns playing the piano with Ilya's sons while everyone danced the waltz and mazurka before going to bed.

One afternoon a carriage drew up outside the farmhouse, and a tall, slim, elegant person who looked to Alla like "a very fascinating foreign lady" stepped out. It was Nina, now sixteen years old. Fluent in French, German, and English, she refused to speak Russian and found Yedintsy terribly backward after the comforts of a fashionable school in Dresden.

"Shocking!" she exclaimed in English when Alla informed her that the farmhouse had no bathroom. Even more shocking, it had only an outdoor privy; Nina decided to wear a hat with a veil and carry a parasol whenever she went there, in case she became "freckled like a peasant" in the midsummer sun.

She traveled with a great quantity of luggage, which Alla watched her unpack. One wicker box contained nothing but cosmetics and a French perfume called Violettes de Parme. "But I use only a soupçon, otherwise it wouldn't be ladylike." It was equally unladylike, Nina added, to eat onions or sit with your legs crossed. Between lessons on etiquette, she displayed the dresses, petticoats, corsets, hats, gloves, fans, and high-buttoned shoes that Yakov had paid for. But at the first mention of their father, the first of their many quarrels began.

To Nina he was the most wonderful, generous man who ever lived, "an aristocrat and a saint," horribly betrayed by Sonya. To Alla he was a devil and Sonya "the real saint in the family." Nina: "I'm not surprised to find you shockingly ignorant after living with Swiss peasants so long." Alla, mocking her tone: "I *am* surprised to find *you* shockingly ignorant after living with millionaires so long." Then, getting angry: "Anyway, your 'aristocrat' was the son of a Jewish peasant." Nina, stamping her foot: "Liar! Take that back at once or I'll tell papa every word you just said." Alla: "Tell that mad dog who should have died years ago anything you like."

They soon made up, Nina saying between hugs and kisses that since they were poor orphans without a mother they must always be friends and never quarrel again. But they soon did. Finishing school had taught Nina the supreme importance of refinement, and she was appalled at the way Alla ran barefoot through the fields, talked to filthy peasants, and enjoyed helping to feed the pigs. "So unladylike!" she complained, and received a most unladylike whack in the face, followed by another furious attack on Yakov. But when Alla described the beatings she endured, her broken arm, the horrible scenes with their stepmother, Nina screamed, "Liar! You're just saying that to upset me!" and fled from the room in tears. After supper that same evening, Alla gave an impersonation of Yakov barking out orders and announcing, "I am the master of this house!" It sent Nina into such violent hysterics that Uncle Ilya told Alla never to do it again.

Between quarrels, Nina could be generous and charming. She lavished gifts on her sister—a lace handkerchief "from Paris," a hair ribbon, a pair of gloves—and dabbed soupçons of Violettes de Parme behind her ears.

She loved the family dances after supper, and waltzed so prettily and gracefully that Alla led a round of applause. But when Nina attempted a song by Schubert, Alla privately found it "not so good, flat, off pitch." She resisted the temptation to parody the way her sister kept hitting wrong notes and settled for a dumb show instead. Mimicking Nina's dainty progress to the privy, she continued to twirl an imaginary parasol while she squatted. The others laughed at first; then Nina left the room in tears, and Ilya told Alla to apologize.

She found Nina sitting on her bed, dabbing at her eyes with a lace handkerchief. Before Alla could say a word, she launched into a pitiful monologue about how lonely she was, how nobody loved or understood her, and how much she missed her best friend at school in Dresden. Feeling guilty and ashamed, Alla offered to become her new best friend. But Nina shook her head. "You're too vulgar," she said, and turned her back. For Alla the rejection was crucial, and she decided never to try to get close to her sister again.

As summer turned to fall, Ilya received a letter from Yakov announcing that he was almost completely recovered and ready to take care of his family again. Alla cried when she said goodbye to Ilya and Sofya, but as the carriage drove off Nina remarked that she couldn't wait to get home to her papa. "Well, let her find out for herself," Alla thought.

Yakov was waiting on the quay when the boat docked. He wore a white silk suit and dark glasses, swung his cane with authority, but his shoulders stooped, his right leg dragged slightly when he walked, and there was an occasional thickness in his speech. He kissed Nina, handed her a bouquet of roses, and said that Dasha hoped to feel well enough to meet her soon. He gave Volodya a brief nod and ignored Alla until they arrived at the house, when he ordered her to the salon, followed her inside, and closed the door. "I won't be able to beat you so much in future because the doctor's forbidden me to get excited," he said. Alla couldn't help smiling, but Yakov had no sense of humor. He grabbed her arm and twisted it. "If you don't obey your elder sister, she'll tell me. Is that understood?"

"That's understood," Alla said. Nothing had really changed, it seemed, except that Yakov treated Volodya marginally better by paying him one ruble (fifty cents) a week to work in the pharmacy. He also gave Nina a weekly allowance of fifty kopecks, but Alla suspected it was partly a reward for spying. Within a few days, Nina announced that she had seen Alla whispering with Tayzi, and warned her not to do it again or Yakov would hear of it. (It was fortunate she didn't hear what they were saying: Alla had wanted to know how long it took a man to die of syphilis.) A week later, she caught Alla and Melanya talking in the salon and threatened to inform Yakov. Alla begged her not to, afraid as much for Melanya as for herself, and once again Nina let her off with a warning. But then, determined to break up a friendship she considered unsuitable, Nina complained to Yakov that Melanya was disrespectful and got her fired.

Finding Alla in tears after Melanya left, Nina gave her a lecture on the kind of "vulgar people" with whom well-bred young ladies must never associate. Servants and store assistants headed the list, followed by actresses. At finishing school, Nina explained, she had learned that girls who went on the stage became "kept women," no better than whores. Then she kissed Alla and presented her with another lace handkerchief.

With Melanya gone and Volodya back in exile at the pharmacy, Alla began confiding her thoughts to a diary. One day she forgot to hide it away with Sonya's photograph, and Nina found it lying open on the desk in the alcove. "My friend must have been wrong about the incurable French disease," she read, "or papa would have croaked long ago." Once again Alla was lucky. When Nina showed the diary to Yakov, he was feeling unwell. Although furious, he could only retaliate by giving Alla a couple of feeble slaps.

Opera singers, unlike actresses, were not on Nina's blacklist. Finishing-school wisdom approved of them as respectable and refined, and she still hoped to become a diva. Hearing that Madame Tatarinova, a teacher and retired singer, was planning to stage a performance of *Eugene Onegin* at the Hotel Russiya shortly after Christmas, she applied for an audition. Madame, no more impressed by Nina's Schubert than was the teacher in Dresden, offered her a place in the chorus. Her hopes set on a leading role, Nina angrily refused. If I had been the one to fail, Alla thought, Yakov would have beaten me. But his favorite daughter could apparently do no wrong, and Yakov dismissed Tatarinova as a provincial fool. All the same, Nina sulked for days and glowered with jealousy when Alla performed at Savelson's next Christmas concert. "Nazimova did not play well that night. I was too nervous with 'two papas' staring at me over the lamps." And as Nina stared, she noticed that her sister's petticoat was showing. She drew Yakov's attention to the fact, and this time he felt strong enough to inflict a serious beating on the daughter who could do no right. Then he almost fainted, and retired to bed for two days.

The day he got up again, Alla's school report arrived. As usual, she had failed her math examination, but when Yakov started to beat her again the effort brought on a seizure, and the doctor diagnosed another attack of sunstroke. "You are driving poor papa to his grave," Nina told Alla.

Papa rallied, but his right leg dragged even more when he walked, his speech sounded even thicker, and Nina feared he would never get really better. "How he must suffer and suffer," she said, so distressed that she struck out at Sonya as well. "Mama broke his heart, and his health. . . ." If Yakov suffered, Alla said, he had only himself and his horrible character to blame. She was reading *The Brothers Karamazov* at the time, found a mirror image of their father in Dostoevsky's vicious patriarch, and thoroughly approved his murder.

That winter, Alla and Nastya began writing poetry. One day, when the sun came out after a week of heavy rain, they huddled in the damp bushes of their secret garden while Alla recited her latest work, the story of two young Roman priestesses chained to a temple altar until they were rescued by angels. Nastya pronounced "The Regeneration of Two Vestal Virgins" as fine as anything by Pushkin ("I did not argue"), and thought it should be printed. "I'll ask my father to put up the money," she said. Nastya also decided that the booklet needed illustrations, which gave Alla an idea. They went to the studio of a local photographer, took off their school uniforms, draped themselves in sheets, and struck a series of dramatic poses for the camera. Carried away as usual by pretending to be somebody else, Alla played her vestal virgin to the hilt. But the photographs were a terrible letdown. They made her look so dumpy and foolish that she hid them away.

Yakov was at lunch when the photographer's assistant arrived with a bill for forty rubles. Insisting that no one in his family had been photographed, he handed it back and told the man to leave. The assistant was about to point to Alla, but Nina proved too quick for him. On one of her snooping expeditions to the alcove, she had discovered the "shocking" and "vulgar" pictures. Now she ran to fetch them, and Alla saw Yakov's face twitch with rage. "So she thinks she's an actress now?" He called Alla a slut and a whore, dragged her across the courtyard, kicked her into the street, and threatened to kill her if she ever came back.

Alla knew that Nastya's father slammed the door on non-Greeks, but she had no other friend to ask for help. As she hurried to the Popandopoulos house it began to rain heavily, and by the time she rang the bell she was soaked to the skin. The servant made her wait outside while he summoned Nastya. In disgrace with her father, who had also received a bill for forty rubles that day, Nastya was in no mood to sympathize. "It was your idea, and you've got to find the money," she said. "Otherwise my father will go to the principal and we'll both be kicked out of school. So get it! All of it!"

Nastya closed the door. It had a glass panel in the center, and Alla came face to face with her own reflection. Locking eyes with herself, she thought: "*Here's a girl kicked out of her home, betrayed by her best friend as well as her sister. She's got no money and I suppose she'll have to try and get a job as a servant. What a story! Enough to make you cry . . .*" And as Alla began to cry, still looking her reflection straight in the eye, she took a step back. "*If you must go on crying, don't screw up your face, it looks awful.*"

It was disorienting to feel suddenly split in two—so desperately unhappy that she couldn't stop crying, and at the same time able to criticize the effect on her appearance. "When I finally walked away from Nastya's house I saw this girl as though I stood apart from her. She went through rain and mud and stopped at every kitchen door, asking if anybody needed a servant maid. Nobody did, and she walked on and on." Hours passed and dusk fell before she understood what had happened. "What I did at that glass door was the same as what I did at every Christmas concert when I stopped thinking of myself. This girl was the same girl I called Nazimova, the girl who played the violin. She was not I. . . ."

A carriage drew up and Dasha leaned out the window. For the first time in two years, she acknowledged Alla's existence by telling her to get in. But it seemed to Alla that "the girl got in first," crying because she was a poor maidservant who couldn't find a job, not because she was Yakov's daughter on her way home to another beating. She had no way of knowing that many actors used this kind of dissociation, or that a few years later she would be using it herself. Obsessed with the need to escape from Yakov, determined to keep up a proud front until she found a way, Alla had taken refuge in a second self, but a self with no conscious identity. "Nazimova" was still only a name, and Alla had yet to recognize the future actress kicking and struggling to be born.

YAKOV WAS waiting in the hallway, cane in hand. After the beating, he told Alla that he couldn't bear the sight of her any more, and was going to send her away to boarding school. But even though his daughter was the black sheep of the family, she bore the great name of Leventon, and Yakov picked a school run by a Greek princess in Odessa, who claimed that her students included "many daughters of the nobility."

Next day, at another "family" lunch, Yakov suddenly choked on his food. He vomited, gasped for breath, then blacked out, and everyone thought he was going to die. Although he rallied again, Yakov began to complain of fatigue and seemed to undergo a mysterious personality

Alla, aged fifteen,
at boarding school
in Odessa

change. The tyrant no longer raged or barked orders, lost interest in his pharmacy, wandered out to the street and tried to engage strangers in conversation. At other times he lay down for hours on a couch in his bedroom, and often invited Alla to sit and talk with him. Drooling with affection over his outcast daughter, Yakov fondled her hair, stroked her cheeks, and kept saying how beautifully she played the violin. Alla found his caresses and his breath on her face repulsive, but not as bad as a flogging, and ticked off in her mind each day that brought her closer to freedom.

In January 1894, she arrived at the princess's school. Nazimova would remember that Alla was determined to be happy there, if only because she was no longer in Yakov's house. But as the only non-Catholic student, she was a spiritual curiosity and with her pudgy figure, untamed bushy hair, and pimply face, made a physically outlandish impression as well. Nicknamed "Anti-Christ," she was cast once again as the outsider, but on a different stage. Although the girls teased Alla, they were not cruel. They looked on the newcomer as a source of entertainment, dared Alla to live up to her appearance by behaving outrageously. She accepted the challenge with a series of acts that would have infuriated Yakov and horrified Nina. When Alla walked up and down the dormitory, sticking out her tongue and making grotesque "Anti-Christ" faces, the girls fell about on their beds with laughter. Accused of neglecting her German grammar and told to stay behind after class, she claimed to speak better German than her teacher and marched out of the room. And when another teacher discovered two banned books (Turgenev's *Fathers and Sons* and a translation of *Leaves of Grass,* lent to her by Volodya) hidden in Alla's desk, she responded with a lecture on the stupidity of censorship.

Reprimands followed from the tiny hunchbacked princess, but no cruel and unusual punishment. It was a new, heady experience to rebel without being beaten, and it gave Alla a sense of her own power. But when the princess refused permission to visit her mother, she felt suddenly helpless again. One of the girls at school was a distant cousin of Sonya and knew her address in Odessa, but Yakov had given orders that Alla must never be allowed to see her. Twice a week, accompanied by a chaperone, she walked a few blocks to the house of her violin teacher, and hoped for a chance meeting in the street. Sometimes she held her breath when a woman with rouged cheeks and a feathered hat came toward her. But it was never the Sonya of the photograph that Alla still kept hidden among her clothes.

With Yakov continuing to frustrate her by remote control, Alla determined to strike back. At least she could kill his hopes for her future as a professional violinist. Outraged by her deliberate wrong notes and hideous screeches, Alla's teacher refused to give her any more lessons and complained to the princess. "You're the biggest problem in my school," the princess said. This was encouraging news for someone high on rebellion, but before Alla could decide on her next move, a fire broke out in the school kitchen. The whole building burned down, and the girls were boarded out with various families in Odessa.

THE FAMILY with whom Alla lived for the next few months consisted of a quiet, genteel widow and her two daughters. Both girls belonged to an amateur dramatic society that gave performances at a local hall every Sunday. Natalie was in her mid-twenties and played romantic leads; Katerina, five years older, specialized in character parts. Settling down to her homework in the evenings, Alla could hear them rehearsing their roles in the next room. At first she tried not to listen, for they brought back a particularly degrading memory from the past.

"So she wants to be an actress now?" Yakov had jeered when he threw her out of the house. Like Nina, he dismissed Russian girls who went on the stage as whores, even though he spoke admiringly of Duse and Bernhardt. But why should only foreigners and divas deserve respect as artists? The girls in the next room were obviously not whores. In the end, curiosity made Alla move her chair closer to the room beyond the half-open door, where she could overhear without being seen.

She soon realized that Natalie and Katerina took acting very seriously, often breaking a rehearsal to discuss a particular line or situation. An even greater surprise was that they found nothing shameful in appearing on the stage, and their mother actually encouraged it. Nazimova the actress gave Alla another impatient kick, and she began neglecting her homework to eavesdrop almost every evening. But it was not only the world of theatre beyond the door that seduced her. When Alla finally got up from her chair to watch as well as listen, she had fallen in love with Natalie's voice.

"I began to adore Natalie. . . . She was not beautiful nor even pretty, but her eyes were soft and her sobs so painful." Kindred spirits with the same thirst for self-dramatization, they both cried when Alla declared her admiration, and Natalie invited her to the next Sunday performance.

Sitting in her friend's dressing room before the curtain went up, Alla witnessed a magic act, Natalie's self-transformation by greasepaint, eye shadow, lip rouge, costume, and wig into a glamorous stranger. And after the play she witnessed the same act in reverse. The wig came off first, followed by the costume, and Natalie, stripped to her petticoat, wiped her beautiful face away with cold cream.

School offered no education to compare to this. The last class of the day over, Alla hurried back to study Natalie rehearsing the next play, to "watch her face, listen to the modulations of her voice and—worship her. . . ." Before every Sunday performance she sat in Natalie's dressing room, helped pin up her hair, tie her shoes, button her dress. And one night the beloved made Alla almost unbearably happy: "To please me, she wore my petticoat under her costume."

That same night, Alla locked her bedroom door and made herself up to look like Natalie in the play, shadowing her eyes with a lead pencil, pressing a red ribbon soaked in water to her lips, and pouring tooth powder over her hair to imitate the effect of a white wig. "I thought I looked beautiful and stared at myself in a hand mirror until I fell asleep, making an unspeakable mess on my pillows and sheets." The next night, Alla imagined herself playing Natalie's roles on the stage, speaking her lines and imitating her gestures. Then she began to feel that Natalie's roles were "not quite sufficient to express all I wanted," and drew on her talent for impersonation to create new characters, copying the speech patterns and mannerisms of her teachers and classmates.

But instead of entertaining others, as she had done in the past, Alla was now performing for herself. Near the end of her life, Nazimova recalled the experience in almost mystical terms. (A typically "Russian" habit, according to the silent-movie actress Dagmar Godowsky.) In Nazimova's autobiography, as the young Alla tries out a series of roles she hallucinates a series of different reflections in the mirror, and hears herself speaking in strange out-of-body voices. "Dealing in emotions seemed to be my destiny. . . ." Her destiny, of course, was Nazimova the actress's finally kicking her way out of Alla's unconscious. "She was not I," but they would be together for life.

WHEN SHE returned home for the summer vacation in July 1895, a few weeks after her sixteenth birthday, Alla was preceded by a batch of spectacularly bad reports from school. But Yakov never read them. He was in a private sanatorium in Odessa after suffering a third stroke, and Dasha had left the house. Settling herself, two sons, and a nurse in an apartment in the town, she looked forward to a life without stepchildren and migraines.

When Nina described how two male nurses had had to carry her adored, helpless papa away on a stretcher, she burst into tears. Although Alla couldn't feel sorry for Yakov, she was touched by her sister's unhappiness. They kissed, hugged, and grew briefly, deceptively close again. But when Alla confided that she was not going back to school and had decided to become an actress, Nina warned that she would end up a whore like their mother. And they moved further apart than ever.

Feeling sure of an ally in Volodya, now her legal guardian for as long as Yakov remained in the sanatorium, Alla asked him to send her to drama school. His refusal stunned her. "You're too young," Volodya said. "But in a year's time, if you still feel the same way, I'll consider it." She couldn't make Volodya understand that a year would feel like a lifetime, or get him to explain why someone who professed to love the theatre should be so discouraging. Sulking in her room, Alla decided that Volodya was playing for time, afraid of the scene Yakov would make if he rallied again and came home. She fired Volodya from the role of ideal elder brother and cast him instead as the cowardly son.

Volodya was certainly timid, and would always be the eternal student,

sincerely idealistic and sweetly impractical. But, with Alla at the most
awkward stage of her adolescence and unlikely to impress anyone as an
actress with a future, was he also waiting for the ugly duckling to show
signs of becoming a swan? If he was too tactful to admit the problem,
Alla soon admitted it to herself. A few more performances before the
mirror made her intensely self-critical: "My face was much too round,
too fat, the nose too thick, the brows too wide, the mouth too small. . . .
I was always tripping over things or hitting chairs and tables with my
hips because my body was too short, plump and awkward."

For years Yakov had insisted that Alla was born ugly, and she had accepted it as fact, but now she determined to look as well as feel like an
actress. She lost weight by training herself to eat less, trimmed her hair,
and styled it with curling irons. Then, with Volodya's permission, she
tried out her new image at the summer dances held on weekends at the
casino. This was a gratifying success. She attracted quite a few college students and army cadets, and although none of them attracted Alla, she accepted invitations to the waltz, carriage rides in the countryside, and
swimming parties at night in the Black Sea. "I had to wait? I'd wait. But
I would have the time of my young life while waiting." For Alla, having
the time of her young life meant performance. Although she went out
with boys, she preferred to play at being "just one of them," her sex disguised by a pair of pants borrowed from Volodya and a beret that covered her hair.

Her brother, meanwhile, tried to disguise the anxiety he felt as a series
of conflicting letters arrived from the doctor at the sanatorium. One
week Yakov was much improved, almost well enough to return home;
the next he'd had a serious relapse. Finally Volodya managed to come to
a decision. He told Alla and Nina they'd better see for themselves, and
the three of them took the boat to Odessa.

On the journey, Alla was obsessed by thoughts of "horrible beatings
for me, endless humiliations for brother," if the tyrant returned. Even
worse, it would mean the death of her future. "I was praying, yes, praying to God to make him incurable!" Waiting on the veranda of the doctor's house, she saw Yakov in the distance, accompanied by a male nurse
as he approached from the garden. She noted how slowly he walked and
how thin he'd grown, but that was all she could tell.

Then he reached the veranda, stopped, and stared blankly at his three
children. After a moment Yakov made them a formal bow and turned to
the doctor. "These are my new tenants," he said. "They've taken the
apartment for the summer." It was the only acknowledgment he made of
the presence of visitors. For the rest of the time, he ignored them and

talked exclusively to the doctor. "I planted this myself, when I bought the house," he said, pointing to a tree. Perhaps Yakov mistook it for his meteorological station, for he went on to explain his formula for concentrated food tablets in surprisingly lucid detail. Resisting the doctor's attempts to change the subject, he talked obsessively of his inventions until a bell rang inside the house. "My wife is calling me for dinner," he said, suddenly alarmed. "I must go now, she gets angry when I'm late."

The nurse led Yakov away, a lost, feeble, harmless old man whom Alla would never see again. But now that she knew the address, she could at last see her mother again. Although Nina wanted nothing to do with the woman she held responsible for driving Yakov out of his mind, Volodya shared Alla's excitement as they walked to the house they'd failed to find before. A plump, happy Sonya answered the doorbell. Unlike Yakov, she recognized them immediately, but when she got over her astonishment seemed ill-at-ease. "Now that we could see her, we found out that it was too late. We were total strangers to each other." No longer the mother that Alla remembered from the lake at Montreux, or even the overly made-up person of the photograph, Sonya had left the past behind. And didn't want to be reminded of it. At the first mention of Yakov she recoiled, then told her children that she had a new husband, a scientist who worked for the government, "and I'm very happy now." A long uneasy silence followed, and "there was really nothing for us to do but kiss and cry a little" before they said goodbye.

Within twenty-four hours, both parents had vanished from Alla's life. Yakov's exit was an answered prayer, but Sonya's left a strange, unsettling void. "There were many tears when we parted, but I think they were tears called up by disappointment rather than anything else. . . . We were all trying to create a relationship which perhaps never existed."

WINTER CAME early to Yalta in 1895. The rains began in October, the sea turned muddy green, the tourists left, the military band no longer played in the park, and there were no more dances after the casino closed. Whenever the sun came out, so did the tuberculars. Wrapped in heavy coats and shawls, they shuffled through the town, holding little glass jars into which they occasionally spat blood. During a storm, huge waves lashed the beach pavilions, saturating the air, and the windows of Yakov's house became caked with salt. Gazing at the blurred world outside, Alla dreamed of another world, then wept with frustration at Volodya's refusal to let her join it right away.

For Volodya, the only thing more difficult than coming to a decision was going back on it. In spite of Yakov's obviously terminal decline, he still insisted that Alla must wait a year before going to drama school. At first she sulked, cried, and struck tragic attitudes sitting by a window or pacing the house. But when none of this made any apparent impression on Volodya, she became "like a tiger cub that burst its cage." Infuriatingly, the pacifist turned his other cheek.

All the same, "poor Volodya did not have a chance. How can you keep a thing like that in hand?" In fact he had two desperately unhappy sisters to keep in hand, for Nina had fallen in love with with Max Hofschneider, the son of Yalta's leading moneylender. Inconsolable after he went back to Kiev to complete his studies at the university, she shed bitter tears at breakfast, lunch, and dinner. If there was nothing Volodya could do about Nina, he could stop giving Alla a reason to claw him every day. So he knuckled under with a promise to send her to drama school as soon as he could arrange it.

With Alla on the verge of release, Nazimova's autobiography breaks off. But one of the later fragments explains how Alla came to apply for admission to the Philharmonic School in Moscow. In a letter to Ivan Keller, an old friend of their father who had moved to Moscow, Volodya asked his advice about drama schools. A wealthy man, "the sole importer of mineral water from Europe," Keller could easily have found out, if he didn't know already, that the Philharmonic was considered the best in Russia. He wrote back offering to arrange an audition for Alla, and, kinky in other respects as Yakov's friend turned out to be, his help was crucial to her future.

When Volodya decided to accompany Alla to Moscow and introduce her to Keller, he already had a passport. As a Jew who had graduated from military academy he was entitled to travel outside the Pale of Settlement, and as Alla's legal guardian he could apply for a passport on her behalf. But the Russian bureaucratic machine must have worked, as so often, in slow motion. In a later autobiographical fragment, Nazimova mentions that Alla had to wait a year after all, and didn't leave Yalta until the end of August 1896, two months after her seventeenth birthday.

In the meantime, a young revolutionary called Vladimir Ulyanov, who later changed his name to "Lenin," was exiled to Siberia for organizing a workers' strike, and Moscow celebrated the coronation of a new tsar, Nicholas II, last of the Romanovs.

4

Incidents

1896–1900

> The first thing you learn in a Russian dramatic
> school is to come out of your corsets. You throw
> them away and you never get them back again.
>
> —NAZIMOVA

AMONG THE PAPERS FOUND AFTER NA-
zimova's death are a few sketches and notes headed "Incidents," sometimes written in the third person, which she planned to use as the basis
for her autobiography of the years 1896–1900. One of them describes her
first day in Moscow. It mentions that she went to see Ivan Keller at his
house on fashionable Miasnitskaya Street, but not what they talked
about or the impression he made. Only one "incident" of that day is
recorded in any detail, and it occurred after Alla left the house.

Walking with Volodya along Kuznetsky Most, the Park Avenue of
Moscow, she stopped to look at a display of "photographs of celebrities"
in a store window. Then Volodya hailed a cab and they went to the hotel
where he'd arranged for her to stay. A few minutes later they said goodbye, for her brother was catching a train back to Yalta that afternoon. As
soon as he left, Alla hurried out to the street, took a cab to the store, and
kept it waiting while she looked through the photographs and "bought
a lot of them."

Two distinct patterns of the future emerge here: a love affair with fame as well as acting, and an inclination to burn the money candle at both ends. Volodya had given her the first installment of a modest allowance, which was supposed to cover Alla's expenses for the next six months, and it comes as no surprise to learn that she went through it in less than three.

THE CELEBRITIES in the photographs were mainly popular actors of the time. No more aware than Alla of a theatrical revolution about to erupt in the wings, they would soon wake up to find themselves out of fashion. The two most important Russian theatres were the Maly in Moscow and the Alexandrinsky in St. Petersburg, funded by the state and virtually controlled by a handful of stars who chose to appear in vehicles written by their favorite hacks. Most of these stars were confirmed scenery-chewers, although they found little scenery to chew. When the curtain went up on a room, the set was minimal, windows, doors, pictures, and sometimes even furniture painted on the walls. The last major Russian dramatist, Alexander Ostrovsky, had been so appalled by the decline in performance standards at the Maly that he began producing his own plays at his own theatre, which died with him in 1886. Ten years later, the Alexandrinsky rejected *The Seagull*, then agreed to present it when the theatre's resident comedy star, Elizaveta Levkeyeva, decided she could get a lot of laughs in the role of Madame Arkadina. Her greedy, exaggerated style, echoed by most of the cast, sank the play. And critics advised Chekhov to stick to writing stories.

When Alla arrived in Moscow, two men were working independently of each other to create a new Russian theatre. Konstantin Stanislavsky had assembled a company of actors that gave occasional performances of Shakespeare, Pushkin, and Ostrovsky. The first director in Russia to insist on authentic period style, commissioning sets and costumes for each production instead of relying on warehouse stock, he believed in "organic" visual atmosphere. Stanislavsky also believed in a unified performance style to create what he called "the feeling of truth." No mannerisms, no playing to the gallery, no pose or gesture without an "inner justification." At the Philharmonic School, Vladimir Nemirovich-Danchenko was teaching his students to replace the external tricks of personality acting with "inner movement" and "emotional merging with the playwright." Different language, similar aspirations, as the two men would shortly discover at an epic meeting that lasted eighteen hours.

When Alla met Nemirovich for the first time, she was an ambitious teenage girl who dreamed of the kind of theatre she had read about in magazines, its flamboyance personified by Sarah Bernhardt on her triumphant Russian tour, wrapped in magnificent furs and applauded by the tsar. But there was no halo of glamour around the man who auditioned her. Short and paunchy, wearing a dark suit and carrying a top hat, an immense black beard fanning out like a broom on each side of his chin, he looked like a bureaucrat and seemed much older than his thirty-eight years.

Nemirovich listened to Alla read a poem by Pushkin, sternly criticized her regional accent, then lapsed into silence. It lasted long enough to convince Alla that her audition had been a disaster, but finally he said, "All the same, you have a beautiful voice. If you work really hard, you should be able to get rid of that accent in diction class." It was Nemirovich's usual way of accepting a novice and left Alla feeling exactly as he intended, aware that she had a spark of promise but a long path to tread.

Diction was one of several extra courses—singing, dancing, fencing, calisthenics—that Nemirovich required all his students to take. Four times a week, at his own classes, he supervised readings and discussions of plays that ranged from Greek tragedy to *Camille* and *Zaza,* whose Fallen Women seemed very "modern" and daring to Alla. Shakespeare and Molière were a problem, for she had no confidence in her ability to speak verse, but she managed to disguise this by "keeping in the background." A more serious problem, at first, was her teacher's insistence on "discipline." Because of Yakov, no word could have aroused more unpleasant associations, and Nemirovich became an equally awesome father figure when she witnessed his expulsion of a student for continual laziness. But sometimes he invited a group of students for a private talk after class, and when he chose to include Alla, she found that Nemirovich dispensed advice and encouragement like a benevolent uncle, and had "a beautiful way of becoming intimate."

On other occasions, private and public, he dispensed shock treatment and made Alla feel like an ignorant stagestruck amateur. Although she had always been proud of her talent for impersonation, Nemirovich despised the actor who merely watched and copied other people. That way, he said, you will never truly create a single role, no matter how many you play. Crying on demand was another accomplishment Alla took pride in, but Nemirovich was equally contemptuous of "easy tears." He liked to quote his friend Chekhov's remark, during a rehearsal for the abortive first production of *The Seagull,* that most of the cast didn't understand "how to act without acting." Old-fashioned actors, Nemirovich explained, were always acting *something*, visibly reaching for a dramatic or comic point. He wanted his students to learn how not to act *anything*, to identify so completely with the characters they played that they no longer seemed to be giving a performance. And when he warned that it would take four years of training in mental alertness and physical control to acquire this technique of "inner movement," Alla came to terms with Nemirovich's idea of "discipline."

One exercise in mental alertness was a weekly play-reading. Nemirovich never told the students in advance what the play would be, because he wanted to see how quickly they came to grips with an unfamiliar text. "Those readings," Nazimova recalled, "were my favorite hours at school. They demanded all my powers of concentration. . . . I would dig my nails into the palms of my hands, draw my toes tight (I still catch myself doing this on the stage at intense moments) and forget all about myself." But not for long. "Oh, the dreaded interruptions of Nemirovich! Just when I thought I was magnificent, he would make fun of my southern accent. . . ." The mentor she longed to please was always more impressed by a troika of star pupils, all a few years older than herself and all soon to become famous in Russia: Olga Knipper and Ivan Moskvin as leading actors at the Moscow Art Theatre, Vsevolod Meyerhold as a director with his own company.

Like most of Ibsen's plays, *A Doll's House* had never been produced in Russia when Nemirovich sprung it on his class. Olga Knipper read Nora, and although Alla had only a few lines as the maid, she found her first experience of Ibsen overwhelming. The heroines of *Camille* and *Zaza*, stricken with tuberculosis or hopeless love for a married man, seemed trivial by comparison. After their novelty wore off, Fallen Women left "nothing to ponder or brood over, nothing to struggle for." Nora, walking out on her marriage and determined to live a free, independent life, left Alla with a great deal on her mind.

But the timing was ironic. Panicked by a letter from Nina that arrived a few days after the reading, Alla began a journey that led to part-time prostitution.

"EVERY UNHAPPY family is unhappy in its own way," according to Tolstoy, and Yakov's ability to inflict peculiar unhappiness on the Leventon family continued after he died. The news of his death, in late September that year, reached Alla in a letter from Volodya. He failed to explain, and she never discovered, whether the cause was syphilis or another stroke. And although Volodya wrote that Yakov left a will naming his three children by Sonya as sole heirs, he remained silent when the roof fell in soon afterward.

Indignant at Yakov's failure to provide for herself and their two sons, Dasha contested the will and claimed a substantial share of the estate. By the time she won her case, Hofschneider the moneylender had conned Volodya into giving him power of attorney, and used it to loan out all Yakov's ready cash at interest. With no legal grounds for suing Hofschneider, Volodya could only denounce him; and Nina, who had just become engaged to the moneylender's son, found herself caught in the middle. Meanwhile, Alla had overspent her allowance and wrote Volodya that she needed another installment right away. Her brother, reduced to living on the pharmacy's daily take, was reluctant to expose himself as a dupe. He asked Nina to reply. Equally reluctant to expose her future father-in-law as a shark, Nina sidestepped the problem of a lack of funds by taking the high moral ground: "Volodya gave you money for six months and you'll just have to manage."

Eventually Alla would get the real story out of Nina, but Nina would never learn how her sister "managed." On the first stage of her journey, Alla moved to a sleazy rooming house in a poor quarter of Moscow, where she helped "empty chamber pots, scrub floors, change foul bed linen" in lieu of rent, and spent her remaining kopecks on bread, sausage, and tea. When she had nothing left, she begged and sometimes stole scraps of food from the other tenants. Not surprisingly, she was often too tired or distracted to concentrate in class. Nemirovich grew impatient with her lack of progress and scolded her for dressing so shabbily. "Too proud and ashamed" to admit her problem to anyone at the school, Alla wondered whom to ask for help and remembered Ivan Keller.

WHERE ALLA'S money went remains a mystery. But her most desperate need, apart from food, was for winter clothes. By November, the temperature in Moscow had dropped almost to freezing point, and made the coldest day in Yalta seem mild by comparison. When Alla walked three miles to Keller's house, she had only a thin coat to wear over one of her cotton dresses.

The importer of mineral water, stout, bald, and pink-cheeked, had just sat down to dinner at the head of a long table with twelve place settings. But Keller wasn't expecting guests. Apparently he dined this way every evening, attended by servants who carried in each course on a silver platter and poured a series of wines. Relieved and grateful to be fed, Alla was less pleased by the way Keller kept interrupting her plea for help with complaints about his own life, the wife who had left him, loneliness, no children or family, and no appetite since he had developed stomach cancer. But finally he promised to give her some money if she "would do what he wanted her to do."

Eager to do anything for a warm coat and new shoes, Alla followed Keller to his study. After locking the door, he asked her to stand in front of a tapestry on the wall. Then he lay back on a couch, told Alla to keep smiling at him, and shouted "words she did not know" while he masturbated.

TEN RUBLES (five dollars) for this seemed like easy money, but Alla had always been hopeless at math. After buying a pair of new shoes, galoshes, and gloves, she was astonished to find herself penniless again. Keller had invited her to come back the following evening, but the experience, which didn't seem particularly repulsive at the time, made her want to vomit in retrospect. Instead, she "sold herself to a tenant" at the rooming house and traded her virginity for a couple of rubles, the price of bread and sausage. But although one client led to another, and Alla "sold herself" a few more times, she never earned enough for a winter coat, only flannel underwear and a woolen dress.

It was life, not drama school, that brought Alla out of her corsets, and the humiliating necessity of "selling herself" that led to her earliest sexual experiences. As Nazimova relates them, they remain "incidents," with no emotional fallout, and no explanation of how or when Alla finally learned the facts of sex. (Most likely from the conversation of those army cadets in Yalta.) In any case, a brutal father and an ineffective brother had inevitably led her to seek affection and support from her own sex. Alla had adored her mother and Melanya, "worshiped" Natalie, and would soon become emotionally involved with a student actress at the Philharmonic. Meanwhile, at the age of seventeen, she found herself in a world where sex with men was a business transaction, the more quickly concluded the better.

Welcoming Alla to the sisterhood, a prostitute at the rooming house occasionally "brought a man to her from somewhere," and after she had spent a few weeks in the lowest ranks of the oldest profession, her sexual education took an upwardly mobile turn. A classmate at the Philharmonic, "a beautiful blond girl, the dressiest and most refined-looking girl in the school," invited Alla to her birthday party at the Hermitage, a fashionable Moscow restaurant. "Come to my apartment first," she said, "and we'll go on together." As well as a bathroom "with a white porcelain tub," the first that Alla had ever seen, the beautiful blonde's apartment had a closet packed with expensive clothes. And as Alla helped her friend into a white satin evening gown, and watched her open an enormous jewelry case, the blonde confided that she owed everything—apartment, wardrobe, diamonds, and pearls—to the man she described as her "guardian."

Moments later he arrived, a middle-aged lawyer with a flower in the buttonhole of his dinner jacket and a bottle of champagne in his hand. After giving Alla her first taste of bubbly, he escorted both girls to his sleigh, wrapped them in fur rugs, and drove them to the Hermitage.

At dinner in a private upstairs room, the only other guest at the party was "a charming man of about forty" who showed Alla how to extract lobster from its shell. The lawyer watched with a faint smile, then startled her by remarking that every race had its own peculiar odor. He pulled his chair closer to Alla's and asked where she came from. "Yalta," she said, and the lawyer supposed she must be Armenian or Tatar. "No! I'm Russian!" Alla insisted. "That's strange," he said, leaning very close. "My sense of smell is very accurate, and I detect . . ." He paused, and knowing what he was about to say, Alla became mute with fear.

It was the first time that anyone in Moscow had suspected her of being Jewish. Volodya had advised her to disguise the fact, for he knew the Moscow theatre was strongly prejudiced against Jews. Alla, born in the Crimea, with its various ethnic minorities, could easily pass for Armenian, Greek, or Tatar. No questions were asked when she registered at the Philharmonic as Alla Nazimova. But as the only Jewish student there, she felt vulnerable. Although the school's royal patron, the Grand Duchess Elizaveta Feodorovna, sister to the tsarina, had a reputation for racial tolerance, she was married to the governor general of Moscow, a notorious anti-Semite who encouraged the police to harass Jews. And the other secret in Alla's life put her doubly at risk. Under Russian law it was a crime for prostitutes to operate without a license, and she had never applied for a "yellow ticket." Already one of her clients had asked to see Alla's ticket, and when she couldn't produce it, the only way to stop him from informing the police was to offer free service. But how to bargain with a rich lawyer determined to sniff her out?

His nose was almost touching her neck. "I detect," he continued, "a strong odor about you that reminds me of something I once . . ." Then he broke off. Alla had fainted.

TEN YEARS later, during the anxiety-ridden months before her Broadway debut, Nazimova wrote in her diary: "Often I can hardly breathe, my heart feels cramped, and then I lose consciousness. The doctor says it's a hysterical condition of the heart or something like that. I think it's a reaction to 'the morning after' of my life."

The first "morning after" of Alla's life, according to Nazimova's autobiography, occurred when she was six years old. Expecting to be reunited with her mother but taken by Yakov to live with the Groelichs instead, she blacked out; for the rest of her life, an emotional crisis could make her lose consciousness. The only other account of these attacks comes from her longtime companion, Glesca Marshall, and apparently Nazimova never confided the traumatic legacies of her past to anyone else until she began reading passages from her autobiography to a few friends. By this time her career was almost over. During the years of fame, in which she gave so many interviews, she always brushed aside questions about her family. But behind her public veil, Nazimova the actress couldn't resist the opportunity to hint at mysterious wounds. And one of her favorite lines to colleagues as well as reporters, "My heart was born in a deep shadow," was unconsciously loaded with subtext: Nazimova died of a coronary thrombosis.

AT THE Moscow restaurant, when Alla recovered from her faint, she made no attempt to explain herself and immediately "ran out of the room and down the stairs and all the way to the Nikitsky Gates where she—well, call it, 'lived.' " Next day she arrived at school expecting the worst, but learned that the lawyer must have decided not to betray her secret. The beautiful blonde merely reproached her for throwing away a great opportunity.

The other guest, it turned out, had been very interested in Alla until she "behaved so badly," and was one of the wealthy Alexeyev brothers. Since the name meant nothing to Alla, she was unaware that another Alexeyev brother had taken the stage name of Stanislavsky. So was the blonde, who knew Alla's admirer only as "a married man with a family, like my guardian. But when they're rich," she explained, "they like to keep a woman on the side. I was as poor as you when I picked up my lawyer outside the Opera. And if I hadn't learned a few tricks to please the old man, I'd be walking the streets again instead of going to drama school."

Nina's equation of actresses and whores began to seem not entirely unfounded after all, but compared with her fellow student Alla felt like a cheap amateur. She resolved to pick up a rich man, and after a few more "incidents" that kept her in food, literally bumped into him on her way home from school. About thirty years old, slant-eyed like a Tatar or Mongol, and wrapped in a spectacular fur coat, he staggered drunkenly out of a bar. Alla took him back to her room, where he pressed a wad of banknotes into her hand before falling asleep on the bed. She kept only two rubles, put the rest of the money back in his pocket, and hurried out to buy bread and sausage. The man was still asleep when she returned, so Alla ate her meal sitting on the bed. Then, as she made tea, he woke up. He had no idea where he was, or who Alla was, but after she filled him in and explained that she'd kept only two rubles of his money, he offered to buy her a really good meal at a restaurant.

"As long as it's not the Hermitage," Alla said, handing him a glass of tea, "and you don't drink any more." A sleigh took them to a restaurant on the outskirts of Moscow, where a gypsy band played and sang. Alla fell in love with their music and persuaded the gypsies to teach her a couple of songs; they stayed until it was almost dawn. Then the "millionaire," as she called him, drove Alla back to her rooming house. She invited him up to her room, but he shook his head, gazed deep into her eyes, and squeezed her hand before turning away. "I'll never see this man again," Alla thought as he drove off. Back in her room, she took off her coat and found the wad of banknotes in one of its pockets. A farewell present, she supposed, and shrugged the whole thing off. Next day she moved to "a nice rooming house" only a short walk from the Philharmonic, and bought her first winter coat.

But within a week the millionaire had tracked Alla down, and from the depths of part-time prostitution she rose to the heights of "kept woman." At this point her lover becomes a very incidental figure in "Incidents," which records briefly that he set Alla up in an apartment, gave her clothes and jewelry, but made few sexual demands, no doubt because he was "drunk most of the time." She felt "free and happy" with him, and apparently the millionaire didn't mind taking second place in Alla's affections to a classmate at the Philharmonic, Olga Zhdanova.

Among the hundreds of photographs in Nazimova's collection, very few relate to her personal life. But she kept a picture of herself and Olga

Amorous friendship:
Alla, aged eighteen,
with Olga Zhdanova
in Moscow, 1897

taken in 1897. Although they look at the camera, not at each other, the expression on Alla's face implies that, on her side at least, it was an amorous friendship. Almost certainly it stayed that way. In the photograph Alla looks surprisingly mature for her age, but she had been slow to discover her vocation as an actress, and all the available evidence suggests she was even slower to come to terms with her bisexuality. She also became deeply attached to Olga's mother, who had a cottage in the country where the girls often spent weekends. A longing for "family," until Nina's behavior cured her of it, was another pattern in Alla's life. But if the longing that Olga aroused was more than sisterly, Madame Zhdanova played the less complex role of a mother figure.

Finally as elusive as the millionaire in "Incidents," Olga reappears in a fragment of autobiography that Nazimova wrote in 1911. She never tried to publish it "for fear of undesirable publicity, fear of amateurish writing, fear of Nina," and only one page of the typescript has survived. It begins with Alla refusing to accompany her millionaire on a trip to his cotton plantations in Manchuria because it would involve too long a separation from Olga. After seeing him off at the station, she joined Olga and

Madame Zhdanova in the country, where she spent most of the summer vacation of 1897. A group of students from the Philharmonic came down for the day, and "dared the fearless Alla to stop the express train from Warsaw. She put on a long white cambric nightie, wore a crown of daisies from the railroad grass and stood between the rails and played Ophelia!" As the train sped toward her, Olga and the other girls screamed, but Alla "stood unafraid, reciting the mad scene with gestures," until the train pulled up close enough for her to touch it.

ALTHOUGH she could defy an express train and keep a millionaire lover on a string, the "fearless" Alla had felt deeply unsure of herself with Nemirovich earlier that year. Material security had enabled her to concentrate in class again, but for months her teacher never spoke an encouraging word. After one of the play-readings, in which she felt sure that she'd done good work, he called her over for a private talk. "Have you read this play before?" It sounded like an accusation. "Never!" she said indignantly. Then had she seen it performed? "No, never!" He nodded, and that was all. It left Alla confused and disappointed. Nemirovich seemed to be losing faith in her, and she had no idea why.

Then, a few weeks later, he assigned her the leading role in *Magda* by Hermann Sudermann. (A popular playwright of the time, he's remembered today, if at all, for the novel *Song of Songs*, which became a movie with Marlene Dietrich.) Alla was convinced that Nemirovich had set her a final test and would write her off if she failed, but quickly became so involved in the part that "I did not care whether he would like my reading or not. . . ." What carried Alla away, of course, was the discovery that a play about a Fallen Woman could give her "something to ponder over" after all. By the end, her nose was red and her eyes streamed with tears.

The usual discussion followed, which Nemirovich began with a remark about "the extraordinary talent of losing one's own personality, of unusual quickness of perception. . . ." At first Alla thought he was complimenting the entire group, or perhaps Meyerhold in the leading male role, then realized Nemirovich had finally singled her out for special praise. "But I could not hear because I was crying like a fool on the shoulder of my friend Olga, who kept pinching my arm to make me behave."

Tears of happiness were followed by tears of frustration. When Meyerhold obtained Nemirovich's permission to stage a student performance of *Magda* at the end of the semester, he gave the part to Olga Knipper.

During the first week of the school's summer vacation, Nemirovich and Stanislavsky had their famous meeting. It began at two in the afternoon on June 22, 1897, in a private room at the Slavyansky Bazaar restaurant. Around midnight it moved to Stanislavsky's house, where it continued until eight the next morning. Nemirovich had suggested the meeting. He knew the commercial theatre had little to offer his students after they graduated, and had heard that Stanislavsky wanted to establish his own permanent theatre but doubted his own capacities as an administrator. Administration was one of Nemirovich's strong suits, and as an admirer of Stanislavsky's work he felt the time had come for them to join forces.

Stanislavsky was enthusiastic. They began by discussing how to raise money for a new theatre, and whether to apply for state funds or approach private backers. Bearing in mind how slowly Russian bureaucracy worked, they decided to move on both fronts at the same time. Then, for several hours, they explored the heart of the matter. "We had to make sure," as Nemirovich said later, "that two bears would get along together in the same den." Although they agreed in principle on the kind of theatre they wanted, they knew that successful collaboration depended on a balance of power, and the time it took for two strong egos to arrive at it was one reason the meeting lasted so long. Stanislavsky the actor-director was interested primarily in imposing his own personality on a play. Nemirovich, who had written several successful plays, believed in the supremacy of the author. Each man wanted a "feeling of truth" in the theatre, but whose truth was it going to be?

As a first step toward solving the problem, they agreed that Nemirovich would direct general policy and Stanislavsky most of the plays. But since Nemirovich had doubts about Stanislavsky's literary judgment, he insisted the plays must be chosen by mutual consent, and gained the right to veto any play he didn't like. In return, since Stanislavsky had doubts about Nemirovich's talent as a director, he gained his own right of veto, which allowed him to correct any mistakes he found in Nemirovich's staging. By six o'clock, they had shaken hands on this, and proceeded to discuss the formation of a permanent acting company. No jockeying for position was involved here. They agreed at once to pool resources, with Stanislavsky contributing the best actors in his own existing company, and Nemirovich his most promising students.

By seven o'clock, Nemirovich had switched roles from playwright-teacher to administrator, and was working out a preliminary budget and making a list of private investors to approach. By dinnertime, both men were jotting down notes for a manifesto on the need to bring "real life"

*Graduation class of 1898 at the Philharmonic School.
Seated left to right: Nemirovich-Danchenko with
beard, Alla Nazimova beside unidentified standing
actress, and, at right, Olga Zhdanova*

into the theatre by staging contemporary plays as well as revitalized classics, lowering the price of seats to attract a wider audience, and scheduling special matinee performances for students. No international conference, Stanislavsky remarked later, discussed world problems more thoroughly than the two of them explored every detail of running a theatre; Nemirovich even wanted to forbid women in the audience to wear hats.

Both men were heavy smokers, and when the air in their private room grew unbearably thick, they adjourned to Stanislavsky's house. There, in the early-morning hours, he proposed that the new theatre should have its own drama school to train a new generation of actors. Nemirovich pointed out that he'd already started to do this at the Philharmonic. Then he showed his administrative hand. Apart from his first choices for the acting company, Nemirovich said, he had several other promising students. They could form the nucleus of Stanislavsky's class, and not only gain valuable experience but save the theatre money by appearing as unpaid extras in productions with crowd scenes.

Stanislavsky welcomed the idea, and before adjourning for a few hours of sleep, each made a list of his candidates for the acting company. Nemirovich wrote down only three names: Olga Knipper, Moskvin, and Meyerhold. But among the students he recommended to Stanislavsky as apprentice extras was Alla Nazimova.

News of the meeting quickly circulated in Moscow, but the two men made no statements to the press until almost a year later, when they had the money in place. (A modest $14,000, privately subscribed. The state bureaucrats took so long to answer a request for funds that the theatre was already in operation by the time they turned it down.) In April 1898, Stanislavsky and Nemirovich announced the formation of the Moscow Open Theatre, whose name they later changed, at Chekhov's suggestion, to the Moscow Art Theatre. They made no mention of their plans for a drama school, and it was only in June, on the last day of class before the summer vacation, that Nemirovich informed his chosen few of "the great opportunity" awaiting them.

For Alla it was a great rejection. She had lost out again to Nemirovich's troika of stars, elected to audition for leading roles in the opening season while she joined the lowly ranks of apprentice extras. Lavish gifts from the millionaire were no consolation. Although he wanted to spend the summer with Alla in Moscow, she wanted to spend it in the country with Olga, and finally agreed to divide the time between them. Going home was out of the question. The Zhdanovas' cottage had already become more like home than Yalta, where embarrassing questions would now be asked.

For more than a year Alla had heard nothing from Volodya or Nina, whose letter telling her to "manage" she never answered. And Volodya had never sent a further installment of her allowance. It seemed to Alla that they couldn't care less what happened to her, and she preferred to answer silence with silence. The only alternative was to lie convincingly about her life, which would be difficult, or to tell the truth, which would provoke horrible outbursts from Nina.

In fact, each side had secrets to keep. Although Nina married Max Hofschneider that summer and Volodya left for Berlin shortly afterward, Alla was not informed. One of the last pages of "Incidents" refers to both events, but its mention of "Nina's husband gambling her money away" provides the key to what had been going on. If Nina had money to gamble away, it could only have come from her father-in-law, when he handed over at least part of her share of Yakov's estate as a wedding gift. And if Volodya could afford to go live in Berlin, he must have settled accounts with Hofschneider in the same way. The fate of Alla's inheritance is never mentioned, but it seems she never saw a penny of it. Two years later, according to "Incidents," she left the millionaire and was soon completely broke again. The long silence of Nina and Volodya could mean that they divided Alla's share among themselves, or that they never bothered to press her claim and the moneylender kept it.

DURING ALLA'S second summer vacation, Stanislavsky began directing rehearsals for his opening season of plays. They included a historical drama, *Tsar Fyodor; The Merchant of Venice;* and at Nemirovich's insistence *The Seagull,* which he considered a masterpiece when he first read it in manuscript. The company had rented the old, dilapidated Hermitage Theatre, in the process of being repainted and wired for electricity when Alla returned to Moscow, and she first saw Stanislavsky at work on a bare stage lit by rows of candles stuck in bottles and a few kerosene lamps. He was directing Moskvin, Meyerhold, and Olga Knipper, whose auditions had won them leading roles in *Tsar Fyodor.* Watching them run through a scene, Alla soon forgot to be jealous and found herself "drinking in every word uttered by Stanislavsky. His directions were so logical, so human, so illuminating. . . . I had the feeling that only with my first day of witnessing rehearsals conducted by Stanislavsky had I begun to take my work seriously."

Five years younger than Nemirovich, and at six feet six inches much taller, Stanislavsky was strikingly handsome—"an Adonis," according to Olga Knipper. Although he always carried a notebook in which he jotted down thoughts on acting and directing, he hadn't yet formulated his "method." Alla never heard him talk about Emotion Memory, Through Lines of Action, or any of the techniques that he first named and codified in a lecture to a group of actors in 1909. But she witnessed them in evolution. Whenever he detected a false note in a scene, Stanislavsky interrupted the rehearsal with a quietly apologetic "No, I don't think so," then reminded the actor of their previous discussions about the character he was playing, explained how he "lost" it at a particular moment and how, by following a different emotional track, he could "find" it again. It was when Alla watched Stanislavsky spend two or three hours on a particular moment that she felt "his discipline knew no mercy."

But she never heard the actors complain. Stanislavsky knew how to

Olga Knipper as Irina in Tsar Fyodor, *the Moscow Art Theatre's opening production in the fall of 1898*

"An Adonis," according to Olga Knipper . . . Stanislavsky at twenty-nine

talk actors' language, to tap reserves of intuition they didn't know they possessed. He was also a religious man, whose call for "the feeling of truth" inspired a kind of conversion, and the company's belief in him was absolute. Nemirovich, it seemed to Alla, had only talked theory, then required his students to demonstrate it in play-readings. Stanislavsky talked creation, and the way he worked with actors made her understand the actual process of inhabiting a character on the stage.

For *Tsar Fyodor* Stanislavsky called seventy-four rehearsals. They began at eleven in the morning, broke for a meal at five in the afternoon, then continued until late at night. The play by Alexey Tolstoy (no relation to Leo) was set in sixteenth-century Russia, and its story of Boris Godunov's plot to assassinate the son of Ivan the Terrible contained some elaborate crowd scenes, including a royal banquet and a public execution. But for Stanislavsky, as Alla discovered, "there was no crowd as we understood the word. Everyone was given a part, often no lines but mostly a 'thinking' part. . . . You received the impression of so many different people, each living his or her own life." Stanislavsky devised a piece of business for each face in the crowd, and Alla's moment came in the execution scene, as "a peasant girl eating sunflower seeds and spitting the empty shells into the river."

Working conditions at the Moscow Art Theatre were "almost monastic," according to a Polish actor who joined it a few years later and eventually directed movies in Hollywood. "We spent our days from morning until midnight without leaving the building," Richard Boleslawski remembered. "There was nothing bohemian about our existence. Both men and women were taught to dress simply, in dark colors. . . ." They were also requested to abstain from liquor and premarital sex. A teetotaler, and happily married, Stanislavsky believed that even occasional drinking and promiscuity destroyed an actor's power of concentration. Delighted when a couple announced their engagement, he was disturbed to hear of an after-hours romance. But by the time *Tsar Fyodor* opened, both Olga Knipper and Alla were directing their own emotions offstage—or being directed by them.

At his friend Nemirovich's invitation, Chekhov had attended a rehearsal of the play. Impressed by Knipper's performance as Irina, he asked to meet her, and shortly afterward wrote to a friend, "I'd have fallen in love with that Irina if I'd stayed on in Moscow." Chekhov had always resisted falling in love, and tuberculosis had aged him prematurely. But Knipper, like many other women, found Chekhov extraordinarily attractive. Unlike them, she realized that she would have to go slow. Over the next two years, they met only a few times but exchanged a great many letters, with each other's work as pretext, and each other gradually emerging as subtext. *The Seagull* was a personal success for both of them and restored Chekhov's confidence in himself as a man of the theatre. After *Uncle Vanya,* he began writing to Knipper as "my dear, sweet actress," and during rehearsals of *Three Sisters* as "my darling." When they finally became lovers, it was Knipper who brought up the subject of marriage; when Chekhov evaded it, she hinted that he might lose her; and when he proposed, by letter, she still had to pin him down to a date for the wedding.

The waiting game was not for Alla. Her first emotional involvement with a man began as a duel that ended in a painful draw, both sides equally wounded. Forty-five years later, Nazimova chose to write about it in the third person, presumably in an effort to be objective. But her account of the affair is far from that. Equivocal, and full of contradictions, it's the only one of her "Incidents" to hide more than it reveals.

Anton Chekhov (center) reads The Seagull *to members of the Art Theatre, October 1898. On his right, Stanislavsky, then Olga Knipper. Seated in right foreground, Ivan Moskvin and Vsevolod Meyerhold*

Stanislavsky's production of The Seagull, *December 1898. Knipper in elaborate hat as Arkadina. At right, Nazimova's walk-on moment as a maid*

Alexander Sanin, ten years older than Alla, was Stanislavsky's assistant as well as an actor in the company. They met when he took over final rehearsals of the crowd scenes in *Tsar Fyodor,* and Alla "fell hopelessly in love." She was "brokenhearted because he could not return her affections," but in the next paragraph their roles are abruptly, inexplicably reversed: Sanin becomes the rejected lover and accuses Alla of turning him down because he's "not rich enough."

Whatever really happened here, Nazimova is not telling. She interrupts the story to give a brief account of her work during the Moscow Art Theatre's first season. When it opens on October 14, Alla makes her professional debut as the peasant girl in *Tsar Fyodor.* She plays two more walk-on parts, a flower-seller in *The Merchant of Venice* and a housemaid in *The Seagull.* At the end of the season, in April 1899, Sanin reappears. Evidently the duel is still on. "To cleanse her soul" of Sanin's wounds, she decides to leave the Art Theatre and "hide from everybody."

"Everybody," it seems, included not only the millionaire but Olga as well. Out of mind since Alla fell in love with Sanin, Olga was out of sight as well, since she was not invited to join the company as an apprentice extra. When Alla informed Nemirovich of her decision to leave, she explained that she wanted to gain experience as a working actress in provincial repertory. Surprisingly, he made no attempt to dissuade her. (Years later, she discovered why. Nemirovich had somehow learned that Alla was Jewish. He knew this would come out sooner or later and would make it impossible for her to continue at the Art Theatre.) He recommended her to the director of a summer-stock company at Bobruisk, a small town several hundred miles west of Moscow. But provincial theatres required actors to provide all their own costumes, and she asked the millionaire for money. Although "as brokenhearted to part with her as she was brokenhearted because of Sanin," he not only came through but made sure that Alla traveled in style. In the first week of June, she took a train to Bobruisk accompanied by a personal maid, a large trunk packed with costumes, a stack of rubles, and a portable rubber bathtub.

"Never be afraid of failure," was Nemirovich's parting advice. "Make up your mind which parts you really want to play and forget the others." But during the journey she tried "to study *Hedda Gabler,* knowing well she'd never get the chance to play it." What Alla got to play was a supporting role in *Camille,* and when the leading man tried to make love to her, she slapped his face. "I came here to work," she said. But the supporting actress soon created a star part for herself in life, as a Hedda of the steppes.

A letter arrived from Sanin, accusing Alla yet again of "needing a millionaire to keep you." She reacted by asking Seryozha Golovin, "a penniless drama student," to come at once to Bobruisk. About this new character on Alla's personal stage, "Incidents" reveals only that he was the son of an impoverished countess, had met Alla in Moscow and fallen "hopelessly in love" with her. When Seryozha arrived, she showed him the letter. He denounced Sanin as a "blackguard," then asked Alla to marry him. She accepted on the spot.

The wedding took place at a "small funeral chapel in the cemetery," with the theatre company in attendance. Seryozha had insisted that Alla wear a white bridal gown and carry a bouquet. Remembering all the "incidents" in her past, she became so disturbed that "she nearly fainted" during the ceremony. She discarded the gown as soon as she got back to her lodgings, where her maid, Simka, had prepared the wedding feast. All the guests, and the priest, got drunk on champagne. When they left, Alla informed her husband there would be no wedding night, and "Seryozha agreed to stay by himself in the inn."

Sanin had heard "the rumors in Moscow of her impending marriage." He hurried to Bobruisk, hoping to prevent it, but arrived too late. He took a room at the inn, where Alla saw him standing by the window. "Overwhelmed with happiness, she ran across the dusty road and burst into his room. When he started making love to her, she showed him the

*Odd couple: Alla Nazimova
and Sergei ("Seryozha")
Golovin a few days after
their marriage in 1899*

thin gold engagement ring Seryozha had placed on her finger. Sanin, too shocked for words, cried and said, 'You are like one of those demented Dostoevsky women!' " He took the next train back to Moscow, leaving Alla "hurt and bewildered."

But Sanin himself appears to have been emotionally fragile. During a rehearsal of *Tsar Fyodor*, a dispute with an actor was enough to drive him to a suicide attempt, as a letter from Stanislavsky to Nemirovich reveals. "Impossible to restrain him. Then I insisted he stay home and rest for a few days. . . ." When Alla "nearly fainted" at her wedding, she was obviously on the verge of what a doctor in New York later diagnosed as "a hysterical condition of the heart."

Although nearing the end of her life when she wrote about the events in Bobruisk, Nazimova was still unable or unwilling to demystify them. Her account never reconciles Sanin's failure to "return her affections" with his jealousy of Alla's millionaire or his anger at her marriage; and although Sanin's behavior suggests that he was "hopelessly in love" with Alla, rather than the other way around, she acts like a woman scorned. Seryozha, also "hopelessly in love," had no better luck and was exiled to

the inn on their wedding night. "Hopelessly" recurs so often that it begins to look like a code word. In Bobruisk, Alla gave the hands-off treatment to two men in love with her. She was never in love with Seryozha,
of course, and manipulated their marriage to spite Sanin. But she *was* in
love ("hopelessly") with Sanin. So why did she run away from Moscow,
then reject him again when he caught up with her? Had she given him
the hands-off treatment from the start, and was this the cause of their
duel?

If Alla felt sexually ambivalent toward men at this time, it would not
be surprising. As a child she had witnessed Yakov force himself on Sonya,
endured his passionate kisses after a beating, and suffered a near-rape by
Otto. At the age of seventeen necessity had driven her to prostitution,
and "Incidents" refers more than once to the fact that she stayed with
"the good, kind millionaire" because he made so few physical demands.
Within a few years she would become sexually free, but her affairs with
men, unlike those with women, usually had a bitter ending. In 1912, an
interviewer asked Nazimova to name her favorite playwright. "Strindberg," she replied. "I love him. He utters a great truth when he says, 'Men
and women hate each other always in the depths of their hearts. . . .'
That is so true!"

WHEN SANIN returned to Moscow he told Nemirovich
what had happened in Bobruisk, and on July 15 Alla's former teacher
wrote her a rather cryptic note: "Life's vagaries are incidents of no importance, but a blunder committed by you in your work would be a matter of deep distress to me."

In a series of undemanding minor roles, Alla committed no blunder
in her work that summer, but failed "to cleanse her soul." Back in
Moscow six weeks later, all she wanted was to rejoin the Art Theatre "to
be near Sanin." Stanislavsky told her that the plays for the second season
were already cast, with only a few walk-on parts still available. "That's all
right," Alla said. "I can study stage management." Which is what she did,
sitting alone in the theatre to watch Stanislavsky direct *Uncle Vanya,*
Twelfth Night, and *Hedda Gabler.* Another historical play by Alexey Tolstoy, *The Death of Ivan the Terrible,* provided Alla with her only onstage
moment of the season, as "an old-old woman in rags" screaming abuse at
a rich merchant.

On the home front, although her millionaire was "miserable" when
she returned to Moscow with Seryozha, he seems to have realized that she

was only nominally a married woman. He didn't even object to Seryozha's living in the apartment that his millions paid for. Instead, he tried to bribe his way back into Alla's life. Usually drunk, "he would come and sit all day on the stoop, holding in his lap his hat filled with jewelry she would not touch." But the duel with Sanin was over, although "Incidents" doesn't explain why. In fact, he had become involved in a new and less frustrating backstage affair. Several years earlier, a young and unsuccessful actress called Lika Mizinova had fallen in love with Chekhov. When he eluded her, she became the mistress of a fiftyish married writer who took her to Paris. After a few months, he abandoned her there and went back to his wife. The situation provided Chekhov with a starting point for *The Seagull,* and he based the character of Nina on Lika. But Lika's own life had a fifth act. She came back to Russia, struggled on as an actress, and eventually auditioned for the Art Theatre while Alla was in Bobruisk. Engaged for a few small parts, she met Sanin and married him a year later.

Meanwhile, another marriage ended. Early in 1900, Seryozha "lost his temper" and told Alla "she was a fool for marrying to 'still a hurt.' " She begged Seryozha not to divorce her, because she was afraid it would make her "do something stupid." Although Nazimova's account doesn't explain what she had in mind, presumably Alla felt that, as long as she remained legally married, she couldn't make the same mistake again. Whatever the reason, there was no divorce until many years later, but the millionaire came in from the stoop and, unlike Alla's husband, was "so happy with so little."

Soon after Seryozha's departure, the Nazimova version continues, Stanislavsky told Alla that he'd decided to add a play called *The Artists* to the current repertory, and offered her the leading role. "I nearly fainted. . . . My chance had come!" Her hopes dashed when he canceled the production, Alla joined "the famous youth rebellion" started by Meyerhold, Sanin, and a few other actors. Equally frustrated by "the impersonal high-handed attitude of Stanislavsky toward beginners," they staged a public protest and resigned from the theatre at the end of the season.

But this is one of Nazimova's self-created legends, and it originally surfaced in a piece she wrote for *Theatre Magazine* after her success in *The Cherry Orchard* in 1928. Glesca supports it by adding a footnote to its replication: "*The Artists* is by Chekhov." In fact it's an Austrian play about circus life that Meyerhold directed after he left the Art Theatre. Either Nazimova slipped up when she told Glesca it was by Chekhov, or her companion's memory faltered. In any case, Stanislavsky and Nemirovich always planned their repertory months in advance and never added a play in midseason. Nor was there a "student rebellion" in 1900. Meyerhold and Sanin, not "beginners" like Alla but important members of the company, didn't resign until 1902. Although they deplored the change in Stanislavsky's attitude toward actors, his tendency to dictate roles instead of discussing them, they were more disturbed by signs that the revolutionary was turning conservative. Both men wanted to become directors, and reacted against Stanislavsky's "feeling of truth," which they felt had become a formula for the same rigidly naturalistic approach to every play. Meyerhold left to form his own company and create what he called "the theatre of fantasy," and Sanin experimented with another kind of fantasy when he began directing operas.

Writing for *Theatre Magazine,* Nazimova also claimed that she "graduated with a gold medal" before resigning from the Art Theatre, and was the only apprentice to win such high honors. But this is another legend that she liked well enough to re-create in "Incidents." During the early years of the Art Theatre, there were no regular classes and no examinations, for Stanislavsky could only find time to conduct an occasional student seminar. Previously, at the Philharmonic, Nemirovich had awarded silver medals as the highest honor. The last of his students to win them were Knipper and Meyerhold, who arrived at the school two years before Alla.

In a period of minimal cultural traffic between the U.S.A. and Russia, Nazimova could get away with inventions that made good copy and were hard to verify. But as early as 1906, before the New York opening of *Hedda Gabler,* she had admitted the truth in her diary. "What was I at home? Nothing, or almost nothing!" Although Nemirovich thought she had talent, he was more impressed by Knipper. We don't know what Stanislavsky thought, except for his comment several years later that Nazimova never seemed happy in the company because she was impatient to become a star. The 1906 diary suggests that Alla's personal life was equally responsible for her impatience and unhappiness: "If I haven't lived beautifully, I must act beautifully, this is my aim, this is what I *must* do!"

Not even her extraordinary success in America was quite enough to compensate for early sorrows, and Nazimova felt impelled to rewrite her past at the Art Theatre. But most of her self-created legends contain a small truth hugely overdramatized. Alla was not the only member of the company who later revised her opinion of Stanislavsky. At the same time as Meyerhold and Sanin, two other actors resigned because they could no longer worship an idol with feet of very hard clay, and Olga Knipper sympathized with them. Writing Chekhov that she'd lost her "blind faith" in Stanislavsky, she complained of the way he kept restaging scenes at the last moment and replacing actors a few days before opening night. So perhaps Alla "nearly fainted" because Stanislavsky asked her to take over a role, and couldn't forgive him for changing his mind. For some actors, some wounds never heal. In her early days, Bette Davis worked for a stock company run by George Cukor, who didn't renew her contract because there were no parts in the upcoming season that she seemed right for. Forty years later, the great movie star was still referring to the humiliation she felt when Cukor failed to recognize her talent.

A MONTH AFTER Alla left the Art Theatre, the director of a stock company in Kislovodsk, a resort town in the Caucasus, offered her a contract for the summer. And in another attempt "to cleanse her soul," Alla decided to leave the millionaire for good. The contract specified leading roles, and "if she really had the talent Nemirovich said she had, she would not let money make it famous." As a parting gesture, the millionaire swore eternal devotion. "He tore a paper rouble in half and said, 'I keep one half and you the other. If you need me, send me your half and I'll come to you.' " As a parting gift he bought Alla "a full theatre wardrobe," including costumes for *The Seagull* and *Hedda Gabler.* Packed into three large trunks, it accompanied her on the train, along with the portable bathtub and her maid, Simka. No stack of rubles this time, but the millionaire insisted that she keep all her jewelry.

Alla had also decided to dye her hair Bernhardt-red, a sign that promotion to starring roles had literally gone to her head. At a party after her enthusiastically acclaimed performance as Nina in *The Seagull,* the local drama critic called her a "genius." He got no thanks. Alla called him an "idiot," said she was good but not *that* good, and advised her stunned admirer to remember a Russian proverb: "In a land without seafood even a shrimp is a lobster." At a subsequent performance she slapped the leading actor's face "in full view of the audience for ruining her best scene." Then she refused to appear in *Hedda Gabler* because "she would rather die than play her worshiped Ibsen half-cooked in three rehearsals," and turned down *The Lady from Maxim's,* a French boulevard comedy that she dismissed as "a piece of ****."

Camille and *Zaza,* however, she graciously accepted, and both plays were so popular that the director proposed to cash in with another sin-

and-repentance drama. Exhilarated by her "rocketing success," Alla
agreed to substitute *Magda* for *Miss Julie*. The next day, Sanin arrived in
Kislodovsk, no longer in hopeless pursuit but passing through on a walking tour of the Caucasus with his brother. All the same, their reunion was
turbulent. Still wildly excited by the artistry of Duse, whom he'd seen on
a recent trip to Europe, Sanin accused Alla of wasting her talent on trash.
Then he ordered her to tear up her contract and "fly across the Milky
Way in search of the 'divinity!'"

Pierced to her dramatic heart and Russian soul, transformed from arrogant star to humble pilgrim, Alla went to see the theatre director. He
agreed to let her go, and they parted with "copious tears" and "passionate kisses on both cheeks." But as a married woman Alla could only obtain a passport for foreign travel with her husband's permission, and to
get it she had to see Seryozha in Moscow. There she also said goodbye to
her maid, who was now two months away from becoming a mother after
a single encounter with a student. Simka's return to her family gave Alla
second thoughts about flying across the Milky Way by herself. Her traveling companion of choice was a middle-aged actress with whom she'd
become friendly in Bobruisk. Out of work ever since, the actress jumped
at the chance of a few weeks in Europe, and Alla pawned some of her
jewelry to pay for the trip.

They caught a train for Vienna, where Sanin had said Duse was playing, but by the time they arrived she had left for Venice on the next stage
of her tour. When they reached Venice, Duse had just left for Milan. In
Milan nobody knew where Duse had gone, and "they took a random
shot at Switzerland." It proved wide of the mark, but Alla discovered that
Duse would definitely be appearing in Berlin the following week. Left
with a few days to spare, she dragged the companion to Montreux, in
search of the hotel where she had once stayed with Sonya. Although she
never found it, she hired a boat to go around the lake, relived a morning
of rare childhood happiness with her mother, then set off on another
journey to the past.

When she arrived at the Groelichs' farm in the mountains above
Zurich, Alla was dressed up in one of her costumes from *Zaza*, pale-gray
suit, red turban, black silk stockings, black high-heeled shoes. But her
new image failed to impress *Die Mutter*. Drab as ever and shrunken with
age, Frau Groelich was only interested in news of Alla's family. Sad to
learn of Yakov's death, she smiled and exclaimed "*Wunderbar!*" when
Alla told her that Nina had found a husband. Then she changed the subject to cabbages and onions. A bumper crop this year, Frau Groelich said
proudly, and led Alla to the vegetable garden.

Otto was working there. "He's completely cured, be kind to him," Frau Groelich said, then left them alone. Like his mother, Otto showed no surprise at Alla's sudden reappearance in stage costume. He spoke matter-of-factly about his treatment for "*Phantasien*" at a sanatorium, apologized for "the great wrong" he'd committed in the forest, and seemed perfectly sane until he reminded her of their vow of Fidelity for Life. Now that Alla had come back to honor it, Otto continued in the same matter-of-fact way, he was ready to "right the wrong" by marrying her.

At first she could think of nothing to say. To tell Otto that she was already married would be like opening Pandora's box, and she preferred to keep the lid on a life "too sordid and too foreign" for him to understand. Finally she said, "But I'm an actress now."

Otto shrugged. "It doesn't matter."

"And I'm very ambitious, you know."

He looked puzzled, then shrugged again. "It doesn't matter," he said.

Apparently nothing mattered to Otto "except a half-forgotten incident which seemed to her now the least of all her incidents." But was he really still insane, or just a stupid, stubborn peasant who expected her to take that absurd vow seriously? Either way it was exasperating. "Look at me!" Alla said. "Can't you see I haven't kept my vow?"

Otto stared at her. "You're still the same," he said.

Then Frau Groelich called them in to supper. Only her husband and Gretl joined them at table, for the other sons had left home. Although Herr Groelich gave Alla a warm handshake, Gretl was cool. A schoolteacher now, starchy and prim, she eyed Alla "as if she knew a whore when she saw one." Otto was silent until the meal ended and Alla made her goodbyes. Then he followed her out to the carriage and said quietly, "You may need a home some day. I'll wait."

She spent that night at a hotel in Zurich, unable to sleep, smoking Russian cigarettes and wondering why she had tried to relive a moment of her childhood with Sonya at Montreux and what had impelled her to see the Groelichs again. "An avalanche of memories from her high alp of memories came plunging, tumbling through the night," scarlet beret flying away over the Black Sea, Yakov beating her after the concert at the Hotel Russiya, Keller masturbating while she smiled, Natalie wearing Alla's petticoat as a gesture of love, the drunken millionaire holding out a hatful of jewelry, Sanin's furious accusations, marriage to Seryozha in a cemetery chapel, and finally Nemirovich's letter. "Life's vagaries," he had written, "are incidents of no importance." But this seemed as obtuse as Otto the peasant saying, "It doesn't matter," even though it came from her distinguished professor. "Were all her trials, hunger, heartbreak, self-abasement, work, struggle, of no consequence? . . . Had not these 'unimportant' incidents become of great importance in the development of her mentality and, too, of her talent?"

Next morning, with her companion in tow, Alla took the train to Berlin and caught up with Duse at last. She doesn't mention the play, only the message that Duse's performance conveyed: "Nothing, nothing was in vain. . . . For the divine Eleanore's art was a mirror of everything she, you, the poor Otto, Alla, the greatest and the least of us, had seen, heard, felt and thought."

5

"High Visibility"
1900–1906

> Love in my own life was unfortunate, and I often
> wonder if the smug bourgeois who envy us know
> that we go to art to forget, and that we work hard
> because the more we work the more we forget.
>
> —NAZIMOVA

A FEW WEEKS AFTER THE DUSE EXPERIENCE, Alla was engaged by a stock company in Kostroma, a town on the Volga two hundred miles from Moscow. She arrived there early in October 1900 with a new self-image, the pure, dedicated actress who lived only for her work. But the wolf at the door was an equally sobering influence. To buy all the additional costumes she would need to appear in two different leading roles every week, she had pawned most of her remaining jewelry.

By the turn of the century, *Camille, Zaza, Magda,* and their recycled versions, *Frou Frou* and *Fedora,* had become enormously popular in Russian provincial theatres, and Alla performed the entire series at Kostroma, rehearsing one play by day and performing another at night. This not only trained her memory but challenged her to create variety and excitement in roles that were essentially the same. When her first entrance became the cue for a standing ovation, Alla knew that she'd met the challenge; and with the Bernhardt-red grown out of her hair, she also succeeded in handling success. The punishing schedule was another aid to good behavior. It left no time or energy for insults to local critics and public slaps in the face for her leading man.

In December, Pavel Orlenev arrived to join the company as guest star in a couple of plays. A popular vaudevillian for many years, he had established himself as a powerful dramatic actor in the St. Petersburg production of *Tsar Fyodor*. Unlike Stanislavsky, he gave the play a subversive, topical slant. As the pathetically weak Fyodor, Orlenev made himself up to look like the current Nicholas II, and created a *succès de scandale* that was closed down when the censor got to hear about it. Orlenev reacted by declaring his belief in "theatre for the people," and formed a company to bring Strindberg, Ibsen, and an adaptation of *Crime and Punishment* to the far corners of Russia. The people responded, but the company fell apart. As an actor, Orlenev displayed an extraordinary talent for suffering, and offstage he suffered from bouts of manic-depression. On the downswing, he sometimes drank so heavily and persistently that he missed several performances in a row. Although audiences who saw him at his most dynamic and compelling could never have guessed that the previous night he'd been dead to the world in a gutter, the news got back to Moscow and St. Petersburg. Managers there turned a cold shoulder, and only provincial theatres, where his name was still a great draw, remained willing to take a chance.

As it happened, Orlenev had spent the night before his arrival at Kostroma in a Moscow jail. But he always found it therapeutic to be arrested for public drunkenness, then sober up in a quiet cell where he could concentrate on his next role or latest project. That night he passed a few solitary hours thinking about *The Brothers Karamazov.* He had recently commissioned an adaptation of Dostoevsky's novel, and intended to use his salary at Kostroma to form a new company and take it on tour. Like Raskolnikov in *Crime and Punishment,* the tormented Dmitri was a part that Orlenev felt born to play, but he hadn't yet found the right actress for Grushenka, the equally tormented whore.

The following night, when he attended a performance at the theatre in Kostroma, it was only to size up his fellow actors. His expectations were low, which made the impact of an actress he'd never heard of even more astonishing. And perhaps the sin-and-repentance drama, in spite of its sentimentality, connected with Dostoevsky in Orlenev's mind. Backstage, he kissed Alla's hand and offered her the part of Grushenka.

> O: "Will you go with me?"
> N: "Yes, to the end of the world."
> O: "And protect me from myself?"

N: "I shall be your maid, your nurse, your mother, your
    lover, whatever you want me to be."
O: "Swear it!"
N: (I crossed myself and said:) "God be my witness, I shall
    stay with you until you tell me to leave you."
O: "Amen." (He kissed me)
N: (I kept my oath)

As remembered by Nazimova in an autobiographical note found among her papers, this conversation with Orlenev occurred soon after their first meeting. The only direct reference to their affair that she left behind, it suggests they were both running a high Dostoevskyan fever from the start. And evidently Orlenev, unlike Sanin, encountered no resistance.

"I had the gift of arousing sympathetic feelings toward myself," he wrote in his autobiography, and contemporary accounts stress Orlenev's personal magnetism, deceptively angelic face, and almost demonic energy. When Alla met Sanin, he was an insecure, unremarkable actor who later discovered that his real talent lay in directing. But at the same age of thirty Orlenev was already a legend in the theatre. Physically seductive, with the extra aphrodisiac of fame, he had everything to offer an unknown actress. And when he offered it, Alla surrendered unconditionally to a lover for the first time in her life.

In her memoir, Glesca tried to portray Nazimova as a woman for whom sexual passion was never a dominating force, unlike her passion for work. Concerning Orlenev, she wrote that Nazimova "made the statement to me on several occasions that though they were lovers their relationship was built on mutual respect for the other's talent and consisted mostly of work and more work." According to Glesca, this set the pattern for Nazimova's subsequent affairs with men. But in a letter that Glesca preferred not to quote, Nazimova described herself as "a woman who all her life followed only one law—the law of impulse. . . . Falling in love and obeying this love down to the last step of self-contempt," she wrote to her niece in 1925, "this was your auntie's only way of living."

It was never Orlenev's way. As he confessed in his autobiography, he lived "under the protection of my very own Orlenev, my only friend, the only one in the world I love, and I'm not ashamed to admit it." And it seems that Alla was the only one in the world for whom Orlenev's love came even moderately close to his love for himself. All his other relationships with women, like his touring companies, fell apart after a few months.

Five feet four inches to Alla's five feet three, Orlenev succeeded in ap-

*"I shall be your maid, your nurse, your mother, your
lover, whatever you want me to be." Nazimova and
Pavel Orlenev in 1901*

pearing much taller because of his high-heeled boots, erect and dominating posture, upswept hair. Determination to stand tall was also a clue
to his character. Orlenev wanted the world to look up to him. "The word
of the star is law," he told Alla soon after they first met. So was the word
of the lover. She had promised to be "whatever you want me to be," and,
on tour with Orlenev's new company from February through May 1901,
she also acted out what he wanted her to be. As well as his whore in *The
Brothers Karamazov*, she played *Trilby* to his Svengali, *Zaza* opposite the
lover for whom she suffered and finally sacrificed herself, and Sonya in
Crime and Punishment, sacrificing herself again when she followed Orlenev's Raskolnikov to the penal settlement in Siberia.

Behind the scenes, since Orlenev was always short of money, he made
free use of Alla's other talents. The expert seamstress was made responsi-

ble for repairing and maintaining wardrobe, the student of stage management was put in charge of props, the violinist provided offstage
musical effects. Maid-of-all-work as well as lover, she also became
nurse-mother when Orlenev had to be sobered up for a performance.

But in obeying a law that imposed total submission on Alla the
woman, Nazimova the actress learned how to impose total submission
on her audience. Personally, Orlenev reduced her to a case of human
bondage. Professionally, he set her free. Stella Adler remembered that,
when she first saw Nazimova on the New York stage,

> She had what we nowadays call "high visibility." So big and
> commanding that it made the audience feel smaller. Only one
> actor in a thousand can bring off that style. Nazimova already
> had it when she played with Orlenev in Russian at a theatre in
> the Bowery. But it was Orlenev who had it first, and taught
> her how.

During that first tour, Orlenev told Alla that she was too inexperienced to play the lead in *Hedda Gabler,* and demoted her to a support-

*Nazimova as Zaza,
on her first tour with
Orlenev's company, 1901*

ing role. She wept with disappointment, then resolved to gain experience by watching Orlenev rehearse every scene with Hedda. Among the effects he devised for his actress was a brief but ominous pause in the doorway at her first entrance; an image of crucifixion when she backed against the living-room wall and stretched out her arms; the victim transformed into a towering angel of death when the last act opened with Hedda alone in the living room at night, wearing a black robe long enough to conceal the fact that she was standing on a footstool. Remembered and elaborated, these became some of the highlights of Nazimova's famous Hedda in 1906.

Physically agile, Orlenev had acquired "high visibility" as a vaudeville comedian. Later he displayed it for dramatic effect, the pratfall mutating to a sudden crumple of despair, the funny walk to a dangerous prowl. Equally adept at vocal gymnastics, he could reach the back of the house with a whisper. In passing on these techniques to Alla, he made her unlearn one of Stanislavsky's basic lessons. Body movement and tone of voice, according to Stanislavsky, had to come from "within," from total involvement with a character. But Orlenev had always believed in standing inside and outside a character, in "becoming" and demonstrating at the same time. Rejecting any theory that set the unconscious against the conscious, he encouraged Alla to draw freely on both. Twenty years later, Stanislavsky reversed his own theory and decided that the route to "inner feelings" was through "physical action." Perhaps Orlenev's revival of *Crime and Punishment* in Moscow at this time influenced him, for Stanislavsky was among several members of the Art Theatre who saw it.

If Orlenev's virtuosity sometimes pushed him over the top, Stanislavsky's cult of restraint led to creeping monotony. It was Alla's good fortune to study under two masters and absorb the best of each, and Orlenev's bad luck never to establish a permanent theatre of his own. But, unlike Stanislavsky, he was too self-infatuated to admit that he needed a Nemirovich, and a Nemirovich would never have put up with him. Nobody, in fact, could put up with Orlenev in the long run, and by sharing his life for five years, Alla established a record for loyalty.

The couple rented an apartment in Yalta for the summer when the tour ended, mainly because Orlenev wanted to visit his friend Chekhov, now one of the hundreds of tuberculars living there on doctors' orders. In a letter to Olga Knipper dated August 21, 1901, Chekhov referred briefly to his first meeting with Alla: "I looked in on Orlenev yesterday, got acquainted with Leventon, she shares quarters with him." The "Leventon" implies that her origins were by now common knowledge. Almost certainly she owed this to Orlenev. When he'd had too much to drink, he often addressed her in public as "my *zhidovka*," Russian slang for Yid.

Chekhov always enjoyed stories of touring companies and their misadventures, and Orlenev took center stage that day. He imitated the earthshaking rumble, like heavy gunfire, that interrupted the company's performance of *Crime and Punishment* on their last night in Samara. Because the police had recently fired on students demonstrating against censorship in the streets of Moscow and St. Petersburg, the actors panicked for a moment, imagining that unrest had spread to the provinces. But the audience reacted with murmurs of relief. It heard the approaching end of winter as ice floes started to break up on the Volga.

While Orlenev entertained Chekhov, Alla studied him. She saw a thin, frail man with pince-nez and a goatee, withdrawn and reserved except when he laughed. Like many chronic invalids, he gave the impression of living at one remove from the world, and she wondered how he could write so authentically about almost all members of Russian society, aristocrats, peasants, actors, soldiers, bureaucrats, criminals, priests, lovers. Finally she asked, "How could you know so much about so many people you couldn't possibly have known?" Chekhov seemed taken aback, then said very simply, "I'm a writer."

That summer Nazimova saw her sister for the first time in five years. Nina was still living in the family house, which her husband had managed to appropriate along with the pharmacy, and the portrait of Yakov still hung in the hallway. She had asked Alla to come alone, so they could have a private talk, and it began with Nina's announcement that she would never allow Orlenev to set foot in her house. Holding her daughter Ludmilla (later Lucy) on her lap, Nina explained that it was out of the question for a respectable married woman to acknowledge a couple living openly in sin. Whether Alla asked any questions about Hofschneider and her inheritance is not known. But she learned that in one way, at least, her sister's view of the world had changed.

It was the Dreyfus case that brought about the change. A Jewish captain in the French Army, Dreyfus had been sentenced to life imprisonment as a spy for the Germans. Even though it turned out that a racist fellow officer had framed him, a military court refused to review the sentence, and the government declined to intervene. When Emile Zola publicly denounced the French Army for its anti-Semitism, and the president of the Republic for betraying the Rights of Man, Nina as a Jew was moved to write him a letter of support. In reply, Zola reminded her that prejudice and militarism had infected many other countries, including Russia, and Nina discovered a cause. The snob from finishing school, who had once angrily denied that her father grew up in the Pale of Settlement, was now a self-acknowledged Jew and a committed pacifist.

Yet the new Nina, sincerely converted to the cause of tolerance and nonviolence, was still the old Nina, a hard-core prude violently opposed to her sister's cause, the theatre. Astonished and puzzled, Alla wondered how the two character aspects could coexist. Although she couldn't find the answer (never found it), the gap between them seemed not quite as wide as before. At least there *was* a new Nina.

In the fall, since Orlenev was unable to raise money to take his company on tour again, Alla joined a stock company at Kherson, in the Ukraine, playing musical comedy on a showboat until winter set in, then moving to the local theatre for *Magda* and *The Seagull*. Meanwhile, Orlenev made a series of star appearances in the Baltic north, where he persuaded a Lithuanian theatre-owner to help him form a new company. By March 1902, investors had been found and actors assembled, and the couple set off on a second tour.

It began in Vilnius, the Lithuanian capital, with Alla and Orlenev playing Napoleon's son in *L'Aiglon* on alternate nights. They wore specially designed identical costumes, and in this, her first and last male role, she became Orlenev's mirror image. At the same time, they began rehearsing an adaptation of Tolstoy's *Resurrection*. Like his performance in *Tsar Fyodor*, this was a deliberate challenge to authority on Orlenev's part, for Tolstoy had recently been excommunicated by the Russian church he attacked as repressive in *What I Believe*. It was also a gamble against heavy odds. Orlenev had commissioned sets and costumes, as well as the adaptation itself, and booked the play into several towns on the Volga circuit, before getting approval from the censor. Although Russian bureaucracy was often technically incompetent, one branch failing to check its directives with another, church and state worked hand in glove. Shortly before *Resurrection* was due to open, all Tolstoy's works were banned from the stage by government order. Orlenev hoped to recoup his losses by hurrying an Ostrovsky play into rehearsal and arranging for it to open in Samara. He took the company there for a final week of rehearsals, but lost another packet when the costumes failed to arrive on time. Although Orlenev claimed that his payment to the designer in Moscow had gone astray through "a twist of fate," this was a familiar alibi. Most likely he had run out of cash and never sent it. Unable to honor the booking, and with no money to pay the refund demanded by the theatre or get his actors out of Samara, he appealed to the investors for help. They bailed him out, but refused to put up any more money, and the company disbanded.

When Alla and Orlenev returned to Yalta that summer, Chekhov was so delighted by Orlenev's account of his latest misadventures that he considered writing a comedy about touring players. But he put the idea aside and started work on an outline of *The Cherry Orchard* instead. In October, Alla and Orlenev again set off on separate provincial tours. This time Orlenev received an offer from the owner of a theatre in St. Petersburg. Victor Nemetti was a man with a mission, to bring the man he considered Russia's greatest actor back to the capital for the first time since his success in *Tsar Fyodor*. In the spring of 1903, he offered Orlenev a contract for a six-month season, an act of faith that included the right to choose his own repertory and a substantial payment in advance. When Orlenev insisted on Alla as his leading lady, Nemetti agreed. It was another act of faith, for he knew nothing about her.

Since rehearsals were not due to begin until October, Orlenev spent most of Nemetti's advance, and the summer, on a European vacation. Before they left, he recalled in his autobiography, "Alla Nazimova suggested I read a play by Ibsen called *Ghosts*. I did not immediately understand the play as a whole, although I found some of it very exciting." Reading it again on the train to Vienna, he found in Oswald the doomed syphilitic another part he was born to play, and chose *Ghosts* for his opening production at the Nemetti Theatre. Alla, his occasional mother in life, was of course too young to play Orlenev's mother onstage, and knew that all she could expect was the small supporting role of Regina the maid. But during the rest of their vacation, in hotel rooms overlooking Lake Como and the Grand Canal in Venice, she stood in for Mrs. Alving while Orlenev worked obsessively on his part. As a reward, he promised to promote her to leading lady in the second production. After considering several plays, he settled on *Rosmersholm*. Himself the rebellious son of a conservative family, Orlenev found another alter ego in Ibsen's Rosmer, the former priest who shocked an orthodox community by renouncing his belief in God. But for Alla, who had already played his whore, hypnotized puppet, and humiliated mistress, the role of Rebecca West was the most double-edged of all Orlenev's gifts. In the final scene, Rosmer challenges Rebecca to prove her love for him by killing herself. When she accepts, he proposes to make it a suicide pact. "But do you really want to go with me? Or want to make me go with you?" Rebecca asks. "That," Rosmer answers, "we shall never know. . . . But we go together."

From Venice they went together to St. Petersburg, the most elegant city in Russia, its cultural as well as imperial center. But the Nemetti Theatre, drab and run-down, was located on the edge of a working-class suburb. Although Alla felt she was still stuck in the provinces when she first saw it, Orlenev seemed hardly to notice. A theatre was a theatre, and theatre was for the people; gilt and chandeliers were for the aristocracy he despised. He immediately began casting *Ghosts* and *Rosmersholm*, then rehearsing them, as well as preparing for the role of Oswald by studying patients in the syphilitic ward of a hospital.

Neither play, written respectively twenty-two and seventeen years earlier, had yet been produced in Russia. All the leading theatres in St. Petersburg and Moscow rejected them as uncommercial, and while Alla and Orlenev were on vacation, the censor refused Nemetti permission to stage *Ghosts*. It was another case of the church's bringing pressure to bear. Always taking offense at even a whiff of anticlericalism, it found more than a whiff in the glib hypocrisy of Pastor Manders. But when Nemetti met with the authorities and went through the play line by line, he persuaded them to reverse the ban by agreeing to make a few cuts in the role of Manders. *Rosmersholm* they licensed intact, since the renegade priest died for his sins.

And in spite of the cuts, *Ghosts* emerged intact, its shock value undiminished, for Orlenev had met this kind of challenge before and knew how to direct an audience to read between the lines. The premiere created a sensation, Orlenev's performance made him a star in St. Petersburg again, and when the enormous demand for tickets virtually guaranteed a run of six months, he decided to cancel the production of *Rosmersholm*.

Alla felt doubly betrayed. She had steered Orlenev to a great personal success by bringing *Ghosts* to his attention, and her reward was a broken promise. But he not only denied her a leading role in the St. Petersburg season. This time Orlenev's theatre for the people drew the fashionable world as well, and Alla was soon denied even a supporting role in Orlenev's life. Grand dukes and society hostesses rode in their carriages to the edge of a slum and came backstage to invite him to parties, and he began drinking heavily again. Throwing himself into the high life he had always despised, he squandered money on gifts of jewelry and champagne to the bored wives and hopeful young actresses he seduced or was seduced by. Some evenings Orlenev arrived at the theatre so drunk that Madame Germanova, who played Mrs. Alving, had to put an arm around his waist so he wouldn't fall down. But the audience saw "only a great genius who swayed so divinely, as if overcome by emotion." A fragmentary note found among Nazimova's posthumous papers records that Alla became "ill and frightened" toward the end of the run. Presumably her illness was the pain of rejection, her fear that Orlenev might self-destruct. The note also suggests that she was on the verge of breaking up with him. "Told him I wanted to go to Yalta *alone*," it continues. "Anything you want," Orlenev replied, apparently never doubting that she would come back.

But she changed her mind about wanting to go to Yalta alone. When Olga and Madame Zhdanova came to see *Ghosts* just before it closed, they decided not to inform her in advance and surprise her with a backstage visit after the performance. Almost four years had passed since their last meeting, and the reunion awakened her old longing for "family." The Zhdanova family now included the illegitimate daughter of Alla's former maid. Soon after giving birth to "Little Nina," Simka had written Alla to ask for help in finding a foster mother. When Alla wrote Olga's mother for advice, Madame Zhdanova replied that she had always wanted another daughter and offered to adopt Little Nina herself. Now Alla suddenly longed for the Zhdanovas to adopt her as well, and it came as an answered prayer to discover that they planned to spend the summer in Yalta.

Alla's real family did not welcome their arrival. The presence of Little Nina appalled Big Nina, who claimed it was common gossip in the town that the child was really Alla's illegitimate daughter by Orlenev, and closed her doors to the Zhdanovas. According to another of Nazimova's posthumous notes, Alla pointed out that she hadn't even met Orlenev when Little Nina was born, but "discrepancy in age, did not count. . . . I told her [Nina] that I was very happy about such gossip! Gave me the feeling that I *could* have a child, had really loved someone sufficiently!" This was surely intended to provoke, and succeeded. The gap between them widened again.

For several weeks there was no letter from Orlenev. Perhaps he was giving Alla time to realize how much she missed him, or perhaps he was simply too preoccupied with the person he loved most in the world. When the novelty of social success wore off, so did the drinking bouts, and he began to think about his professional future. Determined to follow *Ghosts* with an equally daring play, he found it when his friend Maxim Gorky recommended *The Chosen People*. The author, Evgeny Chirikov, belonged to a group of radical writers who shared Gorky's hatred of the tsarist regime, and *The Chosen People* was his response to *The Swindlers,* a violently anti-Semitic government-sponsored play now in the second year of its Moscow run.

With strikes and demonstrations on the increase in Russia, workers demanding higher pay, students protesting censorship, Tsar Nicholas II had sided with the majority of his advisers, who believed that further repression, not reform, was the most effective answer to popular unrest. As well as ordering the police to break up demonstrations by force and arrest their leaders, the government launched a new propaganda campaign against the Jews. *The Swindlers,* which portrayed them as criminal troublemakers, the real enemies of the nation, was part of it; and *The Chosen People* was a counterattack on government-sponsored racism. Chirikov had first submitted it to the Art Theatre, where Nemirovich turned it down as full of good intentions but dramatically heavy-handed. The play has never been translated, and not even perestroika could rescue it from oblivion in Russia, so Nemirovich was probably right. He may also have been afraid of it, but risk was catnip to Orlenev. So was its imitation–*Romeo and Juliet* story of a young Christian from an anti-Semitic family who falls in love with a Jewish girl. When Orlenev finally wrote Alla, it was to tell her that he had a backer for the play in St. Petersburg, and to offer her the role of the girl.

Unlike Orlenev, who was not Jewish, Alla was in danger of racial exposure and its consequences if she appeared in a pro-Jewish play. To show his support for official policy, the governor general of Moscow had passed a new law that several other cities soon copied. It made "audacious conduct" a crime for which Jews could be sent back to the Pale of Settlement. Although the rich and the useful—industrialists, medical and scientific experts—could still count on preferential treatment, for the rest "audacious conduct" was a catch-all offense that even included a Jew's failure to raise his hat when he passed a policeman or other state official in the street.

But Alla decided to follow her own "law of impulse." At first she had felt so bitter about Orlenev, and so happy with the Zhdanovas and "family" life in Yalta, that she even considered giving up her career. Orlenev's letter, which has not survived, evidently convinced her that she still belonged to him and the theatre. Giving up her surrogate family instead, Alla returned almost at once to St. Petersburg, where Orlenev had already formed a new company, his third in three years. Most of its members were young, some of them Tolstoyan pacifists, all of them radical, fired by admiration of Orlenev the actor and the cause of *The Chosen People.*

A few hours before opening night, according to Orlenev's autobiography, mounted police arrived at the theatre with an order from the tsar forbidding the performance. According to an interview that Nazimova gave in New York, "the terrible Cossacks" arrived soon after the curtain went up and drove the actors from the stage, threatening them with "torture and imprisonment" while the audience fled in panic. Orlenev's account sounds more convincing. Why should the authorities have waited for the curtain to go up on the first act before closing the play? The only possible reason is that they wanted to terrorize the actors for daring to present it and the public for coming to see it. But Orlenev himself was no slouch in the art of dramatic exaggeration, and if it really happened this way, he would certainly have milked the scene for all it was worth, and more.

News of the police action reached Maxim Gorky in his home town of Nizhny Novgorod, where the thirty-six-year-old writer was under house arrest for taking part in a student demonstration. If the company had not been thrown in jail, he wrote Orlenev, it was because the authorities had decided on police surveillance instead. He advised Orlenev to keep a low profile for a while, perform only approved plays, then apply for permission to take the company on a tour of Europe. Once outside Russia, he could stage *The Chosen People* and stir up protest at the tsarist government's oppression of Jews and freedom in general.

Orlenev had reacted to the ban by going on a manic bender, but Gorky's letter sobered him up. When he read it to the company, everyone reacted enthusiastically. Afterward, Alla had second thoughts. Until she met Orlenev, she had never known sexual excitement, or the excitement of working with a great actor in the theatre. But she had also endured humiliations as wounding as her father's brutality, and begun to suspect that Orlenev was as doomed as the characters he brought so brilliantly to life. Plays failed to open, his company ran out of money, he arrived drunk at the theatre during a lapse into depression, and not even success, as Alla had learned during *Ghosts,* could protect Orlenev from himself. If she left Russia to tour a banned play and his company fell apart once again, would she reach the point of no return?

When she told Orlenev that she couldn't go with him, she reached it anyway. He still had the power to change Alla's mind by attacking her most vulnerable point, the heart. But in renewing her vow to stay with him "to the end of the world," she made one condition: if Orlenev ever showed up drunk for a performance again, she would leave him for good. In a show of passionate contrition, he swore off liquor for life.

There was no money to take the company to Europe, of course, and

Orlenev had to raise it by putting together a three-month tour of the Volga circuit and the Ukraine. He rehearsed his new actors in old favorites, including *Ghosts*. In March 1904, they played a week in Yalta, and Chekhov, no admirer of Ibsen, went to see *Ghosts* for Orlenev's sake. "A rotten play," he commented later to Knipper, "and the acting not up to much." It may have been an off night, or Chekhov may have been influenced by his belief that even the best actors were defeated by Ibsen, who was "not really a playwright." But it didn't affect his personal feelings for Orlenev and Alla, as he showed when he invited them to a farewell dinner. Orlenev surprised him by refusing a drink, then surprised him again by suddenly handing Chekhov 200 rubles in repayment of a year-old loan. In return, Chekhov promised to take up the comedy about touring actors that he'd put aside, and give the company the rights to perform it in Europe. It would be ready by September, he said. But by July 2, Chekhov was dead.

As for Nina, identification with the Jewish cause allowed her to approve the idea of Alla's going to Europe with *The Chosen People*. But disapproval of the theatre and adultery, which had decided her to bar Alla and Orlenev from her house, now kept her from going to see them on the stage. "She didn't even see me act until I brought her to America," Nazimova recorded in another note, "and even then not until 1911."

AFTER THE usual bureaucratic delay, Orlenev's company finally received permission to leave the country, and arrived in Berlin during the last week of October 1904. They now called themselves the St. Petersburg Players, and their leading lady had decided to appear under the name of Madame Nazimova. In this she followed the example of many Russian actresses. Theoretically at least, it conferred respectability, for, like Caesar's wife, a married actress was above suspicion, not the kind of woman who played sexual politics to advance her career. In practice, the move turned out badly for Nazimova from the start. When *The Chosen People* opened, she appeared on the program as "Mme Nasimoff." Later, the "Madame" would have consequences more serious than a misprint.

Although few of the German theatre critics understood Russian, they all praised the acting of Orlenev and Mme Nasimoff, and Russian Jewish exiles were deeply affected by the play's attack on racial intolerance. But there were only enough of them to support a run of two weeks in a small theatre. Presumably Volodya, settled in the city since 1898, was as indifferent as Nina to his sister's career. Nazimova never mentioned that he came to the play, or that they even met while she was in Berlin.

With no further bookings for the company in Germany or anywhere else, Orlenev decided to gamble on London. He had a letter of introduction to J. T. Grein, founder of the Independent Theatre and author of a manifesto protesting "the iron rod of medieval narrowness and dictatorship" that ruled the British stage. In the man responsible for the London premieres of *Ghosts, Hedda Gabler,* and Bernard Shaw's first play, *Widowers' Houses,* Orlenev sensed a kindred spirit. But since the company had earned barely enough money in Berlin to cover the cheapest fares to London, Nazimova supplied Orlenev with a little cash in hand by pawning the rest of her jewelry.

Bundled up against the cold like poor refugees, lugging battered suitcases packed with theatre costumes, the actors arrived by coal barge from Rotterdam. None of them spoke a word of English, but a Russian dockworker came to their rescue and helped carry their luggage to a dingy, cheap hotel in Whitechapel, the heart of London's Jewish East End. Nazimova found it extraordinarily depressing, with a group of immigrants sitting around in the lobby, one of them playing a mournful violin. The bedroom she shared with Orlenev was equally grim, its small window looking out on the brick wall of a building next door.

Still depressed the next day, Nazimova lay on the bed while Orlenev went to see Grein, expecting him to return with the news that they'd come up against another brick wall. Several years later, Grein wrote an account of that first meeting:

> He [Orlenev] thought that the play would rouse the English people and the Government to send a protest and an appeal to the Tsar. . . . But, I objected, who understands Russian in London except the refugees? . . . Then he proceeded: 'There is a young actress in my company who will set all London talking. Her name is Alla Nazimova—she is beautiful and a genius. I feel sure if you see her you'll be convinced; let me bring her to you.'

Although Grein agreed to meet Nazimova, she failed to impress him at first. He found her "not beautiful" and "*not* elegant." Her German was better than Orlenev's, but Grein still found communication difficult. Dutch-born, he spoke German with his own native accent, and Nazimova had picked up a regional one from the Groelichs. Then, at Orlenev's suggestion, she performed a monologue from *The Chosen People* in Russian. Astonished by an emotional power that completely transcended the language barrier, Grein found himself "carried away":

Never will I forget the impression she made. . . . She had a
voice that sounded like harps in the air, and she had eyes—
so lustrous, so wondrous, so expressive, full of tenderness,
depth and passion—that for a long time afterwards they
haunted me.

He immediately booked *The Chosen People* into the Avenue Theatre,
where it opened on January 21, 1905. "Every actor was an artist," Grein
recalled, "but above the crowd towered the figure of Nazimova." By now
she had not only learned from Orlenev how to stand tall, but followed
Duse's example and created a skillfully "natural" look onstage. Using
makeup to disguise the fact that she used makeup, she blended a light
foundation into her olive skin, then applied a mask of rice powder. The
resulting pallor was in startling contrast to her black hair, eyes that
looked sky- or lavender-blue in the eyes of different beholders, and Se-
mitic but not specifically Jewish features.

"The moment she spoke," according to Grein, "the audience hung on
her lips . . . and when she delivered a speech which in its accents of de-
nunciation equalled Zola's 'J'Accuse' in the Dreyfus case, the audience
rose in a frenzy." (Did Nazimova use an Emotion Memory of Nina here?)
In fact, among the many Russian exiles in the audience that night there
were two at opposite ends of the political spectrum. The anarchist Pyotr
Kropotkin, like all the other refugees, gave Nazimova a standing ovation.
Olga de Novikov, society hostess and secret agent for the tsarist government, walked out in the middle of the speech, blazing with anger and
jewels. After the final curtain, at a backstage party, Nazimova no longer
towered but sat huddled and exhausted in a low chair, tears streaming
down her face as people came to congratulate her. Later she kissed Grein's
hands and thanked him for his help. But her benefactor, like Orlenev,
operated on a tight budget. He couldn't afford to pay living expenses,
only a percentage of profits, and the lovers went back to their "little room
up the rickety stairs."

The Chosen People sold out for its first week. Because another play was
due to open at the Avenue Theatre, Grein arranged a transfer to the
Pavilion, where it played for three more weeks in repertory with *Ghosts*
and *Hedda Gabler*. The critics didn't review the Ibsen plays, which only
Shaw had praised when Grein first presented them in English, and the
majority had abused as "Garbage and offal," "An open drain," and "Ib-
scenity." Nor, as Orlenev hoped, did the press take up the cause of *The
Chosen People*. "Somber" and "depressing" were the critical adjectives of
choice for its subject, although the actors won high praise, especially

Mme Nasimoff, as she again appeared by a mysterious error in the program.

But a well-known writer and several famous actors took up the cause of Nazimova and Orlenev. Jerome K. Jerome was a popular playwright and the author of two oddly dissimilar best-sellers, the farcical *Three Men in a Boat* and the allegorical *The Passing of the Third Floor Back,* about a mysterious boarder in a suburban rooming house who turns out to be Christ come back to earth. Jerome wore yet another hat as a liberal journalist who attacked British colonialism and (just before the St. Petersburg Players arrived in London) predicted a revolution in Russia. Unlike Grein, he found Nazimova "as beautiful in her way as Orlenev," and had the impression they were deeply in love. Orlenev had somehow learned one English sentence, "You remind me of my first love," which he repeated to every woman he met, including Jerome's wife:

> I chaffed him about it. He maintained it was not humbug. All beautiful women reminded him of his first love. But his last love! There was no one like her, and kneeling, he kissed Alla Nasimoff's hand.

The company's impact on an English-speaking country had convinced Orlenev that an even greater success awaited him in New York. He mentioned this to Jerome, who gave him a letter of introduction to Charles Frohman, the owner of several Broadway theatres. But as usual Orlenev needed money. A season in small theatres was earning more prestige than profit, and he could only expect to clear $200, far from enough to buy steamship fares for fourteen actors and keep them in even the cheapest hotel until he found a transatlantic patron.

Although Nazimova had no jewelry left, she had acquired an important admirer in the person of Sir Henry Irving's son Laurence, a Slavophile and author of a play about Peter the Great. The only Russian-speaking Englishman at the first night of *The Chosen People,* he surprised Nazimova by congratulating her in her own language when they met backstage. Later, Irving translated the London reviews into Russian, gave them to her during the run at the Pavilion, and offered to throw a party for the company. Among the stars of the London stage that he invited were Ellen Terry and Sir Herbert Beerbohm Tree. When Nazimova explained they needed money to go to America, Irving promised to arrange a benefit matinee at the Haymarket Theatre. Both Terry and Beerbohm Tree agreed to take part, and Irving's connections made the matinee, like his party, an all-star event.

Last on the bill, alone on a bare stage at one of London's most elegant theatres, Nazimova sang a Russian folk song and was enthusiastically applauded by a full house. She bowed her thanks and exited to the wings, where Ellen Terry stood waiting. When the audience demanded a curtain call, Terry gave Nazimova one last runthrough of a thank-you speech in English that they'd already rehearsed phonetically, word by word. An encouraging push sent her back to the footlights, and Nazimova gave her first performance in a new language: "Deez eez de proudezt day of my live. I tank you verry mooch, God blezz you." It earned her a standing ovation.

Whether Orlenev took part in the matinee is not known, for his autobiography makes no mention of it. Perhaps he felt upstaged. Nazimova had become the center of attention in London, and this signaled a shift in the balance of power.

TRAVELING steerage on a crowded boat to New York in the last week of February 1905, Nazimova learned another English word: "zeazick." The crossing was rough, and she subsisted mainly on ice water for eight days. But "zeazick" made no impression on the medical officer from Ellis Island. Ordered to strip naked, she stood in a freezing cubicle while he examined her. And, like the rest of the company, herded below long before the boat docked, she never saw the skyline of the New World.

Although Nazimova's uncle Osip was now a dentist in Brooklyn, she didn't know his address and had no way of getting in touch with him. Nobody else in the company had relatives or friends in New York, but Orlenev had met a fellow Russian during the voyage who recommended a hotel managed by another fellow Russian. On the way to the Malkin Hotel at the corner of Broadway and 8th Street, Nazimova began to feel like "a spectator in Hell. Streetcars, elevators, overhead railways, noise, and thousands of people always in a hurry." Skyscrapers only twenty years new made the streets below look much older, dingy, and shadowed. Orlenev, his vision tunneled to immediate needs, remembered only that rooms at the Malkin cost $1.50 a week, with heat, light, and daily bath included, and its restaurant "served two generous, tasty courses with a cup of coffee, all for thirty cents."

Next day, Orlenev and Nazimova set out for Charles Frohman's office at the Empire Theatre. The hotel manager had given them directions, but they were afraid to take a streetcar because they had no idea how to ask for fares in English, and walked over thirty blocks, to Broadway and

*The passport on which "Alla
Golovina Nazimova" traveled
to New York in 1905*

40th. When Orlenev handed Jerome's letter to a secretary, she explained
that Frohman was out, then realized they hadn't understood and gestured
for them to wait. She vanished along a corridor, and eventually another
secretary appeared, who spoke to them in German. Jerome's name had
proved important enough for Frohman's partner, Al Hayman, to find an
interpreter and grant the couple an interview.

Hayman was sitting in his office, feet on the desk, hat on the back of
his head. When the interpreter introduced Nazimova, he didn't get up or
remove his hat. "Who is this pig?" Orlenev muttered in Russian. By now
his hopes for success in America were running very high, and he dreamed
of establishing a permanent theatre in New York. But because he was too
proud to plead his own case, he had assigned that role to Nazimova. She
began by explaining that Orlenev was a great star in his own country, and
had left it because the censor banned *The Chosen People,* then described
the conditions under which Jews were forced to live in Russia. While
she talked, Hayman assumed his famous poker face. Even more discon-
certing was the way his swivel chair, the first Nazimova had ever seen,
continually rotated from herself to the interpreter.

"Ask him to let us use one of his theatres, free of charge, for one after-

Charles Frohman, the most
powerful showman of
his time, c. 1907

noon." This was the question Orlenev had instructed Nazimova to lead up to. Their only hope of finding a backer, he reckoned, was to give a single performance of *The Chosen People,* invite the New York critics, then await results. ("With no pleading, no begging from me," he added.) Hayman's response was to light a cigar, swivel back to the interpreter, and confer with her in English for several minutes. Although Orlenev scowled with impatience, Nazimova felt hopeful. At least Hayman hadn't turned them down on the spot.

In fact, he had more than one reason to be interested. With thousands of foreign immigrants arriving in New York over the last twenty years, there was a growing off-Broadway audience for ethnic theatre. Low-budget and high-quality, it connected with the lives of Germans, Hungarians, Italians, and East European Jews who would not have understood *Captain Jinks of the Horse Marines* or *Sherlock Holmes* even if they understood English. But Shakespeare and Ibsen, risky business on Broadway, packed a German theatre, the Conried on Irving Place; comedies by Goldoni and traditional marionette shows ran year after year at the Italian theatre on Spring Street. And at the Grand, Jacob Adler and his Yiddish players attracted the largest and most passionate ethnic following of all, with a repertory extending from folk drama to *The Merchant of Venice* and *The Government Inspector.*

Hayman knew from Jerome's letter that London had a relatively small Russian population, and *The Chosen People* owed its success to Jewish refugees from various European nations. He also knew that no Russian company had yet played New York, and Orlenev could count on additional support from the city's far greater number of Russian immigrants. And although Hayman was not impressed by Orlenev in person, finding him too short to be a star in America and unpromisingly shabby, he liked the look of Nazimova, who had dressed up in her one good suit. He didn't know and didn't ask whether either of them was Jewish, but, like Frohman, he came from a German Jewish immigrant family and was sympathetic to the Jewish cause.

Sympathy apart, as a businessman Hayman thought he might be onto something. If Orlenev's company became a success in New York, the Frohman organization would be interested in managing it. Here was an opportunity, cheap at the price, to test its potential. And when he agreed to give Orlenev the Herald Square Theatre for a matinee of *The Chosen People* in two weeks' time, Hayman's terms cut his costs even further: for all expenses not directly connected with the theatre—rehearsal space, publicity, transportation, and so on—Orlenev would have to find the money himself.

In search of more kindness from more strangers, Orlenev and Nazimova consulted the manager of the Malkin Hotel, who suggested they ask the Kropotkin Society of New York for help. Its members, antitsarist exiles and anarchists who subscribed to Kropotkin's belief in nonviolent revolution, held weekly meetings at the house of a Russian doctor. Gathered around a samovar, they discussed the latest news from Moscow while clouds of nostalgic smoke from Russian cigarettes drifted across the room. When Orlenev told them that Kropotkin himself had seen and approved *The Chosen People* in London, they promised to round up an audience for the matinee by spreading the word to all the Russians they knew.

Among the Russians the doctor knew, as Nazimova discovered, was her uncle Osip. She took down his address and knocked at the door of his top-floor apartment in Brooklyn the following afternoon. It was twenty years since Osip Horowitz had seen Alla Leventon, and he failed to recognize her. She introduced herself; they hugged, kissed, and cried; then he introduced Nazimova to his wife and son. Horowitz had also changed his name: he was now Harvitt, and the family called him Ozzie. Another samovar, more Russian cigarettes, and more tears when they talked of Sonya; more kisses when they marveled at finding each other again in New York. Osip's professional eye noticed that Nazimova's teeth were in need of repair, and he promised to fix them free of charge before the matinee. Unlike Nina, he had nothing against the theatre or "living in sin," and when Nazimova told him about Orlenev, he offered the lovers the spare room in his apartment.

It was an attic room, large enough to provide rehearsal space for the St. Petersburg Players during the day. But although the Kropotkin Society's modest publicity campaign resulted in a less-than-half-full house for the matinee of *The Chosen People* at the Herald Square Theatre on March 23, two critics covered it. Both reviews singled out Nazimova for special homage. An unsigned notice in *The New York Times* called her "an actress of wonderful temperamental and technical quality"; Alan Dale wrote in the New York *American,* "We could not understand the language of the play, but the language of Alla Nazimova is universal. It is the language of the soul. Her name will be a household word." Dale was particularly impressed by "the way she wept." American actresses, he noted, were afraid to ruin their makeup and wept "from their temples and foreheads. . . . Nazimova shed tears from her eyes, mopped them with a handkerchief, and at the end of her grief, she actually had a red nose."

In his autobiography Orlenev sidestepped the issue of Nazimova's success, just as he never referred to her personal triumph in London. Nor did he acknowledge the rows of empty seats. "The success was colossal," he wrote, the press praised "each of the performers to the skies," and producers deluged him with offers. In fact, only Jacob Adler came forward to offer Orlenev the use of the Grand Street Theatre for two matinees a week.

The Chosen People drew good houses there throughout April and, as Jerome had predicted, found a multinational Jewish audience, even though half of it spoke only Yiddish. Orlenev again: "Dollars poured like a river. . . . We [Nazimova and I] often left after a performance with suitcases filled with dollars—gold, silver and paper." Two policemen, he added, escorted them back to Osip's apartment. Reality check: the company turned a modest profit, enough for Orlenev to lease the Murray Hill Theatre on 42nd Street.

Bored with *The Chosen People,* he decided to stage *Tsar Fyodor* there instead. "No sooner said than done, as always in my life. No thoughts, no plans—only feelings. It was enough." It was enough, as Nazimova recalled, only because "Little Alla had to be exceptionally busy." The theatre was only available from the 9th to the 16th of May, and she had ten days to create all the costumes, as well as rehearse the role of the tsarina. Osip's attic became the company's wardrobe department, where she cut

Nazimova and Orlenev in Tsar Fyodor, *New York, 1905. The costumes, notably more spectacular than those in the Moscow Art Theatre production, were designed by Nazimova.*

Nazimova and Orlenev in Tsar Fyodor

and stitched twenty-two court dresses, headdresses, uniforms, and capes with the help of a pair of seamstresses.

But the Murray Hill was a midtown theatre, and *Tsar Fyodor* failed to attract a local crowd or the Lower East Side audience that had supported *The Chosen People*. After three nights of poor houses, according to Orlenev, he realized that he was facing another period "of desperate need and sorrow." According to Nazimova, he fell off the wagon for the first time since leaving Russia. The following night, half an hour before curtain, she heard a commotion outside her dressing room and found Orlenev drunk in the corridor. Already made up but not yet in costume, she announced she was leaving him, threw a shawl over her shoulders, ran out to the street, hurried up the steps of the nearby El station, and boarded a waiting train. But she soon decided it would be wrong to miss a performance, and got back to the theatre in time for her first entrance. Although Orlenev managed to keep himself together until the final curtain, he fell asleep in his dressing room immediately afterward, and Nazimova returned to Osip's attic alone. Next day, when she forgave Orlenev, it was partly because he persuaded her to, and partly because, with no money and no hope of finding work in the theatre without him, she persuaded herself.

Meanwhile, Orlenev was out of work and almost out of money, and a hand-to-mouth existence was straining his company's loyalty. But once again he was rescued at the last moment. The owner of a theatre on the Lower East Side offered to finance a three-week season, which opened toward the end of June with *Crime and Punishment*. Within a few days the company had recaptured its ethnic audience, and by the end of the season Emma Goldman had added Orlenev to her list of causes.

A fearless campaigner for birth control and the rights of workers, women, and homosexuals, this Russian Jewish immigrant called herself an anarchist but was disapproved of by the Kropotkin Society. Emma's record contradicted her official belief in nonviolence. As well as being arrested for inciting unemployed workers to riot, she had aided and abetted Alexander Berkman, her fellow anarchist and lover, in his attempt to murder the "prototype capitalist" Henry Frick, chairman of the Carnegie Steel Company. She gave Berkman money to buy a revolver; he fired one shot that hit Frick in the shoulder, but was apprehended before he could fire again, and sentenced to eighteen years in jail.

Thirty-six years old, only five feet tall but huskily built, Emma concealed a powerful erotic drive behind plain, unfashionable clothes and shell-rimmed glasses. Deeply stirred by Orlenev's performance as Raskolnikov at the Talley Theatre, she went backstage to congratulate him and decided that he was "a naive, unworldly creature living only in the realm of art." Emma cared passionately about the art of the theatre, and had lectured on Shaw, Ibsen, and Strindberg. Orlenev, who had heard about Berkman, told Emma that he considered her lover "a character for a great tragedy," adding of course that he saw himself in the part. And since Berkman's sentence still had several years to run, Emma soon began to see Orlenev as the man to take over the role of her lover in life. Not surprisingly, her reaction to Nazimova was guarded. Emma's autobiography pays a brief, restrained tribute to the actress, a longer one to the "resourceful" designer of costumes for *Tsar Fyodor.*

When she discovered that Orlenev had no prospects after the season ended, and would soon run out of money again, Emma not only promised to launch a fund-raising campaign but invited the entire company to spend the rest of the summer at her campsite on Hunter Island in Pelham Bay. During August and most of September, according to Orlenev, the St. Petersburg Players lived there "as a commune," cooking their meals in a brick oven, sleeping in tents, and plagued by mosquitoes.

But there was one significant absentee. Many years later, Nazimova and Orlenev gave conflicting accounts of the reasons behind her sudden departure for Russia. Nazimova claimed that a repertory theatre in Moscow had offered her a contract to play leading roles in its forthcoming season, and she decided to accept it. Personally unhappy with Orlenev, convinced that his "eternal ill luck" would never change, she walked out on him for good. Several other actors in the company, she added, were disillusioned and had left to find other work in New York. Orlenev denied her whole story. Certain that his dream of "a permanent Russian theatre" was about to be fulfilled, already making plans for a season of new plays, he needed to expand the company and sent Nazimova to recruit ten new actors in Moscow.

Orlenev's version was confirmed by Osip's son Henry Harvitt. He remembered that Nazimova left for Russia "to bring back a new group of actors." Where the money came from, he didn't say. By this time, presumably, Emma had raised enough to pay steerage fares. But according to her autobiography, only "some" of Orlenev's actors were living on Hunter Island when she joined him there. So it seems probable that several had in fact defected, and Orlenev was too proud to admit that he needed to replace them.

Nazimova's version is one of her boldest rewrites of the past. A theatre in Moscow, the most anti-Semitic Russian city, offered a contract to a relatively unknown actress who was appearing in a pro-Jewish play in New York? And at a time when the pogroms had begun again? A few months earlier, on "Bloody Sunday," police had killed or wounded several hundred workers marching to present a petition to the tsar. As usual, the government accused the Jews of inciting unrest, and they suffered the consequences. In 1900, Nemirovich doubted that a Jewish actress could establish herself at the Art Theatre. Five years later, her chances in any Moscow theatre would have been nil.

Pride, of course, also played a part in Nazimova's story. By claiming that a Moscow theatre had offered her starring roles, she once again exaggerated her professional standing in Russia. But besides sustaining a legend, she concealed a fact. When Orlenev sent Nazimova to recruit new actors, he enabled her to rejoin a lover of whose existence he was unaware.

Maurice Sterne was the son of a Latvian Jewish couple who emigrated to the United States in 1889 and settled in New York. Eleven years old at the time, Sterne was already determined to become a painter, but his parents could only afford to offer moral support. Eventually, by working in a factory, he saved enough money to enroll at the National Academy of Design. He graduated in 1904, at the age of twenty-six, won a traveling scholarship shortly afterward, and decided to study art in Paris. Sterne's memoirs, which he didn't live to complete, make no mention of where he first met Nazimova or when their affair began. Since he left New York at the end of May 1905, it must have been during that spring; and since he was interested in the theatre and spoke Russian and German, most likely he went backstage after a matinee at the Grand Theatre. Although he sailed for France a few weeks later, it was *au revoir* and not goodbye. The lovers kept in touch, as Sterne's memoirs reveal, and in the summer of 1905, "Alla Nazimova came to join me in Paris. We had an idyllic two weeks together, enhanced by love and also by Alla's wonderful dramatic readings."

Short and powerfully built, Sterne had a "handsome look of suffering" that would prove immensely attractive to his first wife, Mabel Dodge Luhan. "Skillful and ruthless in my pursuit of physical pleasure," was the artist's self-portrait as a young man. "I have on occasions behaved like a son-of-a-bitch. . . . It took many years for me to learn to see women as friends and not as prey." Physically and psychologically, it seems, he had not a little in common with Orlenev. But although Sterne still regarded women as prey during his affair with Nazimova, he recollected her with friendly admiration:

*Maurice Sterne, soon after his
arrival in Paris*

The night she arrived we sat up until dawn while Alla "acted"
Uncle Vanya for me. On another night she read a scene from
Evgeny Onegin and I saw then with deep intensity how gifted
she was. Every nuance of the poetry was dramatically expressed, not only in the many different vocal inflections, but
in the constant change and movement of her body.

One afternoon, when Nazimova read Nina's final scene in *The Seagull*,
"the tears were rolling down her cheeks." But at dinner that evening,
when Sterne "marveled at how deeply she must have felt," Nazimova
laughed. As he stared at her, a waiter came up to ask if they would like a
cognac with their coffee.

With tears spilling out of her eyes, Alla whispered, "No,
thankyou, no cognac." The waiter was startled and asked her
what was wrong. Alla's face was lit with a sad smile. She said,
"I am crying from happiness. This is my first honeymoon."
The spiritually uplifted waiter left and I nearly exploded with
laughter.

Nazimova the actress was clearly more than ready to emerge from Orlenev's shadow. And during those idyllic two weeks, when Sterne asked

her to marry him, she gave what he failed to recognize as another "wonderful dramatic reading." She accepted his proposal, but said she had to go back to New York almost at once for career reasons. A few days later she left Paris, "promising to return in the spring when we were to be married." In the months that followed, Sterne received "a few passionate letters, the last of which announced her decision to stay in the United States." Since Nazimova never mentioned that she was still married to Golovin, and Sterne's memoirs betray no trace of bitterness at her deception, both were evidently playing a game.

Sterne had made his conquest, and would make several more until he was conquered by Mabel Dodge Luhan in 1916. But what exactly was Nazimova's game? By her own account, possession of a passport allowed her to move around freely, and she spent the first part of that summer in Yalta, instead of going directly to Moscow to sign a contract with the theatre. A strange decision, if the offer really existed and she was so eager to accept it. Nazimova's account also mentions that she received a letter from Orlenev before leaving Yalta. "He wrote that some multimillionaire had become interested in his company and had decided to build a theatre to honor them," and begged Nazimova to change her mind about leaving him and return as soon as possible with the new actors. She didn't answer the letter. Finally, in mid-August, she went to Moscow and made an appointment to sign her contract. The following morning, as she was about to leave her hotel for the theatre, Nazimova heard sounds of a violent disturbance and agonized screams in the street outside. She ran to a window and saw mounted Cossacks brutally attacking a group of student demonstrators, trampling them underfoot and lashing them with whips. Horrified, she decided not to stay in a country where such things happened, sent a cable to Orlenev promising to engage the actors he needed, and sailed to New York with them a week later.

Reality check: In his autobiography Orlenev confirms that "the troupe invited from Russia arrived," and lists the actors' names. But he doesn't mention that Nazimova traveled with them. In fact, she left Moscow for Paris, where she spent two weeks with Maurice Sterne. And when she explained why they couldn't get married right away, she was really turning him down because she had made up her mind to go back to Orlenev after all.

Once before, after the St. Petersburg run of *Ghosts*, she had tried and failed to break his hold on her life. The most likely explanation for Nazimova's unlikely story of her trip to Russia is her reluctance to admit that

*Nazimova as Regina
in* Ghosts, *during the
"Orlenev's Lyceum" season
of 1905–6*

she tried and failed again. And the offer from a Moscow theatre is another legend with a faint gleam of reality behind it. Although stardom in Moscow was out of the question, Nazimova could have resumed her career on the provincial circuit. But she was too ambitious to settle for such a modest future. Although it cannot be verified, the incident of the Cossacks probably happened. In addition to the mutiny on the *Potemkin,* strikes and street rebellions occurred in several cities that summer and were brutally suppressed. The only certainty is that Nazimova's final option was Sterne, and she couldn't settle for him either. "The law of impulse" still bound her to Orlenev.

MEANWHILE, Orlenev's hold on Emma Goldman's life had grown stronger. On Hunter Island she found him "literally afire with inspiration," and Emma's autobiography is afire in its account of those "unforgettable weeks." Sometimes he woke her in the middle of the night, standing at the entrance to her tent and shouting, "I have it!" What he had, she discovered, was a new inflection for one of Raskolnikov's speeches, or a new gesture for Dmitri Karamazov in his drunkenness. Evenings, the company sat around a bonfire, "with Orlenev in the center, guitar in hand, softly strumming an accompaniment to his own singing, the whole troupe joining in on the chorus, the strains echoing far over the bar as the large samovar buzzed. . . . Russia filled our souls with the plaint of her woe."

Orlenev's account of that summer is less romantic. No mention of Emma. "Accustomed to solitude," he refused to share a tent with anyone, conducted acting classes in the open air, and occasionally left the island "to visit the shareholders signed up for the future theatre" in New York. In an interview with a reporter from the Boston *Transcript* he announced that Orlenev's Lyceum would open on October 20:

> It will be a small playhouse, with a seating capacity of about nine hundred. . . . Madame Nasimoff, the leading lady in the company, [has] returned to Russia to procure the rights of new plays by Gorky and Chekhov, and also to obtain the services of ten actors and actresses of standing in Russia, to add to the strength of the company.

Since Emma arranged the interview, she was obviously confident of raising sufficient funds. But the "multi-millionaire" that Orlenev mentioned in his letter to Nazimova did not exist. For her various campaigns, Emma relied on two groups of wealthy supporters: Jewish immigrants who had become successful businessmen, and the radically chic liberals of the day. She expected the first group to sponsor Orlenev the spokesman for racial tolerance, the second to rally behind his cause of "theatre for the people." Emma's autobiography does not reveal how much money she hoped to raise, but the checks that came in were evidently less generous than she hoped.

When Nazimova returned to New York in mid-September and asked to see the new theatre, Orlenev and Emma looked "mysterious. . . . 'Wait one week, and all will be ready.' " Orlenev had moved out of Osip's apartment and was living in the house of a German couple. Friends of Emma, Osip said, implying that Orlenev and Emma were also a couple. Nazimova had guessed as much, but after her affair with Sterne she was in no position to play the injured party. The mystery of the theatre was another matter. A week later, when they told her it was still not completely ready, she became angry and demanded to see it.

What she saw from the outside, on East 3rd Street in the Bowery, was a derelict lecture hall flanked by a saloon and a bowling alley. From the inside, rows of wooden benches, a gallery with a low iron railing, and a small stage with a tattered draw curtain. Below the stage, Russian workmen were converting a cellar space into cramped, windowless dressing rooms. A violent dispute broke out when Orlenev accused them of working too slowly; the workmen threatened to quit, and Emma stepped in to calm both sides down. "What could I say or do?" Nazimova wondered. "Russia I would not go back to—I could not go elsewhere. . . . I was trapped, and had to make the best of it." Making the best of it, she soon discovered, would involve the hardest work of her life to date. After taking a lease on the hall, paying for the construction work, the wooden benches and draw curtain bought from a thrift shop, and the materials Orlenev had ordered for sets and costumes, and keeping a sum in reserve to cover the company's living expenses over the next few weeks, Emma had no money left. There would be no costumes unless Nazimova made them, no sets unless she helped to paint them, no incidental music unless she arranged it, no stage manager unless she took over the job, and, besides rehearsing several new plays, she would have to translate one of them into Russian—the only available text of Ibsen's *The Master Builder* was in German.

All this she agreed to do, after a major row with Orlenev over her living expenses. When he claimed that she didn't need any since she was living with Osip's family, Nazimova threatened to go on strike. She was not only embarrassed at the prospect of continuing to depend on Osip, but refused to work twelve hours a day unless she could take a room close to the theatre. Orlenev gave way, and she rented a walk-up apartment in a rat-infested tenement on East 4th Street. By the time the season opened, Orlenev had moved in with her. There is no record of Emma's reaction, for, like Orlenev, she wrote her autobiography long before the era of "telling all," and neither was explicit about the relationship. (Emma hinted at it by writing that she only found true happiness with men who shared her ideals while "loving the woman in me.") But she remained loyal to Orlenev's cause after he went back to Nazimova, acting as publicist for the theatre and interpreter at interviews, and traveling with the company when it went on tour.

Orlenev's Lyceum opened on November 3, only two weeks behind schedule, with *Uncle Vanya, The Seagull, The Master Builder,* and Gorky's *The Lower Depths* among the new plays in the repertory. "The public clamored for us," according to Orlenev, but Henry Harvitt remembered that the company played to half-empty houses at first, and on one night he and his father were the only members of the audience for *Uncle Vanya.* "We give this performance just for you," Orlenev said. Afterward, Osip commented: "One of the greatest performances I ever saw."

By the end of the month, Emma had persuaded a few theatre critics to make the journey to the Bowery. James Huneker was the first to review the St. Petersburg Players, and devoted most of his column in *Public Opinion* to praising Nazimova's "splendid emotional power" in *The Seagull*. Richard Watson Gilder echoed him a few days later in *Century Magazine,* and also wrote a letter to *The New York Times:* "Those who care for acting as an art should take a trolley car to Orlenev's Lyceum. There may be enjoyed some of the best acting ever seen in New York."

"IBSEN BY RUSSIAN ACTORS DRAWS CROWDS TO THE BOWERY. NEW TRAGEDY QUEEN IS FOUND ON EAST SIDE." Newspaper and magazine features were one result of Gilder's letter. Another was a dramatic rise in attendance when Orlenev lowered the price of a ticket from twenty to ten cents. (Later, at Nazimova's suggestion, a pack of cigarettes secured a seat in the gallery. She had run out of cigarettes before a performance, and was frantic.) The press reported that in spite of the theatre's "primitive smell," a surprising number of Americans could be spotted among the audience of "Slavs and Poles . . . with big animal nostrils and thick lips." But at the end of December, the New York Fire Department declared the theatre a public hazard and ordered it to close.

Apart from the actors, everyone had worked without pay. Stagehands, musicians, and box-office staff were all Russian immigrants whom Orlenev had met at neighborhood cafés and persuaded to volunteer their services. But at ten cents a seat, the company had a long way to go before breaking even; the sudden closing of the theatre left Emma without funds to lease another space, and the St. Petersburg Players at the end of the line. The last of their last-minute rescues came from Al Hayman and Charles Frohman, who had kept an eye on them since that first matinee at the Herald Square Theatre and written them off as unlikely to succeed. The press coverage of Orlenev's Lyceum changed their minds. They organized a relief fund and booked the company into another of their theatres for a series of matinees. Among those who sponsored the fund were John Pierpont Morgan, Andrew Carnegie, and Otto Kahn, as well as Mrs. Stanford White, wife of the architect; Mrs. Douglas Robinson, sister of President Theodore Roosevelt; and Edith Wharton. Their names guaranteed advance publicity and a fashionable audience. At the Criterion Theatre, where Frohman presented the matinees, Ethel, John, and Lionel Barrymore were appearing in a double bill of plays by J. M. Barrie, but after Mrs. Harry Payne Whitney saw *Tsar Fyodor* on January 31, 1906, she declared Orlenev and Nazimova the greatest actors she had ever seen. The matinees sold out and Frohman decided to send the company on tour. But since Nazimova had proved the star attraction, especially in

The Seagull and *Zaza*, he insisted that she receive equal billing with Or- lenev. Henry Harvitt, who saw both plays, remembered that Nazimova "displayed stage presence to the nth degree," commanding more audi- ence attention than Orlenev; he also remembered Orlenev "drinking quite heavily" by the time the company left for Chicago.

By now Orlenev was on the brink of a situation that would eventually be mythologized in the Hollywood movie *A Star Is Born*. When *The Cho- sen People* opened in London, public reaction to Nazimova had forced Orlenev to share the spotlight with his protégée. He would find himself barely on the edge of it during their two-week engagement in Chicago, followed by two weeks in Boston. In both cities Nazimova became the star attraction, not only onstage but at several receptions given for the company. Mrs. Hobart Chatfield-Taylor, a leading Chicago socialite and passionate fan, endorsed a local critic's suggestion that Nazimova should learn English and aim for a career on Broadway. If the idea first entered her mind that night, Nazimova did not let on. "But I would have to leave Mr Orlenev, and that is impossible," she replied. Emma, acting as inter- preter, no doubt reported the conversation to Orlenev, who made little attempt to ingratiate himself on social occasions. "Now we will sit down and keep silent on a number of interesting subjects," he would mutter in Russian, and ask Emma to fetch him some vodka. (Posing as "Miss E. F. Smith," since she feared her real name might alienate high society, Emma disguised herself so effectively that a Chicago journalist believed her pseudonym concealed "the daughter of a noble Russian family in re- duced circumstances.") At another reception, when asked why so many Russian plays had unhappy endings, Orlenev answered with a stream of Russian obscenities. Nazimova covered for him: "In Russia the people who come to the theatre laugh and weep, not for the characters but for themselves, and they usually weep." Throughout the tour she provided reporters with good copy. "The church will never talk as plainly to its people as Ibsen talks in *Ghosts*." "Must the stage be only a commercial in- stitution, without at least an artistic undercurrent in the ocean of money- making?" "Your [American] stage, I think, has many personalities but very little individuality."

But Orlenev made headlines when he was arrested for grand larceny after the company returned to New York. According to the New York *Daily Mirror* of March 24, 1906, a subscriber to the relief fund organized by Frohman accused Orlenev of fraud and breach of contract. Joseph Goldstein, after being promised a percentage of the profits in return for his investment of $1,500, had only received $50. He checked the box-

Nazimova in New York, October 1906.
"In front of me lies fame, a great career."

office receipts, found more than $1,500 unaccounted for, and charged
Orlenev with diverting money to his own pocket. Because the case never
came to court, the details remain murky. According to Orlenev, he spent
two days in jail, but "when the District Attorney learned from his wife
that I was the actor Orlenev, he wrote a check for $5000 and . . . said in
French, 'You are free—this is your bail.' " Then, at the request of the
DA's wife, the three of them had breakfast together. According to
Emma—whose autobiography doesn't mention Goldstein, only "problems with creditors"—she herself wrote the check, amount unspecified,
for Orlenev's bail. Neither of them explained how the money was raised
for a settlement out of court, but Frohman was evidently angered by the
publicity. He cut his connections with the company, and after going on

another manic bender, Orlenev decided that his American dream was over.

When Nazimova's admirer Richard Watson Gilder heard that Orlenev was determined to take the St. Petersburg Players back to Russia and needed to raise boat fares, he offered to find sponsors for a benefit performance. But, like several of Nazimova's admirers, Gilder had come to view Orlenev as an obstacle to her future, and saw an opportunity for cloak-and-dagger work. He contacted Henry Miller, general manager for the Shubert organization, and suggested setting up an interview between Lee Shubert and Nazimova. Miller contacted Owen Johnson, a popular novelist who spoke German, and asked him to act as interpreter. Although Shubert had never seen Nazimova onstage, he was primed in advance, tipped off by a leading critic, a best-selling novelist, and his own general manager that she was a potential Broadway star. When they met at his office, the potential star looked incongruously shabby, for her one good suit was threadbare by now, her shoes down-at-heel. But Shubert took what Nazimova later described as "a gambler's chance" and offered her a five-year contract on the spot.

Although she was equally quick to accept, no announcement appeared in the press until three weeks later. Presumably Nazimova needed time to prepare for her final break with Orlenev. We don't know exactly when she made it, but the interview with Shubert took place in early April, and a benefit performance of *The Master Builder* at the Berkeley Theatre had been set for April 30. The day after the couple made their last appearance on the stage together, *The New York Times* announced that Orlenev's company would shortly be leaving for Russia without Nazimova, who had decided to pursue her career in the United States.

In her autobiography, Emma wrote that Nazimova's defection revealed "the gap that must always exist between a truly creative artist and one interested mainly in material success." But this is a view from the wilder shores of infatuation. "Material success" was not yet within Nazimova's grasp, only the chance to escape from total poverty as well as Orlenev's total domination of her personal and professional life. He still had a future to go back to in Russia, but he ended by destroying it, and would surely have destroyed what little future remained for Nazimova there.

The rest of Orlenev's life is the story of a few brilliant successes between long intervals of depression and drunkenness. And if Nazimova often blurred the line between fact and fiction, Orlenev often obliterated it. In his autobiography, he wrote that he returned to New York in April 1912 with a new company, and had "colossal success" in Ibsen's *Brand* and

Lee Shubert in his office, c. 1907.
Shubert told Nazimova, "Ibsen is
not a money-maker."

another play banned in Russia, Dmitri Merezhkovsky's *Tsar Pavel*, about the assassination of Catherine the Great's son. According to Orlenev, he was even offered a contract to star in a silent film of the Merezhkovsky play but turned it down. In fact, the two plays lasted less than two weeks, the movie contract was a fantasy no doubt inspired by Nazimova's stardom in Hollywood, and Orlenev returned to Russia. When his autobiography appeared there in 1932, he was on tour in Siberia, sixty-two years old and syphilitic, but still playing Raskolnikov and Oswald. He died a few months later.

ON MAY 5, 1906, Orlenev and company left New York. On May 14, Nazimova signed her contract with Shubert, who agreed to pay the salary, until November 5, of "a competent and suitable teacher of English, who shall give instruction in the English language to the said party for two hours each day." To Nazimova he agreed to pay a salary of $100 weekly, plus 20 percent of the profits, for a guaranteed twenty-five weeks during the 1906–7 season. A final clause gave Shubert an option on Nazimova's services for the next four years, with a weekly salary increase of $75 each year, and "proportionate increases" in her share of the profits.

When Shubert learned that Goldstein was not Orlenev's only creditor and Nazimova had been paid nothing since the beginning of the year, he offered her an advance of $100. She immediately spent some of it on a new suit and new pair of shoes, then returned to her tenement flat, where the rats remained but the costumes that used to litter the living room had gone back to Russia with Orlenev. Nazimova never disclosed, and neither did Orlenev, what they said to each other on the day she announced that she would not be going back with him. But a few days after signing the contract with Shubert, she recorded in her diary: "My heart is so heavy that I feel like bursting into tears every moment—and this won't help me either, as I've had plenty of opportunities to notice. . . . There is no medicine for it, is there? For this utter loneliness I have to go through?"

Although Nazimova felt a "gnawing pain" when she realized that "I have torn myself away from everything I have been attached to," she never referred directly to Orlenev. Perhaps because she had resolved "to make an end of my old life . . . and it is my unalterable determination to leave the old world behind me!" But to make sure she had really left the "old world" behind, Nazimova had to lash herself into an act of exorcism. "I closed every window, locked my door and for half an hour gave myself up to the luxury of rolling on the floor in an agony of despair, tearing my hair and yelling like someone possessed."

6

"A Modern Woman"
1906–1912

Ibsen's women ... are to be found everywhere.
You may have met Nora on the street or taken
Hedda Gabler to dinner. But you did not recognize them because Ibsen was not at hand to introduce them to you. That is why you have to go to
the theatre to see them ... and often see something of yourself too.

—NAZIMOVA

A MONTH AFTER ORLENEV LEFT FOR RUSSIA,
Nazimova began her English lessons. Less afraid of loneliness by then,
she decided to "live" entirely in English, refused to speak Russian, and
even cut herself off from the Harvitt family until the end of October.
Much of the time she spent alone, going to the theatre to listen to actors'
speech patterns, sitting in restaurants to study the lip movements of people at nearby tables. But for the first few weeks Nazimova could communicate only with herself, in her native tongue. "I shall write in Russian
if I cannot speak it," she noted in her diary, "shall feel as if there is at least
one person I can really talk to who will surely understand me." As the
lessons progressed, she began translating the diary into English, and
combined homework in a new language with an attempt to reach a new
self-understanding: "I feel that no matter what happens to me, I shall
never return [to Russia], shall never even be the same, shall live differ-
ently, have a different outlook upon life and people. . . ." All the same,

memories of the past and all its "most regrettable incidents" continued to trouble her.

"Something cruel to myself awakens sometimes within me," she wrote, "as if I like to hurt myself, create pain stronger than anyone ever could. . . ." Clinging to the pain of her childhood and youth, in fact, became a habit that took years for Nazimova to shake off, even though she had already begun to suspect that only acting could heal the wounds of the past. "If I have lived not beautifully, I *must* act beautifully. . . . In front of me lies fame, a great career." Staking her future on her English-speaking debut, Nazimova was convinced that she could achieve "everything I have been longing and working for." But she worried that Shubert and Miller, whose ideas about the theatre were so different from her own, had the power "to decide for me what the play should be—the play in which I must either win or lose."

Shubert's first idea had been to launch her as a new Bernhardt in an old-fashioned romantic role. Nazimova wanted to play "a modern woman," and was thinking Ibsen. At first she thought *The Master Builder*, the last play in which she had appeared with Orlenev. But although she found a strong personal subtext in the role of Hilda, gradually disenchanted by a man she idolized, Nazimova began to feel that the win-or-lose part should be one she'd never played before. "I know that I have not shown yet all I can do. . . . Every part leaves me unsatisfied, untouched, un-emptied, as if the play had stopped just when I was going to open my innermost soul." Could *A Doll's House* open it? Nora struck another personal chord, but not as deeply as another of Ibsen's women:

> Hedda Gabler! Yes, that's it. Hedda Gabler, not in the sense of being possessed with the idea of controlling someone else's destiny, but to mold my own destiny in the most wonderful way, into something worthwhile and unexpected, even to myself!

Although Hedda's destiny was suicide, Nazimova was the first actress to find it "wonderful" and "unexpected." The most original and controversial aspect of her performance was its insistence on Hedda's refusal to admit defeat, and on her suicide as a final, spectacular, triumphant act of revenge. Trapped in a repressive small town, with a husband she despises, alternately bored, angry, proud, cunning, this Hedda found temporary compensation in the power game, manipulating weak men and shocking provincial women. (Nazimova had played this game herself, with Golovin and the millionaire, and with her own sister.) The first major test of her strength comes when she succeeds in driving a man to suicide, the last when she kills herself, secure in the knowledge of all the shattered lives she will leave behind, their deceptions and hypocrisies brutally exposed.

With scores of her own to settle, Nazimova responded to Hedda's anger with a shock of recognition. When she first read the play is not known, but in 1898, during her "hopeless" relationship with Sanin, she was studying it on the train to Bobruisk. She knew then that "she'd never get the chance to play it" in repertory there, and six years later hadn't forgotten that Orlenev denied her a chance to play it because he thought her too inexperienced. Now, with more than enough experience behind her, in life and the theatre, Nazimova felt so ready for "a great climax" that she struggled for breath, then blacked out in her hotel room. As soon as she regained consciousness, she moved into even higher dramatic gear. "I always think that I shall die soon, so I have the right to hurry." And hurry she did, straight to Shubert's office, where she summoned enough English to tell him before the interpreter arrived: "I play Hedda Gabler, Ibsen. No Hedda—I do not play!"

"Isben," said Shubert, who never got the name right, "is not a money-maker." Even the popular Minnie Maddern Fiske had failed to attract an audience when she gave the New York premiere of *Hedda Gabler* in 1903; and by this time Shubert had a new idea for Nazimova, a play with great commercial possibilities and a suitably exotic role that would not over-tax her command of English. Its title was *Miss Pocahontas*. Instead of ar-guing, Nazimova repeated her ultimatum. Several times. Not without misgiving, but awed by her baleful Hedda-like determination, Shubert finally threw in the towel.

BY THIS TIME Nazimova was living at the Judson Hotel on Washington Square, thanks to her Chicago admirer Mrs. Hobart Chatfield-Taylor, who formed what the New York *Mirror* described as "a little syndicate of Chicago women" to move the future star out of her tenement flat and foot the bill at "a good address." There, for three hours six days a week, Nazimova had begun her English lessons with the teacher engaged by Shubert. A Southern divorcée and out-of-work ac-tress with a ten-year-old son, Carolyn Harris didn't want to leave Dickie alone at home, so brought him along to the Judson with a cage of white rats that Dickie didn't want to leave alone at home. Like the Zhdanovas, Carolyn and Dickie reawakened Nazimova's nostalgia for something she had never really known. They became "family," and she grew particularly fond of Dickie, who, as Richard Barthelmess, had his first acting role in Nazimova's first silent movie, three years before D. W. Griffith cast him opposite Lillian Gish in *Broken Blossoms.*

As a language teacher, Carolyn Harris was ahead of her time. "There was no grammar," Nazimova remembered. "It was all conversation and reading books and newspapers and magazines." Sixteen years earlier, at Yakov's house in Yalta, Melanya had given Alla her first Russian lessons in the same way. Acting in repertory had made Nazimova's oral memory even sharper, and within four months her English was remarkably confident if not always correct. She also found Carolyn's lessons an education in American manners, especially for women, as she remarked to Charles Darnton, drama critic for the Boston *Transcript,* when he interviewed her in September:

> They tell me it is all right to say "My God" in French, but that it is wicked to say the same thing in English. . . . Here if I want to call on God I must use another language. . . . Another thing I cannot understand about is that little word "Damn." . . . If [an actor] wants to make the audience laugh when the play is not funny enough, he just puts in a few "Damns." But ladies are not supposed to say it except in private.

By this time Nazimova had also learned that ladies were expected to put on a show of modesty. In her diary she confessed that she was ambitious and longed for fame, but she told Darnton that she "didn't want to become a star—no, that is the fatal thing, to be a star!" And at the first rehearsal of *Hedda Gabler,* in late October, she charmed Henry Miller and the cast (which included Laura Hope Crews, later Prudence in Garbo's *Camille* and Aunt Pittypat in *Gone with the Wind*) by asking for their help and patience because she was "ver-rr-y frightened by the new language." Then she pretended surprise when they were surprised by her fluency. Skillfully usurping male authority without ruffling male feathers, she soon had Miller in her power. In 1906, there were no women directors in the New York theatre, and it was equally unheard of for a producer to allow an unknown foreign actress to direct her own debut. But although assigned by Shubert to direct *Hedda Gabler,* Miller first agreed not to direct Nazimova's performance, then allowed her to direct everyone else's. Realizing that she knew far more about Ibsen than he did, he sat out front and puzzled over her "unique methods."

Nazimova began by telling the cast that there were no small parts, only

Two faces of Hedda. Nazimova as Hedda Gabler in her English-speaking debut, 1906

small actors. Every role was equally important, she said, all the characters were interrelated, and she wanted the actors to play to each other, not to the audience. She also asked them to "play simple" and avoid "the singing voice." Basic Stanislavsky, of course, but "unique" to Miller and the actors because they knew nothing about him. Just as they had no experience of basic Orlenev, and were stunned when Nazimova produced the footstool effect to make Hedda appear taller, and played an important moment with her back to the audience, something that no leading actor in the New York theatre had done before.

Truly unique was something else they had never witnessed before, a star personality with a dynamic instinct for theatre who was also an actress with an equally dynamic instinct for characterization. Other stars of the time owed their success to creating a fixed image within a fixed tradition. Gentility and caution prevailed. Maude Adams had cornered the market in wistful sweetness; Ethel Barrymore patented dignified glamour; and even the more adventurous, versatile Minnie Maddern Fiske firmly distanced herself from Hedda by portraying her, as she told Alexander Woollcott, as a "poor, empty, little Norwegian neurotic." But in Nazimova's view, Ibsen had created a subversive character of almost mythic proportions and "had to make her smaller to get her on the stage." Where Fiske saw only a pathetic, "enormously unimportant" creature driven to suicide, Nazimova embraced Hedda as a woman who drove herself, a Medea of the North, icily rejecting sympathy and consumed by aggression. In performance she was always dangerously on the move, apart from a few sudden, unnerving pauses, a freeze at the suggestion that she might find happiness in motherhood, a rigid stare at the pistol she'd just loaded. And to the image of crucifixion originally devised by Orlenev, Nazimova added an ornament of her own. Left alone onstage, Hedda backed against a wall, and as she extended her arms, her black robe fell slowly open to reveal a blood-red lining.

"Here at last, in the very flesh, was that nightmare-lady, Hedda Gabler," wrote Alan Dale of the New York *American* in his review of the first performance, at the Princess Theatre on November 12. *The New York Times* agreed: "Great creative acting . . . One of the most illuminating and varied performances which our stage has seen in years." Two critics dissented sharply from the majority view. William Winter of the New York *Tribune*, who considered Ibsen's plays the product of "a disordered brain," found only "reckless violence" in Nazimova's "twisting, turning, grieving, serpentine" Hedda. In the New York *Sun*, John Corbin faulted her for portraying "a writhing (or insinuating) serpent that hungrily devours" instead of "a graceful cat." This Hedda, he concluded, "was not Ibsen." Obviously he had never read the play. Ibsen's stage directions define Hedda as a highly theatrical predator with "clear, cold eyes" and "a contemptuous laugh," habitually pacing the room, "clenching her fists with anger," firing her pistol at imaginary targets through the open French windows, and after her final exit strumming "a wild dance tune" on the piano, then shooting herself.

Eugene O'Neill, eighteen years old at the time, hadn't read the play either, and Nazimova in *Hedda Gabler* provided his first exposure to Ibsen. He saw the production ten times, partly for its own sake, partly because he found it such a powerful antidote to the old-fashioned, artificial American theatre of his father, James, who had toured the country for years in *The Count of Monte Cristo.* "That experience discovered an entire new world of drama for me," O'Neill recalled later. "It gave me my first conception of a modern theatre where truth might live."

Shubert, doubtful that truth could live very long at the box office, had advertised his new star's debut as "IBSEN IN THE AFTERNOON WITH NAZIMOVA," and she played matinees only, four times a week. A month of packed houses, and heavy advance bookings, called for a change of plan. Since Shubert had another play occupying the Princess at night, he decided to present Nazimova in a season of repertory at the Bijou Theatre. "You can play your Isben as long as you like," he told her, "as long as you need only a small cast and one set." It was all she needed for *A Doll's House,* which opened the season at the Bijou on January 14, 1907, and alternated nightly with *Hedda.*

Although Henry Miller again received sole credit as director, he had allowed Nazimova to take charge of rehearsals. The result was another star performance, but with a completely different image. No trace of the commanding figure in a severe dark gown, hair drawn back starkly, high heels adding to her stature, a glare of scarlet lipstick enlarging her mouth. Instead, at her first entrance, a child-wife with a fluffy halo of hair, frilly white blouse, and skirt, stature diminished by low heels, mouth by absence of rouge. Discarding frills and froufrou for Nora's last scene, Nazimova chose to walk out the door in a plain winter coat and head scarf. Before leaving, she took out a hand mirror, glanced at her reflected face, and, to emphasize the moment of self-illumination, had a spotlight trained on the mirror.

On the way she handled Nora's inner transition from first entrance to final exit, several critics made the same point. *The New York Times* praised Nazimova's "natural dramatic instinct" combined with "intellec-

Two faces of Nora. Nazimova in the "Tarantella" scene, and on her way to slam the door, in A Doll's House

tual appreciation." Owen Johnson, an admirer since he first saw her perform with Orlenev, wrote in *Century Magazine* of her "amazing virtuosity" allied to "calm, clear intellect," and *Cosmopolitan* ran a special illustrated feature on Nazimova. "In Nora there was no suspicion of Hedda," it noted. "Each was a clean-cut, cameo-like portrait. That, of course, is the real object of acting. Its perversion—every part exactly the same—is what we get today."

For Laurette Taylor, five years younger than Nazimova and hoping to make a career in the New York theatre after working in a Seattle stock company and touring the West, these two performances were a revelation. "There was courage," she remembered, "courage of one who was willing and able to tread unknown paths." But although she could applaud Nora for leaving her husband, as Laurette herself had recently done, she couldn't forgive a woman who walked out on her children as well.

The great public dissenter was again William Winter. He launched another attack on Ibsen, finding a threat to American morals in the playwright's ideas about women's independence, and dismissed Nazimova as an actress admired only by "judges who care nothing for form, but are quickly responsive to hysterics." From May Webster, the future Dame May Whitty, came an enigmatic private verdict: "A great actress, with a revolting personality." She did not elaborate, but Webster was rooted in the English tradition of genteel theatre. Also in private, another member of the audience thought Nazimova's "Slav temperament did not suit the role." But neither, as Alice B. Toklas admitted, did Nora suit her own temperament. *A Doll's House* was her first encounter with Ibsen, and she decided to make it her last.

Although the critics found a strong intellect at work in Nazimova's performance, her comments on the play imply an equally strong personal involvement: "It was the misfortune of Nora that she had been made into a doll through her training first by her father, then by her husband." Nora, she added, "can change. . . . But how can [her husband] change when he thinks everything he does is exactly right? She could not help him, he could only hinder her. That is why she never came back." And in spite of her technical virtuosity, there were times when Nazimova's unconscious took over. "I didn't know, for example, that I had caressed the door with my hands when Nora starts to leave her husband for the first time, until one or two critics mentioned it." A similar moment had occurred in *Hedda Gabler*, when Hedda steals the manuscript of Løvborg's book and plans to burn it. William Archer, London's leading Ibsen critic, was unaware that she usually hid the manuscript under a sofa pillow, and at the performance he saw, Løvborg entered before Nazimova had time to reach the sofa. She slipped the manuscript under her gown instead, and clasped it to her breast. Løvborg, believing he's lost the manuscript and too humiliated to admit the fact, claims he destroyed it because he decided it was no good. Mrs. Elvsted, overhearing this as she enters, is appalled. "For the rest of my life," she tells him, "I shall think of this as if you'd killed a little child." Then, Nazimova later wrote,

> The thought of clasping a dead child to my breast filled me with such horror that my hands shrank from the touch of the manuscript and it almost fell to the floor. . . . I thought no more of it until Mr Archer spoke of it as the greatest moment in the play.

Once Nazimova knew what she'd done, Hedda almost dropped the manuscript and Nora caressed the door every night. "It's impossible for me to be mechanical," she realized, "but I need watching. Sometimes I do the right thing, and it's left in. Sometimes I do the wrong thing, and it's cut. I must be told. I do not remember."

Years later, she also realized that, whenever she'd done the wrong thing in life, the same kind of emotional seizure was responsible. But since nobody was watching, nobody told her so, and she left it in.

WITH *Hedda* and *A Doll's House* still playing to capacity houses after two months, Shubert knew he had a major star on his hands. If Nazimova could attract a sizable audience for "Isben" at the Bijou, he thought, she could create an even bigger one in a comedy to which he'd recently acquired the rights. This was *Comtesse Coquette*, high-society fluff that had proved a popular success in Paris and London. Nazimova read the play, told Shubert that the part "would be like resting," and welcomed the chance to add a comedy to her repertory. Henry Miller was again assigned to direct, and this time she made no attempt to take over rehearsals, recognizing that he knew more about streamlined popular theatre than she did.

When *Comtesse Coquette* opened on April 12, most of the critics praised her expert timing and the way she "played up and down the scale of feminine fascination." As usual, William Winter was hostile, and the anti-Nazimova faction followed its leader in denying her both feminine fascination and comic skill, as well as complaining of her "imperfect command of the English language." The attacks on her diction were not new. Reviewers who disliked Nazimova's Hedda had described her voice as "nasal" and "harsh," her accent as "heavy," whereas those who admired it found her voice "expressive" and her accent "slight." In her last movies, as well as the recording of a 1939 radio play, her voice has a light, far from nasal register, and its accent sounds no more foreign than Garbo's. All-or-nothing, it seems, was the critical response that Nazimova provoked from the start, and, perhaps not coincidentally, so did Martha Graham. Both women were artists of the extreme, hurt, aggressive, and fearlessly theatrical.

In 1907, if Nazimova's command of English was still fallible, audiences evidently overlooked it. Their response to Nazimova in comedy was to pack the house for every performance until the end of June, when New York theatres closed for the summer. Shubert's response was to insist that Nazimova open the fall season with *Comtesse Coquette,* and play it more often. She agreed, but only on condition that he allow her to add *The Master Builder* to the repertory. Earning considerable money for the first time in her life, and due for a raise in salary and percentage profits in September, she was feeling her power as a star, and beginning to live like one as well. She had moved from her room at the Judson to a suite at the more luxurious Hotel Collingwood, and from austere self-imposed solitude, while learning English and studying *Hedda Gabler,* to exuberant publicity-consciousness. Her scrapbooks record more than twenty interviews during the first six months of 1907, in which she replied to criticisms of her English ("If my performance is bad, please don't ascribe it to my poor linguistic abilities, but rather to my inability to act"), discussed Shakespeare ("His heroines seem to me more like types, ideals, than real persons, but I would like to be a man to play Hamlet"), and meeting Theodore Roosevelt at a White House reception ("I learned something from the way he prepared himself for his public, taking care to remember people's names"). She also denied that she brought any personal experience to her roles, claiming to approach them objectively, through analysis of "the plot and the central theme and the play of the characters upon each other." Nazimova knew this to be untrue, of course, but was anxious to dissociate her private self from the public image that success as Hedda had created. Louis Untermeyer's "Nazimova as Hedda Gabler," which appeared in the August issue of *Theatre Magazine,* was only one of several absurd poems about the First Femme Fatale of the American theatre:

> Woman of stone! Sphinx of the marble mien!
>   Empress of hate, you turn men's blood to ice
> Lithe as the sensuous serpents that entice

With fearful fascination. Never queen
So soulless, soiled with cowardice, was seen
So far beyond the hope of Paradise. . . .

At this time, in fact, as Nazimova's cousin Henry Harvitt remembered, "she liked the boys." But the woman of stone had felt "like resting" in *Comtesse Coquette* after Ibsen, and she also needed a rest from deep personal involvement after her experience with Orlenev. In search of relaxation through variety, she had "a series of affairs" during 1907, according to Harvitt. None of them was "serious," although "a relative of B. Altman, founder of the department store," fell in love with her and made a proposal of marriage. Harvitt was surprised when she turned it down, for he didn't yet know that the twenty-eight-year-old Madame Nazimova, as the press generally referred to her, was legally still Madame Golovin. Nor, of course, did her lover. Harvitt also remembered that the idea of marriage seemed to attract Nazimova, who hesitated for several days before breaking off the relationship with a final No. Perhaps she thought about divorcing Golovin, for only a few years later she was clearly feeling the need for "husband" as well as "family." Although an emblem of the New Woman onstage, and proud of it, she was not completely sure that she wanted to play the same role in life.

Before her English-speaking debut, the legal Madame Golovin had often been referred to as Madame Orlenev, for the press assumed they were married. Nazimova never denied it, alerted to the power of American puritanism by Maxim Gorky's experience in New York. He arrived there shortly before the first matinee of *The Chosen People,* to give a series of lectures on the evil empire of the tsars. Accompanying Gorky was Marya Andreyeva, a former actress at the Moscow Art Theatre, officially his wife as well as his interpreter. The day after a reception in his honor at Columbia University, a New York newspaper revealed that Gorky had a legal wife in Russia and Andreyeva was his mistress. The land of freedom viewed adultery as a far more shocking crime than tsarist violence and repression. A group of religious leaders, the Christian Coalition of the day, called for Andreyeva's deportation as "a female of bad character," the lectures were canceled and the couple turned out of their hotel. Moral outcasts in America, *personae non gratae* in Russia, Gorky and Andreyeva fled to Capri.

Their humiliation had aroused an intense fear of scandal in Nazimova; and yet, by continuing to pose as Orlenev's wife without divorcing Golovin, she seemed to court what she feared. A year later, when fame had made her particularly vulnerable, she still did nothing to lessen the risk of exposure as a "female of bad character." Presumably Nazimova was discreet about the affairs mentioned by Harvitt, for nothing about them appeared in the press. But she gave some deliberately provocative interviews on the subject of marriage and motherhood. Her "ideal woman," Nazimova announced, was Hilda in *The Master Builder*, who chose to become "a man's ever-inspiring companion." This set her above most women, who preferred to play the subservient role of "his wife, the mother of his children, in one word, his *comfort*."

The only star of her time to challenge convention so openly and get away with it for so long, Nazimova seemed dazed when scandal eventually broke over her head. "I have been living on top of a volcano," she said, but never explained why she chose to live there. Perhaps, as Djuna Barnes suggested, it was because Nazimova had no choice: "There has never been any reasonableness in her 'fate'; a glance backward shows a meteoric condition that almost no one could cope with."

AFTER *Comtesse Coquette* reopened in the first week of September, Nazimova quickly grew bored with it. Plays in which "people were married and lived happily ever after," she remarked in an interview with Alan Dale, forced her to act "night after night in a mechanical way," because there was no "idea to work out." On September 23, she returned to the world of Ibsen and gave the American premiere of *The Master Builder*. Apart from Winter and company, the critics greeted Nazimova's performance with superlative praise and the play with guarded respect. At the beginning, Hilda hero-worships Solness the great architect, whom she first saw standing at the top of a tower. But at close quarters he soon disillusions her. She realizes how desperately he clings to fame, how vain he is, how jealous and afraid of potential rivals. Finally she turns on Solness, who tries to restore the image that Hilda once had of him by climbing to the top of another, higher tower. As she watches, he slips and falls. To see Ibsen's women in the theatre, Nazimova believed, was to "see something of yourself too." She could hardly have failed to see a great deal of herself in Hilda, dazzled and eroticized by an artist's fame, then discovering her own strength as she exposes his weakness. Dominating the man who once dominated her, she finally becomes the agent of his downfall. And Nazimova's comment on Hilda, "She triumphs even though he fails," suggests how completely she perceived the play as a parable of her life with Orlenev.

Shubert wanted her to follow *The Master Builder* with a "daring" new

Brandon Tynan, c. 1908

play by an American writer, and believed he had found it in *The Comet.* Famous actress returns to the remote small town she left as a sixteen-year-old girl, determined to revenge herself on the man who seduced and abandoned her. Young man falls in love with her, turns out to be the son of her former seducer. Actress decides to alienate young man from his father and "lead him up as high as he can go." Father, who's been out of town, returns unexpectedly, tells son he was once actress's lover, and invokes a "sacred" law: "Father and son must not share the same woman." Devastated son rushes offstage and kills himself. Nazimova said later that she agreed to do *The Comet* partly because the author was Owen Johnson, her early supporter and friend in New York, partly because Shubert convinced her that an American play would be a good career move. And perhaps they simply couldn't find anything better. The best American playwrights of the time were at best passable, and they wrote almost exclusively for American actors. At least Johnson's actress, born "in the Spanish Pyrenees," was as sensationally foreign as Hedda Gabler.

Unfortunately, his play opened the same night, December 30, as *Rosmersholm* with Minnie Maddern Fiske. Neither production was a success, but even the critics who disliked *Rosmersholm* beat Johnson over the head with it, attacking *The Comet* as "undigested Ibsen." For Nazimova's admirers it was a waste of her talent, although the *Times* applauded her for having the courage to "look like the Whistler portrait of a human vampire."

The Comet lasted only two weeks in the repertory—unlike Nazimova's affair with her leading man, which lasted almost four years. Cast opposite her was Brandon Tynan, playing eighteen to her thirty-five when in fact they were both twenty-eight. Physically he resembled Orlenev—short, powerfully built, with dark intense eyes and a shock of dark curly hair. His father was an Irish nationalist who joined the Fenians, the IRA of the time, fled Dublin in 1887 to escape arrest by the British, and smuggled himself, wife, and eight-year-old son on board a ship sailing from Cork to New York. Brandon Tynan began his acting career in stock, landed a few minor roles on Broadway, then wrote a major one for himself as the Irish revolutionary Robert Emmet. His performance impressed David Belasco, who offered him a contract. Tynan accepted, but turned down every play that Belasco proceeded to offer him. They remained at loggerheads for two years, Belasco refusing to let him work for anyone else, Tynan doggedly sitting out his contract. As an actor he would always go his own way, but his way was not Orlenev's. A true artist, he once said, "feels his shortcomings." Orlenev, of course, never believed he had any, but Tynan felt that he lacked the magnetism to become a star, and set out to establish himself as a leading character actor. He seems to have been the only man who shared Nazimova's life for several years and caused her no pain. Glesca recorded that she spoke affectionately of him as modest, humorous, and good-natured, although Glesca didn't record that the affair caused Tynan considerable guilt: he was a married Catholic, and his wife suffered from tuberculosis.

In February 1908, Nazimova and Tynan went on tour together in *The Master Builder, A Doll's House,* and *Hedda Gabler.* The tour was Shubert's idea. In theatres across the country, a star from New York was always a major event, and he anticipated major profits from audiences who had heard about but not yet seen Nazimova in Ibsen. Tynan as her leading man was Nazimova's idea. She didn't want to be separated from him; he shared her enthusiasm for Ibsen, and was naturally eager to share it onstage. They opened in Washington, where the plays sold out for three weeks. "There is not a town of any consequence in the United States today," a columnist wrote in the *Washington Post,* "where the coming of this young actress would not create interest among theatregoers, for her fame has spread over the land." As well as creating interest from New Orleans to Toronto, Nazimova was invited by D. W. Griffith to visit his Biograph Studios, and by the Yale Drama Department to lecture on Ibsen. At Biograph, Griffith advised her, "Don't come to do pictures yet, they're not ready for you." At Yale, she read from a prepared text that was later published in *Independent Magazine* under the title "Ibsen's Women":

> Ibsen has no heroines; he has women. Shakespeare has heroines. There is a simplicity and grandeur about them, [and] perhaps women really were like that three hundred years ago

and Shakespeare drew them as he saw them. But the position of women has changed so much since then. . . . The modern woman is more complex. She knows more; her nerves are exaggerated.

She also explained why the Russian censor was wary of Ibsen: "In Russia you can make love on the stage in the wildest way, but you must not touch on politics or religion. Here you have to be very conventional in lovemaking, but you can say anything you please about politics and religion." She defended Nora for walking out on her children: "She had to go away to grow up . . . Her children were better off without her. She saw that. What could she do with them except spoil them as she had been spoiled?" The talk ended with a comment on critics who attacked Ibsen: "We shut our eyes that we may not see what we do not like. Ibsen forces them open. That hurts. Then we say we do not like Ibsen, or we pretend we do not understand him."

With her share of the profits of a highly profitable six-month tour, Nazimova bought a property near Rye, New York. She called it Who-Torok, Russian for "little farm." *Theatre Magazine* called it "Madame Nazimova's American Doll's House," but, although small, the eighteenth-century house stood in six acres of parkland. Nazimova built a covered veranda on each side of the porticoed entrance, bought Russian antiques for the living room (no obvious props like icons or samovars, but a desk, a tea table, and chairs with curved wooden backs that might have come from the country houses in Chekhov's plays), and remodeled the bathroom in up-to-the-minute American. She created an apple orchard and a rose garden, acquired three carriages (the Port Chester railroad station was several miles away), two black thoroughbred horses, a blue parakeet, "an industrious cow," and a live-in maid.

Who-Torok, Nazimova told a reporter from *Theatre Magazine,* was "home," and she would never go back to live in Russia. But Tynan's frequent presence was not enough to make Who-Torok "family." Then, in December, a desperate letter arrived from Nina. Her husband had died after gambling away most of her inheritance, leaving her with two young children to support; and Volodya, struggling to support a family of his own in Berlin, was unable to help. Nazimova was able and almost desperately willing. She not only invited Nina and her children to Who-Torok, and booked and prepaid passage for them, but decided to move out of her new home, which had two bedrooms, to a one-bedroom cottage on the grounds. The cottage was in need of extensive repairs, and the work had to be completed before Nazimova and Tynan began another Ibsen tour in February 1909. Remodeled after her own design, the

Happy days at Who-Torok: Lucy
Olga and Val Lewton in 1912

main space of the new interior became half bedroom and half conservatory, with a skylight, potted plants, wicker chairs, and a convertible sofa-
bed. And before Nazimova left for the Midwest and California, she also
bought a pony for the children and filled their bedroom closet with new
clothes. Nina arrived a few weeks later and wrote a letter of thanks. "You
are the only family I have," Nazimova replied. "Why shouldn't I be good
to you?"

When she returned to Who-Torok that summer, after another successful tour, they met again for the first time in four years, and Nazimova
experienced "a real feeling of sister-love." But it wasn't easy to be good to
Nina when it was difficult for Nina to be wholly dependent on a younger
sister of whom she had always disapproved. In Yalta it was always Nina
who knew best, but at Who-Torok she had to let Nazimova know best.
Nazimova, who was paying for the children's education, decided they
would feel less out of place at school if they changed their first names

from Ludmilla and Vladimir to Lucy and Val; and the family name of Leventon, to which Nina had reverted after her husband's death, Nazimova insisted on Americanizing to Lewton. A change that Nina found it more difficult to adjust to was Tynan's presence at Who-Torok, for in spite of an unhappy marriage she still strongly disapproved of adultery. At Yalta she had refused to entertain Nazimova and Orlenev, because she considered them an immoral couple. At Who-Torok, obliged to let Tynan entertain her own children by teaching them to ride and taking them to the beach, she saw Nazimova's lover become the father their real father had never been.

But what really turned Nina's world upside down was that Nazimova, scorned by her family as "ugly" and "vulgar," had become a famous actress. Soon after arriving at Who-Torok, Nina made her own attempt at self-transformation by deciding to dramatize Bertha von Suttner's novel *Lay Down Your Arms*, which had won the 1905 Nobel Peace Prize. To aid the cause of pacifism, she said, but Nina had never shown any interest in the theatre before, and her real cause was a lost cause, competition with Nazimova. "My interests have taken me to things you have not had any share in at all," as Nazimova would write her sister a few years later. "You do not understand it, dear, this is the trouble and always was." By then Nina had given up hope of finding a producer for her play. No longer quite so sincerely grateful to Nazimova, she was becoming more sincerely jealous.

THAT SUMMER, Tynan finished writing a play, with leading roles for himself and Nazimova, which he'd begun during their tour. Evidently Shubert had misgivings about *The Passion Flower,* for he would commit himself only to a tryout production in Albany, where it opened November 29. Set in the world of high finance, with Tynan playing a bank president and Nazimova his social-butterfly wife, it was advertised as "A Realistic Play of New York Life Today," but the critics found it notably unrealistic. Charles Housenn of the Cleveland *Leader*, a passionate Nazimova fan, wrote her an anguished letter: "Oh, Madame Nazimova, how could you put on a play like *The Passion Flower?*" She had put it on for Tynan's sake, of course, but presumably their affair was not common knowledge. "You are cheapening and hurting yourself by appearing in it. . . . For the sake of your own reputation, do not take this play to New York."

Nazimova had been absent from the New York stage for two years, touring in Ibsen and bringing the total of her earnings for the Shubert organization to more than $4 million, a notable amount for 1909. As a reward, Shubert decided to name his newest theatre Nazimova's 39th Street Theatre. Equipped with the latest lighting system, 750 seats upholstered in rose-red velvet, its walls decorated with imitation Louis XVI tapestries and bronze candelabra, the building was now complete. All it lacked was a play to celebrate Nazimova's return to Broadway. *The Passion Flower* was clearly not a contender, and Shubert closed it after a run of two weeks in Albany followed by a month in Washington and Philadelphia. "Isben," whom Shubert once considered death at the box office, had become his safest bet, and he was delighted when Nazimova proposed to open her theatre with the American premiere of *Little Eyolf.*

The first night, April 18, 1910, was a gala event. Huge bouquets of flowers were massed on each side of the orchestra pit, and a tribute from Shubert to Nazimova headed the program: "Unquestionably much of the success obtained by the plays in which Madame Nazimova has appeared is due to the fact that she personally supervised the productions and acted as the stage director." As the curtain rose to the sound of chimes, dried autumn leaves were released from the flies and floated down to the (vacant) orchestra pit. Then the lights went up on another of Ibsen's deceptively ordinary living rooms, the first-act setting for his powerful and bitter study of a disintegrating marriage.

Little Eyolf was "not a joyful occasion," Melville Ellis wrote in the *Sun,* although "the Russian actress, in the first act particularly, caught and held her audience by an extraordinary display of nervous force." And after admiring Tynan's performance, "the most artistic success of his career," Ellis blamed Ibsen for leaving the audience "bored, fatigued and apathetic." He spoke for the majority of critics, but not for subsequent audiences. *Little Eyolf* played to capacity houses for three months, which meant that almost seventy-five thousand people came to see it. *Cosmopolitan* attributed its success entirely to Nazimova: "She stands without a peer on the American stage as the delineator of soul-harassed women." Nazimova disagreed, and insisted that audiences flocked to her theatre on account of Ibsen. "I do not think there is any other writer who understands the soul of women as he does, [and] there is a mighty purpose in every one of his dramas far above any considerations of acting."

Nazimova's 39th Street Theatre, Shubert announced, would be "devoted exclusively to dramatic productions of the 'intimate' order." But none of them, as it turned out, would star Nazimova, and she never appeared at her own theatre again. On September 15, she opened Arthur

Schnitzler's *The Fairy Tale* in Chicago, the first stop on a pre–New York tour. Nazimova herself chose the play and arranged for Shubert to commission Nina to translate it from the German. (Schnitzler was unknown in America, and never caught on. Two years later, John Barrymore had a moderate success in *The Affairs of Anatol,* but only *La Ronde* reached a wide audience—on film, in Max Ophüls' brilliant 1950 adaptation.) In *The Fairy Tale,* Nazimova played another famous actress (Viennese this time) involved in a love affair that ends badly. (Love affairs in Schnitzler's plays always end badly, or sadly.) Chicago's leading critic, Percy Hammond of the *Tribune,* was fairly warm to Schnitzler and fairly cool to Tynan as the lover; but to Nazimova, whom he had admired in the past, he was positively arctic: "[She] gives vent to grotesque and inexplicable facial convulsions. . . ." At a production that had somehow gone wrong? At an audience that "Mac's Gossip" in the *Herald* described as notably unenthusiastic?

There are no clippings about *The Fairy Tale* in Nazimova's scrapbooks, as if it were a disaster she couldn't defend and preferred to forget. Shubert, who closed the play after two dispiriting weeks, fell back on a sure thing and sent Nazimova off with Tynan on a third Ibsen tour. From November through April 1911, they were on the road in Texas, Arizona, Colorado, Utah, and Ohio. From Canton, Ohio, where they played one of their last one-night stands, Nazimova wrote a curious letter to her sister:

> I feel that I need strength, I need will, I need spiritual hope— I need you. What I think of you I can express only in a dream. You know sometimes I sit in a railway carriage, there's a lot of noise around, conversation, and in front of my eyes there pass telegraph poles, naked trees, fields, fields, fields with dried up stalks of last year's corn, and I see only your face. I see only your face with your dear half-grey hair, with your eyes which have cried so much and I would like to embrace you and say like Chekhov: My beautiful sister . . . Nina, I don't know what's the matter with me. Sometimes I'm all love and tenderness and it seems to me that I will melt and fall asleep and melt and never wake up. I shut my eyes and I see everything that is dear and precious to me. Sometimes on the stage I speak words, but think about you, about the children, about Who-Torok. . . .

What provoked this Chekhovian aria, Nazimova doesn't say. But when the tour ended, she seemed less in need of "spiritual hope," from Nina or anyone else, than of reassurance about her career. Instead of returning to Who-Torok, she rented a New York apartment at 2 West 40th

Street. At the corner of Fifth Avenue, it was only three blocks from the Empire Theatre and the offices of Charles Frohman, where six years earlier "Mme Nasimoff" had shown up with Orlenev.

Now, during the first week of May, Frohman's office became the scene of what the press would soon describe as "secretive negotiations" with Madame Nazimova. The last of Shubert's options on her services was due to expire, and he had no idea that she was going over to Frohman until Frohman made an announcement to the press on May 15. Allegedly so angry that he never spoke to her again, Shubert countered with a press release of his own: "Mme Nazimova is to be stripped of the honor of having a New York theatre named after her. . . . The name 'Nazimova' is to be dropped from the New York house and it is to be called 'The 39th St Theatre.' "

Press clippings are the only source for this episode, and once again Nazimova didn't collect them, maybe because she felt guilty about her treatment of Shubert. But a comment by her loyal fan Charles Housenn in the Cleveland *Leader* suggests that Nazimova had strong reason to be anxious about her professional future. Under the Shubert banner, he wrote, Nazimova had "faded from public sight," thanks to bad plays like *The Comet* and *The Passion Flower,* "and now it is Frohman who will try to re-establish her in public favor."

The first and most successful star-maker among American producers, Frohman had a contract list that included John Drew, Ethel Barrymore, Maude Adams, Billie Burke, Marie Doro, and William (*Sherlock Holmes*) Gillette. By the early 1900s, he had become the most powerful showman in America, for, unlike Shubert, he was a member of the Syndicate, an investment group which controlled more than thirty of Broadway's forty houses, as well as the largest chain of theatres across the country. But the man with a famously sweet tooth, always snacking on chocolate cake and Smith's Delicious Cream Patties, had an appetite for saccharine plays. J. M. Barrie was his idol, Ibsen his bête noire. "We [Americans] have not felt the corroding touch of decadence," he said in 1905. "There is no real taste among us for the erotic and the decadent."

Frohman's real taste, in addition to Barrie, was for *The Dollar Princess, Charley's Aunt,* and *Madame Butterfly* (the play by Belasco on which Puccini based his opera). But he also had a yearning for cultural prestige, which made him a forerunner of movie moguls like Louis B. Mayer, at that time a nickelodeon owner in Boston. Again like the future patriarch of MGM, Frohman expected his family of stars to look to him for guidance, and paid special attention to his actresses: "I have often helped those young women to take a brighter view of things, and it makes me feel I am not just their manager, but their friend." And as an expert on "star material" and how to market it, Frohman kept a sharp eye on the marketplace. By 1911, as he remarked to a colleague, comedy and melodrama were still gilt-edged but the public had tired of high-minded sentiment and developed a taste for "sex conflict."

Frohman clearly bore this in mind when he proceeded to market Nazimova. The press reports do not reveal who made the first approach, but the intrigue surrounding the whole affair suggests there was a go-between. Strong internal evidence points to the literary agent Elisabeth Marbury, who was ideally placed to bring them together, a friend of Nazimova as well as a close professional associate of Frohman. Marbury, who had previously sold *Comtesse Coquette* to Shubert as a vehicle for Nazimova, was the only agent to cover the theatrical season in London and Paris every year. She represented more than thirty British and French writers, and always gave Frohman first bid on their successful new plays. But, like Napoleon, whom he greatly admired, Frohman always took sole credit for his victories. Although he announced, after signing Nazimova, that he'd found the ideal play to bring her back to New York, it was Marbury who'd seen *Witness for the Defense* in London earlier that year and suggested Nazimova for the role of the mysterious Stella Ballantyne.

In "completing" Nazimova's life, Glesca made no mention of Marbury, for the same reason that she barely acknowledged the existence of Mercedes de Acosta. Both were lesbians, and it was Marbury who encouraged Mercedes to write her autobiography. According to an unpublished section of de Acosta's autobiography, Marbury told her, "You could say a lot if you wrote with courage"; and in her own autobiography of 1923, Marbury wrote with some courage about her love for Elsie de Wolfe. But *My Crystal Ball* is basically the history of a tireless and fearless operator, the first woman to become a major behind-the-scenes influence on the American theatre, and later on Tammany Hall.

In 1911, "Bessie," or "Granny Pop," as Mercedes affectionately nicknamed her, was fifty-six years old and weighed well over two hundred pounds. On account of her unusually dainty feet, she had to walk with the support of two canes, but nothing else slowed Marbury down. With offices in London and Paris as well as New York, she once calculated that she'd made forty-two transatlantic crossings by the time she was fifty. Marbury had inherited a house on Irving Place, where she and Elsie de Wolfe lived together for part of the year. The rest of it they spent at the Villa Trianon in Versailles, which they owned jointly. When they first set

*Elisabeth Marbury and Elsie
de Wolfe at home*

up house together, in the early 1890s, de Wolfe was an actress, but, as Marbury jovially confided to Mercedes, "Both for her [Elsie's] sake and the sake of suffering audiences, I took her off the stage and started her on a career of interior decorating." And in *My Crystal Ball* Marbury paid loving tribute to de Wolfe's talent for self-decoration: "A simple cotton frock upon Elsie de Wolfe became a poem, and a shawl thrown across her shoulders an inspiration."

"Bessie knew Nazimova well," according to Mercedes; according to Marbury, Nazimova often visited the house on Irving Place, but it's not known when they first met. In any event, Marbury would have heard about Nazimova soon after she arrived in New York with Orlenev. Early in 1905, Marbury had moved her office to the Empire Theatre, directly above Frohman, "my best customer," and she also knew Nazimova's benefactor from Chicago, Mrs. Chatfield-Taylor. Another of Marbury's talents was to know *everybody*, from Henry James to Bernhardt, from Henry Adams to Duse, from Henry Irving to Pola Negri. On one of her first trips to England, she met George Eliot and struck up a friendship with Oscar Wilde, who found her "a brilliant delightful woman." She became Wilde's American agent and remained loyal after his release from jail, visiting him several times in Paris. By 1911, when she sold *Witness for the Defense* to Frohman, and sold him on Nazimova for the lead, Marbury was at the height of her power. Her clients included Bernard Shaw, H. G. Wells, Somerset Maugham, J. M. Barrie, Jerome K. Jerome, and the leading French playwrights, Sardou and Feydeau.

In Marbury's (and Nazimova's) time, "bachelor girl" was the discreet term for independent career-minded women who never married or had affairs with men. Sexual deviation was a taboo subject in America, as Nazimova hinted in her lecture at Yale when she remarked, "Here you have to be very conventional in lovemaking." The opposite, as she also remarked, was true of Russia, where in fact a widely tolerated homosexual and lesbian subculture had sprung up by the 1890s. Alexey Apukhtin, a popular poet (and former lover of Tchaikovsky), the tsar's uncle Grand Duke Sergey, and one of his chief advisers, the journalist Prince Meshchersky, were all openly homosexual. Diaghilev and Dmitri Filosov, cousins and lovers, edited the influential *World of Art* magazine. A leading feminist, Anna Yevreynova, lived with the writer Maria Feodorova. Lydia Zinovyeva-Annibal wrote *The Tragic Zoo*, about two young women falling in love, and Mikhail Kuzmin in *Wings* described a young man coming to terms with his homosexuality and beginning a relationship with an older man.

Novels like these could never have been published in early-twentieth-century America, which was not the land of the sexually free; and friendship with Marbury would have taught Nazimova that even a powerful, successful lesbian had to lead a strictly closeted life. There is no evidence to suggest that Nazimova became actively bisexual before she reached her mid-thirties. Perhaps American puritanism created fears that held her back, or perhaps her bisexuality was the kind that Freud described in "Three Essays in Sexuality," making "its first appearance late in life after a long period of normal sexual activity." In the case of women, whose sexuality he described as a "dark continent," Freud offered no explanation for the delay. And for a long time Nazimova's sexuality seems to have remained a dark continent to herself. In 1925, plunged into a personal and professional abyss, she wrote that for many years she had dismissed her private life as "something that *does not matter.* Only my work mattered. . . . I climbed very high as an artist. And the scales went rather low on the other side. And here is something funny. I had never noticed this other side until my work became of less and less value to me and I wanted more recognition for myself as a woman."

But in 1911, Nazimova was not yet aware that more women than men would offer her the kind of recognition she wanted. "As soon as she lets you into one unexplored crevice of her personality, she closes the door and you can permeate no further," one interviewer commented that year. "She is unknowable." Unknowable to herself as well, except metaphorically. On Nazimova's dressing table stood a framed photograph that she had bought in an antique store and kept until she died. It showed a rockbound pine tree, dramatically twisted first by the way it was forced to grow, then by the wind.

Praised as an actress for her insight into character, Nazimova was often surprisingly naïve about people in life, and never suspected, when she signed a contract with Frohman, that she was going over to the enemy. "Mme Nazimova has had her first disappointment under the management of Charles Frohman," the New York *Tribune* announced on June 17, explaining that Ethel Barrymore had expressed a wish to star in *Witness for the Defense,* and "Miss Barrymore usually gets from Mr. Frohman whatever she wants." Madame Nazimova, the writer speculated, would have to go back to the "Norwegian gloom" of Ibsen. In fact, where Nazimova really wanted to go, if she couldn't find an American or British play, was to some of the other great European playwrights, Chekhov, Strindberg, Wedekind. But no American producer would touch *Three Sisters, Miss Julie,* or *Pandora's Box,* which were considered too remote or "immoral" for Broadway audiences. Whereas the great American novelists Henry James, Theodore Dreiser, and Edith Wharton explored the real world, the most successful American playwright of the time, Clyde Fitch, relied for "inspiration" on his collection of reference books, *Twelve Bad Men, Twelve Bad Women, Celebrated Poisoners,* and *Famous Crimes.*

Although similarly "inspired," *Witness for the Defense* at least contained a showy leading role, but Frohman gave it to Ethel Barrymore, and chose a first play by Algernon Boyeson called *The Other Mary* to reintroduce Nazimova to Broadway. It never got there, in spite of his boast to have discovered a work that would "set both the North and East Rivers afire." The play opened in Utica on September 15 and closed in Chicago three weeks later. Set in New York, its leading characters were two women called Mary, a Virginal type and a Magdalene type (foreign, of course, and therefore suitable for Nazimova), and a man (played by Tynan) torn between them. The press clobbered the play and mocked Frohman's claims for its author, who was never heard of again. For Nazimova, perhaps, it was some consolation that Ethel Barrymore in *Witness for the Defense* lasted only six weeks at the Empire.

Onstage, the big surprise was that Brandon Tynan finally chose the Other Mary (Magdalene) but after the play closed he went back to his wife. "Whether it was she [Nazimova] or Tynan who ended the relationship," Glesca wrote in her memoir, "I do not know." Apparently she never asked, only speculated that Tynan felt professionally overshadowed by his lover. Whatever the reason, professional tensions or Catholic guilt, it seems the parting was amicable. Each continued to speak well of the other, and Tynan (who died in 1957, aged seventy-eight) had a long, honorable, if not brilliant career in the theatre.

Three weeks after they broke up, Nazimova begen rehearsing another play for Frohman. Evidently Marbury got to work behind the scenes again, for the author, Pierre Wolf, was one of her clients. *The Marionettes,* like *Comtesse Coquette,* was a high-society comedy that had been successful in Paris. Promoted to the rank of marquise, Nazimova won back an indifferent husband by pretending to be an indifferent wife. She also won back her audience when the play opened at the Lyceum on December 14. *The Marionettes,* Alan Dale commented in the New York *American,* would have been "drab enough without the illumination of Mme Nazimova's genius," and *The New York Times* found that "she creates characters where others would miss them; she impersonates where others only read."

But by the end of its four-month run, Nazimova had grown impatient with her first Broadway success since *Little Eyolf.* Pierre Wolf was no Ibsen, and "I would find myself, in the middle of my lines on the stage, saying to myself, 'Oh, why do I have to repeat these stupid words? Why do I have to pretend to be this uninteresting creature—making myself abominable and mean and vulgar?' " She had also come to realize that Frohman was far more inflexible than Shubert. He ordered his actors into the plays he felt were right for them, and could never be swayed by a threat of "No Hedda—I do not play!" He also dictated the casting. Believing that all he needed for a hit was one star, Frohman regarded two stars in the same play as a waste of money. In Frohman's view, a play "went on the shelf" after it served its purpose as a star vehicle, and so did the actor who played opposite a star. Nazimova had acted for four years with Tynan, and before that, in *Comtesse Coquette* and *The Master Builder,* her leading man had been the young Walter Hampden, later the most famous Cyrano of his time. But for *The Marionettes,* Frohman forced her to accept a leading man, Frank Gilmore, whom she found profoundly uninteresting.

During the last week of the run, in April 1912, another of Nazimova's former leading men arrived in New York with his new company. The Broadway star went by herself to see Orlenev play Ibsen's *Brand* at a small East Side theatre, the Garibaldi, but apparently did not go backstage after the performance. Later she remarked that Orlenev, whom she remembered as thin and "nervous as the surface of water," had put on weight. In the past "you could see the reflection of every thought, every feeling, in his face," and now his face seemed less expressive, although "he had the same grip on his audience—that he will never lose."

Emma Goldman, who saw a different performance of *Brand*, found Orlenev as magnetic as ever and went backstage to congratulate him. "His eyes had more Weltschmerz in them," she noticed. When she mentioned that Nazimova had a house in the country, he looked very bitter. "And I live in hunger," he said. In Orlenev's autobiography, as Nazimova discovered when she read it, Who-Torok became "a villa by the sea." And in Emma's autobiography, Orlenev's final New York appearance became an excuse for a last dig at Nazimova. After he went back to Russia, Emma wrote, there was no true artist left in the American theatre.

THE SAME month that Nazimova opened in *The Marionettes*, Mrs. Patrick Campbell had premiered a new play in London. When she first read *Bella Donna*, Mrs. Pat found it so bad that she "threw it into the slop pail," then fished it out because she needed the money. Based on a novel by Robert Hichens, author of *The Garden of Allah* and a specialist in erotic intrigue against an exotic background, it was the story of Mrs. Chepstow, married to an Englishman living in Cairo, who takes an Egyptian lover and tries to poison her husband. *Bella Donna* ran for over six months in London, and after reading the play, Frohman promised the leading role to Ethel Barrymore, who was eager for a change of pace from drawing-room comedy and J. M. Barrie. Then, in a reversal of the situation with *Witness for the Defense*, he decided that *Bella Donna* would make an ideal "sex conflict" vehicle for Nazimova. She didn't like the play, and told Frohman she would be hopelessly miscast as an Englishwoman. When Frohman merely shrugged, she tried another tack: "I look more like the Egyptian than the man who is my lover." Frohman shrugged this off as well. As he explained to a colleague, he was convinced that he had the ingredients for a major hit: "Nazimova is a murderess. She poisons her husband because she's in love with a nigger." And Nazimova had no choice. She was under contract to Frohman, and behind Frohman stood the Syndicate, which had been known to blacklist actors who got out of line.

Bella Donna. *Suspicious
doctor (Charles Bryant), dying
husband, and murderous wife
(Nazimova)*

Was it Marbury who advised Frohman that Ethel Barrymore would
certainly be more convincing than Nazimova as an Englishwoman but
far less persuasive as a femme fatale? There is no evidence one way or the
other in Marbury's autobiography, or the "biography" of Frohman, a series of worshipful anecdotes supplied by his brother and partner, Daniel.
In any event, it was Frohman who cast the New York production of *Bella
Donna,* signed a British actor called Charles Bryant for an important
role, and introduced Nazimova to the central mystery of her life.

7

"Happily Married"
1912–1918

I am a feminist, but I am happily married.

—NAZIMOVA

SHE WAS THIRTY-THREE, RUSSIAN-JEWISH, FIVE feet three inches, rich, famous, unattached but still legally married. He was thirty-one, British, six feet three inches, not rich, not famous, unattached and unmarried. Apart from the fact that both happened to be unattached when they met, Nazimova and Charles Bryant were polar opposites in every department—background, looks, temperament, abilities.

Bryant's father was a lawyer, and Bryant himself worked in a bank before deciding to become an actor. As a member of Mrs. Patrick Campbell's company when it toured America in 1902, he played supporting roles in *The Second Mrs. Tanqueray* and two plays by Sudermann, *Magda* and *The Joy of Living*. Nine years later, as the doctor who exposes Mrs. Chepstow's attempt to poison her husband, he was cast in a leading role opposite Mrs. Pat in *Bella Donna,* and later claimed he had "a fling" with her during the run. Considered at best a solid actor, at worst a wooden one, Bryant was probably signed for the New York production less on account of his talent than through the influence of Mrs. Pat and his brother-in-law, J. B. Fagan, who wrote the play based on Hichens' novel.

Bryant was tall and well built, with an angular nose and jaw, a hearty, breezy manner, and a very British drawl. He looked and sounded more like a cricketer than an actor but, in the popular expression of the time, had "a way with women." During the second week of rehearsals of *Bella Donna*, Nazimova wrote Nina, "Charles Bryant is very charming." Soon, in private, he was calling her "Allikins," and at Bryant's request Nazimova was calling him "Chumps." Glesca's account of the first stage of the affair, based on what she claimed Nazimova told her, is that, although Nazimova found Bryant very attractive, they were "not sexually compatible, and in the ten years they lived together as would-be partners, although they tried for a time, their physical union was never consummated." A letter from Bryant to Nazimova written shortly before they separated, with its reference to "*the trouble*" and its wish that she "had found someone who could replace whatever happiness I could give you with the happiness that I could not and which was essential to you," bears this out. But it doesn't explain, of course, why she agreed to pretend they were married and kept up the pretense for so long.

Bella Donna. *Mrs. Armine (Nazimova, in the "serpent's-tail" gown she designed for herself) and her Egyptian lover*

Physically and personally, Bryant was unlike every other man with whom Nazimova became involved. He was not conspicuous for talent—except, according to some observers, when it came to spending Nazimova's money. He seems to have been intellectually dull, although she claimed he "reads all the time. He simply gloats over books." Until 1921, photographs of Nazimova with Bryant often show her playing the child-wife, like Nora in the first act of *A Doll's House,* sitting on his knees, smiling with adoration, leaning against his shoulder. They suggest that, in clinging to the pain of her childhood and youth, Nazimova relived not only her longing for "family" but for "husband," the ideal protective male figure she had never known. When the relationship began to sour, she could no longer play out her fantasy of domestic bliss, and by 1923 Nazimova the silent-movie star was posing for some deliberately ambiguous photographs with Bryant and her intimate friend Natacha Rambova. "Husband" and "wife" glare at each other while Rambova sits enigmatically between them.

Tattle in the movie colony by this time was that Bryant had advanced his career by posing as the husband of a famous star, and Nazimova posed as his wife to deflect attention from her lesbian affairs. Although this explains Bryant, there is no evidence that Nazimova was actively lesbian at the time of their "marriage," and strong evidence that she found him attractive. When they first met on the stage of the Empire Theatre in October 1912, Nazimova was friendly with two members of Marbury's circle, Anne Vanderbilt and Anne Morgan, but not involved with either of them. "I can count my friends on the fingers of one hand," she had recently told a reporter, without naming names. In fact, she would have needed two hands to count Marbury and her chums, Nina, the Harvitts, Carolyn Harris and her son, and Gertrude Berkeley, who played Aline Solness in *The Master Builder* and the Rat Wife in *Little Eyolf.* Significantly, Berkeley was another divorcée with a young son, sixteen-year-old William, known as Buz or Busby.

Bryant may not have been much of an actor, but offstage he gave an expert performance in the role of admiring comforter to a high-strung actress increasingly troubled by the character she was rehearsing onstage. Nazimova's letters to Nina stress Bryant's "angelic disposition" and "patience" with her extreme nervousness about *Bella Donna.* On opening night, in fact, she had one of her worst attacks of stage fright, and, in Frohman's words, "we almost had to carry her onstage." Less than a month later, during an interview with a reporter from the New York *American,* Nazimova revealed that she had married Bryant the previous afternoon, December 5, in her apartment, and the wedding took place in the presence of her sister, Nina Lewton. The reporter, who commented that "neither has been married before," reminded Nazimova of her previous skepticism about marriage and asked whether she now believed that "art and marriage mix. . . . She replied calmly: 'I am unable to answer the question now. As yet my perspective is not properly adjusted. Perhaps I can reply later.' "

On December 14, the New York *Dramatic News* announced, without revealing the source of its information, that Nazimova had after all been married before—not to Pavel Orlenev, as had once been generally supposed, but to "Count Serge de Golovin." Wisely, she didn't deny it, and everyone assumed that she had divorced Golovin. Falsely reported as a witness to the ceremony that never took place, Nina must have raised some awkward questions, but Nazimova evidently convinced her that she'd been misquoted and that the wedding *did* take place, for there are many letters to Nina in which Nazimova refers to Bryant as her husband. But Frohman wrote a rather ambiguous letter to Bryant's brother-in-law J. B. Fagan: "Mr. Bryant is giving an exceptionally good performance . . . and is so much taken with my theatre and company that I have the newspapers' word for it that he married my star." Still, if Frohman had any doubts, they remained private, and for twelve years Nazimova continued to skate on very thin ice without falling through.

When the ice finally broke, she tried to explain the marriage that never was. To the press—and to the IRS, who questioned their joint tax returns—Nazimova claimed that, after informing several friends of their intention to marry, she applied for a divorce from Golovin through the Russian consul in New York. But when it failed to come through, "we both permitted the impression to remain that we had become married." Later, she told a far more bizarre story to Glesca: "The first night they spent together they were caught. A Negro janitor saw a Russian priest coming down the hall . . . and knew Bryant had gone into her apartment earlier. Putting the two together, he assumed that Nazimova and Bryant had secretly married and gave the 'scoop' to the press."

Just as she never really explained why she married Golovin, Nazimova never seemed to make up her mind why she pretended to marry Bryant. But when Nazimova lied, it was not always with the intent to deceive. Sometimes she couldn't find her way to the truth. The actress who perceived Hedda and Nora and Madame Ranevskaya and Christine Mannon so completely had only scattered insights into her own self. Nazimova never connected, for example, the need she confessed in her 1906 diary, "to hurt myself, create pain stronger than anyone ever could," with the equation of sex and cruelty, demonstrated by Otto as well as her father, that shadowed her childhood. Nor did she see how they connected with Orlenev. Although Bryant was not cruel, merely selfish and calculating, when she allowed herself to become involved with him in spite of "*the trouble*," Nazimova took on yet another cargo of pain.

IN LIFE Bryant had established a powerful hold on Nazimova, but in the theatre *Bella Donna* reinforced her public image as a mysterious, ruthless femme fatale. It was celebrated in *Vanity Fair* with another absurd poem:

> Her sunken train a serpent seems,
>   Her scarf, a spider's snare;
> The mystic wreathings of the smoke
>   Unite to beckon where
> This dark enchantress of the East
>   Seems fashioned to decoy
> The most elusive man of all
>   And make of him a boy. . . .

Almost every critic evoked the serpent or the cobra to describe Nazimova when the play opened at the Empire on November 12, and the *Evening Mail* headlined Burns Mantle's review "WITH THE SINUOUS GRACE OF A REPTILE STANDING ON ITS TAIL RUSSIAN ACTRESS MOVES THROUGH POISON PLAY." But, like most of the other critics, Burns Mantle found more exhibitionism than real acting in her performance. "We have patiently waited for this gifted woman to get back to the simple, sane, forceful method that was hers when she first became known," he wrote, "but it seems a hopeless wait." Although Nazimova later claimed that she deliberately burlesqued the role, it seems more likely that she decided to trick it out with some extreme stylization and razzle-dazzle. According to Djuna Barnes, the performance worked on its own terms. "Her artistry was so extraordinarily flexible and persuasive that she could make a common vampire of melodrama, seem, for the moment, as great a creation as Hedda." But it was a dangerous kind of success, especially when she decided to repeat it in another, even more garish melodrama. "With that divine gullibility common to those who are greatly of the stage," she didn't realize that she lowered her own art by trying to elevate kitsch into art.

Among the effects she created in *Bella Donna,* an evening gown that Nazimova designed for herself was a notably spectacular example of kitsch. She wore it in the last act, when Mrs. Armine (as Mrs. Chepstow was inexplicably renamed for New York) has been exposed for attempting to poison her husband. Its long, tapering, glittering, sequined train swayed like a serpent's tail as she hurried to the house of her Egyptian lover. Distant exotic music filled the brief pause before Mrs. Armine came out again. In the wordless scene that followed, Nazimova walked toward center stage, her face masklike. Then she stopped, turned, and deliberately stepped on the train like an angry serpent biting its own tail, and the audience knew she'd been rejected. After a moment she turned back and walked proudly through a gateway leading to the Nile embankment. (No sound of a splash, except in the collective mind of the audience, before the curtain fell.) The anger and the pride were her own characteristic touches. In London, when Mrs. Pat emerged from the house, she slumped, then made a slow, defeated exit through a gateway leading, improbably, straight to the desert.

Even more stylized was Nazimova's offstage performance soon after *Bella Donna* opened. Wearing "a clinging, reptilian garment," her eyes "great black coals of intellect," her throat "a long, sinuous expression of sensuality," she talked in her dressing room with a dazzled reporter from *Vanity Fair:*

> Interviewer: It must have taken much study and hard work, Madame, to acquire such perfect poise, such unerring grace of movement and of posture?
>
> > (Not the faintest glimmer of a smile disturbs the artistic melancholy of her complete repose)
>
> Nazimova: No. (with a rising inflection and after a pause) It is natural.
>
> Interviewer: What do you like, Madame?
>
> > (The delicately outlined black eyebrows rise slowly, ever so slightly, yet quite perceptibly. Nothing she does passes unnoticed. Every move has its instant effect)
>
> Nazimova: Everything. (And then, as if commenting on my laugh) Why not enjoy it (long pause) while we are here?
>
> Interviewer: Then you believe in the future? (Madame looks at me steadily for a full minute and says quietly, convincingly)
>
> Nazimova: Yes.

And here, as described in *McCall's*, is her entrance into the Plaza Hotel tearoom with "her husband Charles Bryant":

> Her gown of black fell in straight simple lines from her shoulders to her feet. . . . She wore a veil of which the lower half was

so heavily embroidered as practically to conceal her features. The upper part was of sheer net, nothing more than a film. Between her wonderful arched eyebrows was a large beauty patch, and her eyes—deep blue eyes they were, shaded with their long black lashes—shone out with startling distinctness. . . . She might have been a Turkish woman, shrouded from the world, and gazing out at it from her yashmak.

After *Hedda*, Nazimova tried to distance herself from her public image. But after *Bella Donna*, which she claimed to "despise myself artistically for doing," she exploited it with the kind of artifice that would become her trademark, on and off the screen, as a silent-movie star. The route she now began to travel was almost certainly due to Bryant's influence. Lucy Olga Lewton remembered that he liked her to wear "couturier gowns," and enjoyed showing off "Mrs. Charles Bryant" in public; Patsy Ruth Miller said that he viewed "Mrs. Charles Bryant" as "a commodity."

"I hate *Bella Donna* more and more—hardly got through with it opening night," Nazimova wrote Nina, who apparently had no interest in seeing the play. This was in early December, when "business was so-so" as a result of the unfavorable reviews. Although it picked up toward the end of the month, Frohman closed the play in mid-January 1913. A great believer in the "mystery" of stars, he advised them not to make any kind of public appearances outside the theatre and, above all, not to get married. Nazimova's highly publicized "marriage" he regarded as a serious betrayal, and, partly out of anger, partly because he anticipated a decline in business, he sent the production on tour. It was supposed to last, with a two-month summer break, until the end of the year, but "the corroding touch of decadence," which Frohman once denied had any appeal for Americans, proved so popular in the heartland that he extended the tour for another year.

"We are happier than ever, always together in heart, soul and body and all the rest," Nazimova wrote Nina from Buffalo on January 28, 1913, during the first week of the first tour:

> He [Charles] is so kind, so considerate, so loveable—I never thought one could be in one room with a man day after day and night after night and never have the want of being alone. In little things like jumping up in the morning and getting ready a hot cup of tea for you to have in bed or caring for you being warm enough, comfortable, asking and worrying about your slightest want . . .

The same letter describes a romantic visit to Niagara Falls by moonlight:

We stood alone on a bit of ground projected over the water and gazed and pondered over it and felt as if we were witness of the creation of the world. . . . He stood behind me with his arms embracing my shoulders and I felt so safe and guarded against everything leaning against that strong man who loved me.

And in Minneapolis, according to a letter dated March 2, "Everything in our life is so quiet and charming, full of love and understanding."

Granted Nazimova's talent for self-dramatization, and her desire to validate her marriage in Nina's eyes, it seems obvious that at first Bryant satisfied her fantasy of a husband who would protect her, and although he disappointed her sexually, he made up for it by being thoughtful and affectionate.

From Syracuse, a letter of April 2 describes Charles as "an angel," but Nazimova was getting "tired to death" of touring:

Performances in rotten towns with storms and wind and rain and the constant dread of the flood. Our baggage car was burglered [sic] and every bit of jewelry belonging to the company (more than 2000 dollars worth) stolen. . . . Happily I had my personal jewelry on me.

In Baltimore she told an interviewer that for audiences "nothing is more tiresome than thinking," and that they enjoyed *Bella Donna* because "it does not make them think." In Chicago she announced that, as soon as the tour was over, "I'm going to have a big studio in New York with a tiny stage, and produce the plays I love. Many by Strindberg . . ." Shortly afterward she wrote Frohman to ask if he would back a season of classic repertory in New York. He refused, doubting that the kind of plays she had in mind would cover the cost of producing them. If Nazimova failed to point out that Shubert had made a great deal of money from Ibsen, it was probably because she'd decided that Frohman would never see things her way.

Denied Strindberg and condemned to another year of *Bella Donna,* pretending to be married to a man who couldn't satisfy her, Nazimova still insisted to the world that she was completely fulfilled. Headed "Nazimova's epigram," the following appeared without explanation in the Seattle, Washington, *Times* of May 25: "The woman who attains success in a professional career and happiness in marriage has found the ideal of human existence."

The last stop on the tour before the summer break was Victoria, British Columbia, where she wrote Nina on June 12: "I've never been so fond of anyone and will do everything in my power to make his holiday in Europe a happy one." A subtle and perhaps unconscious change of mood is apparent here. "Fond" is surely cooler than "always together in heart, soul and body," but Nazimova seems determined to play the role of subservient wife opposite the husband who signed his letters "your always loving 'easy going' Chumps."

"His" holiday was spent mainly in England, where Bryant still kept an apartment. His mother came to stay with them, and "Charles is the happiest man now you ever saw," Nazimova wrote her sister on August 17. "It must be hard for him to be away from his dear old England. Charles loathes the thought of going back and I don't blame him, but I, oh! . . ." While his mother served tea, sandwiches, and "homemade pastries," Bryant contentedly smoked a pipe and Nazimova felt homesick for Who-Torok. Later in the month they went on a trip through the dear old English countryside, and Bryant taught her to ride a bicycle. For "her" holiday they paid a brief visit to the lake at Montreux, where Nazimova relived one of the happier experiences of her childhood. Then they sailed back to New York and opened the second *Bella Donna* tour in Detroit on September 23.

"One night stands and three week stands—what terrible work that is," Nazimova wrote Nina from Ogden, Utah, on January 30, 1914. "In some towns we arrive at 7.30 pm and leave at once after the performance." Three weeks later, she was hoping to get rid of Frohman when the tour ended: "I think I'll propose to come to an amicable parting of the ways. I need something great and to stay in New York—to put me back where I was when I played Ibsen—something I can throw myself into and which will give me back my self-respect."

If Nazimova wrote letters to anyone except Nina during these years, they have not survived. Marbury, Carolyn Harris, or Gertrude Berkeley would surely have been more interested in her career problems, and better equipped to offer advice, but in spite of their differences Nazimova appears to have confided only in Nina. Lucy Olga Newton claimed to know the reason, and in this case Lucy Olga Newton may be believed. Bryant, she insisted, was jealous of Nina, and although he failed to "undermine" their relationship, he succeeded in convincing Nazimova to be wary of confiding in friends. There was always the risk, he warned, that their secret might be exposed. He also wanted to isolate her from other influences.

After the second tour ended in June 1914, it was "his" holiday again, and they went back to England for the summer. Bryant wanted to buy a cottage in the country, and they looked at several, while Nazimova again felt homesick, as she wrote Nina, for Who-Torok "and my tiny cottage, the lawns, the maple trees, dogwood and poplar trees we planted. Charles will never stay during the summers in America—he is happiest in England—it's heartbreaking. I was so happy in Who-Torok. . . ." They were still looking at cottages on July 30, when Germany declared war on Russia. Two days later, the German Army invaded France and Belgium, and when Britain declared war on Germany on August 4, World War I began. Bryant gave up the idea of a country refuge, and they returned to London. "The war is horrible—I can't bear the eternal talk about it," Nazimova wrote Nina on August 22, and wondered what would happen "to our brother, his wife and children in Berlin." Next day, the couple sailed for New York on the *Lusitania*, and soon after arrival Nazimova asked Frohman for a release from her contract. "He assented on the condition that if he found a suitable new play, I would return. Neither he nor I could find the elusive drama, however."

What she found instead was *That Sort*, a play commissioned for Nazimova by an ambitious new producer called George Tyler. At first she was unsure about it, and wrote the author, Basil Macdonald Hastings, that the play seemed to lose momentum after Act One. He disagreed: "From a commercial point of view both the latter acts are much stronger. . . . If the play is to succeed financially it must be deliberately written for the market. There isn't a penny in good work, at any rate on this side." It was one thing, Nazimova now discovered, to escape from Frohman, but another to escape from his values. "It has cost me a lot of hysterics and regrets for my high ideals and so forth," she'd written a few months earlier to Nina, "but I have come to the conclusion that they [American audiences] are children and want to be treated like children, except the spanking." And since Nina was very discouraged about the lack of interest in *Lay Down Your Arms*, Nazimova advised her to write something else and "give them light or strong entertainment, but only entertainment. When some day they will be used to your food they'll take your purgatif [sic] or your music, but that is a long way off, so put all that aside, dearest."

Unable to find "something great," Nazimova followed her own advice and yielded to the pressures of the marketplace. She was also under pressure from Bryant. By now her business manager, he insisted that the expenses of Who-Torok, and of providing for Nina and her family, had left her low on funds. And she dutifully explained to a reporter:

> When one is a star, one lives like a star should live, one dresses
> as a star is expected to dress. What does that mean?—that
> most stars are up to here (she touches her throat) in debt.

Although Bryant may have been right—Nazimova had no business
sense and was a reckless spender—she not only failed to make much
money out of *That Sort* but suffered a further loss of prestige. The first
act was virtually an extended monologue for Diana Laska, "the most notorious woman in Europe," drug addict and would-be suicide, after her
marriage breaks up. In the second act, she's reunited with the daughter
she hasn't seen for sixteen years and cleansed by "a mother's love." In the
third, to protect her daughter's good name and ensure her happiness,
Diana does a Madame X–Stella Dallas and bows out of her life.

On its pre–New York tour (Buffalo, Atlantic City, Hartford), the play
was popular with audiences, but it was poorly received when it opened
at the Harris Theatre in New York on November 6. "A play's success or
failure is like tossing a coin," Nazimova commented when *That Sort*
closed a month later, "not much fun when you are the coin tossed." And
she'd been violently tossed by most of the critics, who complained of the
posturing and grimacing that had come "to disqualify her for any sort of
play," according to the New York *Sun,* "in which realism . . . was an important element."

EARLIER THAT year, Nina had left Who-Torok for
Rochester to work as translator for an American corporation building
railroads in Europe. In March, she wrote Nazimova that she was worried
about her ten-year-old son, Val, who kept playing hooky from school,
used four-letter words, was sulky and disobedient. Nazimova wrote back
that Val needed "a masculine hand to guide him into a straight channel,
to clip off all those 100 moods a day, which are very interesting to read
about but not at all practical for home life or even companionship, and
which if left to develop will *ruin* him." She added, perhaps with Orlenev
in mind: "He is training you to apply yourself to *his* moods."

Nina took offense at this advice and accused her sister of "trying to
take Val away from me." A few months later, she decided to give up her
job, and offered to pay her way at Who-Torok by acting as housekeeper.
Now it was Nazimova's turn to take offense:

> I do not need material proofs of your devotion. I do not need
> your looking after my place—hired people can do this and
> better than you ever could. Things that can be paid for I do

Who-Torok, the original eighteenth-century house, with covered veranda at back added by Nazimova

Who-Torok, the main entrance

> not buy from you. But what I cannot buy and what you have
> not yet given me, this is what I want—your absolute trust,
> your faith in my unselfish devotion to your family, and most
> of all give me the feeling that I have accomplished in a small
> way something toward your happiness.

She welcomed Nina back to Who-Torok but begged her, "if I am busy with somebody or something, not to feel hurt or wounded or replaced, but simply feel and know that I am busy, that's all!" Feeling rejected, it seems, had become Nina's specialty. "In my heart I have never replaced you, nor have I let anyone stand between us. This you never did understand."

Nina returned to Who-Torok at the end of the year, but Nazimova and Bryant stayed at her apartment in New York after *That Sort* closed. From friends in Moscow, she wrote her sister, came news that "S. Golovin is safe on account of superfluous flesh, but is serving in a military office." She didn't identify the friends, but they were probably the Zhdanovas, with whom she kept in touch. "The irony of it all," the letter continued, was "when I think of the eternal fear that Charles may leave or even be summoned to leave any moment." In fact, Bryant had a mild case of irregular heartbeat, which was not life-threatening but made him ineligible for military service. Keeping his condition a secret from Nazimova, he talked about volunteering for the British Army and incited her to some high-voltage drama. "I am happy and thank God for every minute I am stealing from war and death," she wrote Nina, "for that's how I must look at it, to be brave and to be able to live my life—when he does not come back. . . ."

And then, with unconsciously perfect timing, came an offer to star in a one-act pacifist drama, *War Brides*. "I am not merely doing something as an actress," she told the New York *American*, announcing her decision to appear in the play, "but for the womanhood of the world." After protesting in general "the miseries and brutalities that war entails on women," Nazimova declared her particular reason for wanting to spread the message of peace: "My idolized brother is with the Russian colors at Warsaw." This was untrue—Volodya had been interned as an enemy alien in Germany—and Nazimova's particular reason was Bryant, who decided not to volunteer for the British Army after all when she offered him the role of her husband, who gets killed in the trenches.

Out of lies, fantasy, and elaborate confusions of theatre and life came one of Nazimova's most celebrated performances, widely admired for its simplicity and truth. But because the play lasted only thirty-five minutes, it was on the vaudeville circuit that she won back her self-respect as well as the respect of critics. Once the last resort of run-down actors, vaudeville had been made respectable by Bernhardt, who toured the circuit in 1905, even performing in tents and skating rinks rather than pay the enormously high rentals the Syndicate demanded for its theatres. More recently, both Ethel and Lionel Barrymore had shared billing with the same kind of acts that made up the program when *War Brides* opened at the Palace on January 25, 1915—Chinese jugglers, singer-comedienne Trixie Friganza, an "Irish minstrel," a troupe of acrobats, and a trained chimpanzee.

The play was set in a peasant cottage in an unnamed European country during a time of war. Joan, played by Nazimova, loses two brothers and then her husband (Bryant) on the battlefront. When the king orders women to bear more children to fight in future wars, Joan organizes a protest and finds a strong ally in The Mother (Gertrude Berkeley). Finally, threatened with jail if she doesn't obey the order, Joan shoots herself. *War Brides,* in the majority critical view, was "principally Nazimova." Totally deglamorized, wearing a drab Mother Hubbard, she found her way back to the direct emotional power of her Ibsen roles and according to the New York *Telegraph,* broke the house record: "It was the first time a dramatic attraction has been retained for more than one week at the Palace, with the single exception of Sarah Bernhardt."

Not yet known to Nazimova or each other, Tallulah Bankhead and Mercedes de Acosta were in the audience during its twice-daily, four-week run. Many years later, when she starred in a revival of *The Second Mrs. Tanqueray,* Bankhead inserted a note in the program that "her only theatrical training at seventeen consisted of running away from home to see Nazimova's *War Brides.*" In fact she was thirteen and managed to sneak out of school without being discovered. (School, improbably, was the Holy Cross Academy, near Washington.) Mercedes, aged twenty-one, perceived in Nazimova "a great soul as well as a great artist," and "could dream of nothing but meeting her." A drab getup, it seems, could not disguise Nazimova's erotic impact, and the feminist in Mercedes was equally stirred by the play, which had attracted strong support from women's organizations. When the president of the New York Association of Suffragists called *War Brides* "the Magna Carta of Woman," Nazimova acquired a new if temporary public image, and the veiled enchantress of the East was transformed into a champion of women's rights. "Those women who don't believe in suffrage, they're not awake, that's all," she told the Brooklyn *Eagle.* "The woman is counting for more and more

every day. . . . She has real work to do and she has found it out, and is
not going to give it up."

A six-month tour of the Keith-Orpheum circuit, for which Nazimova
was paid $2,500 a week, followed the New York run. Visceral pacifism fit-
ted the country's isolationist mood, and in many cities members of
women's organizations turned out in force. In Pittsburgh an interview
with the star was headlined "SAYS WOMEN WILL END WAR—FAVORS EQUAL
FRANCHISE"; in Boston, "MME NAZIMOVA WORKING TO END WAR"; and
the play's militant author, Marion Craig Wentworth, inscribed Nazimova's copy of *War Brides*, "In beloved gratitude. 'This righteousness
shall be shown unto the nations: *Let the earth be moved.*' "

Nazimova was playing Pittsburgh on May 7 when a German subma-
rine torpedoed the liner *Lusitania* off the coast of Ireland, and Charles
Frohman was one of more than a thousand passengers sailing from New
York to London who went down with the ship. The casualties included
more than a hundred Americans, and as the Germans continued their in-
discriminate attacks on world shipping, public support for American
neutrality began to lessen—like audiences for *War Brides* during September, the last month of the tour.

Had the relationship between Nazimova and Bryant also begun to
change by the end of the tour? Maurice Sterne, back in New York that
year after a trip to Bali and India, visited the couple at Who-Torok in October. Alone with Nazimova, "I asked her whether she loved her husband. She admitted that she did not, and when I pressed her further she
said, 'I thought having him around would improve my English.' "
Sterne's only reaction was that Nazimova always "had a humor about
herself that was very attractive, nor did she take her gifts so seriously that
she was not able, for example, to laugh at her own love of publicity."

After two years of "*the trouble*," it would not be surprising if Nazimova
found Bryant less romantic, and as boring as almost everyone else did.
But according to Glesca, "Nazimova needed someone to handle her
business so she could concentrate on her 'work,' Bryant had a business
background . . . and they decided it would be better to pretend they were
married and live together rather than cause a scandal, as it would have
ruined their reputations." This is unconvincing. After "marrying"
Bryant, Nazimova could have "divorced" him, and a more qualified business manager would not have been difficult to find. In hindsight, several
of her friends had explanations to offer. Patsy Ruth Miller, who first met
Nazimova and Bryant in 1921, believed that in spite of everything she still
loved him. "She was very fluttery around him, which wasn't her usual

style at all." Josephine Hutchinson, who knew Nazimova well in the 1930s, detected "a streak of respectability" that made her want "everything to *look* right, whether in relationships or lifestyle. And she was *always* fearful of what Nina would say!" Isabel Hill, who accompanied Nazimova on her 1926 vaudeville tour, remembered that "she never wanted to be alone. Really frightened of it."

Though none of these explanations can be discounted (Nazimova may have been putting on a "fluttery" act around Bryant), none of them, singly or together, seems sufficient. The whole truth will never be known, for it was buried deep in the ambivalence of Nazimova's nature. But it seems likely that, by the time she told Sterne she didn't love Bryant, she had begun to explore her bisexuality. A few months later, she met Mercedes de Acosta and had her first known lesbian affair—which is not to say that it was her first.

In the meantime, Nazimova allowed Bryant to spend a great deal of her money on remodeling and enlarging the main house of Who-Torok, and making what he considered improvements to the property. It became less of a farm and more of an English country estate, the apple orchard cut down to make way for a lawn, a tennis court replacing the vegetable garden. When the work started, Nazimova moved Nina and her children to an apartment in New York, and at Bryant's suggestion she bought a two-story apartment in the Hotel des Artistes. Also at Bryant's suggestion, in February 1916 she informed Nina that when the work on Who-Torok was completed there would be another change:

> We shall live in the main house and you and the kids in the cottage. . . . [The main house] is not really a small house any more but a little mansion and will take servants to keep it going. On the other hand, the cottage is now perfect and is easily managed . . . Charles says he knows that you will prefer it.

Nina did *not* prefer it, even though Nazimova officially deeded her the cottage. She accused her sister of going back on a promise, and seventy-five years later Lucy Olga was still echoing the charge. In Nina's case, jealousy almost certainly triggered the outburst. She must have found it bitter, after being unable to interest a producer in *Lay Down Your Arms,* to see Nazimova triumph in the pacifist *War Brides.*

The same letter also referred to "the double bed that Charles and I found" for their new master bedroom at Who-Torok. Whether they also shared a bed at the Hotel des Artistes is unknown, although Nazimova's description of the apartment there is significant: "By locking the door upstairs it makes 2 separate apartments, [with] their own telephones and their own entrances." And as it turned out, the couple spent very little time together at Who-Torok before moving to Hollywood.

IN THE SPRING of 1916, Jane Wallach, a friend of Marbury and a rich socialite devoted to the theatre and good causes, organized a benefit in aid of European war refugees at Madison Square Garden. Among her helpers was Mercedes de Acosta, and among the performers was Nazimova. Mercedes had asked Marbury to introduce her to Nazimova after seeing *War Brides,* but Marbury declined because she was "frightened of the two Annes. They think they own Nazimova and they would be angry with me for introducing her to a young person." This is one of several passages from an earlier draft of Mercedes' autobiography, *Here Lies the Heart,* that the publishers asked her to cut. It remains the sole reference anywhere to Nazimova's friendship with the two possessive Annes, respectively the second wife of William K. Vanderbilt, a noted philanderer, and the daughter of J. P. Morgan. Anne Morgan was a good friend of Marbury and de Wolfe, and stayed with them at the Villa Trianon frequently enough to excite rumors of a *ménage à trois.* But the cast of a rumored *ménage à trois* changed when Anne Vanderbilt became a frequent guest at Villa Trianon during Marbury's absence, and jointly hosted dinners with Morgan and de Wolfe.

Perhaps it was not only Mercedes' youth but also her reputation as a lady-killer that decided Marbury not to rock the Nazimova-Morgan-Vanderbilt boat. The eighth and youngest child of aristocratic Castilian Spanish parents living in New York, Mercedes wrote in *Here Lies the Heart* that "at an early age I had violent attacks of psychological suffering and, going into a corner of the room, put my face to the wall and moaned." Omitted from the final draft was her reason: Mercedes had discovered that she was not a boy. In her late teens she became a voracious celebrity-hunter, and celebrity for Mercedes was highly aphrodisiac. Luckily, as Dagmar Godowsky later attested, many women found her irresistible. Dark-eyed, romantically pale, black hair slicked down with brilliantine, she had the air of a toreador, especially when wrapped in a black cape and wearing buckled shoes. Although many biographers of her most famous lovers, Dietrich and Garbo, have questioned Mercedes' veracity, friends and/or lovers of both actresses, including Erich Maria Remarque, Cecil Beaton, and Douglas Fairbanks, Jr., have confirmed it. The same biographers have tended to caricature Mercedes as a

Mercedes de Acosta, painted by
Abram Poole, 1927 (Santa Barbara
Museum of Art)

vegetarian–astrology–wisdom-of-the-East freak. In fact, she tried various diets because she suffered from poor health, and although she talked (and wrote) too much about The Way, her admiration for the Buddhist teacher Ramana Maharishi was shared by Jung. "Persistent" is the word most commonly used to describe Mercedes, and as a woman-chaser she could be persistent to the point of absurdity, but among her male friends were Stravinsky, Aldous Huxley, and Krishnamurti, none of whom had any patience with fools or frauds.

At Madison Square Garden, the twenty-two-year-old Mercedes saw Nazimova, costumed as a Cossack and personifying imperial Russia, make a solo entrance into the arena:

> As the band struck up the Imperial Anthem, she waved the
> Russian flag as a great spotlight played over her. Then the music
> changed to a wild cossack strain and, still carrying the flag high,

she ran the entire distance around the arena, leaping into the air
every few steps. . . . People jumped to their feet, applauding
and shouting her name. They called her out over and over
again, and as she stood at the door to acknowledge the enthusiasm, instead of bowing she gave the Roman salute.

Knowing she was desperate to meet Nazimova, Jane Wallach had
asked Mercedes "to take care of her" after the performance. Mercedes arrived at her dressing room "in a trance":

> She had taken off her fur hat but was still in costume. She had
> thick black hair which stood out from her head and her eyes
> were the only truly purple-colored eyes I have ever seen . . . and
> at this first meeting they made a great impression on me. She
> held out both her hands and said she had heard about me from
> Bessie and Jane.

If Nazimova had heard about Mercedes from Bessie and Jane, she
clearly knew what to expect. But Mercedes was surprised to find Nazimova, in her flat Russian boots, so "tiny and more like a naughty little
boy." In 1960, when *Here Lies the Heart* was published, Mercedes had not
only to cut several passages that would seem tame today, but to write in
code. Those in the know quickly got (and spread) the message of Nazimova as "a naughty little boy"; of Marbury, who "seemed more like a
man"; of the holiday that Mercedes and Eva Le Gallienne enjoyed in
Brittany, staying in a country cottage whose owner "got out her linen
wedding sheets" to put on the bed; of "Daisy, You're Driving Me Crazy"
as the record to which Mercedes and Garbo danced together; and of the
reason why Dietrich "sent me flowers sometimes twice a day, ten dozen
roses or twelve dozen carnations."

Mercedes' account of her first meeting with Nazimova ends with another coded sentence, "She asked me to walk home with her," followed
by another passage omitted from the final draft:

> The weeks after our first meeting were wonderful ones for me.
> Alla was looking for a play. . . . She read me Hauptmann's *The
> Sunken Bell*, and all her Ibsen roles. And she read me Chekhov's
> *The Cherry Orchard, Three Sisters* and *The Seagull*. And some-
> times as she read them she acted out the parts.

Like Maurice Sterne beguiled by Nazimova reading and acting out
Uncle Vanya and *Eugene Onegin* during those "idyllic" two weeks in Paris,
Mercedes couldn't separate the actress from the woman, or illusion from
reality. And Eva Le Gallienne would soon find Nazimova's appeal so
powerfully theatrical that "sometimes you're not sure where you are or

what you're thinking." Sometimes Nazimova was not sure either, and the actress cast the same spell on herself, but she seemed sure enough of what she was doing with Mercedes. And the ease with which they became intimate, as well as the Wallach-Marbury connection, makes it unlikely that Mercedes was Nazimova's first lesbian lover.

But perhaps Mercedes was a liberator, for Nazimova's sexual life became predominantly lesbian after their affair ended. Her later involvements, always with artists or actresses, followed the pattern of other great lesbian romances between creative personalities of the time, Stein and Toklas, Natalie Barney and Romaine Brooks, Janet Flanner and Solita Solano, Djuna Barnes and Thelma Wood. But, unlike the others, Nazimova's affairs never lasted very long. Her situation made it inevitable. While keeping up the pretense of marriage with Bryant, she couldn't live with anyone else, and her other affairs (especially with women) had to remain secret. And in the surviving letters from Bryant to his "wife" after they separated, his most insistent demand (apart from money) is for discretion.

Mercedes was dazzled by Nazimova, but her really grand passions, for Dietrich and Garbo, would come later. That summer, when she was introduced to Isadora Duncan on a beach on Long Island, the dancer "stretched her arms wide with a quick, spontanous gesture as if we had known each other all our lives." It encouraged Mercedes to begin a courtship that another coded passage in *Here Lies the Heart* suggests was successful. During this time, Nazimova was making her first movie at the Fort Lee studios in New Jersey. A year earlier, she had turned down an offer from the Chicago-based Essanay Company to make a movie of *That Sort* because she considered the money not good enough; in May 1915, answering an inquiry from producer William N. Selig, Bryant had written that "Madame Nazimova contemplated posing in Pictures," but apparently Selig's offer was not good enough either. Thirty thousand dollars to make a movie of *War Brides*, with a bonus of $1,000 for each day the production went over its thirty-day schedule, was a different matter. This offer came from Lewis J. Selznick Enterprises, and Lewis J. was a big spender, a trait that his son David O. inherited. To direct the movie he proposed Herbert Brenon, a thirty-six-year-old Irishman who had made his name in 1914 with *Neptune's Daughter,* a vehicle for the swimmer-dancer Annette Kellerman and her one-piece bathing suit. Brenon had just completed a second Kellerman movie, *A Daughter of the Gods,* and invited Nazimova to a screening. She liked it, and in late June they held a press conference to announce the project and exchange compliments, Nazimova praising Brenon's "imaginative faculty" and Brenon praising Nazimova as "the foremost tragedienne of the American stage today."

At Nazimova's request, he signed Bryant and Gertrude Berkeley to repeat their stage roles, and auditioned Richard Barthelmess, still in college and expecting to make a career in business, for the young brother. Getting the part changed his life:

> Nazimova, who had been a splendid friend to both my mother and me, gave me the opportunity, and I intended at the finish of the engagement to return to college. . . . But Herbert Brenon offered me a part in his next picture. I've acted ever since.

Filming began on August 7, and among Nazimova's posthumous papers are some diary notes headed "First Movie." Having trained herself "never to act *for* the audience, never to look at the audience," she wrote, "I find it almost unbearable to say or rather act out things 'to the front.' " Unexpectedly, her nearsightedness proved helpful: "I can't even see the camera or the people around it." But Brenon, like most silent directors, continually bellowed instructions to actors through a megaphone while the scene was being shot, and he was disappointed that Nazimova couldn't see him clearly. She "told him that his voice will give me all I shall need," for Brenon was a relentless whipper-up of emotions:

> "Berkeley," shouts Mr B., "your boy is gone, there he goes out of the door, out of your house, out of your life. They've taken him, your little boy, your youngest. . . . See, Nazimova, this is what a mother feels, see, this is what you would feel were it your boy! Take her over, Nazimova, she *needs* your help. Come, Berkeley, you are still strong, don't show the young mother how deeply it hurts. Tell her it's for the country, show her your simple peasant patriotism. . . ."

Brenon shot almost every scene several times, beginning with a master shot, moving in for a closer shot, finally for close-ups:

> Here is where I learned of the usefulness of a director. No human being could possibly work himself up for the third and fourth and fifth time for the acting of a highly emotional scene, with the constant interruptions necessary for the moving of the camera . . . and the fixing of the make-up ruined by the combined heat of the sun pouring through the glass roof and the electric light too strong even for a Turkish bath.

And just as Nazimova fears she's losing it, Brenon makes himself useful:

"Lights! Get into the atmosphere!" How can I? "Come on, Nazimova. . . . You are weak, dear, worn out, body and soul, you haven't slept for nights, have you?"

"No, I can't sleep."

"Why can't you, child?" He calls me 'child' and I feel so little, so weak, I feel so sorry for myself, I need comfort and am not ashamed to ask for it.

"What are you thinking of, dear, why can't you sleep?"

"I am thinking of my Frank."

"Your husband, the one man you loved in all your life, the one who is gone and you may never see again?"

"Yes, of him, of him alone . . ."

In the final scene, when Joan decides to kill herself rather than comply with the king's orders to bear a child, Brenon's voice booms again as Nazimova picks up the prop gun:

"Slowly, slowly, Nazimova, the whole world is looking at you, this is what they will see and remember, this is how you will live, through this work, this is your great chance, Nazimova. . . . Look at me, Nazimova, let me see that you want to die!"

Oh yes, this is to make me look to the front—I hate it but it is necessary. I looked—saw not Mr. Brenon but all the people I knew since childhood, there in Switzerland in the Alps . . . and in Odessa, my teachers in the boarding school thought I was such a lazy and bad pupil; and in Yalta, the neighbors, and my brother and sister to whom I was such a terrible undertaking as a hoyden of 16; and in Moscow, my professors in the dramatic school who put so much hope in me; and Olga, my friend who believed in me. . . . They were all there, watching, watching.

If the scene stills from *War Brides* look wildly theatrical, Brenon's advice to his players was no doubt responsible. "Stage technique *emphasized* and *enlarged*," according to Nazimova, was his definition of film acting. But he didn't need to remind her that she was acting for posterity. In an interview with *Photoplay* she had already commented: "Our only means of living after death among our successors is to put records of our work upon the film." Unfortunately, no copies of *War Brides* have survived, and Minnie Maddern Fiske's *Vanity Fair* and Ethel Barrymore's *The Kiss of Hate* are also lost, along with the opportunity to see how three Broadway stars performed in a new medium that year. They would probably all look hammy today, like every transplanted theatre artist in silent movies before 1920, Duse in *Cenere* and Lillian Gish excepted.

For the first New York run of *War Brides,* Lewis J. Selznick leased the "legitimate" Broadway Theatre, to compete for prestige with Griffith's

Intolerance, which had opened at the Liberty a few weeks earlier. In a typically appalling publicity gimmick, for the November 11 premiere he even decorated the lobby with bouquets shaped to form the word "Success." It was the only thing *The New York Times* found to criticize in a review celebrating "the marvelously mobile face" that made Nazimova "a priceless asset for the dumb show of the screen." Almost every review of the movie and her performance was highly favorable, although there were some complaints about Nazimova's eye makeup ("overdone") and the scenes of trench warfare ("unrealistic") that Brenon added to the play. But two other new scenes were widely admired: a hospital ward packed with maimed and wounded soldiers, and a spectacularly staged climax as Joan leads a delegation of women to the king's palace. Just before they reach it, the king drives out in his royal limousine. Joan runs forward to block the way, the driver brakes, she pulls out a pistol and shoots herself in the heart. The women catch her body before it falls and raise it high above their heads in protest.

After a long New York run, *War Brides* went on general release in April 1917. A month later, the U.S. declared war on Germany, and the movie was immediately withdrawn from circulation. Although it had grossed more than $300,000, a major sum for any producer at the time, Selznick was unwilling to stop there. To make its pacifist message acceptable to America at war, he inserted new titles that placed the action in Germany, and sent the movie back to the theatres. "People were willing to think of Germans suffering—but not of ourselves or our allies," Nazimova remarked to an interviewer. "It is ver-rr-y interesting to study human nature, isn't it?"

IN THE MIDDLE of a highly emotional scene between Nazimova and Gertrude Berkeley during the filming of *War Brides,* Joan expresses a hope that the war will somehow end soon, her husband will come back, and she can bear his child. "Show her those baby clothes," Brenon shouts at Berkeley; "she always wanted a baby so much, didn't you, Nazimova?" Then the sun goes behind a cloud and the cameraman shouts "Stop!" Waiting for the cloud to pass, Nazimova suddenly wants "to cry a little for my own sake. . . . Oh, this unsatisfied longing in my heart! All my life I have been waiting for this miracle to happen—to have my own dear baby, and by the man I love—and what it means to me to know that I have missed woman's greatest happiness."

Did Nazimova mean that she could never bear Bryant's child because

*Nazimova with Nila Mae, an early "protégée," in
Herbert Brenon's 1916 film of* War Brides

of "*the trouble*," or that she was barren? Or was the longing for motherhood another fantasy, a compensation for the early loss of her own
mother and the pain of her childhood? She had never mentioned the
subject before, and a few years later would announce that "no woman
who desires to create anything worthwhile in art or literature should
hamper herself by bearing children." So perhaps Nazimova was simply
carried away by the reality of theatre when she played that scene in *War
Brides,* and continued to "live" it after the movie finished shooting—for
back in New York she not only came to the rescue of six hungry girls, but
acted as "godmother" to an orphan by making a gift to an agency that
specialized in finding homes for abandoned children.

The hungry girls were students from Isadora Duncan's dance school
in Paris. They hoped to make careers for themselves in America, and
Isadora had persuaded her wealthy lover Paris Singer to bring them over.
She moved them into a large apartment at the Hotel des Artistes, but
shortly afterward quarreled with Singer and was left without funds. Mercedes couldn't help, for she had little money of her own. She was also
temporarily estranged from Isadora. No reason is given in *Here Lies the
Heart,* where Mercedes writes only that, after their euphoric experience
in a deserted barn on Long Island, "I never saw Isadora in any intimate

way in New York." But it was presumably Mercedes who alerted Na-
zimova to Isadora's plight, and Nazimova donated some of her *War
Brides* salary to feed six girls in Greek tunics and sandals until Isadora and
Singer reconciled a few weeks later.

   Although there was no estrangement between Mercedes and Nazimova, after a three-month romance they settled into a lasting friendship. In the fall of 1916, Mercedes began working for the National
Woman Suffrage Organization and taking her first steps along The Way
by studying *The Bhagavad Gita,* but she found time to introduce Nazimova to the twenty-two-year-old Walter Wanger. The future movie
producer was then working for the unsinkable Bessie Marbury, who had
branched out into personal management, with clients ranging from Fritz
Kreisler to Vernon and Irene Castle, and had also produced Jerome
Kern's first musical, *Nobody Home.* Nazimova had read and liked a play
called *'Ception Shoals,* which according to Mercedes "wasn't a good play,
but Alla and Wanger thought that it was." Nazimova also found Wanger
receptive to the idea of repertory theatre, and on October 21 they an-

War Brides. *The climax of Brenon's film, as Joan
(Nazimova) defies the soldiers. Behind her, Gertrude
Berkeley, mother of Busby*

'Ception Shoals. *Nazimova
(aged thirty-seven) as Eve the
sixteen-year-old virgin*

nounced *'Ception Shoals* as the opening play in a "Nazimova season" that
would include works by Strindberg and Goldoni, as well as revivals of
Hedda Gabler and *The Master Builder.*

But as Wanger later recalled, "In those days there were no independent
theatrical producers," and his access to private financing angered the
Syndicate. It refused to lease any of its theatres to Wanger, so he had to
settle for the 299-seat Princess, where Nazimova had made her Broadway
debut. The Princess still belonged to Lee Shubert, who had not forgiven
Nazimova and was in no mood to do her a favor, but couldn't resist doing
the Syndicate a disservice.

In *'Ception Shoals,* which opened on January 10, 1917, Nazimova at
thirty-seven played a sixteen-year-old virgin named Eve. Her first entrance was in dramatic contrast to the chic femme fatale of *Bella Donna*
and *That Sort,* and to the shabby, heroic woman of the people in *War
Brides.* She "emerged dripping from the sea, clad merely in an abbrevi-
ated bathing suit," according to the reviewer for *Theatre Magazine,* who
described her as "astonishingly slight and girlish-looking." But, like most
of his colleagues, he found the play underwhelming. H. Austin Adams,
the author, was a former Episcopalian minister who left the church to
preach the gospel of sex education. In *'Ception Shoals,* Eve is an orphan

brought up by her fanatically religious uncle, the keeper of an island lighthouse and ideally placed to isolate her from the world, the flesh, and the devil. A motorboat is stranded on the nearby shoals, its only passenger a pregnant woman. Eve sees the woman give birth, but Uncle Job refuses to explain the facts of life and sends away the boatman (Bryant), with whom she's fallen in love. Driven mad by frustration and ignorance, Eve kills the old man and walks into the sea, clutching a dishrag that she imagines to be her baby.

Besides the chance it offered to show off her figure, slimmed down from *War Brides,* the play's symbolic treatment of an unhappy childhood seems to have attracted Nazimova. "Little Eve [was] foredoomed at birth," she explained, "to perish for want of light in a lighthouse." As a foreigner, perhaps, she wasn't fully aware of the creaky dialogue. But the future producer of *Queen Christina, The Long Voyage Home,* and *Scarlet Street* might have been expected to veto a line like "There can be no deception about conception."

In spite of the reviews, *'Ception Shoals* played to packed houses, for Nazimova now had the additional box-office value of a movie star. And the production itself was admired for the sets and costumes (including Nazimova's bathing suit) by the young Robert Edmond Jones, soon to establish himself as one of Broadway's most brilliant designers with the Arthur Hopkins–John Barrymore *Hamlet.* Although Bryant's performance made little impression, he also appeared on the program as director, and for the first but not the last time took credit for Nazimova's work.

Wanger had rented the Princess on a monthly basis, and early in February Shubert suddenly declined to renew the lease because he'd booked another production into the theatre for later that month. Sweet revenge on Nazimova? The timing certainly suggests it. Wanger added extra matinees during the final week of the run and looked around for another theatre, but none was available. He managed to arrange a tour of the Midwest, planning to bring the play back to New York when he found a theatre. Then, as well as interrupting the release of *War Brides,* America's entry into World War I put an end to the projected Nazimova-Wanger repertory season. Wanger joined the Committee of Public Information, the film branch of the government's propaganda agency, and after the war became a producer at Paramount.

IN THE AUDIENCE at one of the last matinees of *'Ception Shoals* in New York was the eighteen-year-old Eva Le Gallienne. She was

Walter Wanger, taking time off from Elisabeth Marbury's office

brought up in London and Paris, and her first inspiration in the theatre had been Sarah Bernhardt. Nazimova became her second. She saw the play several times, and was due to meet her idol after the February 8 matinee, having heard from Wanger that Nazimova wanted her to join the company.

Both Eva's parents were writers, her mother the London literary correspondent of a Danish newspaper, her father the alcoholic poet and critic Richard Le Gallienne. When they divorced in 1900, Le Gallienne went to live in New York. Eva made her professional debut on the London stage in 1914, and arrived in New York with her mother a year later. After a couple of minor roles in unsuccessful plays, she attracted the attention of critics and producers in *Mr. Lazarus*, which Nazimova had either seen or heard about. She had also heard of Eva's father, an admirer since her first Ibsen season. Pasted into one of Nazimova's scrapbooks is an article in which Le Gallienne described her as "the greatest virtuoso on the American stage today."

Audience response to *'Ception Shoals* had made Eva aware, as she noted in her diary, that there was a passionate Nazimova "cult." Eva had joined it by the time she met Nazimova in her dressing room, but was as unprepared as Mercedes for the star's impact at close quarters. "God, she is marvelous! . . ." Eva also noted in her diary that Nazimova was "not beautiful but elfin," with a "tremendous magnetism" and no less powerful intelligence. Already committed to go on tour with *Mr. Lazarus,* Eva couldn't accept Nazimova's offer to join the company. A great professional disappointment to her, it turned out not to matter, for the "Nazimova season" never materialized, and this in no way dampened the personal attraction that sprang up between the two of them that afternoon. It was a meeting like the first meeting of Nazimova and Orlenev, perhaps even more intense because they knew they'd be going separate ways within two or three weeks. In fact, they would often be separated over the next four years, but between separations Nazimova was the mentor-lover of a youthful mirror image of herself, with a slender boyish figure, blue eyes, and fierce ambition, determined to play both Hedda Gabler and Hamlet before she turned forty.

Nazimova's influence, in fact, is reflected in many of the roles that Eva eventually chose to play. In 1926, she appeared in *La Locandiera,* the Goldoni comedy Nazimova was planning to present after *'Ception Shoals;* in the thirties, she toured the same three Ibsen plays that Nazimova first toured, *Hedda Gabler, A Doll's House,* and *The Master Builder;* in 1944, she played Madame Ranevskaya in *The Cherry Orchard;* and in 1948, Mrs. Alving in *Ghosts.* Also from Nazimova, Eva seems to have derived a mystical belief in theatre as destiny. In a letter to a friend before opening in a new play, her language is an almost exact echo of her mentor's: "God knows what I'm doing it all for—except that I feel it should be beautiful and *must* be done—for something stronger than myself *wills* it."

DURING THE tour of *'Ception Shoals,* Nazimova compensated to some extent for Eva's absence by forming a close friendship with twenty-nine-year-old Edith Luckett, who played the small part of the pregnant passenger in the motorboat. Like Eva, Mercedes, Marbury, and Nazimova herself, Edith was a New Woman, a suffragist and careerist who refused to grow up female in the accepted sense. But her circumstances were very different. Born to a railroad clerk and his wife who ran a boarding house in a working-class suburb of Washington, D.C., Edith had failed to graduate from high school. Although she chose acting as a means of self-advancement, her real talent was in the theatre of life. Edith invented an aristocratic childhood on a plantation in Virginia, an education at an exclusive private school, and an almost absurdly refined

Southern accent. She dropped her guard, but not her accent, to use four-letter words and tell breathtakingly dirty jokes, passing on a taste for them to Nazimova. A few months before *'Ception Shoals* opened, Edith had married the only son of a genuinely aristocratic New England family. In theory it meant upward social mobility, but in practice the family had fallen on hard times and Kenneth Robbins was working as an insurance salesman. Before ending in divorce, the marriage would produce one daughter, Anne Frances Robbins, known later as Nancy Davis and finally as Nancy Reagan.

A deceptively innocent-looking blonde, Edith was "not a beauty but very attractive, in spite of her heavy legs," according to her friend Lester Weinrott. The friendship with Nazimova led to rumors that they were lovers, but Weinrott thinks it unlikely. "They were just two very dynamic women who appealed to each other, genuinely liked each other, and had no areas of conflict because they were ambitious in very different ways." The tone of Nazimova's letters to Edith bears him out. "Knowing you has been a great happiness to me," she wrote in 1919, "because one rarely meets a person as unselfish and bighearted as you, so kind and considerate to everybody, big and small." Like Isabel Hill, another young actress who became a close friend, Edith always responded to urgent requests from Nazimova on tour, to pick up "the gold evening dress trimmed with black fur" from her New York apartment, take it to a dressmaker for alterations, then send it to the Hotel Mayfair, St. Louis, or look for "3 pair white woolen understockings from upper *left* drawer in blue chest" and mail them to the New Bismarck Hotel in Chicago.

Enormously proud of her friendship with a great star, Edith (also like Isabel Hill later) seems to have felt privileged to do favors for her; and Nazimova, apart from admiring what Weinrott called Edith's "moxie," felt relaxed in the company of someone so exuberantly unshockable. The friendship lasted until Nazimova's death, and their correspondence over the years makes it clear that Edith was one of the very few people with whom she was frank about her sexuality. In 1917, after the end of the *'Ception Shoals* tour, Nazimova wrote that Bryant had again decided "to enlist in the British army. . . . I feel very miserable." In 1920, she confided the reason for her breakup with Jean Acker, and in 1930 thanked Edith for the "warmth and love you have given me and Glesca."

To judge from the hundreds that survive, Nazimova kept almost every letter written to her. In the archive created by Glesca, there are many from Eva, intimate but not "compromising," but none from Edith. And because Edith was probably Nazimova's main confidante for more than ten years, it's impossible not to suspect that her letters were destroyed, casualties either of Glesca in her role as keeper of the flame, or of an agreement with Nazimova that certain tracks had to be covered after her death.

NAZIMOVA and Eva were reunited in New York during the summer of 1917, but not for long. In September, as Eva began rehearsals for *Lord and Lady Algy,* Nazimova went to New Orleans to star in her second silent movie.

Maxwell Karger, in charge of production at Metro Pictures Corporation's East Coast studios, was one admirer of Nazimova who didn't admire her movie debut in *War Brides.* He was shocked by her choice of a role that he feared would restrict her celluloid future to character rather than starring parts. Then he watched her emerge like Aphrodite from the sea in *'Ception Shoals* and changed his mind. Three years earlier, William Fox's company had launched Theda Bara as the half-Arab, half-French Vamp of Vamps in *A Fool There Was,* and made a fortune. But Theda lacked the talent to sustain a hugely fraudulent success. The more exotic she pretended to be as Carmen or Cleopatra, the more Theodosia Goodman, former movie extra from Chillicothe, Ohio, showed through. By 1917, the public no longer cared for the star billed as "The Woman Who Did Not Care," and the three most popular movie actresses were Mary Pickford the child-woman, Norma Talmadge the misty-eyed romantic, and Ruth Roland the tomboyish, pistol-packing serial heroine. In Karger's view, none of them filled the sexual gap left by Theda, and *'Ception Shoals* convinced him that Nazimova, a genuine exotic who could also act, still had the looks to fill it. Metro's president, Richard Rowland, agreed, and authorized Karger to offer her a five-year contract.

After the collapse of her plans for a repertory season, Nazimova's only firm offer in the theatre was "to go on the road in *Eternal Magdalen . . .* a mediocre drama." She turned it down in favor of Metro, and Bryant recovered from his second attack of patriotic fever when he learned the terms of the contract. At $13,000 a week, Nazimova would not only top Mary Pickford by $3,000 and become the highest-paid movie actress of the time. Metro also gave her the right to approve director, script—and leading man.

Since its foundation in 1915, Metro had earned high profits from low-budget pictures and was now eager for prestige. (The company also made a successful bid to lure the director Rex Ingram away from Universal.) In a press release, Rowland was "proud to announce the association of so great an artist as Nazimova with Metro Pictures. . . . I can assure the public that the Nazimova pictures will be of the very highest type, large in scope of theme and of an artistic treatment so necessary with such a star." And Nazimova defended herself against the inevitable charge of selling out to a medium incapable of art: "On the speaking stage there have always been more bad plays than good ones, but no one ever argued from this that the drama was a failure. We must always judge an art by its best examples, not its worst."

Like many other companies, Metro was gradually transferring its operations from New York to Los Angeles, where Carl Laemmle had built Universal City and Louis B. Mayer had acquired his first studio. Before being transferred to the Metro lot on Cahuenga Boulevard, Nazimova made two movies at its studio on 61st Street near Broadway, although the first of them, *Revelation*, was shot mainly on location, with the Vieux Carré in New Orleans doubling for the Latin Quarter in Paris. "Have

Revelation. *Charles Bryant as artist, Nazimova as his model, in her first film for Metro*

THE SUPREME
NAZIMOVA
"REVELATION"
Jury's Imperial Pictures Ltd

succeeded in keeping Ch with me for a little longer," Nazimova wrote
Edith on September 23, "as he is going to be in my first picture. . . . With
all my heart I hope that your husband stays with you, for I do know how
it feels, oh, oh!" This is the last time we hear of "Ch" playing hard to
keep, and he would be Nazimova's leading man in nine of her eleven
Metro pictures.

In *Revelation*, Nazimova played Joline, a "cabaret singer" (i.e., prostitute) and favorite model of an American artist (Bryant) during the first
months of World War I. He paints her as Cleopatra, Salome, and Sap-
pho, then smuggles her into the grounds of a monastery disguised as a
boy, puts a shawl over her head, and asks her to pose as the Madonna.
When she touches a sacred rosebush it immediately blooms, a miracle is
declared, and another follows. Joline renounces life in the Latin Quarter
"cabarets" and sets out for the battlefield as a Red Cross nurse.

A likely story, but it allowed Nazimova, in the words of one reviewer,
"to run the gamut between Vice and Virtue with dazzling effect." And at
the premiere of *Revelation* in February 1918, *The New York Times* reported
that, when the lights went up for intermission halfway through the
movie, the dazzled audience at the Lyric Theatre spotted Nazimova sitting in a box, and "greeted her with shouts and handclapping." The same
thing happened at the end, and "not until she had left the theatre did the
people stop their applause." *Toys of Fate,* made back to back with *Revelation* and premiered three months later, was equally successful at the box
office. An even more lurid sexual melodrama, it allowed Nazimova to
run the gamut between dual roles. Fade in on a wild, passionate gypsy
who deserts her tribe when she falls in love with a wealthy Englishman
(Bryant again) and commits suicide after he abandons her. Fade out, and
fade in again, twenty years later, on the gypsy's wild, passionate daughter
intent on revenge.

Like most of Nazimova's silent movies, *Revelation* and *Toys of Fate* have
been lost, but her own opinion of them survives in a 1918 interview with
Motion Picture Magazine: "So long as the stories are false, the actor cannot be blamed for acting the part and not living it." Yet in the same interview she described Metro as "a splendid company to work for and they
let me have my own way." Although Nazimova's contract gave her script
approval, she accepted the stories of *Revelation* and *Toys of Fate,* and later
chose others no less false. In *Bella Donna* and *That Sort* she had fallen
back on external tricks, and by the time she made *Stronger than Death* in
1920, she was "acting the part" to the edge (and sometimes over it) of self-
parody. But audience response to Nazimova's first silent movies made her

Toys of Fate. *In the first of her dual roles,*
Nazimova played a gypsy and (seen here) her daughter.

a star as popular as Pickford and Talmadge, and the critic of *The New York Times* was a lone dissenting voice when he ended his review of *Toys of Fate:* "Can it be that she hasn't much respect for the movies?"

In fact, during her first successful year at Metro, Nazimova claimed that in some ways she preferred movies to the theatre. Retakes, she felt, offered a unique opportunity to "improve your work, where if a line is once spoken on the stage you cannot go back and do it over. [And] Metro say that I use up more film than anyone they ever had."

But before moving to Hollywood, Nazimova returned briefly to the

theatre. The studio agreed to release her for a season of Ibsen directed by
Arthur Hopkins, who was then at the start of a remarkably adventurous
career. Hopkins had his first success in 1914 with Elmer Rice's first play,
On Trial, for which he commissioned Robert Edmond Jones' first Broadway set. After the Ibsen season they would work together on several other
landmark productions, John Barrymore's *Hamlet* and *Richard III,* Philip
Barry's *In a Garden* with Laurette Taylor, and two early O'Neill plays,
Anna Christie with Pauline Lord and *The Hairy Ape.* George Cukor, who
saw many of these productions, remembered that Hopkins' work "really
electrified me. . . . [It] introduced a whole new look into the theatre,
[and] in his presence actors began to discard the tricks they'd learned and
the play itself would emerge without any artificial aids."

The season opened at the Plymouth Theatre on March 11, 1918, with
the American premiere of *The Wild Duck,* Hopkins' favorite Ibsen play,
followed by revivals of *Hedda Gabler* and *A Doll's House.* In *The Wild
Duck* he had planned to cast Nazimova as Gina, the mother, but "she
elected to play the fourteen-year-old Hedvig. The idea was at first startling, but I soon saw the wisdom of it. She was a slight person of no age
[and] one actress who never had to find again the histrionic gifts of childhood. They had never left her. If anything, they had expanded with ma-
turity. She was sensitive, timorous and afraid of herself." Interestingly,
Hopkins seemed to connect Nazimova's fears with her childhood, and
went on to describe her intense stage fright, which Nazimova traced back
to her eleventh year, when she was beaten by Yakov after giving her first
concert. Almost thirty years later, according to Hopkins, she quickly recovered once she was onstage, "but the knowledge that this would in-
variably happen was of no use to her in subsequent performances."

Hopkins found Nazimova "touching and beautiful" as Hedvig, and
most of the critics agreed. So did Pauline Lord, to whom Nazimova had
recently sent flowers after seeing her for the first time in *Spellbound.* "I
did not know I was able to feel so humble—so very very little," she wrote
on an accompanying card. On March 12, Lord returned the compliment:
"Having seen you in *The Wild Duck,* I see no reason why anything on the
stage today should make you feel 'humble.' " But the reaction to *Hedda
Gabler,* in which Lionel Atwill gave a widely admired performance as Eilert Løvborg, was much less favorable. Although William Winter had retired, Nazimova's old enemy John Corbin was now writing for *The New
York Times,* and seized the opportunity to attack her entire career. "She
has touched no character without debasing, distorting it," he complained, and this time around accused her of transforming Hedda "into

*Nazimova as Hedda Gabler in Arthur Hopkins' 1918
production. With Lionel Atwill (right) as Løvborg*

a Continental lounge-lizard." And *The New Republic* commented, "To
see the part twisted and wrung for effectiveness is to suffer unnecessary
pain."

Eva, appearing in a comedy with Ethel Barrymore, was able to see
Hedda during the season. What she said to Nazimova is unknown, but a
few years later she told Alexander Woollcott that she found Mrs. Patrick
Campbell less "neurotic" and more "real" in the part. If Hopkins was unable to prevent Nazimova from settling for exhibitionism as Hedda,
however, he guided her to a performance as Nora in *A Doll's House* that
the critics found remarkably self-effacing, subtle, and true. Julie Nørre-
gaard, Eva's mother, told her that Nazimova was the only actress she'd
seen who succeeded in playing "both ends of the character," the spoiled
child-wife and the "grave young woman" who slams the door on her husband. So impressed was Thornton Wilder, aged twenty-one, that he

Nazimova as the fourteen-year-old Hedvig in Arthur
Hopkins' 1918 production of The Wild Duck

began writing a play "with a magnificent fierce love scene" for Nazimova, but didn't know how to finish it.

Also in the audience for *A Doll's House* was the journalist and theatre critic Rebecca Drucker Bernstien. By 1992, when she celebrated her 102nd birthday, Rebecca was probably the only living witness of performances by Bernhardt, Duse, Olga Knipper, Ethel Barrymore, the Lunts, and Eva Le Gallienne as well as Nazimova:

> In 1918, the New York theatre was still very provincial, domi-
> nated by the English style of acting. A diversion from life, un-
> like the Yiddish theatre, which was a mirror of life. Ethel
> Barrymore was the supreme example of gentility in the Amer-
> ican theatre. That kind of actor always "played" emotional
> parts and made you aware of the fact. Always the barrier of
> formality. Nazimova was the first to appeal more directly to
> the emotions, and she introduced a new style of acting. She
> was very small, but so *vivid,* a great theatrical presence com-
> bined with an intensely inner analysis of the parts she played.
> She added her own individual personality to the character,
> unlike Knipper, who played and analyzed her characters with
> great care, but in a more impersonal way. And unlike Bern-
> hardt, a commanding star personality but often at the expense
> of character. Closer to Duse, although Duse seemed to me
> very intense and very remote at the same time.

Rebecca disagreed with the critical reaction to Nazimova's Hedda, a performance she found "very disturbing, much too powerful for fans of the genteel style. If Nazimova made Nora much less theatrical, and scaled her down, that's because Nora is a very different character and can't be played the same way." A few years later, Rebecca saw Eva Le Gallienne play Hedda—"A fine actress, but you admired her without being really excited by her. Like Knipper, she didn't have that mysterious, necessary star personality."

TOYS OF FATE advertised as "The World's Greatest Actress in Her Greatest Play," opened May 30, just after the ten-week Ibsen season closed. At a party after the premiere, Nazimova met the extraordinarily flirtatious Fannie Hurst, whose novel *Humoresque* had just become a best-seller, and who wrote next day:

> Dear Nazimova the Unforgettable: Last evening was fairly exotic with the lovliness [sic] of you in cinema and flesh. Thankyou for being you! We're neighbors. Why not a dish of five o'clock tea—here—soon—just you and me—knee to knee?

It seems unlikely that Nazimova accepted the invitation, since by June 2 she was back at Who-Torok for ten days before leaving for Los Angeles and her third Metro picture. And a letter written to Edith Luckett on June 3 suggests that by now Eva was not the only young actress in whom Nazimova had become interested: "Nila Mae had the chance of her life with me in Hedda Gabler [she played Mrs. Elvsted], but truthfully speaking she was a disappointment to herself and others, and I am *very* sorry for her for she'll never have another chance like this. Have you seen *Revelation* and *Toys of Fate?* She was with me in the second but has not impressed the managers so she won't have more work with Metro."

This is the first and only mention of Nila Mae in Nazimova's letters, although in fact she had a small role in the movie of *War Brides*. Since Nazimova doesn't refer to this, presumably the attachment sprang up later. In any case, the letter makes it clear that Nila had been a subject of discussion on one of Edith's occasional visits to New York. Edith was now living in upper New York State, in a farmhouse belonging to the Robbins family, her husband a sergeant in the army and her career on hold. Nila's career, if it continued after *Toys of Fate,* is not on record. The first of what the press would soon be referring to as "protégées" of Nazimova (just as it had already referred to Marion Davies as a "protégée" of Hearst), she would not be heard from again. But much would be heard from her successor, Jean Acker, whom Nazimova met a year later. By then the box-office returns from her pictures had caused *Motion Picture News* to comment, "Never has a star new to films jumped right into the center of the spotlight as she did," and *Motion Picture Magazine* to raise its eyebrows at her "seemingly overwhelming appeal for the feminine sex."

8

The 8080 Club

1918–1921

Nazimova—the quintessential Queen of the
Movie Whores. It was the only time Hollywood
let a star come near to orgasm on the screen.
                                —DARRYL F. ZANUCK

Aware that the success of *REVELATION*
and *Toys of Fate* had made her Metro's most important asset, Nazimova
issued a series of demands (or commands) before leaving for Los Angeles. For her next picture she wanted the studio to acquire the rights of
L'Occident, a play by Henri Kistenmaeckers; to adapt it she wanted June
Mathis; and she wanted Metro to put Nina on its payroll. Karger and
Rowland agreed to everything, including a job for Nina in the foreign
department of their New York office, where she read and reported on the
latest French and German plays and novels.

June Mathis, the writer chosen by Nazimova, was a former child
vaudeville star who graduated to adult roles and went on the road with
the female impersonator Julian Eltinge. In 1916, they both gave up the
stage, Eltinge for movies and Mathis to take a writing course at City College of New York. She began writing screenplays, and sold her first to
Edwin Carewe, a director at Astoria Studios, and her second to Metro.

*June Mathis in her office at Metro, "magical" opal
ring on third finger of her right hand*

This was *Toys of Fate*, and it so impressed Karger that he put her under
contract. Nazimova and Mathis also impressed each other when they
met at the Metro studio in New York, and by the time Nazimova asked
for Mathis to work on *L'Occident*, she had been promoted to head of the
scenario department on the Hollywood lot. Only twenty-six, Mathis had
the additional title of "artistic supervisor," becoming in effect a production executive, a position that no other woman in Hollywood would
achieve for many years to come. According to a contemporary account,
"She watches with a narrow eye the filming, cutting and titling of each
production. Her assistance is deemed invaluable." The productions,
about fifteen of them that year, included vehicles for Metro's other contract stars, Mae Murray, Francis X. Bushman, Milton Sills, and Viola
Dana.

The first of two women as powerful as herself with whom Nazimova
collaborated in Hollywood, Mathis was stocky, rather plain, famously
short-tempered and proud of it. She liked to tell a story about herself
as a seventeen-year-old actress on tour, rebuffing the attempt of her

drunken leading man to make love in her dressing room during inter-mission. "I sank my teeth into his shoulder and hung on like a desperate little bulldog until the blood streamed out of his flesh into my face. He begged for mercy and I let him go." When the curtain went up again, they had to play a love scene together, and Mathis was amused to see "blood trickling down his shoulder as I ran into his arms crying in my best ingenue manner, 'I don't know why I love you so, but oh I love you so!' " In her career as a screenwriter, kinky moments became her trade-mark, and Mathis was proud of this as well. She wrote a shot of two les-bians into a café scene for *Four Horsemen of the Apocalypse,* and in the banquet scene at the French château, "I had the German officers coming down the stairs with women's clothing on. To hundreds of people that meant no more than a masquerade party. To those who had lived and read, and who understood life, that scene stood out as one of the most terrific things in the picture."

But Mathis' sexual imagination does not appear to have carried over into her life. Falsely rumored to have been in love with both Valentino and Rex Ingram, she eventually married an Italian cameraman whom she met in Rome during the filming of *Ben-Hur.* Forever frumpish and mak-ing no effort to appear attractive, Mathis didn't allow marriage to change her style. Yet she was not one of those women or men whose philosophy is: Only power matters, and if you have it, forget charm. Mathis also in-habited worlds above and beyond. She believed in the "magical" proper-ties of an opal ring that she always wore when writing, and in reincarnation, spiritualism, and the Book of Revelations, one of the rea-sons she insisted on Metro's buying the rights to Blasco Ibañez's *Four Horsemen of the Apocalypse.*

Although falsely rumored in her turn to attend séances with Mathis, Nazimova had no interest in the supernatural. But she admired Mathis' flair for sexual melodrama in exotic surroundings, and felt sure it would be stimulated by *Eye for Eye,* as *L'Occident* was retitled. Hassouna, the daughter of an Arab sheik, falls in love with an officer in the Foreign Le-gion (Bryant, of course). Rejected by her tribe and left in the desert to die, she's rescued by Bedouins who sell her into slavery. She manages to escape and becomes a dancer in a café in Tangier. The rest of the story takes place in Marseille, where Hassouna gets a job in a circus, discovers that her legionnaire has married, and plots vengeance until a last-minute happy ending reunites them. Mathis added a few characteristic touches of her own, notably the sinister, depraved Bedouin who first spots Has-souna in the desert, and anticipated Valentino's tango scene in her script

Nazimova, in her gypsy costume for Toys of Fate, *on the back lot at Metro with Rex Ingram, soon to begin preparing* Four Horsemen of the Apocalypse

for *Four Horsemen* by writing a sword dance into one of the Tangier café scenes. All that survives of *Eye for Eye* is the trailer, which presents the dance as a high point in the movie. Bare-legged, wearing a distinctly non-Arab costume (jeweled bandana, tight-fitting satin top, matching sarong), Nazimova performs a kind of hootchy-cootchy while brandishing the sword above her head. But then "The Untamed Desert Child" responds to a customer's lecherous grin by threatening to bring the blade down on *his* head.

Nazimova's first two Metro pictures had been directed by the competent but undistinguished George D. Baker, who remained in New York to make *The Cinema Murders*, produced by Hearst's Cosmopolitan Pictures and starring Marion Davies. In her capacity of artistic supervisor, Mathis assigned Albert Capellani to *Eye for Eye*. Capellani had made his name in France with adaptations of *Les Misérables* and *Germinal*, then at the Fort Lee studios with *The Common Law*, starring Clara Kimball Young, the current queen of high-society drama. Mathis admired the picture's visual sophistication, which earned Capellani a special tribute in *Photoplay*, praising his "stealthy artistry" and the way he coaxed his actors "to be natural, to walk and talk like real people."

To make the characters of *Eye for Eye* behave like real people was beyond even Capellani's coaxing, but when the picture premiered on December 22, 1918, most of the critics agreed with *The New York Times* on the "forcefulness" of Nazimova's acting as well as her "lithe, plastic body and [at thirty-nine] youthful appearance," and admired "the glowing sands and nomadic tribes shown to splendid advantage" of Capellani's desert scenes (shot near Palm Springs). Although most of the critics also agreed with the *Times* that "whatever Kistenmaeckers wrote has become on the screen a photoplay of little merit," the movie's success at the box office led *Motion Picture Classic* to feature Nazimova on its cover with a solemn boldfaced caption:

> With the advent of Motion Pictures, the public and the crit-
> ics, as well as our Editorial Staff, have been eagerly looking
> for one artist who would embody everything that the art
> of the silent drama should have. The search is over. In Alla
> Nazimova we have beauty, we have a depth of emotionalism
> never depicted before, and we have art with such little touches
> of finesse that she unconsciously stands alone.

The Nazimova-Mathis-Capellani combination proceeded to top itself by giving the public two Nazimovas in her next picture. No doubt eager to immortalize the image of herself as a girl of sixteen in a bathing suit, Nazimova wanted to film *'Ception Shoals*, and Mathis invented a prologue to allow her to play, as in *Toys of Fate*, both mother and daughter. Fade in on Faith, the lighthouse keeper's sister, seduced, made pregnant, and abandoned by a sailor. She gives birth to Eve, but a ferocious lecture on mortal sin from her puritanical brother drives Faith to throw herself off the lighthouse during a storm. Fade out, and fade in sixteen years later on Eve emerging from the same ocean. Not content to show two generations of women suffering the same fanatically "Christian" male tyranny,

Eye for Eye. *Nazimova as Hassouna, the Arab girl
sold into slavery*

Eye for Eye. *Hassouna, escaped from her slavemaster,
performs a sword dance in a Tangier café*

Mathis added one of her kinky touches by hinting at the lighthouse keeper's incestuous fixation on his sister.

Retitled *Out of the Fog*, the movie opened in New York on February 9, 1919. Although there were reservations (surprisingly mild) about the story, Capellani was praised for his direction of actors and atmospheric location work, Nazimova for her "strength and subtlety" in both roles. For a forty-year-old actress to get away with portraying a teenager was even trickier onscreen than onstage, but *The New York Times* found that she made the daughter as "real" as the mother. Although cameraman Eugene Gaudio's exteriors of the Massachusetts coast also won praise, his interiors of Nazimova must have been equally deserving. Like all her preceding movies at Metro, *Out of the Fog* has been lost, but a few weeks after it finished shooting she performed a solo dance in *Screen Snapshots*, a monthly news "featurette" on Hollywood and the stars. This piece of film, "Putting the Hooray in Cabaret," survives. By now Nazimova had cropped her unruly hair so she could wear all kinds of "character" wigs in movies, and this one shows her with a fringe, long fluffy waves falling to her shoulders, and a bandana. She wears a typically exotic, gypsy-Arab costume—embroidered blouse, diaphanous shawl, fancy knee breeches with tassels, and black stockings. Although she doesn't dance barefoot like Isadora Duncan, or bare-naveled like Ruth St. Denis, at times her style reflects both their styles. Large dramatic effects alternate with sinuous Oriental arm movements, and once she seems about to break into a cancan. Nazimova's self-confidence and energy almost disguise some fairly amateurish dancing, but when crudely photographed on a bare stage hung with streamers, she can't disguise her age. In "Putting the Hooray in Cabaret" she looks only a few years short of forty, and slightly overweight. For a while, weight seems to have been a problem, and she would look a bit heavy again a year later in *Stronger than Death*. Then she became a vegetarian, with results spectacularly visible in *Camille*.

"GREAT IS ALLA!" commented *Theatre Magazine*, pronouncing Nazimova 1918 Actress of the Year for her Ibsen season, but fearing she was now lost to the movies, "her principal profit." And by the end of that year, she had spent $65,000 of her principal profit on an imposing California Spanish house at 8080 Sunset Boulevard. She spent half as much again to remodel the interior, build a swimming pool, and landscape the property's three and a half acres. This area of Hollywood, at the end of the Big Red Cars trolley line from Los Angeles, was still

*Another kind of dance, half gypsy,
half cancan: Nazimova "Putting the
Hooray in Cabaret" in the 1919*
Screen Snapshots

countryside. To the north a narrow dirt road wound up Laurel Canyon with its avocado and citrus orchards; to the east lay poppy and bean fields and occasional farmhouses; and to the west, on each side of what later became The Strip, Japanese nursery gardeners leased land to grow and sell flowers. The orange grove, lily pond, cedars, and palms on her land Nazimova left as she found them, but she added a terrace with an aviary, a rose garden, and masses of semitropicals—mimosa, birds of paradise, hibiscus, poinsettia. She jokingly called it The Garden of Alla, a nickname that stuck. Although she supposedly designed the pool in the shape of the Black Sea, photographs suggest the resemblance was minimal. But the interior of Who-Torok West became a classic movie star's showplace, its immense tiled hallway dominated by a Mexican chandelier and two massive antique chests, its vast living room with another tiled floor, beamed ceiling, couch and armchairs upholstered in purple velvet, gilded wall candelabra, baronial fireplace, a grand piano. A broad tiled stairway led to the upper floor, and in Nazimova's bedroom the pièce de résistance was a huge circular window that she installed above her bed. A photograph shows her posed below it, hazy sunlight pouring through to heighten an already soft-focus effect.

The regular staff at the Garden of Alla, apart from Nazimova's personal maid Ada Scobie and secretary Peggy Hagar, comprised a gardener, a cook, a housemaid, and a butler who doubled as Bryant's valet. The garage housed a new Rolls-Royce, and since Nazimova never learned to drive, Bryant doubled as "husband" and chauffeur. In public, a reporter observed, "she flirts intensely and convincingly" with Bryant, but in private they had separate bedrooms and led separate lives. Nazimova later told Glesca that it became even more important to keep up the pretense of marriage because she was earning so much money, and had so much more to lose if the truth came out. Once again the main advantages seem to be Bryant's. Although the critics usually described his acting as adequate or colorless, or failed to mention it, he was assured of work. Never ambitious as an actor, he was more interested in living well. One fan magazine slyly reported that Bryant earned $1,000 a week as "Madame's husband and leading man. (Of course, the salary is paid him for being the latter.)" Another claimed that as Madame's business manager he was paid 10 percent of her salary.

By now Bryant was mainly useful to Madame as a convenient if expensive "beard." Like many other stars, she found that a public façade of marriage guaranteed private freedom, and when rumors of her bisexuality ripened on the Hollywood grapevine, it even amused Nazimova to

*Nazimova in her role as Mrs. Charles Bryant,
with "husband," in The Garden of Alla*

Pruning The Garden of Alla

"Helping" a workman at The Garden of Alla

The pool, vaguely shaped like the Black Sea,
at The Garden of Alla

The living room of The Garden of Alla

titillate the gossip columnists. "Most of my friends are young girls," she told *Photoplay*, and confided to Gladys Hall, of the *Telegram*, that "my friends call me Peter and sometimes Mimi." (In an aside, Hall noted that the actress was wearing "a blue serge suit of mannish cut.") On Sunday afternoons Nazimova hosted poolside parties, occasionally mixed, more often "young girls" only. Like Nila Mae, some were hopeful actresses who never made it; others achieved a measure of fame—Mildred Davis by marrying Harold Lloyd, Virginia Fox by marrying Darryl F. Zanuck, Lois Wilson by losing Valentino to Bebe Daniels in *Monsieur Beaucaire*.

As well as playing First Lady of the Silent Screen, who in fact liked to be called Madame and not Peter or Mimi, Nazimova was the first to cultivate an image of the "foreign" sexual sophisticate, and supplied the original theme on which Pola Negri, Garbo, and Dietrich created variations. Offscreen all four actresses were bisexual, Nazimova and Negri ending their lives with female companions, Garbo and Dietrich preferring solitude. Onscreen all four represented dangerously seductive women who not only pursued sexual pleasure as openly as men, but betrayed men as ruthlessly as men betrayed women. Offscreen Garbo found it easier to manipulate men by never marrying, Dietrich found that marriage made it easier for her to manipulate lovers, Negri found it good publicity to marry (and divorce) a prince, and only Nazimova was outsmarted. The one way to understand a person's "apparently senseless actions," Louise Brooks believed, is to understand "that person's sexual loves and hates and conflicts." Nazimova's apparently senseless loyalty to Bryant bears this out. The "Rosebud" of her life was a fantasy that she only abandoned when Bryant abandoned her. In spite of his inadequacy, Bryant *looked* like her fantasy of an ideal husband, handsome and protective, and knew how to play the part in public. At the same time, his failure to play the part of her lover in private drove another nail in the coffin of Nazimova's trust in men. Ironically, it took a woman to become the real man in her life; and until she met Glesca, her involvements with both sexes were essentially makeshift, passions that soon burned themselves out. The final irony, revealed in her later diaries, is that, because Glesca's attraction was not primarily sexual, Nazimova never found her ideal partner.

In the theatre Nazimova descended from Ibsen to the lust-and-revenge melodrama of *Bella Donna,* and at Metro she continued the same downward trend with a series of silent-movie equivalents. What survives most strongly in the work of this period is a formidable narcissism, so perhaps Bryant's mediocrity made him an ideal leading man. Onscreen she didn't want male competition, and when she got it from Valentino in *Camille,* she cut him out from her death scene. She didn't want competition from a director either: after one more film with Capellani, she dismissed him and worked only with impersonal technicians.

Their last picture, again adapted by Mathis from a best-selling novel, *The Red Lantern,* was even more popular than its predecessors, and inspired a "Red Lantern" theme song ("The Chinese tell a story / That's full of mystic glory"). Set in Peking during the Boxer Rebellion, it provided Nazimova with her most spectacular dual role. Instead of mother and daughter, she played half-sisters, the high-yellow Eurasian Mahlee, born to an English father and his Chinese mistress, and the pure, white, and blonde Blanche Sackville, born to the same father and his English wife. Predictably, both fall in love with the same man, an American diplomat (*not* played by Bryant, perhaps because it was a minor role). Losing him to Blanche and disowned by her father, Mahlee takes revenge on the white world by joining the Boxer Rebellion. But she still loves her American, and when he's killed by the rebels just after they declare her Goddess of the Red Lantern, Mahlee takes poison. As she lies back in a peacock chair and closes her eyes, an intertitle translates her final lip movements: "East is East and West is West. . . ."

When *The Red Lantern* opened in New York on May 4, 1919, critical reaction was generally very favorable, the last scene singled out for its

Another dual role: Nazimova as the Eurasian Mahlee and as her half-sister, the "pure white" Blanche Sackville, in The Red Lantern

"poignancy," Nazimova's Mahlee for her perfect "imitations of the Chinese feminine manners," and Capellani's direction for its faithful reproduction of the "mystic soul" of China. But *The New York Times* found it improbable that "a Chinese half-breed stamped with the Occident" would be deified by the nationalistic Boxers, and in a letter to the Baltimore *Sun* a Chinese student complained of another distortion of his country's life: "Chinese women would not show bare legs as Nazimova did when portraying the Goddess." Although one print of the movie survives in good visual condition at the Cinémathèque Royale de Belgique, the celluloid is too fragile for viewing even on a moviola, and funds to restore it are not yet available. Scene stills make it clear that *The Red Lantern* was sumptuously photographed by Eugene Gaudio, and that the sets by Henri Menessier, who later worked with Rex Ingram, were splendid, if no more authentic than all the Oriental characters impersonated by Americans, among them Noah Beery as a Boxer chief. Only the extras, including the twelve-year-old Anna May Wong, were genuine Chinese.

The final day of shooting actually occurred at night, on the back lot at Metro, where more than a hundred members of the press were invited to watch Capellani direct Mahlee's coronation procession. Elected a goddess by the Boxers, wearing a brocaded gown and elaborate headdress, she arrives at a temple by palanquin, while six cameramen film the ceremonial journey. A few days later, Nazimova wrote Nina:

> Capellani is no more. The thing that I could not bear any longer was seeing, and having to work with, a man who—no matter what one did—was constantly wearing an unhappy and unsatisfied face. Everything was not to his liking—the country, the people, the firm [Metro]—until one day I asked him, "Is there anything that would ever make you happy?" And he said, "Yes—to be my own boss! . . ." On account of my pictures being such a success he maintains that it is due to him and therefore he ought to be treated like Griffith. He constantly speaks of the adoration the latter is given in his studio, called "Master" instead of Mr. Griffith etc. Also he wanted an increase of salary (750 a week instead of 500) and many other things which were impossible.

Nazimova was earning $13,000 a week, so it seems she thought Capellani's talent worth only a twenty-sixth of her own. As for wanting "to be my own boss," was he referring to Metro or his star? In any event, *The Red Lantern* was Capellani's last Hollywood picture, and he went back east to form his own company at the Fort Lee studios. Nazimova's letter

*Chaplin visits Nazimova and Charles Bryant
on the set of* The Brat.

to Nina continues with the news that Bryant will become assistant director on her next movie, "and study hard for 2–3 pictures so that in the
future he will be my director—which he ought to have been long ago—
it's the only solution to this problem." In fact, Bryant was later credited
(twice) as Nazimova's director and (three times) as her scenarist. In every
case it was a courtesy title. From now on, up to and including *Salome,*
Nazimova in effect became her own director. She pretended otherwise to
deflect criticism after a blistering open letter from *Photoplay:* "In the
opinion of many who have worked with you, you have tried to do too
much. . . . Perhaps you have come, unfortunately, to that place where
you believe the whispering chorus that says 'the Queen can do no
wrong.' " Unfortunately, Nazimova had also come to a place where she
believed that directing herself in movies was no different from directing
herself in the theatre.

And Bryant, of course, was on his way to becoming Nazimova's
professional as well as personal "beard." Her letter to Nina ends with
an account of the joys of "married" life in California. "It is wonderful. . . . I look through my windoes [sic] upon the mountains where here
and there peep out white villas like in Yalta, mimosa trees in our garden
in full bloom below. . . . Charles rides a good deal in the canyons and
brings delicious honey which people living on top of mountains

The Brat. *Charles Bryant as the high-society writer;*
Nazimova as the girl from the slums

sell. There are thousands of beehives for the sage honey and Ch loves it."

On Nazimova's next picture, "Ch" was again her leading man and may also have served as assistant director, but in those days assistant directors were not credited. *The Brat* was Nazimova's first comedy for Metro, based on a play that had been a Broadway hit the previous year and that owed an obvious debt to *Pygmalion*. She played a chorus girl from the slums down on her luck, and Bryant the writer who decides to study her as "material" for his next novel, introduces her to his snobbish family, and finally turns her into a "lady." Herbert Blaché, a run-of-the-mill director under contract to Metro, was Nazimova's choice to replace Capellani, and the movie was less warmly received than the Art Deco interior of the New Capitol Theatre, which opened with *The Brat* on November 1. "Frequent dreary spots in the story's fabric," the New York *American* proclaimed, and the *Times* accused it of sentimentalizing the play. In a 1931 remake directed by John Ford, Sally O'Neil played the hard-edged Brat of the Broadway production, not a chorus girl but a prostitute. The softer profession of Nazimova's Brat allowed her to perform two musical numbers: a "classical" Greek dance on a glass runway, lit from below by massed klieg lights, and a comic "rabbit dance" in a furry costume with whiskers and long pointed ears. Unlike her films with Capellani, *The Brat* made only a modest

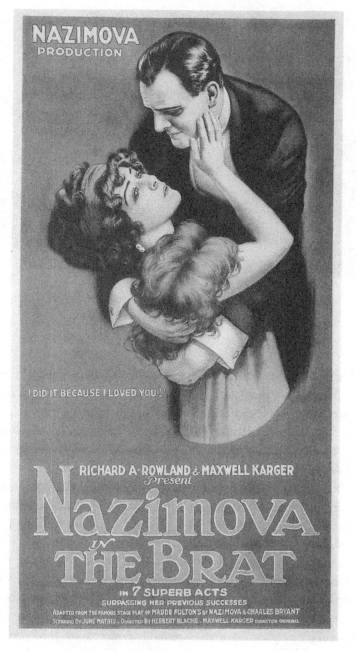

Poster for The Brat

Jean Acker, the "protégée" Nazimova discovered in New York in September 1919, brought to Hollywood, and introduced to the "8080 Club"

profit, perhaps because her public didn't really approve of Nazimova venturing into Mary Pickford territory.

IN SEPTEMBER 1919, *Photoplay* reported that Nazimova had recently visited New York and brought back "a new brand of perfumed cigarettes, together with a protégé [sic] who used to be known to the world as Jeanne Acker, but who now prefers to call herself Jeanne Mendoza."

At this time Acker was twenty-six years old, part Cherokee, a dancer in vaudeville and small-part actress in summer stock—and hardly known to the world at all. Photographs show just another pretty face, and she seemed the least likely person to set off an emotional brushfire that would burn not only Nazimova but Valentino, Natacha Rambova, and June Mathis. Although Dagmar Godowsky remembered that she had "great charm," Acker left a very different impression on Patsy Ruth Miller: "She wore severe tailored suits and looked very mannish. But it was only later I heard stories she was a lesbian." Nazimova installed her at the Hollywood Hotel and persuaded Metro to put her under contract at $200 a week. But the studio found her not exotic enough for a Jeanne Mendoza. It launched Jean Acker with some all-American publicity photographs that featured her barefoot in shorts, striped blouse, and a Louise Brooks hairstyle.

Even before Prohibition became federal law in June 1919, local laws had severely cramped public nightlife in Los Angeles, most municipalities forbidding dance halls and nightclubs to serve liquor. To drink, listen, and dance to a first-rate band with Paul Whiteman playing violin, it was necessary to drive out to the Vernon Country Club, a ranch-style building surrounded by beet fields, where Valentino worked as a tango dancer when he first arrived in California. And on the private circuit, Nazimova created the movie colony's first salon. Pickfair didn't open its doors until 1926, the same year that Hearst and Marion Davies began entertaining at Ocean House in Santa Monica.

The Garden of Alla also became known as the "8080 Club," and at first Acker inevitably felt threatened or outclassed there. The ambitious but relatively inexperienced girl found potential rivals splashing around in the pool on all-girl Sunday afternoons; and at the weekend dinner parties with an international guest list, Nazimova conversed in Russian and French as well as English, talked of her childhood in Yalta and Switzerland, of Ellen Terry and Duse, Stanislavsky and Chekhov. Among the regulars at the 8080 Club were thirty-year-old Mae Murray and her director husband, Robert Z. Leonard; future director Robert Florey, then Hollywood correspondent for a French magazine; Lilyan Tashman, a talented actress who preferred her own sex and whose "outrageous" personality her friend George Cukor relished; June Mathis; Chaliapin when in town; pianist Leopold Godowsky and daughter Dagmar; Norma Talmadge and sister Constance; and the Mdvani brothers, who claimed to be Georgian princes. Patsy Ruth Miller remembered the Mdvanis as "real spongers," each determined to marry a rich movie star. (David managed to take Mae Murray away from her husband and a good deal of her money. Serge got Negri to the altar, but it was a case of cheating cheaters. Princess Pola basked in the publicity of a royal marriage, then of a royal divorce.) Florey remembered that a new European movie was often screened after dinner, Patsy Ruth that Nazimova sometimes sang Russian folk songs "in a beautiful voice," Dagmar Godowsky recalled a costume party at which "we were all in white powdered wigs and the Court of Louis XV came alive. I was Madame du Barry—so were five others. . . . Of course, Madame was Marie Antoinette."

Dagmar engagingly compared her own life to "an express train going

Members of the "8080 Club":
Lilyan Tashman, Dagmar
Godowsky, Constance and
Norma Talmadge

*Above, another member
of the club, Mae Murray,
in* Fashion Row *(1923),
clearly under the influence
of Nazimova's 1921*
Camille, *left*

nowhere," but it made some interesting stops along the way, with her father at the eleven-year-old Jascha Heifetz's debut in Berlin, at the 8080 Club, later as one of Valentino's leading ladies on film and one of Stravinsky's in life. Nazimova, according to Dagmar, "moved through your life like the moon, lighting your way, controlling your moods, and quite often going behind a cloud. . . . The Nazimova story was a script that she herself had written as a starring vehicle. We were all her supporting players and no one minded."

Except Jean Acker. Her sense of security already undermined by poolside parties and high life at The Garden of Alla, she had to wait around until the end of the year before Metro put her to work, while Nazimova began shooting *Stronger than Death* in late August, and began a brief affair with the picture's script girl. It cannot be known for certain that Acker was aware of this, but it seems likely. In September she began an affair of her own with Grace Darmond, an actress who would achieve nominal stardom in a few low-budget movies during the early 1920s. (One of them was *Handle with Care;* Patsy Ruth, who had a supporting role, found Darmond "pleasant if not talented.") Also unknown is

*Nazimova as femme fatale Sigrid ("I am afraid of
nothing in word or deed—except ugliness") in*
Stronger than Death

whether Nazimova was aware of Acker's affair, but in the last week of October they were still together. She brought Acker, along with Bryant, to a dinner party given by Maxwell Karger of Metro to celebrate the end of shooting on *Stronger than Death*.

Karger's other guests at the Ship Cafe, a fashionable restaurant built in the style of a Spanish galleon on the pier at Venice, were two Metro stars, Viola Dana and Milton Sills, and Dagmar, who played a small part in the film and a major one in a scene that occurred during the evening. (In her memoir, Glesca refused to believe Dagmar's story, but Viola later confirmed it.) On the dance floor was a handsome young Italian who had met Dagmar at a New York nightclub. He noticed her and came over to the table to say hello. "I started to introduce him, but Nazimova lowered her head and froze. Her little frame was rigid and she looked as if she were having a divine fit." The other guests followed her lead, and when the young man retreated Nazimova turned on Dagmar. "How dare you bring that gigolo to my table?"

By this time Rudolph Valentino had appeared briefly with Clara Kimball Young in *Eyes of Youth* and Mae Murray in *A Delicious Little Devil* without creating much of an impression, except on June Mathis, who later recommended him to Rex Ingram for *Four Horsemen of the Apocalypse*. But two years previously his name had appeared all over the New York tabloids, when the police raided a house belonging to one Mrs. Georgia Thym and arrested her for blackmail. Finding Valentino in the house with her, they arrested him as an accomplice. After he spent a week in jail, the charge was dropped, but several months later Valentino hit the headlines again as a friend of Mrs. Bianca de Saulles, arrested for murdering her wealthy and socially prominent husband. After he became a star, the police files on Valentino "disappeared," thanks to a handout to the NYPD from Metro, and, like much of his life in New York, the nature of his connection with Mrs. Thym and Mrs. de Saulles remains a gray area. But before Mrs. de Saulles went on trial, Valentino decided to avoid further publicity by leaving New York. He got a job as a dancer in the road company of a musical comedy bound for the Midwest and San Francisco, moved on to Los Angeles, and got his next job at the Vernon Country Club.

When Nazimova snubbed Valentino at the Ship Cafe, the "streak of respectability" that Josephine Hutchinson observed in her seems to have been showing. It was at once understandable and ironic in someone with a not very respectable secret of her own, and equally ironic that Karger also decided to snub the future star of *Four Horsemen*, which would become the most profitable movie in Metro's history. Even more ironic was the result of a chance meeting between Valentino and Jean Acker only twenty-four hours later.

One of the legends that grew up around Nazimova was that (for reasons never satisfactorily explained) she "stage-managed" both Valentino marriages, the first to Jean Acker and the second to Natacha Rambova. But a letter from Nazimova to Edith Luckett makes it clear that in Acker's case she was surprised and angry. "Perhaps you've heard of Jean Acker's marriage? It was the worst thing she had done on top of all the other worst things she has done from the day we arrived here. [Was one of them the affair with Darmond?] You remember how I warned her that I would absolutely break with her if she did not behave? Well, we weren't here 4 weeks [eight, in fact] when she forced me to do it! She married a proffessional [sic] 'lounge lizard'—that's how she herself called him only 1 week before her marriage! Haven't seen her and don't know even if she is still here. . . ."

Two of Valentino's bachelor friends, director Douglas Gerrard and cameraman Paul Ivano, later described the sequel to that standoff at the Ship Cafe. Next evening, Gerrard took Valentino to a party celebrating the end of shooting on another movie, Pauline Frederick's *Madame X*. Jean Acker was also at the party, alone. Both were depressed, Valentino because his mother had recently died and his movie career was not going well, and Acker, according to Ivano, because she had quarreled with "her girlfriend" and "wanted to return to her." (Presumably Darmond wanted Acker to break with Nazimova; Acker had refused and was now regretting it.) Valentino never suspected she was lesbian, Ivano said, and "thought it was a good idea to marry Jean because she knew a lot of people, and that could help his career." She was also attractive, and earning $200 a week. Acker later claimed that she accepted Valentino's sudden proposal "simply because I loved him." But she made this statement in court when she was suing him for separate maintenance. If she loved him, she wouldn't have told Nazimova that she was going to marry a professional lounge lizard, but if she wanted to revenge herself on Nazimova, it was an ideally wounding thing to say. And in her obvious state of emotional confusion, Acker might also have seen the marriage as a way of escape from Nazimova *and* Darmond.

After marrying him on November 5, all Acker wanted was to escape from Valentino. That evening, she allowed the bridegroom to get only as far as the door to her room at the Hollywood Hotel, then ran inside and locked him out. A few hours later, she arrived weeping at the house of

Dorothy Arzner, script girl on
Stronger than Death

Karger and his wife, and said she'd made a terrible mistake. The next day, she reconciled with Darmond and moved into her apartment. Every evening for the following week, Gerrard recalled, Valentino "would call her up but she always declined to meet him." On November 22, he wrote Acker, "I am at a complete loss to understand your conduct towards me," and asked her "to come to her senses." She never answered, and in early December began work on her first film for Metro, *The Roundup*, starring Fatty Arbuckle. It was shot on location at Lone Pine, and when Valentino once again pleaded for permission to come and see her, she answered by telegram: "HOTEL ONLY HAS ROOM FOR THE COMPANY." But when Darmond came to stay, Acker made room in her own room at the Lone Pine Motel.

THE SCRIPT girl on *Stronger than Death,* which opened January 11, 1920, in New York, was twenty-year-old Dorothy Arzner, formerly a script typist at Paramount. She would soon take another step up, to the editing room, where she developed great technical skill. Later, of course, as the only female director in Hollywood during the late twenties and the thirties, Arzner became a feminist icon. More remarkable as a "case" than as a director, she cultivated a stereotypical lesbian image— short-haired, sometimes severe in a suit, shirt, and tie, sometimes breezier in a man's hat, sweater, breeches, and boots—while always expressing indifference to feminism and covering her tracks even more thoroughly than Nazimova. But their affair became known to George Cukor, that great connoisseur of the secret life of Hollywood. As scrupu-

lous as an art expert called in to authenticate a newly discovered painting by an old master, he always separated falsehood from truth before
passing on a story.

According to Cukor, the affair didn't last long. And at this time, anyway, Nazimova had started to make other connections. In *Stronger than
Death* she was due to perform an Indian temple dance, with Dagmar
Godowsky as her attendant, and arranged for Theodore Koslov to give
both of them lessons. One of Koslov's students, Flower Hujer, was prac-
ticing at the barre on a day when Nazimova arrived by herself, "wearing
this marvelous perfume, something like lemon verbena":

> She was known in Hollywood to be bisexual, and I found out
> years later that she had a crush on a few of the girls at the stu-
> dio. She invited one of my friends, named Virginia, to come
> and spend an afternoon with her at her house. And Nazimova
> looked at me and said, "Bring her along too." So I
> went . . . and was thrilled to be a guest there. We spent the af-
> ternoon painting leaves with iridescent colors. Nothing unto-
> ward happened. But at one point she asked Virginia to do
> some oriental movements. So she had her dance in silhouette
> before a bright window shade in a room where all the lights
> were turned off. Then we went home.

Nazimova chose to make *Stronger than Death* after being unable to obtain the rights to Pierre Louÿs's novel *La Femme et le Pantin,* later the
basis of the von Sternberg–Dietrich *The Devil Is a Woman* and Buñuel's
Cet Obscur Objet de Désir. Concha, obsessed with tormenting a lover by
flaunting her promiscuity, and a character whom Buñuel saw as so deeply
conflicted that he used two actresses for the role, would have been Nazimova's most extreme femme fatale. Sigrid, in the novel by I. A. R. Wylie
that became *Stronger than Death,* doesn't begin to compete.

Mathis being unavailable, Nazimova gave Bryant credit for a script
that she all but wrote herself. Her copy of the *The Hermit Doctor of Gaya*
is full of notations, breaking it down into scenes, marking cuts and fade-
outs, underlining dialogue to be used for intertitles. The plot is bizarre,
even for a Nazimova picture. Sigrid ("I am afraid of nothing in word or
deed—except ugliness") is a famous dancer who develops a heart condition and has to give up her career. She travels to a remote British military
outpost in India under the surely mistaken hope of finding a rich husband there. She rejects a lecherous Eurasian merchant, then falls in love
with a poor doctor (Bryant) who treats children and animals and lives in
a hut on the edge of the jungle. The brutal colonel in charge of the outpost whips a crippled dog to death and dies shortly afterward under mys-

terious circumstances, and the doctor is accused of murdering him. The Eurasian tells Sigrid that he knows the identity of the real murderer, but will only reveal it if she marries him. To clear the man she loves, Sigrid consents. But on her wedding night she pulls a gun on her husband, orders him to sit at a table, and keeps him covered until dawn. By then a native mutiny has broken out. Sigrid stops it by distracting the rebels with a temple dance. Although she collapses, love proves stronger than death, and the doctor rescues her from the brink.

The sole surviving print of this movie shows a Nazimova who's gained a few pounds since *The Brat* and looks close to her actual age of forty. She doesn't really attempt to "act" a character who defies characterization, but relies on a show of personality. At her strongest when coolly aggressive, keeping her husband at bay on their wedding night, or raising a contemptuous eyebrow when the colonel orders four native soldiers to be shot for disobedience ("Wasn't the execution a trifle ostentatious, colonel?"), she is less persuasive when obliged to "melt" with love for the uninteresting Bryant. There are two dance scenes. The first is a flashback to Sigrid's farewell performance in Paris, with Nazimova again in Isadora mood, whirling scarves and veils. But the temple dance (with Dagmar visible only in two shots) is mainly wrist-and-finger stuff, hardly energetic enough to bring on a heart attack.

The British outpost in India looks more like an early Spanish settlement in California, but Nazimova evidently approved of the way Metro's contract cameraman Rudolph Bergquist photographed her, for she used him on all her subsequent pictures at the studio. If her appeal in *Stronger than Death* seems hard to account for today, the same is true of Gloria Swanson in Cecil B. De Mille's *Why Change Your Wife?*, another box-office success of 1920. Although a notably plump and absurdly over-dressed Swanson looks ten years older than her actual age of twenty-three in this Jazz Age drama, for contemporary moviegoers she represented an ideal, the chic and sophisticated young American woman, just as Nazimova embodied foreign sexual politics.

But the Nazimova of *Stronger than Death* is in one way atypical. Because of the weight problem, she wears soft, flowing gowns and never displays that extraordinarily supple, slim-hipped, androgynous body. When Darryl Zanuck called her "the quintessential Queen of the Movie Whores," he was certainly not thinking of this picture, or of the over-stylized, nonorgasmic *Camille* and *Salome*, but of some of her now lost films. The scene stills of *Toys of Fate* and *Madonna of the Streets*, and the trailer for *The Redeeming Sin*, suggest three likely contenders.

"The quintessential Queen of the Movie Whores" in Madonna of the Streets

Like Mae West, the only other actress to become a movie star at forty, Nazimova was never beautiful. Nor were most of her younger popular contemporaries, such as Mary Pickford, Colleen Moore, Lillian Gish. Although Norma Talmadge and Mae Murray were pretty in different ways, sweet and tinsel, only Swanson manufactured herself into a beauty through dieting and the advice of Elinor Glyn, who steered her to better designers, hairdressers, and makeup artists. What Nazimova displays in *Stronger than Death* is a more primitive version of the *allure* that startled Broadway and that Djuna Barnes described as a "splendid physical ability to look 'dangerous' and inexact, that look that is necessary to the popular conception of a thoroughly able adventurist." In silent movies there was, quite simply, no one like her. Until Pola Negri, who emerged later that year in the first foreign film to be widely distributed in the U.S.A., Ernst Lubitsch's *Madame Dubarry* (retitled *Passion*). Just as Nazimova had been publicized as Russian to account for her "mystery" (although in fact the Leventon family traced its ancestry to the Levanderas, Sephardic Jews of medieval Spain), Negri's calling card was her Polish gypsy blood. And when Paramount signed Negri to a Hollywood contract, it launched her in one of Nazimova's most successful stage vehicles, *Bella Donna*.

About *Stronger than Death* it only remains to note the very curious relationship between Sigrid and her longtime English female companion, Smithy. A sketchy, incidental figure in the novel, she becomes the object of Sigrid's warmest affection in the movie, kissed and hugged far more frequently than the doctor. Hefty and grizzled, Smithy acts as Sigrid's dresser on tour, as housekeeper and confidante at home, and is fanatically devoted to the woman she describes as "the greatest dancer in the world."

PERHAPS NOT coincidentally, *Stronger than Death* inspired a female admirer of Nazimova to write the words and music of "Alla," which became a best-selling phonograph record and piano roll. From Anita Owen's verse:

> When the stars are shining,
> My heart ceases pining,
> Your soft arms entwining
> Around me steal. . . .

From her refrain:

> Alla my heart is lonely
> I want you only
> Your eyes are e'er before me,
> Alla I'll pray to Allah
> To keep you safe for me.

At the peak of her popularity, Nazimova was even more firmly in the driver's seat at Metro. She wrote Nina soon after *Stronger than Death* finished shooting:

> First 5 weeks of working on the story, then 9 weeks of filming and now I am daily in the projecting room "cutting" it. . . . The trouble is not with the organization [Metro] but in finding a good director, and they are so few that you can count them on one hand. As a class they are an ignorant, conceited lot . . . who simply have acquired no knowledge of continuity and light effects. It is very hard pulling for Ch and me for the actual direction of the film lies practically on our shoulders, and what with writing, acting and cutting—well, if we are not nervous wrecks in a year it will be a miracle. Of course, you know that all the remaining 5 pictures of this contract are bought and have been in our hands [since] the day we signed in June. . . .

In claiming that "Ch" made any serious contribution in any department, Nazimova was of course keeping up the pretense that they were a team in every department. Under the new contract mentioned in the letter, she had her own production unit at Metro, with Bryant appearing on the letterhead as "Manager." But a new figure was about to enter her personal life.

After a series of Young Women (Mercedes, Le Gallienne, Nila Mae, Jean Acker, Dorothy Arzner) came the first of the Young Men to arouse Nazimova's libido since her "marriage." Nineteen-year-old Sam Zimbalist was a projectionist at Metro's East Coast studio who introduced himself to Nazimova when she was in New York for the opening of *Stronger than Death*. A genuine fan as well as genuinely ambitious, Zimbalist explained that he was eager to work in Hollywood. Finding him personally engaging as well as sexually attractive, she followed "the law of impulse" and took Zimbalist back with her on the train to Los Angeles, where she gave him a job as assistant editor for Nazimova Productions.

To Zimbalist, as to her other lovers, Nazimova made it clear that she didn't consider sexual relationships binding, but interludes of pleasure in a life dedicated to work. Although the idol of her school days, George Sand, had done the same thing seventy years earlier, in 1920 it was still a daring approach for a woman, especially to a Young Man half her age. Evidently Nazimova had the fascination and power not to be resented for it, or not for very long. Zimbalist, like his successor Paul Ivano, was picked up, dropped, and then picked up again. But he spoke of Nazimova with great affection to the end of his life, cut short by a heart attack in 1959, when he'd been a successful producer at MGM for over twenty years and was halfway through production of *Ben-Hur*.

Although Nazimova Productions was now entitled to 2 percent of domestic profits, on its next three movies the bonus was purely theoretical. *Heart of a Child*—the first of them, and the first on which Zimbalist worked—was based on a magazine story about an ambitious cockney girl from the London slums who schemed and slept her way to the top, finally marrying a monocled English aristocrat (Bryant) who mistook her for a sweet young thing. Since Mathis was now working with Rex Ingram on *Four Horsemen*, Nazimova again broke down the story into scenes and gave an "Adapted By" credit to Bryant. To direct she chose Ray C. Smallwood, a former cameraman who had directed some of the crowd scenes in *The Red Lantern* and recently made his first movie. He evidently knew about "continuity and light effects," for when *Heart of a Child* opened in New York on April 10, 1920, *The New York Times* noted that Smallwood "appreciates that his medium is moving pictures, [and] in many places he uses pictures effectively where others would use text dully." But, like most of his colleagues, the reviewer found the story "preposterous."

In Madame Peacock, *Nazimova played another
dual role: Broadway star (seen here) and her
actress daughter.*

The downward box-office trend continued with *Madame Peacock* and *Billions,* both directed by Smallwood, and a year later Nazimova had dropped from fourth to twentieth in the annual popularity poll conducted by *Photoplay.*

In *Madame Peacock,* also based on a magazine story, she saw an opportunity to repeat her earlier triumphs in a dual role, and not only wrote but took credit for the adaptation. Determined on a career as an actress, a woman (Nazimova 1) deserts her small-town husband and baby daughter. She becomes a glamorous Broadway star, but eventually a young actress begins to steal her thunder. The newcomer turns out, of course, to be the abandoned daughter (Nazimova 2). But when the movie opened in New York on October 23, 1920, *The New York Times* commented that "*Madame Peacock* will not give anyone an impression of reality," and her performance(s) received generally cool reviews. All that survives of the film is an out-take marked "Sc. 83" on the clapperboard, which certainly gives an impression of the reality of Nazimova's glamour. A head-and-shoulders shot opens on her profile, a turban covering her hair, the contour of her bare shoulders making it clear she's lost weight, her facial contour equally firm and suggesting a woman of around thirty. When she turns directly to the camera, the face looks a few years older, but gorgeously strange. Playing the actress at the height of her success, she is unmistakably The Actress, and her eyes meet the camera eye with the same confident, proprietary gaze that, when she played Salome three years later, they level at the severed head of John the Baptist. But the reality of Nazimova playing her own daughter, of course, is another matter.

Billions had its New York premiere two months later, with only one Nazimova but two Bryants on the credits. Bryant 1 was the leading man; Bryant 2 supposedly adapted this French romantic comedy about a Russian princess who falls in love with an American poet and dissuades him from giving up poetry for the good life when he inherits a fortune. Another critical and box-office failure, the movie provoked a sharp personal attack on Nazimova from *Motion Picture Magazine.* "The whole story is impossible and Nazimova played it impossibly. And not only was Nazimova bad, but nearly everyone else in the cast was bad." The most unkind cut of all came at the end: "Nazimova should do all her future pictures in long shots. This is the only way in which she can make us remember the Nazimova of old."

None of these three movies has survived, and exactly why each was so unpopular remains a mystery. Their stories were obviously no more absurd than the stories of some of Nazimova's greatest successes, *Eye for Eye* and *Stronger than Death.* Several reviews suggest that her acting had grown too mannered, their adjectives of complaint ranging from "eccentric" to "inhuman." Surprisingly, no critic pointed out that, except for one of her roles in *Madame Peacock,* Nazimova continued to play girls in their twenties after she'd turned forty. Or perhaps not so surprisingly, at a time when Mary Pickford was still impersonating juveniles at twenty-eight. But, whereas audiences adored the "Little Mary" persona, it seems they were alienated by the characters Nazimova now chose to play. When Karger summoned Nazimova to his office after the failure of *Billions,* he accused her of losing touch with the public, for whom a Russian princess lecturing a poet on artistic conscience, a ruthless cockney girl, and a cold, selfish actress were all equally remote or unsympathetic. It seems the public also had a problem with Bryant, and Karger shared it: one of the demands he made was that Nazimova replace him with a more popular leading man in her next movie.

Karger also demanded that she replace both Bryant and herself with a "professional" screenwriter, and give Metro the right of story approval. Since Nazimova still owed the studio one more picture, she risked being sued for breach of contract unless she came to terms. But even when she didn't have the stronger hand to play, Nazimova always stood up to pro-

ducers. The unknown foreigner had insisted that Lee Shubert launch her
American career with *Hedda Gabler*. A few years later, dissatisfied with
Shubert, and with her career in crisis, she negotiated her own contract
with the more powerful Charles Frohman. Now, with her box-office appeal on the wane, she agreed to Karger's demands but secured an important concession in return. Once he approved her choice of story, writer,
and leading man, Metro would have no "artistic control" over production and editing. And although Karger vetoed *Hamlet* as Nazimova's next
starring vehicle, in principle he approved *Aphrodite*, probably because
the play had been a great success on Broadway, and a romance set in pre-
Christian Alexandria promised a return to the style of her earlier, exotic
triumphs. What Karger didn't know was that the play sanitized Pierre
Louÿs's novel, and Nazimova intended to return to the original, which
dramatized the cruelty of a pagan culture with some extremely bloody
scenes of murder and torture, and celebrated its pansexuality with an
orgy scene and a lesbian subplot.

To write the script, Nazimova approached Mathis, who found the
subject highly stimulating. For the costumes and sets she turned to
Theodore Koslov, the dancer now beginning to make a second reputation for himself as a designer. In 1917, after his Imperial Russian Ballet
went bankrupt, Koslov had founded a School of Dance in Los Angeles.
De Mille cast him as an Aztec prince in *The Woman God Forgot*, then in
two more pictures for which Koslov also designed his own costumes.
When he gave Nazimova lessons in temple dancing for *Stronger than
Death*, he had just been engaged to work on a fantasy sequence in De
Mille's *Forbidden Fruit*, and showed her some of his sketches. She was
struck by their originality, and a year later engaged Koslov to design a
dream sequence in *Billions*.

For several years, Koslov had been the lover of Natacha Rambova, first
his student and later a member of his short-lived Koslov's Imperial Russian Ballet. Although she taught at his School of Dance, Nazimova never
met her until Koslov sent Rambova over to Metro to deliver the first
sketches for *Aphrodite*. Once again Nazimova was very impressed, but
made a few suggestions for changes in her own costumes, and asked
Rambova to pass them on to Koslov.

Under the circumstances, it had been incredibly arrogant of Koslov to
use Rambova as his delivery girl. Close to breaking point in the relationship anyway, she now had an impulse to betray his secret, and told Nazimova that Koslov was not responsible for the sketches. He had passed
off Rambova's work as his own, as he'd previously done with De Mille

and with Nazimova herself on *Billions.* Then, as Nazimova watched, she proved her point by making the changes on the *Aphrodite* sketches. By the time she finished, Nazimova had decided that the Young Woman was personally no less fascinating than her talent. Forgetting Zimbalist and following "the law of impulse" again, she offered Rambova the job of art director on the movie.

For both Nazimova and Valentino, the emotional brushfire set off by Jean Acker two months previously had almost died down. But by accepting Nazimova's offer, Rambova would cause it to flare up again, and spread.

ALTHOUGH she looked like a Natacha Rambova—tall, slant-eyed, hair braided in "ballerina" style—she was born Winifred Shaughnessy in Salt Lake City, to a Mormon mother and an Irish American colonel. In 1899, Mother Winifred left the colonel and took her two-year-old daughter to San Francisco, where she set herself up as an interior decorator. After divorcing Shaughnessy, she married Edgar de Wolfe, brother of Elsie, a marriage of convenience that gained Edgar a "beard" and Mother Winifred a major professional connection. When Elsie appointed Edgar business manager of her New York office, the couple

*The laying on of hands: Rambova and
Nazimova in 1921*

moved to Manhattan, and Mother Winifred secured several commissions through her sister-in-law. In 1905, at Elsie's suggestion, she sent young Winifred to boarding school in England, and to the Villa Trianon for her long summer vacations, where for surrogate parents the child had Elsie and Marbury and whichever of the two Annes was also in residence. Sometimes Elsie took her to the theatre in Paris, and when young Winifred saw Anna Pavlova in *Swan Lake* she decided that she wanted to become a dancer. Elsie enrolled her in ballet class at the Paris Opera, where she studied until World War I broke out in 1914.

Back in New York with her mother, young Winifred continued her studies at Theodore Koslov's dance studio on 42nd Street. Once a member of Diaghilev's Ballets Russes, Koslov had left the company to form his own. When it went broke, he decided to try his luck in New York, and supported himself as a teacher while trying to raise money to assemble another company. In 1916, he succeeded, and young Winifred, whose name Koslov changed to "Natacha Rambova," joined his new Imperial Russian Ballet. By that time Koslov had become her first lover, and when Mother Winifred heard about it she threatened to charge Koslov with statutory rape and have him deported. But, with Koslov's help, Rambova did a vanishing act, and for six months Mother Winifred's Pinkerton detectives were unable to find her. (She was in England, staying with Koslov's estranged but remarkably accommodating wife.) Finally Rambova sent word that if Mother Winifred would drop the charges she would meet her in Chicago. Mrs. de Wolfe agreed, in the hope of persuading Rambova to give Koslov up. But she failed; and Rambova went back to Koslov, whose Imperial Russian Ballet went broke again a few weeks later.

Koslov, like Orlenev, was a magnetic tyrant and a brilliant performer-teacher. Unlike Orlenev, he had great sexual energy. In 1921, Agnes deMille attended his School of Dance, and later remembered that he was surrounded by a "ménage of females." All, for a while at least, completely in thrall. Even Koslov's wife would still do anything to please him, and Rambova not only accepted her role as just one female in the ménage but agreed to become Koslov's ghost-designer. As a painter and draftsman he was uninteresting, but very interested in the money that working for movies could bring. And although he awakened Rambova's talent as a designer by exploiting it, he was apparently unaware of her growing resentment at his control over her life.

Or perhaps Rambova concealed it. She had also grown frightened of Koslov, and when she perceived Nazimova's offer as a way of escape, she

*Nazimova and Natacha Rambova at The
Garden of Alla. Nazimova's pajama suit was
designed by Rambova.*

planned that escape on a day when he'd gone hunting with De Mille. But
he returned sooner than expected, rifle in hand, as Rambova and a female
friend sat waiting for a taxi. It arrived a moment later, and when Rambova ignored Koslov's order to stay where she was, he fired. She ran to
the next room, and her friend struggled with Koslov long enough for
Rambova to jump out the window and drive off in the cab. Her arrival
at Nazimova's office with bloodstains on her dress, buckshot lodged in
her knee, "in tears and almost hysterical," was witnessed by Paul Ivano,
who'd been engaged as camera assistant on *Aphrodite*.

Michael Morris, the biographer of Rambova whose research uncov-
ered the story of her life with Koslov, believed that she was strictly het-
erosexual and never had an affair with Nazimova. But Cukor insisted
that she did, and Irene Sharaff said it would be very surprising if she
didn't: "*Exactly* what happened between them I don't know for certain,
and nor I suppose does anyone else. But they were both very deeply involved with each other for a while, and they were both sexually free."
And when photographed together they seemed to enjoy creating the impression that they were lovers. But if Nazimova was sexually free because
she recognized the importance of sex in her life, Rambova was sexually

The *"Rabbit Dance"*
in Billions

free because sex never mattered very much to her. Toward men she appears to have been extremely cool—like Mother Winifred, who had married the colonel for his money and Edgar for his connections, and was now the wife of Richard Hudnut, a cosmetics tycoon with an enormous mansion in the Adirondacks and a considerable villa (Château Juan-les-Pins) on the Riviera. Rambova's memoir of her marriage to Valentino is remarkable for its asexuality. She wrote that they "found a common ground for mutual friendship and understanding" because they had both been brought up in Europe, and spoke French and Italian. Not even a sentence to suggest her feelings were romantic, but page after page devoted to Valentino's career and her own part in it. After their divorce, Rambova became increasingly absorbed in Egyptian mythology, Hinduism, Buddhism, and the teachings of Gurdjieff, the philosopher of the paranormal. She came to believe, like Gurdjieff, in the lost continent of Atlantis and the approach of the Aquarian Age. She studied Navajo sand paintings in New Mexico, pre-Columbian culture in Guatemala, and the symbolism of pharaonic scarabs in Egypt. Finally she synthesized all this research and discovered "The Real," as her friend Mercedes de Acosta had discovered The Way. And "The Real," she wrote Mercedes, "brings with it . . . a new kind of ecstasy which far outweighs the false and emotional."

SCENE STILLS, and a contemporary account of Rambova's set for the dream sequence in *Billions,* show that her style as a designer was already formed. A "nocturne in black and silver," it anticipates some of the effects in *Camille* and *Salome,* as well as suggesting that Nazimova and Rambova, at this stage of their lives, shared a taste for Aubrey Beardsley and 1890s "Decadent" art. When the reporter from *Motion Picture World* visited the set that day, Nazimova's costume consisted of "a white suit bordered with crimson poppies" and "a curious mandarin-shaped hat." She led him past a chair labeled JAZZIMOVA to the Garden of Dreams:

> Black walls, merging into the night sky, encircled a pool of water that moved and gleamed with oily sheen like some green reptile crawling from out a clump of golden-splotched bamboo. Silver reeds, edged and shining as swords, pierced through its surface, and Gargantuan flowers bowed silver faces. . . . Whispering together in a group were girls with slender throats and glistening silver hair.

Rambova had completed only a few costume sketches for *Aphrodite* before Metro abruptly canceled the production. Although a press release stated that it was "not suited to the requirements of Madame Nazimova," in reality it was not suited to the requirements of Metro. Karger had been shocked to discover just how perversely erotic and violent a movie Nazimova, Rambova, and Mathis were planning, toning up everything in the novel that had been toned down for Broadway. But he approved another project that Nazimova and Mathis had already discussed, and the three women immediately set to work on a "Paris 1921" version of *Camille.*

The role of Armand Duval could not be cast without Karger's approval, and when *Camille* began preproduction in late February 1921, two weeks before the New York premiere of *Four Horsemen of the Apocalypse,* Rudolph Valentino was still unknown. Mathis, a shrewd politician who was convinced that the picture would make him a major star, went first to Karger to propose Valentino for Armand. He had seen *Four Horsemen* and agreed. So, after Mathis screened it for her, did Nazimova.

When Mathis introduced them, Nazimova behaved as if the incident

Two scenes from the dream sequence in Billions, *designed by Natacha Rambova and bearing her unmistakable signature, but credited to Theodore Koslov*

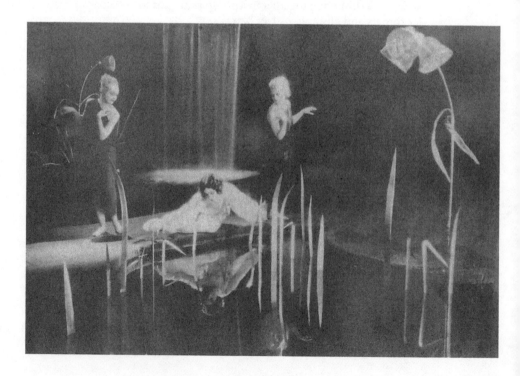

at the Ship Cafe had never occurred, and Valentino was both too polite by nature, and too eager for the chance to act with her, to mention it. But many years later, reduced to playing small parts in Hollywood movies and up to her old trick of rewriting the past, Nazimova claimed credit for launching his career. "He was fat and far too swarthy . . . yet I saw that if he could reduce and pluck his eyebrows, he would be the perfect Latin lover. . . . He was so good [in *Camille*] that he went from that picture into *Four Horsemen*." But in *Four Horsemen,* which of course was made first, Valentino's eyebrows are not bushy enough to need plucking, and he doesn't look overweight. According to Rambova, when Nazimova first introduced her to Valentino, "I found it very difficult to understand why so much fuss was being made to get him for Armand." She thought his hair too slick and pomaded for a naïve young man from the French provinces, and Nazimova ordered him to restyle it for a screen test, which they both found satisfactory. Rambova's account is convincing and unintentionally ironic. It suggests that both women, at the time passionately interested in each other, were interested in Valentino only as a visual object. But it was disingenuous of Rambova to write that she thought, on first seeing him, "Madam at times had strange ideas." By this time she must have known that "Madam" was predisposed in Valentino's favor from the start. Casting him as her leading man was one in the eye for Acker.

For *Camille,* as for *Four Horsemen,* Valentino was paid $350 a week. A clotheshorse frequently in debt to his tailor, he saved money by sharing a two-bedroom apartment at the Hollywood Formosa Apartments with Paul Ivano. Born in 1900, Ivano had been a photographer for the French Signal Corps during World War I, and in 1919 immigrated to the U.S.A. His friendship with Valentino got him the job of technical adviser on the French scenes of *Four Horsemen,* but his ambition was to become a cameraman. Through Valentino he met Bergquist, Nazimova's regular cameraman at Metro, who engaged Ivano as an assistant. And shortly before *Camille* started shooting on March 10, Bryant (who had no role behind or in front of the camera) left for New York, clearing the floor for a Nazimova-Ivano-Rambova-Valentino quadrille.

"Why Rudy fell for her [Rambova] I could never figure out. But then, so did Madame," Patsy Ruth Miller said later. "And it's also a mystery to me why Rudy fell for Jean Acker or Madame for Charles Bryant—a real stinker, by the way." At first, Rambova was equally cool to Valentino and Patsy Ruth: "I had a fairly small part in the film, and she never gave me the time of day, made me feel completely unimportant. But it was her bossiness that got to me—and a lot of other people—most of all. She had a very grand prima-ballerina manner, always walked in flat shoes with her toes pointed out, and wore long skirts because she had lumpy legs." But when Rambova acted the grand prima ballerina to Valentino, it was not only because of her closeness to Nazimova. After her experience with Koslov, she felt threatened by the idea of involvement with another man.

At the time, Patsy Ruth had no idea that Valentino was smitten with Rambova, any more than she suspected Nazimova of being lesbian, something she was still finding hard to believe fifty years later. "I was only sixteen and very innocent then, of course, but, without meaning to boast, very attractive too, so why didn't she ever come on to me?" One reason was Patsy Ruth's innocence. It would have been reckless, even if she'd wanted to, for Nazimova to "come on to" a girl living at home with her solidly middle-class parents. The other reason was Rambova, whom Patsy Ruth disliked too much to admit that Nazimova could have found her more attractive.

When *Four Horsemen* opened in New York a few days before *Camille* started shooting, it became an instant box-office hit and an extraordinary

Happy days at the Garden of Alla pool: Nazimova's future lover Paul Ivano, her current "husband" Charles Bryant, and a visiting Charles Chaplin, c. 1920

Changed partners on location for the Manon Lescaut sequence in Camille. *Left to right: Nazimova and Paul Ivano, unidentified actress, Valentino and Rambova*

Camille. *Nazimova and Valentino ("I wish I were a servant—a dog—that I might care for you.")*

Camille. *With Patsy Ruth
Miller as Nichette.
"A distinctly erotic tenderness."*

personal triumph for Valentino. This was one reason why Rambova began to thaw. With Nazimova's example awakening in her an ambition to produce as well as to design movies, she realized what an asset Valentino could be. The other reason was that she also realized Valentino the man could never be a threat. Her perception was shared by Patsy Ruth, who commented that "he was never the lady-killer type; the ladies killed *him,*" and by Colleen Moore, who attributed Valentino's fascination with women much stronger than himself to the fact that he was "a weak man, and a bit on the stupid side as well."

Adela Rogers St. Johns and other gossip columnists later reported that Nazimova was furious when Rambova and Valentino became lovers; St. Johns even claimed Nazimova warned Valentino that Rambova "would swallow him like a boa constrictor." But this is another legend. Both women were sexually as sophisticated as the Bloomsbury set. Nazimova was the only one of her friends that Rambova invited to the wedding, and shortly after Rambova and Valentino became lovers, Nazimova and the twenty-year-old Ivano began an affair. "Alla preferred women most of the time," Ivano said later, adding that the affair lasted only six

Nazimova and Valentino in the "Paris 1921"
apartment designed by Rambova

months. In fact it continued—on again, off again—for several years, during which Nazimova saw Ivano through hard times by loaning him thousands of dollars that were never repaid. Nazimova later told Glesca that he was "a good lover," and although their eventual parting (on Nazimova's side, at least) was angry, Patsy Ruth remembered them at the time as "very cute together. Paul was very charming, looked very boyish, and Madame used to tease him about being so much younger than she." On location for a scene in which Marguerite and Armand imagine themselves as Manon Lescaut and Des Grieux, the two couples were photographed during their lunch break, a picnic on the grass. Nazimova wears an unbecoming eighteenth-century powdered wig and looks uncharacteristically doll-like, but period costume suits Valentino, who looks as if he knows it. Next to him sits Rambova, enigmatic and faintly amused, wearing a cloche hat. Next to Nazimova sits Ivano, smiling and dapper, a short dark man in the Orlenev-Tynan mold.

When Valentino became Rambova's lover, he moved out of the Formosa Apartments to the two-room bungalow she was renting on Hollywood Boulevard. To save money, Ivano moved in with them, and slept on the couch when not spending the night with Nazimova. He remembered an episode that sheds light on the physical side of the lovers' relationship. At four o'clock one morning, his friend ran out of the bedroom and shouted, "I have killed Natacha!" Ivano woke to see Valentino naked and sweating. "He had an erection. . . . I asked him if he and Natacha had been making whoopee. Rudy said yes, but I should hurry into the bedroom because he thought Natacha was dead." Apparently overpowered by Valentino's passion, her hair "unbound and flowing over the bedsheets," Rambova had fainted. And after that night she started a rather intimidating collection of pet animals, which meant that soon Valentino had to share her with two Great Danes, a bull snake, a monkey, and a lion cub. The lion cub, a female, became deeply attached to her and slept at the foot of their bed. As she no doubt intended, this was hardly conducive to lovemaking. For Ivano, sharing the living room with the rest of the menagerie was hardly conducive to getting a good night's sleep, and he soon moved out.

Meanwhile, Patsy Ruth developed what she viewed as a "mother-daughter relationship" with Nazimova:

> Somehow I always remember myself sitting at Madame's feet. It seemed the natural thing to do: she was so *impressive*, with those incredibly blue eyes, long red nails, long cigarette holder, and that incredible air of self-confidence. When I was first introduced to her, at a dance at the Hollywood Hotel, I sat on a stool while she sat queenlike in a fake Spanish chair, surrounded by courtiers. I'd seen *The Red Lantern* three times, and she was surprised that I admired her so much, because she appealed mainly to older "sophisticated" audiences. When I confided that I hoped to become an actress, she seemed to think I had possibilities. "Maybe I will have a part for you in my next film," she said, and arranged for me to make a test.

After seeing the test, Nazimova cast Patsy Ruth as Nichette, Marguerite's young milliner friend. "Madame became fond of me," Patsy Ruth believed, "partly because she'd never been allowed to be a young girl, and I obviously had. I could never imagine Madame as a young girl, although she could be very playful and very funny and had a pixie side to her wit." But Patsy Ruth had no time for Bryant:

> Very pompous, ultra-British, extremely good-looking, or so people thought at the time. He had a self-important managerial air, but did nothing for Madame except spend her money. I could never imagine what she saw in him, and neither could Rudy. Once Rudy and I were sitting by the pool at her house, and he made some crack about Bryant. Madame overheard

and looked very offended. Rudy quickly dove into the pool. . . .

On another poolside occasion, Patsy Ruth remembered, "Madame, who became very fond of Rudy, told him, 'You have great charm, and that's a wonderful gift, but don't use it for the wrong reasons. Don't think you *have* to charm. It'll get you into trouble.' Madame was right, of course," Patsy Ruth couldn't resist adding. "He charmed Rambova and that got him into a lot of trouble."

Faithful to her image of Patsy Ruth as an uncorrupted child, Nazimova usually discouraged "adult" talk in her presence. "At one of Madame's dinner parties, when Valentino began telling about something that had happened before he came to America, involving himself and a ballerina, Madame cut him off in Italian. He said, 'Oh, *scusi,*' and that was that. And at another dinner, when Eva Le Gallienne had come out to stay with Madame, she started to tell some story about the theatre, then glanced at me and switched to French. But Madame said, with another glance at me, 'Although she speaks it abominably, she understands it quite well,' and that was that again."

When Eva paid her first visit to Hollywood, she hadn't seen Nazimova for three years, and found her much changed. As a "pure," dedicated theatre actress, she had already written off the movie world as corrupt, and all her prejudices were confirmed by seeing Nazimova play to the hilt her role of $13,000-a-week silent-movie queen. (Eva was then earning around $250 a week on Broadway.) At the 8080 Club dinners she felt like an outsider, with Rambova, Mathis, Valentino, and Ivano all in orbit around Nazimova in her new "hostess" costume, black silk pajamas designed by Rambova; and at an all-girl poolside party Eva would not have wanted to be an insider. After ten days, she arranged for a friend to send a telegram summoning her urgently back to New York, and left without even visiting the set of *Camille.*

There, as at the 8080 Club, everyone orbited around Nazimova. Ivano said later that she directed the picture in all but name, and Patsy Ruth confirmed that "we called the nominal director 'poor Mr. Smallwood,' because she gave him so many orders and he had to take them." They would "scrap and argue," according to Smallwood's actress wife, Ethel Grandin, "and Ray was very upset all the time. It made him nervous working with her." And Patsy Ruth saw "Madame turn into a tiny, angry tsarina" when somebody's technical error caused a delay on the set:

> She tongue-lashed everyone, poor Mr. Smallwood included,
> and closed down production for the day. She took me back to
> her house in her limousine and didn't say a word during the

drive. At the house, she asked if I thought she'd behaved badly. I said she'd certainly succeeded in scaring a lot of men. And then she smiled. "Quite a performance, wasn't it?" And as I stared at her, she went on: "But tomorrow I shall apologize very nicely to everyone, and everyone will say, "How wonderful of Nazimova to say she's sorry, what a character she is." Then her smile vanished. "But there'll be no more mistakes on my set."

Valentino was also nervous during *Camille*, but on account of Jean Acker. She had filed suit for separate maintenance, claiming that Valentino deserted *her* immediately after their marriage. Although he hired an attorney to file a cross-complaint, he realized that Acker was out for money and would make humiliating accusations to get it when the case came to court.

Yet, in spite of all the offscreen emotional tension, *Camille* is a very unemotional movie. Onscreen, the opening shot establishes a mood of total artifice, as Nazimova makes her first entrance at the head of a stairway leading down to the lobby of a theatre. Extraordinarily slim, huge curly black wig above a deathly-pale face with bee-stung lips, she wears a gown with a camellia pattern and a black fur train that opens out like a fan. Nothing more remote from a courtesan in the Paris of Dumas or the 1920s can be imagined, and Rambova's set is German expressionist. She based its semicircular stairway, supported by pillars like enormous candlesticks, on the lobby designed for Max Reinhardt's new theatre, the Grosse Schauspielhaus, which had opened two years previously in Berlin. The next scene takes place in an Art Deco no-man's-land. Marguerite's cool and spacious apartment is dominated by three curved archways, the main one separating the living room from the bedroom with a semi-transparent, camellia-patterned curtain. The circular camellia motif recurs in the headboard of Marguerite's round bed and the window that Rambova copied from Nazimova's own bedroom, in the decorations surrounding the archway that leads to the dining room, in light fixtures, mirrors, throw rugs, and fireplace. Later, there's an equally striking, equally abstract casino set, again dominated by three archways. This time the central one separates the gambling tables from a stage where two dancers perform in silhouette behind a scrim. Across the second archway, a gauzy black curtain decorated with white spiderwebs rises to reveal another stage and a black jazz band. Behind the camellia-patterned curtain of the third archway is a bare, melancholy corridor where Marguerite and Armand meet again and part again.

Only the task of designing the lovers' country cottage apparently failed to stimulate Rambova. Her conventionally realistic set breaks the visual style, and its solidity emphasizes the fragile artifice of Nazimova's performance. A bare shoulder shrugging with elegant disdain, bare arms rippling and fluttering like a ballerina's when she dances, a lithe bare back arching when she laughs display a body in remarkably good shape. But Nazimova seems so proud of it that her body language is more narcissistic than seductive, and although a vivid apparition in medium shot, she becomes unexpectedly remote in close-up, when Bergquist's extreme soft focus makes her face almost disappear behind a veil of mist.

Dramatically, Valentino carries the film. As in *Four Horsemen,* he seems a real person rather than the personality manufactured later for *The Sheik.* No doubt this is why Nazimova exercised "artistic control" in the editing room and snipped him out of Marguerite's death scene. But Valentino felt no resentment, only gratitude. "She rehearsed me until she actually got me to act, not to strike poses but to express genuine emotion," he said after seeing the picture. And even though Nazimova brought no genuine emotion to her own performance, only a series of profoundly superficial effects, she brought out the curious submissive streak that made Valentino so susceptible to powerful women, and so right for an Armand who falls to his knees in front of Marguerite and speaks a characteristic Mathis-Nazimova intertitle: "I wish I were a servant—a dog—that I might care for you."

Valentino's submissiveness also allowed Nazimova to pluck his eyebrows, an unnecessary act that slightly feminized him. But when Rambova virtually produced two of his later movies, she took feminization a stage further. For *Monsieur Beaucaire* she pruned Valentino's eyebrows again until they matched her own, placed a beauty spot on his cheek, fitted him with a gleaming silver wig, and decorated its ponytail with a black satin bow tie; for *The Indian Rajah* she costumed him in nothing but pearls, ropes of them twined around his body from neck to toes. In life already "a very sharp dresser," according to Robert Florey, under Rambova's influence he soon developed a taste for "antique florentine rings and heavy chain bracelets."

But even with plucked eyebrows, Nazimova's Armand turns unexpectedly macho when he believes Marguerite has betrayed him. In the casino scene he becomes the brutal avenger and makes *her* submit, first to a violent kiss and then to public humiliation, throwing in her face all the money he's just won. It provides one of the rare "modern" touches in a movie with an opening title that asks, "Why not a Camille of today?" And in the first scene between Marguerite and Nichette, Nazimova fondles and kisses her friend with a distinctly erotic tenderness, giving their relationship a subtext of which Patsy Ruth was unaware. The same subtext between Sigrid and old Smithy in *Stronger than Death* is merely bizarre, but here it titillates because Patsy Ruth responds with such innocent, eager affection.

When *Camille* opened at the Ritz Carlton Theatre in New York on September 12, 1921, Nazimova also titillated the press at a reception in the theatre's Crystal Room after the screening. Wrapped in an opera cloak, her hair cropped short, waving a long cigarette holder, she told one reporter: "I am to play a boy in my next picture." To another, who commented that Marguerite's apartment didn't look like "a real home," she replied: "Women like Camille do not have real homes—they merely have places where they exist. . . . Now come with me and admire the artist who created the settings. She is a charming girl."

Critical reaction was polarized, the daily press on the whole favorable. Carl Sandburg, then a reviewer for the Chicago *Daily News:* "This *Camille* movie is far and away ahead of anything Nazimova was ever seen in when she played the tragedies of the irreckonable [sic] Norse dramatist." No less incomprehensibly, the New York *Mirror* found Nazimova "direct and without affectation." But the fan magazines were hostile, with *Photoplay,* the most influential of them, spearheading the attack: "What has happened to the great actress, the splendid genius, the incomparable artiste? . . . It is not fair to offer the public pictures bearing the name Nazimova that possess nothing that name stands for." *Photoplay* also complained of her "Fiji Island make-up," an odd way to disapprove of someone appearing in extreme whiteface. Her *Camille* image, in fact, had a great influence on Mae Murray, who reproduced it a year later in *Fashion Row.* Wearing a curly black wig to conceal her blond hair, beestung lips in a continuous pout, Mae carried an ermine cloak that trailed behind the skirt of her gown like a train.

Although *Camille* was a moderate box-office success, either Metro did not renew Nazimova's contract (the studio's story) or Nazimova declined to renew it (her story). According to Metro, the company could no longer "cope with her whims and vagaries," and its star had become unbearably autocratic and temperamental. According to Nazimova, Metro wanted to limit her artistic freedom even further, and rejected her idea of filming *A Doll's House.* At an emotional press conference, she explained how important the play had been in her life, and claimed that the famous Polish actress Helena Modjeska had come backstage after a performance, embraced her, and announced, "I came, I saw Nazimova, I was conquered." Metro countered by planting a series of anti-Nazimova stories in the fan magazines. They complained that her extravagant production methods had made *The Red Lantern* and *Stronger than Death* the most expensive movies in the company's history (although *Stronger than Death* looks like one of the cheapest), and that she considered herself "too great" to accept suggestions from directors or screenwriters. Other stories were veiled personal attacks, reports that Nazimova and her friend Natacha Rambova consulted psychics, and that her swimming pool, "crowded with Hollywood ingenues," was illuminated at night by underwater lights.

It was the start of a campaign against a woman who the Hollywood male establishment decided had grown too powerful. And, commercially at least, too successful. Only three of Nazimova's eleven films for Metro lost money, and several were among the studio's most profitable. A cliché of film history is that women were enormously influential in silent movies, the number of female screenwriters being cited as proof. Yet none of them had more than very limited independence. Jeanie MacPherson's situation was typical. She worked for De Mille; all the ideas she brought to him, and all the scripts she wrote, were designed for De Mille to make De Mille movies. Only Nazimova, Rambova, and Mathis achieved real power, and they were unable to keep it for more than a few years. Nazimova and Rambova were undeniably arrogant, but Mathis the expert political operator lasted no longer. (She left Metro to become "editorial director" and "studio manager" at Goldwyn Studios, but when both companies were absorbed into MGM, there was no room for a female executive at the Mayer-Thalberg inn.) And as soon as Nazimova left Metro, Karger ordered a new advertising campaign for *Camille*. Intended to exploit Valentino's success in *Four Horsemen,* it was also a symbolic gesture. As well as giving Valentino top billing, the new posters cut Nazimova down to size by printing her name in much smaller letters.

9

"Money Matters"

1921–1925

A FEW DAYS BEFORE THE NEW YORK PREMIERE
of *Camille,* there was a special screening at the Ritz Carlton Theatre of
J'Accuse, French director Abel Gance's antiwar film. Among those invited
were Nazimova and Valentino, who went out for a drink with Gance
after the screening. In his account of their conversation, Gance made no
mention of Rambova's presence, and since her presence was not something easily overlooked, she must have been otherwise engaged that
evening, most likely with Mother Winifred and Richard Hudnut.

Valentino told Gance that he was unhappy in Hollywood and longed
to work in Europe, where artists were respected. Rambova was the main
influence behind this, of course, but Valentino also felt humiliated by
Metro. Immediately after *Camille* finished shooting, Karger had assigned
him to *The Conquering Power,* and refused to raise his weekly salary from
$350 to $400. When Nazimova echoed Valentino's desire to work in Europe, Gance warned them that producers in France were not as respect-

ful of artists as they imagined. "You're doing well in America," he advised Valentino, "and you should stay." He didn't advise Nazimova, whom he admired, to work with better directors, although he felt she needed them. As a friend of Capellani, he no doubt realized that she wouldn't listen. And Gance turned down Valentino's suggestion that they make a film together in Hollywood. "I didn't like the feel of the place any more than he did. . . . To make a film you must be independent."

Although Gance could not be brought to Hollywood, Nazimova, Rambova, and Valentino had already tried to bring the European art film to Hollywood with *Camille,* and now they determined to try again. But Valentino was forced to wait his turn, desperately in need of money after his recent divorce from Jean Acker, whom the court awarded a single alimony payment of $12,000. June Mathis helped him negotiate a $750-a-week contract with Jesse Lasky's Famous Players company at Paramount, incidentally pioneering the Hollywood package deal when she also persuaded Lasky to buy Blasco Ibañez's latest novel, *Blood and Sand,* with Valentino as star and herself as screenwriter. Lasky agreed, on condition that Valentino's first film for the company would be *The Sheik.* Although Rambova strongly disapproved of the project, Valentino could not afford to refuse.

Before the break with Metro, Nazimova and Rambova had planned to collaborate on two more projects, *A Doll's House* and *Salome.* After every major company refused to finance them, Nazimova decided to produce both films with her own money. Although "lashed by extravagances," she still had over $300,000 in the bank, which granted her a loan of an additional $100,000 when she secured a distribution guarantee from Allied Producers and Distributors Corporation, a subsidiary of United Artists. She signed with Allied against the advice of Robert Florey, whose friends Max Linder and Charles Ray had made similar deals with the company and been wiped out.

Two years earlier, Nazimova had written Nina that Bryant was going to "study hard" so he could become her director. On *A Doll's House* he received his first directing credit, as misleading as the screenplay credit to Peter M. Winters, aka Alla Nazimova, still mindful of *Photoplay's* accusation that she tried "to do too much." When Florey visited the set at the poky Brunton Studios on Melrose Avenue, he noted that Bryant had little to do except call "Lights! Camera! Action!" and thought it just as well. "He was the last man I would choose to direct Ibsen, and the first to do a picture about an English cricket match."

Two problems developed during the first week of shooting, both connected with Nazimova's age. Nora slammed that door quite a few years before she reached forty-two, and Nazimova hoped to age herself down by casting thirty-seven-year-old Wallace Beery as her husband. But at the end of the first week, Beery decided he was miscast, and when she viewed the dailies, Nazimova decided she was badly photographed. The parting with Beery was amicable, for he suggested not only his own replacement, Alan Hale, but a new cameraman, Charles Van Enger, with whom he had recently worked on Maurice Tourneur's *Last of the Mohicans.*

"She [Nazimova] knew nothing about photography," Van Enger said later, "but had perfect confidence in my judgment. . . . I was warned that she was difficult, but she never was—at least not with me or anyone that I know of." He would soon become Lubitsch's cameraman (on *The Marriage Circle, Forbidden Paradise, So This Is Paris,* and *Lady Windermere's Fan*), but remembered that "the two films I did with Nazimova were the most pleasant of all." And on December 8, during the final week of shooting, Nazimova cabled Eva, "VERY HAPPY DOING DOLL'S HOUSE AM SURE YOU WILL LIKE IT BETTER THAN ON THE STAGE NEVER FELT SO ENTHUSIASTIC."

A Doll's House is yet another lost film, but scene stills suggest that one reason for Nazimova's happiness was Van Enger's photography. He made Nazimova look ten years younger, not by obvious soft focus but by subtle control of lighting. In contrast to her Camille, she also looks like a real person. Rambova, although more excited by the visual possibilities of Wilde's *Salome* than by a realistic Ibsen play, designed some effectively simple costumes and supervised construction of the sets, which have an authentically solid, middle-class look. In the final scene, after Nora slams the door, the camera follows her outside to the street. It's snowing. Wearing a fur-trimmed hat and coat and black stockings, and carrying a suitcase, she walks off into a wintry world.

When the movie opened in New York on February 12, 1922, to mainly enthusiastic reviews, it restored Nazimova's prestige as an actress, although some critics detected a sense of strain in the early scenes of Nora as a child-wife, where, according to *The New York Times,* she became "a jumping jack." But in 1920 women had won the right to vote, and in the euphoric years after World War I the character of Nora lost its shock value. Jazz Age audiences took a woman's freedom for granted, and wanted to see how Gloria Swanson and Mae Murray handled it when they got it. *A Doll's House* was a box-office failure in spite of an about-face by *Photoplay,* which congratulated Nazimova for "curbing her Camille tendencies. . . . As Nora, one of the drama's most absorbing women, [she] really acts."

As Nora in A Doll's House, *photographed by Charles Van Enger, who helped Nazimova to look thirtyish at forty-two*

She also acted very successfully when a reporter from *Photoplay* interviewed her at 8080 Sunset. "Adverse criticism of her last Metro pictures cut her sharply," he wrote. "Some thought that her ego was running rampant, unbridled. That is not true. . . . She may not have as clear a perspective or understanding of production as, say, Mary Pickford, but she will gain it or die in valiant defeat. There's a strain in her that will not let her pass up a challenge where her art is concerned. . . . She's a misunderstood woman who wants to be understood."

In person, the interviewer noted, when "the august Madame entered, whistling," the effect was "boyish." She wore her hair in an Eton crop, had on a white Eton collar over a dark blouse, plaid skirt, and flat-heeled brogues, and greeted him with "a handclasp, direct and energetic, which any politician might envy. It's the essence of sincerity." But if this was another lesson Nazimova had learned from meeting Theodore Roosevelt at the White House in 1907, it was also another example of theatre and life as a two-way mirror. Refusing to pass up a challenge or to bridle her ego, she invested $250,000 on a second independent project in spite of the commercial failure of *A Doll's House.*

Nazimova had been determined to play *Salome* since 1906, when

A Doll's House. *With Alan Hale, who replaced Wallace Beery as Tørvald Helmer*

A Doll's House. *Nora and her children*

Orlenev planned to direct it at his theatre in the Bowery, then changed his mind. The play appealed to him partly because it had been banned in Russia, where the church condemned it as sacrilegious, and partly because he saw the author of *The Soul of Man Under Socialism* as a political victim, deliberately silenced by the establishment. Meyerhold had tried unsuccessfully to change the censor's mind in 1908, and *Salome* could not be produced in Russia until after the 1917 revolution, when Alexander Tairov staged an enormously successful production in Moscow.

"I am writing a play," Wilde had told a friend, "about a woman dancing with her bare feet in the blood of a man she has craved for and slain." This was right up Nazimova's alley. For both her and Bryant *Salome* was at once a fable of forbidden love, and a coded personal fantasy. Did Bryant suspect the parallel between his failure to respond sexually and the fate of John the Baptist when he scorned Salome? Nazimova certainly provided a strong hint when she explained to the press that "Salome was willing and eager to give all, [but] her love was repudiated scornfully. Since she could not rule, she was impelled to ruin the life that might have saved her." The feminine instinct "to command and rule that which she loved," Nazimova added, "persists in the race from the legend of Eve to the newest divorce story in the latest issue of today's newspaper."

And Salome herself, according to Nazimova, had a kind of innocence in spite of her savagery, because she was "the one pure creature in a court where sin was abundant." To emphasize the point, she decided to play Salome as a fourteen-year-old girl ("otherwise she would already have been married") brought up in a society ruled by lust. In Wilde's play, Salome's stepfather and the Syrian captain of the palace guard lust after her, but Nazimova widened the circle to show both Salome's mother and a Roman soldier lusting after the Syrian captain. Nazimova also wanted the sets and costumes of the movie to reflect Aubrey Beardsley's illustrations to the published edition of the play. She had a copy of it, as well as an account of Tairov's production that described the sinuous, balletic movements of Alisa Koonen in the title role.

Rambova not only admired Beardsley, whose drawing *La Dame aux Camélias* had inspired Nazimova's first costume in *Camille,* but was no stranger to "the feminine instinct to command and rule." Photographs of Nazimova and Rambova taken during preproduction suggest a pair of conspirators, and Rambova was clearly inspired to create a series of almost hallucinatory ambisexual costumes. For the Syrian captain, black tights, a beaded necklace, and a fine mesh jersey that accentuated his painted nipples. For the Roman soldier, sleeveless lamé armor with a short metallic skirt that left him bare-armed and bare-legged. Tightly curled white wigs and silver lamé loincloths for the black slaves, and for the Negro executioner, a white actor painted gleaming black, a satin loincloth, a string of beads as large as eggs, and a silver sword more than three feet long. The court musicians accompanying Salome's dance were dwarfs in harem pants and plumed helmets, and the court ladies, three of them played by men in drag, sported wigs as elaborate as Marie Antoinette's or RuPaul's.

The most ambitious costume that Rambova designed for Nazimova was for Salome's Dance of the Seven Veils, a pearl-studded gown composed of several layers of semitransparent white silk, with a long train. Nazimova rejected it as totally impractical for dancing, and didn't want to wear the yashmak that went with it. But she definitely wanted to show off her figure, and asked Rambova to create something as form-fitting as the Syrian guard's jersey. Rambova's solution was a sheathlike tunic of white satin, with a rubber lining (specially made by a manufacturer of automobile tires) that clung to her body. Nazimova liked it so much that she asked for another in the same style but dark in color, to wear in the earlier scenes. In every case expense was no object, for Rambova insisted on importing all the fabrics from Maison Lewis in Paris. Initially less costly was her composite set, the banquet hall in Herod's palace separated from the terrace beyond by her trademark archway with gauze curtains. In the banquet hall, smoke drifted up from incense in huge urns, and on the terrace, what looked like an enormous birdcage was the entrance to the cistern where Herod imprisoned John the Baptist. Since all the action took place at night, only the outline of two cypresses was visible in the surrounding darkness. But the set covered a considerable area and needed extra lighting equipment, a total of more than twenty arc lamps and a hundred spotlights.

Salome was shot during January and February 1922, again from a script nominally by Peter M. Winters, with Bryant the nominal director, Van Enger the cameraman, and Paul Ivano his assistant. Ivano remembered that the lighting effects, especially for the court scenes and the "Shadow of Death" that had to fall across the Baptist in the cistern, were time-consuming. "Several times when we were shooting big scenes, we stayed in the studio until four o'clock in the morning and returned at nine." The nights were cold, many of the actors seminaked, and a system of "fifteen immense electric stoves" was improvised to heat the entire stage. Perhaps because so many of the actors wore nothing but loincloths, and

*Forty-two-year-old Nazimova as
a teenage Salome, recorded by
Van Enger's camera, 1922*

either Nazimova or Rambova had the idea that some of the court ladies should be played by men in drag, another legend grew up: the entire cast of the picture was said to be homosexual, in homage to Wilde. According to one of the extras, however, "some of the cast were gay, and some of the extras as well, but there's nothing surprising or unusual about that."

That year, on his first visit to Hollywood, Samson de Brier was taken by friends of one of the gay extras to visit the set, and "persuaded to put on a costume and strike a pose as one of the ladies at Herod's court." Later in the day, the actor playing the Syrian captain was found drunk in his dressing room, and de Brier was asked to change costume and "stand in for him in the background of a couple of shots. But after an hour or two he sobered up."

Before shooting had started, the arrangement between Nazimova and Bryant had been under strain because of her continuing affair with Ivano. Bryant moved out of 8080 Sunset and took rooms at the Hollywood Athletic Club, and when his work as "director" ended, he left for New York. In his luggage was a chin strap that Nazimova had asked him to deliver to Mother Winifred. In her letter of thanks to Nazimova, Mrs.

Salome dances on the terrace designed by Rambova.

Hudnut recommended a new diet that her doctor promised "will absolutely hold back change of life which should not commence with any woman until after fifty, so take heed and start your vitamine diet at once. . . . The reason we are all so anemic is because we haven't the life-giver." The life-giver of the moment was a patented drink called Zoolak, but she later converted to rice, just as, having been born a Mormon, she converted successively to Catholicism, Christian Science, and Theosophy.

Mother Winifred dated her letter May 11, 1922, and was evidently unaware that her daughter was due to marry Valentino two days later, for she made no mention of the fact. Under California law, they were supposed to wait a year, until Valentino's divorce from Jean Acker became final, but Dagmar had advised them to follow her example and get around the law. She had recently married actor Frank Mayo in Mexico, and although Mayo had been granted a divorce from his previous wife only three months earlier, the marriage was recognized as legal when they returned to the United States. On May 12, Rambova and Valentino drove to Palm Springs, followed by Nazimova with Paul Ivano at the wheel of another car, followed by Douglas Gerrard at the wheel of a third. The wedding party spent the night at the house of Dr. Fioretta White, a friend of Rambova's, and next morning crossed the border to Mexicali, where Rambova and Valentino were married at the mayor's house.

After the ceremony, they all returned to Palm Springs, where Valentino received a phone call from the legal department at Paramount, summoning him back to Los Angeles at once. Thomas L. Woolwine, the Los Angeles district attorney, was running for re-election on a morality platform, and as a self-serving political move had decided to charge Valentino with bigamy. On the advice of Valentino's lawyer, Natacha removed herself to New York the next day, and Valentino pleaded guilty in front of a JP, who set bail at $10,000. But it was Saturday, and he had to remain behind bars until Monday, when June Mathis and Douglas Gerrard arrived to pay in cash.

Paramount, of course, could have settled the matter right away but, like Woolwine, was in the business of publicity, and its new star detained behind bars for forty-eight hours made gratifying headlines. By the time the case came to court a week later, Valentino's attorney had conceived an ingenious defense. A marriage could not be said to exist until it was consummated, and he arranged for the wedding guests, as well as Dr. White and her servants at the house, to testify that Rambova had been unwell during the trip and spent the night in a separate bedroom. Ivano and Nazimova were reluctant witnesses, foreigners who ran the risk of deportation if they were exposed as perjurers, and Nazimova actually tried to leave town. Heavily veiled, she was served with a subpoena at Union Station on her way to board the Super Chief. But the defense strategy worked, Valentino was acquitted, and Nazimova left for New York to discuss distribution plans for *Salome* with the executives at Allied.

On July 22, she wrote Eva, now Mercedes' lover and spending the summer with her in France: "I heard you are going to appear in Joan d'Arc and that it is written by a very good friend of yours. You know I wish you only the best in everything and I would love to see you do 'The Maiden.' Hope the play is worthy of her." This was naughty, for it cast doubt on the talent of Eva's "very good friend," who Nazimova knew was the author. (And in fact Nazimova had little regard for Mercedes as a writer.) "I stayed in NY five weeks," the letter continued, "the most terrible five weeks I have experienced in a long time. The rain kills me and lightning and thunder send me into hysterics."

But it was not only thunderstorms that unnerved Nazimova. When Allied refused to set a release date for *Salome*, comments about the delay began to appear in the press, and the New York *Herald* reported that "members of the film gentry are eloquently silent concerning its present whereabouts, or its ultimate destination. . . . What, we repeat, has happened to it? Is it too flagrantly artistic to be profitable?" The writer didn't ask whether the "members of the film gentry" were trying to put Nazimova out of business after the commercial failure of *A Doll's House,* something made obvious by the way they finally marketed it.

At Ivano's suggestion, Nazimova screened *Salome* for the critics, hoping to impress Allied with the reviews. As it happened, they ranged from highly favorable to totally dismissive. Robert E. Sherwood in *Life:* "The persons responsible for *Salome* deserve the whole-souled gratitude of everyone who believes in the possibilities of the movie as an art." Alan Dale in the New York *American:* "Nazimova is witheringly unusual. This is the very apex of her harrowing originality." Thomas Cranen in *The New Republic:* "Degrading and unintelligent. Nazimova has attempted a part for which she has no qualifications. . . . Try as she will, she cannot be seductive. . . . The deadly lure of sex, which haunts the Wilde drama like a subtle poison, is dispelled the instant one beholds her puerile form."

When Allied finally gave *Salome* a very restricted release in February 1923, the only effective feature of its publicity campaign was Rambova's poster. Beardsley's illustrations had a satirical edge, and in his drawing of the moon that hangs above the palace like "a dead woman" in the sky, Wilde's face appears as the Woman in the Moon. In Rambova's elegant adaptation of Beardsley, Nazimova replaces Wilde. But the advertising copy Allied used in conjunction with her poster was a crude promise of sexual titillation, and the mainly youthful audience it attracted was left severely disappointed.

A movie *Salome* is not. In the credits, Nazimova described it as "A Pantomime after the Play by Oscar Wilde," and also said that she conceived it "in the style of the Russian ballet." Obstinately theatrical, the style is derived partly from what she knew of Tairov's production, with its emphasis on ritualized movement and mime, and partly from Beardsley filtered through Rambova. There are some individually striking, powerful shots—the introduction of Herod's court, a huge close-up of Salome's eyes filling the screen with anger, the image of the Baptist in the cistern as he stands in a circle of light with reflected prison bars casting dark stripes across it—but they look frozen, like scene stills. The whole film, in fact, is like a succession of scene stills, and apart from the final scene it lacks dramatic momentum.

Nazimova's performance, even more stylized than in *Camille,* might have worked better in the theatre, for in medium or long shot she lives up to the introductory title defiantly announcing Salome's age. As long as the camera keeps its distance, forty-two manages a vivid impression of a precocious and rather sinister fourteen. Lying on her stomach and impatiently kicking her legs in the air, padding around the cistern entrance and suddenly swinging on the bars, this Salome might grow up into the Hedda Gabler of Galilee. But close shots break the illusion, and she becomes a remarkably well preserved woman in her thirties trying to look younger. Although carefully lit, the face doesn't match the body, whose movements now suggest only a calculated impersonation of adolescence.

For the Dance of the Seven Veils, Nazimova changes tunics, wears a platinum-blond wig, and falls back on her interpretive Isadora-style routine. A choreographer was needed here, for it's low on invention and even lower on sensuality. But then, after she demands the Baptist's head, Nazimova suddenly becomes electrifying and *Salome* turns (at long last) into a movie. Carrying his enormous sword, the enormous executioner disappears into the cistern. Salome waits outside in another change of costume, turban and dramatically flowing cape with a Beardsley design of peacocks. A cut to the cistern, where the executioner confronts the Baptist. Cut back to Salome, whose eyes dilate in orgasm when she hears "something fall." In long shot, the executioner emerges from the cistern, carrying a silver shield with the Baptist's head bathed in a mysterious white light. Salome takes the shield, kneels, and in a loving gesture slowly covers the head with her cape. Intertitle (from Wilde): "Thou wouldst not suffer me to kiss thy mouth, Jokanaan. Well! I will kiss it now!" And Salome's head slowly joins the Baptist's under her cape. Dynamically paced in the editing, it's the only nonstatic scene in the film.

And it gains force from Nigel de Brulier, the only supporting actor of any talent. In a previous scene he has established the Baptist as an obsessed, ascetic presence, similar to the Christ-like figure he played in *Four Horsemen*. But Mitchell Lewis and Rose Dione as Herod and Herodias leer and bicker like vaudeville comics, and Earl Schenck's Syrian, drunk or sober, seems far more responsive to the Roman soldier than to Salome. Dione, a lesbian friend of Nazimova and an understandably unsuccessful actress, was surely cast out of kindness. Perhaps Mitchell and Schenck were needy friends too.

NAZIMOVA had spent more than $400,000 of her own money by the time Allied put *Salome* on the shelf in June 1922. To recover part of her losses she hoped for movie work, but had no offers. Her other option was a return to the theatre, but she had burned too many bridges there as well by "selling out" to Hollywood. Her only offer came from Minnie Maddern Fiske, who proposed they share a season of Ibsen plays. On October 22, she cabled Nazimova that the season would open with Fiske starring in *Pillars of Society,* and "WOULD YOU PLAY MARTHA A BEAUTIFUL SYMPATHETIC ROLE QUITE EQUAL TO MINE OF LONA HESSEL THIS WILL RUN A FEW WEEKS AND WE CAN FOLLOW IT WITH A DOLL'S HOUSE OR ANOTHER IBSEN PLAY OF YOUR CHOICE IN WHICH YOU WOULD HAVE THE LEADING AND I THE SECONDARY ROLE." *A Doll's House* was not the most tactful suggestion, considering the recent commercial failure of Nazimova's film, but in any case she had no intention of sharing a stage with the fifty-seven-year-old Fiske. Her cabled reply, after thanking Fiske for the proposed honor, continued with mounting acerbity: "MY ABSENCE FROM STAGE FOR NEARLY FIVE YEARS DEMANDS MY SINGLE APPEARANCE OTHERWISE WILL BE MISCONSTRUED SURELY YOU UNDERSTAND STOP MOREOVER I AM IN GREAT NEED OF SOMETHING NEW TO ME STOP I HAVE NOTHING NEW TO GIVE IN MY OLD IBSEN PLAYS AM TIRED OF THEM AND AM SURE SO IS EVERYBODY ELSE STOP THOSE I HAVE NOT PLAYED DO NOT INTEREST ME SUFFICIENTLY TO JUSTIFY MY APPEARANCE STOP.

The cable ended with the news that she had chosen "a rather curious and unusual play" for her return to Broadway, although in fact Bryant had found it, and *Dagmar* was most curious or unusual only in being so completely out-of-date. Unable to dissuade Nazimova from making "art films," Bryant believed that a play in the mold of *Bella Donna* would return her to commercial favor. And if Nazimova hadn't so completely lost her way, in art and life, she would never have agreed to spend even more of her own money on the "Charles Bryant Production" that opened at the Selwyn Theatre on January 22, 1923.

This English version of a Hungarian melodrama about a femme-fatale countess (Hungarian in the original *Tilla,* Russian in *Dagmar*) who betrays one lover after another until the last of them murders her, was nominally directed by Bryant, who also played the murderer. It was lurid enough for Alexander Woollcott to remark during intermission, "In the next act Nazimova will strangle her Pekinese," and for Charles Darnton to sum up the critics' view of her performance and the play in the *Evening World:* "She was alluring, gorgeously picturesque and unmistakably dangerous, but there was nothing in her role to make her really interesting."

Ironically, the eight-week run of *Dagmar* was almost concurrent with the first New York season of the Moscow Art Theatre, which opened on January 8 at the Jolson Theatre with *Tsar Fyodor*. It was the same production, with Moskvin and Olga Knipper, that Nazimova had first seen Stanislavsky rehearse by candlelight twenty-five years earlier. Meyerhold was no longer with the company, but little else had changed, including the sets and costumes, which showed their age even more in *The Cherry Orchard*, with Knipper still playing Ranevskaya. Nazimova's first reunion with her past was at a reception given by the Soviet trade delegation, which was headed by Stanislavsky's nephew. Afraid that no one would recognize her, Nazimova didn't go over to introduce herself, but Moskvin caught sight of her and shouted "Alla!" He came over and led her by the hand to Stanislavsky, who embraced her. Then, she recalled later, "Olga Knipper-Tchekhova put her arms around me and said, 'Think of her not coming to see us!' 'Oh,' I said, 'you have forgotten all about me.' They replied, 'We saw everything you did in the movies.' "

Later Stanislavsky wrote Nemirovich, who remained in Moscow: "She has grown old, but is very sweet." (Nazimova was forty-three.) And Bertenson, his business manager, told Rebecca Bernstien, who was the company's publicist for the American tour: "We were all astonished by her success over here. She was a very minor actress in our theatre." In her turn, Nazimova commented to a friend, "I was a much better actress than Knipper, but she was Chekhov's wife and she got the parts."

Stanislavsky was unable to see *Dagmar*, but on opening night sent flowers and a note: "To you, Alla Nazimova, who were with us in our artistic childhood." Later they talked for over an hour one afternoon, and she asked about conditions in Russia. Nazimova herself had once told *Photoplay*, "I have not yet made up my mind whether or not to like Lenin," and more recently a reporter from the New York *Telegram*:

> My old mother lives in Odessa. There is much of hardship and discomfort for her in spite of the help I am able to give her. She knows that I have a comfortable home for her in this country if she will but come, yet she prefers to stay. . . . I have artist friends in Moscow who might come away and find living easier but they will not. How can one explain it except that those with a viewpoint larger than their own petty circle are enthralled by the life in a society which dares to promise freedom for the coming generation?

Nazimova's mother, to whom she occasionally wrote and sent $200 every month, was married and provided for. But her stepmother, Dasha,

was a tubercular widow whose fragile nerves and health had been shattered by the famine of 1921. Wandering the countryside around Yalta in a
vague search for food, she collapsed and died in a ditch. But now, meeting Stanislavsky again at a very uncertain point in her career, it was life in
the Russian theatre that Nazimova wanted to hear about, as if trying to
imagine what it would be like for herself; and, no doubt because he had
decided to stay and come to terms with the Soviet regime, Stanislavsky
was evasive.

In fact, while Nazimova was having her first great success in New York,
with *Hedda Gabler*, Meyerhold's production of the same play opened in
St. Petersburg two days later. It was the start of a new and adventurous
movement in the Russian theatre, encouraged by a relaxation of censorship after the 1905 uprisings. Antirealistic, like Tairov's first productions
a few years later, Meyerhold's theatre was not actor-friendly, more concerned with visual effect than the psychology of character. This would
not have suited Nazimova, nor would the official Soviet style with its emphasis on collectivism. This did suit Stanislavsky's theory of ensemble
acting, although within a few years he would come under attack for staging politically incorrect plays.

Like most of her exiled compatriots, Nazimova had moments of intense nostalgia for Mother Russia, and often talked of going back there
for a visit. Another thing she would obviously have wanted to hear
about, and could obviously never have discussed with Stanislavsky, was
the Soviet regime's attitude toward personal sexuality. But she had recently been reading a book on the French Revolution, and probably suspected that the Soviet leaders were no less puritanical than most
revolutionaries. In fact, the very few works of gay or lesbian literature
that had appeared in Russia since 1917 were ignored by the press, and although the regime had legalized homosexuality between consenting
adults, an official government publication in 1923 defined sexual deviation as mental illness. When Stalin came to power, homosexuality was
criminalized again, and Maxim Gorky, back in favor since the revolution, wrote an article for *Pravda* approving the new law and blaming homosexuality for the rise of fascism. Did Nazimova hear about this from
friends in Russia? Even after she became an American citizen, she said
that she would never go back to Russia again for fear the authorities
would deny her permission to leave. Her American friends found this ir-
rational, and she could never explain it, but perhaps the subconscious
had its reasons.

Nazimova also learned that two members of Stanislavsky's company defected at the end of the New York season. They were helped by Richard Boleslawski, who had left Russia in 1919 and founded the American Laboratory Theatre in New York. The twenty-year-old Akim Tamiroff worked as an office boy there while he learned English, then began playing small parts in Broadway productions, and eventually settled in Hollywood. The forty-seven-year-old Maria Ouspenskaya became a teacher at the Laboratory Theatre. One inch shorter than Nazimova, and also lesbian, she was a formidable presence who entered the classroom wearing a monocle and carrying a pitcher of what looked like water but was in fact gin. Her opening line to the class, delivered without a smile, became famous: "Make for me friendly atmosphere please." Later Ouspenskaya also settled in Hollywood, where she landed a role that Nazimova had hoped to play, the Maharani in *The Rains Came.*

ACTING TOGETHER in *Dagmar,* Nazimova and Bryant continued to play the happy couple. Their marriage survived, she told a reporter, "because we are of vastly different temperaments. . . . He likes to take long walks, adores exercise, while I—well, I abhor it. . . . I want to curl up on the couch to read. So we each do what we please, [and] when we come together, we are fresh for each other." But before the play opened she had written Nina: "All those money matters nearly spoiled our personal lives—Ch's and mine—made me so small and petty and quarrelsome and unjust, and distorted my real attitude toward him. On the other hand it has made Ch into a sort of 'manager,' which he ought not to be." Even though Nazimova never really leveled with her sister, this is peculiarly baffling, for it was Nazimova who encouraged "Ch" to become her business manager. And although the "money matters" referred to her discovery that for years "Ch" had paid all his personal bills out of her salary, which he kept in a separate bank account, she supplied the money to present *Dagmar* as "A Charles Bryant Production."

At the same time, she devised a bizarre secret plan. In 1912, Nazimova had tried through the Russian consulate in New York to obtain a divorce from Golovin so she could marry Bryant. Now she tried again, but in order to get rid of Bryant. Divorced from Golovin, she could go to Europe, announce she had "divorced" Bryant there, and return to the U.S.A. legally single. Bypassing the consulate, she enlisted the help of a cousin in Moscow, Anna Rabinovich-Meisel, who contacted Golovin. He agreed to start proceedings from his end, "but wanted Nazimova to write him herself that she will free him of his vow to obstruct a divorce."

Since she was an exile without Russian papers, Golovin also needed an old passport or travel permit "with a record of the marriage" to establish her identity. Luckily, she had kept the passport with which she entered the U.S.A. under the name "Alla Golovina Nazimova."

Meanwhile, the supposedly happy couple was seldom seen together outside the theatre. Nazimova arrived alone at parties, and made a great impression at Laurette Taylor's house. Laurette liked her guests to perform after dinner, so Nazimova played both parts in the last scene of *Dagmar*, where the countess tries to escape her murderer, and terrorized an audience that included Noël Coward and the Lunts. "My God, Alla, I could never do that!" Laurette exclaimed, and Coward was so impressed that he determined to write a play for her.

Dagmar lasted eight weeks, doing little for Nazimova's prestige or her pocketbook. Early in April, she returned to Hollywood for another try at making quick money in the movies. Bryant came with her, presumably hoping for a piece of the action, but this time the doors were even more firmly closed. In mid-April, while Bryant was driving Nazimova in the Rolls, he collided with a trolley car. "Thrown from the machine," she received a deep gash in her cheek, and was terrified when a surgeon told her it would need several stitches to heal properly. She settled for adhesive tape, which left a welt over three inches long when it was removed a few days later. Mrs. Ella Harris, who specialized in facial peeling and renovation, came to the rescue. Nazimova spent two weeks at her clinic, and "came away not only with the scar removed but with soft, pink skin the texture of velvet."

Although she employed a photographer to take "before and after" pictures and publicize her new face, there were still no movie offers. Convinced that it was time to leave a sinking ship, Bryant returned to New York, then went to England for the summer. During his absence, Nazimova's divorce papers arrived from Russia, recording the decision of a People's Court on May 11, 1923, to dissolve the marriage of "citizeness Leventon Alla Alexandrovna" and Sergius Arkadyevitch Golovin, "consummated between them in the City Church of Bobruysk June 30, 1899."

Nazimova was now free to go ahead with her plan. But she was apparently in no mood to do anything except celebrate Bryant's departure. On June 19 she wrote Eva:

> All I want is to sleep, doze, lie around, and kiss! Don't laugh,
> my dear, but all through winter I coveted so much the sun and
> the caresses that I became greedy! Nothing is enough for me!

I want more and more! . . . It seems to me that not only is it
my house but everything, the sun, the moon, the stars shine
only for me. . . . I drink the beauty around me like a drunk.

A few days later, Bessie Marbury sent Nazimova a two-character one-
act play by her client George Middleton. If she liked it, according to
Bessie, the Keith-Albee vaudeville circuit would book it for a minimum
of eight weeks. *Collusion* was an attack on the New York law under which
divorce could only be granted on the grounds of infidelity. Nazimova's
role was the prostitute whom a man picks up and takes to a hotel room,
having previously arranged for them to be caught in the act by the police. The prostitute discovers his plan and angrily refuses to go along with
it, until the man explains that his wife wants her freedom because she's
fallen in love with another man. This way, he adds, "you are making it
possible for my wife to remain decent." And the prostitute, who can
never be "decent," is deeply moved and sacrifices herself.

Nazimova liked the role and the $3,000-a-week salary that went with
it. She decided to postpone her trip to Europe again, and *Collusion*
opened at the Orpheum in San Francisco on August 25. Her costar was
Herbert Heyes, a minor fallen idol of the silent screen, and the other acts
included performing seals, Egyptian acrobats, and "Miss Juliet," a female
impersonator.

It seems that the on-again, off-again affair with Ivano was off again.
Even if Nazimova had missed his "caresses" in New York, and enjoyed
them on her return, by August she was on again with Sam Zimbalist. He
took a leave of absence from Metro to become her "stage manager" for
the tour. Perhaps because of being in his company, movies and her possible return to them were on Nazimova's mind. "When the synchroniza-
tion of voice with the action on the screen has been perfected," she told
a reporter from the San Francisco *Bulletin,* "no more theatre for Nazimova." In Denver, the feminist Nazimova went into action. "There are
only twelve states [in the U.S.A.] that define prostitution as an act that
is committed by the man as well as the woman," she told the *Colorado
Rocky Mountain News.* "In most states women are punished while the
men who employ them go free." And when she announced her intention
of joining the National Women's Party, a conservative local paper accused Nazimova of being influenced by "the rise of Communism in Russia" and intent on "the tearing down of all the props of society." As she
intended, it was excellent publicity for the play. Business was already
good, but this kind of thing made it even better.

Collusion, retitled *The Unknown Lady,* opened at the Palace in New

York on October 29, and Nazimova took twelve curtain calls. But Catholic groups protested so violently, predicting the play would have "a negative effect on impressionable youth," that E. F. Albee withdrew it after three days, canceled subsequent bookings in Washington and Philadelphia, and paid off Nazimova in full. That same week, Lawrence Langner of the Theatre Guild, which was planning to produce *Saint Joan*, received a letter from Bernard Shaw. He wrote that he'd seen several of Nazimova's movies (which he didn't name) and suggested her for the part. Langner and his associate director, Theresa Helburn, caught Nazimova's final performance in *The Unknown Lady*, and Langner replied:

> [We] are somewhat dubious about her playing the part of Joan. It is not merely a question of age. . . . She has been acting in moving pictures for quite a long time, and that always makes it difficult to get out of habits which are all right for the screen but bad for the stage. I think she is a good second choice, but I believe we can do better.

Ironically, Langner's first choice was Eva. She was unavailable, but in any case would have turned it down, committed to Mercedes' version of the Saint which hadn't yet found a producer. On November 12, Langner wrote Shaw again, incidentally reflecting the current view of Nazimova among "serious" New York producers:

> Joan was a real problem, but I think we have solved it satisfactorily. [By choosing an unknown actress, Winifred Lenihan.] As to Nazimova: We did not reject your suggestion but went into it very thoroughly. She has had a very peculiar career. She commenced in the Yiddish theatres and built up a really fine artistic reputation which was afterwards capitalized by the moving pictures. Since then she has played largely exotic parts. Nobody in the Guild regarded her as eminently satisfactory, but out of deference to your wishes, we saw her in New York and discussed the part with her. It transpired that she was tied up in a music hall engagement for two months, and we were anxious to open with *Joan* during Christmas week. . . .

Because she was anxious to recover more of her personal losses on *A Doll's House* and *Salome,* Nazimova had postponed her trip to Europe yet again and accepted another engagement on the vaudeville circuit, this time at $2,000 a week. On December 23, she opened at the Palace Music Hall in Chicago in a revised and shortened version of Basil Hastings' *That Sort*. With most of the second and third acts jettisoned, "the most notorious woman in Europe" had the stage to herself for almost half an hour, contemplating suicide in a drug-addicted haze until the surprise last-minute arrival of her ex-husband. The play was generally dismissed as trash, but as the Chicago *Post* critic commented: "Strange—or is it?— that some of the worst plays seem to provide the best acting media. . . . Nazimova is the show." She took "insistent" curtain calls. Among the first-night audience was Fannie Hurst, who happened to be in the city. They finally had a dish of five o'clock tea together, but Nazimova's engagement book for January 3, 1924, records nothing more. Two days later, it records her verdict on Mercedes' latest work, *The Dark Light:* "No good." (The play was never produced.) Then she moved on to St. Louis, Kansas City, and San Francisco, where the tour ended in the last week of February.

Sam Zimbalist was not with her this time, having returned to his job at Metro after *The Unknown Lady* closed in New York. They remained friendly but were never lovers again, and Nazimova returned to Ivano. Now that she was no longer the great movie star and hostess, she decided to put The Garden of Alla on the market, but no buyers came forward. "Lashed by extravagances," she closed the house and spent the money she'd earned in vaudeville on building a smaller one on the western edge of the property, imagining the move would be economical in the long run. But she designed a grand entrance to 1438 Havenhurst, wrought-iron driveway gates embossed with a large "N."

If Nazimova had gone to Europe and procured her "divorce" that spring, she could still have spared herself extreme humiliation. She not only delayed once more, but wrote Bryant that she had moved out of 8080 Sunset. From New York, where he was now living in Nazimova's apartment at the Hotel des Artistes, Bryant wrote: "You must certainly have built a fine mansion out there with that $30,000. What are you doing? Starting an organized effort to beautify Hollywood or what?" Since she couldn't sell 8080 Sunset, he advised mortgaging the property, "but only mortgage just what you intend selling with the house. You will need to have an estate engineer make a plan for you showing the exact amount of ground you are selling with it, so that the mortgage will only show just the right amount."

By this time, the press had begun to comment on Bryant's absence from Nazimova's life and Ivano's presence at The Garden of Alla, and it seems that Bryant had discovered her plan for a "divorce." The letter continues with a reproach: "Apparently you have told a great number of people many things. . . . No one need know whether we are together or apart except those that have to know. I really think we are better advised if we let people mind there [sic] own business and keep our affairs to ourselves. . . . If you keep your clever head about things—especially Paul—things will straighten out from lack of curiosity."

Obviously Nazimova had confided in Ivano, but whom else? Almost certainly Dagmar Godowsky and Mae Murray, who could never keep their mouths shut, and perhaps "Norma and Theda" (Talmadge and Bara), with whom her engagement book records a March 19 lunch date, again with no comment. "You will find, Allikins," Bryant warned in the same letter, "that however we try to justify ourselves we can't escape the conventional tar. I know it is easier for me to handle (it always is for a man) but—not a soul gets an inkling out of me." Then, after referring to "the trouble," and the "essential" happiness that he was never able to give Nazimova, Bryant wrote: "In the event of my suddenly getting a job out there [in movies] your situation with Paul makes it hard for me to be in the house with—much as I would enjoy being with you." The solution he proposed was to pretend to be living with Nazimova, who would rent a bungalow at Santa Monica for him and "let it be known as a place we are using over weekends."

But there was no job for Bryant in Hollywood or anywhere else for several years, although "Charles Bryant Productions" maintained an office in the Longacre Building at Broadway and 42nd Street and occasionally announced movie and theatre projects that never materialized. Nor did Nazimova take Bryant's advice about mortgaging 8080 Sunset, because a new "business representative" she hired on May 6 advised against it. Jean Adams had been recommended by an actress named Theodora Warfield, who played a small part in *War Brides* and was now living in Hollywood. Later (too late to help) Nazimova remembered Warfield's telling her that Mrs. Adams was a person "whose honesty was above board and whose managerial abilities would help me to get on my feet."

Mrs. Adams thought that Nazimova should retain complete ownership of her property as long as she could afford to, and for the moment Nazimova could afford to, since she had just received her first movie offer in over a year. It came from Edwin Carewe, who had a producer-director contract with First National, and the deal was for two pictures, for which Nazimova would be paid $25,000 each. (At Metro she had averaged $65,000 a picture.) Determined to erase her "temperamental" reputation, she told the Los Angeles *Times:* "I am glad to be back on the screen. . . . In *Madonna of the Streets* I have one of the greatest opportunities of my career. The role is different from anything I've ever played."

Hardly. The role was routine sin-and-repentance, with Nazimova (aged forty-five) as a girl on the make in the slums of Limehouse, a popular setting since the success of *Broken Blossoms*. She lures a preacher into marriage when he inherits a fortune, leaves him when he gives all the money away to the poor, takes to the streets, and is finally redeemed by the preacher when they meet again by chance. *Madonna of the Streets* opened on October 19 to generally poor reviews. In the Los Angeles *Times,* Harry Carr suggested that Nazimova was trying to recapture the public she had lost after *Salome* with a cheaply sentimental role. "Personally," he wrote, "it gives me gooseflesh to see a woman of her predominant genius doing it." For Nazimova the attempt was particularly demeaning because it failed just as both Natacha Rambova and June Mathis were reaching the peak of success. Rambova was now legally married to Valentino and exerting total control over the production of *Monsieur Beaucaire* at Paramount's Astoria Studios in New York. She had chosen the story, designed the sets and costumes, approved the director and leading actresses, and even insisted that the crew address her as "Madam." Encroaching even further on Nazimova's territory, she invited Stanislavsky to visit the set. (But Stanislavsky privately told his interpreter that Valentino had no idea how to wear period costume and summed up his impressions in one word: "Abominable.") After leaving Metro, Mathis had written the screenplay of *Blood and Sand,* then became an executive at Goldwyn Pictures, where she not only wrote the screenplay for *Ben-Hur* but cast the director and leading players, and was now supervising preproduction in Rome.

And now Nina was doing well enough for their situations to be reversed when Nazimova turned to her sister for help. Before Nazimova left Metro, she had acquired the rights to *The World's Illusion,* a novel by the Austrian Jacob Wasserman, much admired at the time and forgotten today. Then she sold them back to Metro and put the money into *A Doll's House.* Later the rights passed to the newly formed MGM, the result of Loews Inc.'s acquiring and merging Metro, Goldwyn Pictures, and the Mayer Company. After the merger, Nina was promoted to the head of MGM's New York foreign department. "Anything you can do," Nazimova wrote her in June, "to influence MGM to let me play in *World's Illusion* will be helping me realize the only really artistic ambition I have left." Victor Seastrom, she added, was "the only director who can do it, as they would not give it to Stroheim," who was angrily disputing the studio's decision to cut *Greed* from five and a half hours to three. But

Nina wrote back that there was nothing she could do: MGM had placed
The World's Illusion "indefinitely" on the shelf.

Instead, Nazimova accepted $20,000 to appear in *The Redeeming Sin*,
a low-budget lust-and-vengeance melodrama for Vitagraph, before making her second movie for Carewe. "Not the kind of film I like to do, nor
the kind of part I like to play, but I need the money," she told Robert Florey when he visited the set. In fact, it was the kind of part she'd often
played before, an Apache dancer "whose sinuous grace fascinates the un-
derworld of Paris." The director, J. Stuart Blackton, had begun his career
as Thomas Edison's assistant when he invented the Kinetoscope in 1889,
and Florey thought him very old-fashioned. For one of her cabaret numbers, Blackton asked Nazimova to burlesque Salome's dance, with a
painted Halloween pumpkin as the head of John the Baptist, and she
agreed because "she no longer seemed to care what happened." But to
Nina she kept up a front: "I am almost certain it will be a hit. Everyone
in the office is crazy about it—I look about 16. . . ." She looks about
thirty-five in the trailer for *The Redeeming Sin*, which is all that survives
of Nazimova's post-*Salome* silent movies. The trailer doesn't feature her
Salome burlesque, but although Florey felt that "Alla did what she was
told, and no more," she's a forceful presence in the dramatic scenes. As
well as a restraint that critics found missing in *Madonna of the Streets*, she
displays a sexuality that was missing in *Camille* and *Salome*. When *The
Redeeming Sin* opened on January 22, 1925, *The New York Times* commented that the story required "a less heavy hand, [but] Nazimova re-
deems the picture. The fact is, the picture would be a sin without her."

For her second picture with Carewe, Nazimova reluctantly deferred to
his argument that a role with some connection to reality would do more
for her career than another attempt to recycle her exotic past. In *My Son*
she played a fisherman's widow whose son (Mary Pickford's twenty-
seven-year-old brother, Jack) becomes infatuated with a flapper (Constance Bennett in a black satin bathing suit and rope of pearls). The story
itself had little connection to reality, but looked as if it did because
Carewe shot much of the film on location. Cast and crew spent three
weeks on an exterior set that reproduced a New England fishing village
on the northern-California coast near San Francisco, then returned to
Hollywood for the interiors. By the end of shooting, Carewe was so
pleased with Nazimova's performance that he proposed directing her in
a play, but soon afterward he fell in love with the unknown nineteen-
year-old Dolores Del Rio, and occupied himself with launching her
movie career.

*Burlesquing Salome's dance,
one year later, in*
The Redeeming Sin

*As the Apache dancer who "fascinates the under-
world of Paris" in* The Redeeming Sin

IN THE FIRST months of 1924, Eleanora Duse (aged sixty-five, and in poor health) was playing *The Lady from the Sea* and *Ghosts* on an American tour that began in New York and was supposed to end in Los Angeles. *The Illustrated Daily News* had asked Nazimova "to act as our special representative and critic at the Philharmonic auditorium during the three performances to be given here," but halfway through the tour Duse died of pneumonia in Pittsburgh. Nazimova had never met Duse, but Eva had got to know her well and was devastated. On May 12, she wrote Nazimova in need of spiritual comfort: "I can't yet realize that one will never *see* her again—never *hear* her—It is a thought almost too desolate to bear." Nazimova's reply, dated October 8, was written while filming *My Son,* and reflects an abysmally low point in her own life:

> If I knew what to write to you, I would have written long ago—in May, [but] what you need—*this* that I cannot give—is *something that I have not yet found myself.* . . . Love, ambition, work, friendships, charity, everything I turned my hand to gradually lost all charm, all meaning. Oh, I had many "periods," but the worst failure was the period of "giving." Years, years, years—and it invariably ended by disappointment in the one I gave to.

The letter names no names, but apart from Bryant it is most likely referring to Jean Acker; to Rambova, who had become totally preoccupied with managing Valentino's career; and, in the light of what Nazimova writes about her own emotional state, to Ivano as well:

> Even if all the people—women, men—who ever loved me, people I ever loved and lost—even if they all came back to me *such as they had been,* I would be lonely and lost all the same.

Although she hadn't lost Ivano, it seems that she hadn't found real happiness with him. "*How can I help you when I don't know how to help myself?*" the letter continues. The old remedies—music, books, art, "a debauch, a passion"—are no longer enough. "We need a different attitude toward things and people. We must come to the full realization of what we have done. . . . What did I really give? What real value did it have? Can anything of *real value* be thrown away?"

Throughout her life, Eva flirted with the occult, and during her stay at The Garden of Alla while Nazimova was filming *Camille,* she paid a visit to Krotona, a commune of Theosophists and self-styled mystics in the Hollywood hills. Among the inhabitants of this "place of promise"

As Jack Pickford's mother in My Son

with a psychic lotus pond was a man called Rudyard. He impressed Eva, who evidently mentioned him in her letter, for Nazimova writes that she "spent an evening with Rudyard, but the idea of reincarnation does not find me receptive." And although she found Rudyard personally sympathetic, he couldn't help her "to get away from this terrible, terrible feeling of being lost, this walking in mid-air, this loneliness" that nothing could relieve:

> Rudyard says: where there is nothing—there is God. Well, of course. But even God has nothing to do with this. . . . Perhaps it's better to get there all alone, Eva. Without any help. Just thinking. And weighing.

When she described her method of thinking and weighing, Nazimova became what Dagmar called "Russian—*completely.*" Before falling asleep at night, she told herself that, although she enjoyed "my beautiful home, my garden, pool, clothes, my car—money . . . if it came to the point, would I part with this statuette? Or my lovely tapestry? Or my emerald necklace? Or this? Or that? And who would I rather see?" She decided that she wouldn't really miss any of the people she presently saw, or the statuette, or the necklace, but would like to keep the tapestry a *little* longer. Then she closed her eyes, lay "still as memory," and had another

Nazimova, who never learned to drive, poses at the
wheel of her new Stutz, c. 1925.

out-of-body experience, confronting her second self like the fifteen-year-old Alla Leventon meeting Nazimova the actress reflected in a mirror. "I slowly see *myself*, just my face, right close, looking at me, and I find that my own eyes are open—*wide*—and I am looking right into my own eyes. *And I don't have to ask any more questions.* I just look. And I *know*."

But although Nazimova knew that the answer lay "not with prayers, crosses, holy pictures, readings of the Bible, believing in miracles, not with any of the ways we've been brought up with," she could not tell Eva where to find it. How could you describe "feelings that are *only being 'born'?*" And the letter ends:

> We'll go up and down, up and down, but every time we'll go up we'll stay there a little longer. . . . Yes? Whatever comes of it, dear—*it can't be worse than what we know.*

AT A LOW point in her personal life, Nazimova apparently reached a high point in her silent-movie career. When it was released on April 19, 1925, *My Son* earned her some exceptional notices, including a seal of approval from *Photoplay:* "After a career of strange pretensions and exotic posings, Alla does her best acting in this simple offering." Only *Variety* praised everything about the picture except its star: "Nazzy over-acts at times and her grimaces in close-up are not at all pleasant to see." In those days, *Variety* was ventriloquized by the industry, and it seems more than coincidence that, although *My Son* had a modest commercial success, it earned Nazimova no further movie offers.

During April, she was in New York, but not for the opening. (No longer rating gala premieres, Nazimova movies went straight into na-tionwide release.) A few weeks earlier, she had received a letter from Bryant:

> Allikins, if it worries you to sign this don't bother about it. . . .
> I made it up casually so as to pretend to attach no importance
> to it. . . . Sign Alla Nazimova and use the same heavy ink I
> have. . . . I won't use it if I don't have to. . . .

"It" was a document on an old, wrinkled sheet of paper that he wanted Nazimova to pretend to have signed in 1918, when she moved to Holly-wood and began earning $13,000 a week, and it stated that she agreed to pay both her own and Bryant's income taxes in future. In fact, Bryant had filed joint returns for himself and Nazimova as a married couple since 1912. Her plan for a "divorce" had made him nervous that the re-turns might be audited, and he wanted to make sure that, if the IRS de-manded back taxes, Nazimova would have to pay the bulk of them.

Why did Nazimova sign the faked document? Although she had no head for business, she must have realized that it could get her into trou-ble. And since she was no longer in love with Bryant, or her fantasy of an ideal husband, the question raises further questions. Why did she allow him to go on living in her New York apartment? What had made Bryant so certain, in a previous letter, that Nazimova would rent a bungalow in Santa Monica for him if he came out to California? He had given Na-zimova every reason, as she said about Salome, to feel "impelled to ruin the life that might have saved her," and yet she repeatedly agreed to all his demands and postponed carrying out a plan that could set her free.

On the surface at least, Chumps was a gentleman and would never have used the word "blackmail" to his Allikins. But it seems almost cer-tain that he realized he had the whip hand, and let Nazimova know it. If he exposed their false marriage, she would be the big loser, and not only because of her fame. Bryant was in a position to reveal the "other women" as well as the "other men" in her life. (He seemed to be hinting at this by remarking that it would be easier for him to "escape the conventional tar.") For all their genial tone, his letters to Nazimova are full of similar veiled warnings, to "keep your clever head about things," and in the case of the faked document, "I won't use it if I don't have to." His lawyers, Bryant adds, had assured him that the document "will hold even in New York where there are no community laws, [unlike] California." But it seems unnecessary to have mentioned this, unless it was Bryant's way of issuing another warning. If Nazimova "divorced" him, he would have legal rights under the California law of community property.

For two years, Nazimova had worked at an almost frantic pace, three movies and two vaudeville tours bringing in $110,000, minus the $30,000 she blew on 1438 Havenhurst. After finishing *My Son,* she wrote Nina, "I have become very avoracious [sic] and I only think about money," perhaps not only from a need to recoup personal losses but to pay off Bryant when the time came. Early in April, that time seems to have come, and Nazimova arrived in New York on her way to Paris. With Bryant in residence in her apartment, she stayed at the Hotel Chatham, which the press took as confirmation of the rumors it had already printed. Nazimova countered with a claim that she planned to make a film in Paris, and Bryant refused to make any public statement. But in private he told Nazimova that he'd consulted his lawyers about his rights in the event of a supposed divorce, and they believed he was entitled "in the eyes of the public" to 50 percent of everything she owned.

Apart from whatever money remained in her bank account, Nazimova owned two houses in Hollywood, Who-Torok, and the New York apartment. But when she reminded Bryant that he had never paid for anything during their twelve years together, he only joked that the bank account in which he kept all his earnings as an actor was "A Widow's Brief." The joke fell flat, because he had to explain it. Nazimova had never heard the expression, used in Scotland by wives who salted money away for future security. She later told Glesca that Bryant finally settled for the New York apartment and half of her remaining cash in hand.

Nazimova and Bryant never met again. But their final interview left her humiliated, and fearful that, if her plan somehow misfired and a scandal broke, she risked deportation. A few days later, the press reported that Nazimova had applied for American citizenship. It did not report how long she had hesitated over one question on the application form. Asked to state whether she was single, married, or divorced, she finally opted for the truth, writing "divorced," and hoping not to arouse suspicion when she announced another divorce (from Bryant) in two months' time.

Before leaving for Paris on the *Aquitania* on April 27, Nazimova also saw her sister, although it's not known what or how much she told Nina; spent a few days at Who-Torok; talked several times on the phone with Ivano, now occasionally employed as a second cameraman; and wrote Jean Adams, authorizing her to try to sell or at least rent The Garden of Alla. A diary note discovered after Nazimova's death, headed "New York April 1925" and presumably written around the same time, echoes the alienation of her letter to Eva: "My life has no relationship with my inner life. It is outside me. I am alone. How stupid, how unharmonious my life has turned out to be. . . ." And then, in what may be a reference to the meeting with Bryant: "Why do I find myself in circumstances where I have to hide?"

IO

"A Little Lonely"

1925–1928

When I first came to America I had so much luck
it frightened me. . . . And then the luck turned.

—NAZIMOVA

OR TWO DAYS THE CROSSING WAS ROUGH,
and Nazimova noted in her diary, "Swaying from side to side. Headache.
In bed all day. Nearly ill but not quite." The third day was calm. She took
a walk on deck and was recognized by an American woman, Clara
Denby. They hit it off, and Clara introduced Nazimova to her husband,
Harry, a millionaire who had made his fortune in a bizarrely original way,
buying up Chinese pigtails and using the hair to make hairnets. They
seemed intelligent, generous, and kind. "Is kindness, *kindness without expectations,* what I needed?" Nazimova wrote in her diary. "Was this sent
to give me back just what I have lost? . . . By refusing everything *material* Clara and Mr D want to shower upon me—can I make them understand that they are giving me something bigger than what can be
bought?"

She had planned to stay at the Hôtel Montalembert on the Left Bank,
but the Denbys had taken a suite each at the Crillon, and Clara insisted

that Nazimova share hers. When the *Aquitania* docked at Cherbourg, they helped her through a crowd of reporters asking questions about Bryant. "Deny divorcing CB," Nazimova noted, and added, "*Of course.*" (It stopped them from asking further questions.) In Paris the Denbys continued to be unbelievably kind, and confessed they were equally lonely, with few friends they really trusted. "I who have stopped even to *like* people, I who have become suspicious of even a smile given to me. Here, with them, *nothing* is wanted of me. . . . They, people with all the money one can spend—I, a 'famous' actress—both thinking the other has everything and looking like into a mirror—only to see our reflections as constant companions—is this what threw us together?"

"If only," Nazimova wrote after taking a drive in the Bois de Boulogne with Clara, "it did not end 'ugly' . . ." But it did. One evening the Denbys invited her to a "club" in a fashionable quarter of Paris. Very cosmopolitan, known as "The House of All Nations," they said, and formerly patronized by Queen Victoria's son Edward VII. In fact, it was a pansexual whorehouse where customers could either take part in or watch the act of their choice, and the Denbys were passionate voyeurs. Nazimova was not shocked, only disillusioned. As a way of compensating for loneliness, it seemed very second-rate. Next day she moved out of the Crillon to the Hôtel Montalembert, and she never saw the Denbys again.

Falling back on "the old remedies," she started going to art galleries, concerts, and music halls, buying clothes, and seeing an extraordinary number of people. On May 19, she attended the opening of the Folies-Bergère "in Georges Carpentier's party." The boxer's guests included actress Estelle Taylor and her fiancé, Jack Dempsey; actress Carlotta Monterey, who would soon marry Eugene O'Neill; Mae Murray; former queen of the serials, Pearl White; and Sessue Hayakawa. Afterward Nazimova met Raquel Meller, the star of the show, in her dressing room. They all went on to a nightclub and "I danced! Home at 4.30 . . . I *can* laugh, be simple, wholeheartedly contented, enjoy myself!" On May 31, she had dinner with Eva and Mercedes, whose *Jéhanne d'Arc* had finally found a producer in Paris. The play was due to open June 12 at the Odéon Theatre, translated into French by Eva, but Nazimova does not record that she saw it. (It was poorly received, and the relationship between Mercedes and Eva ended soon afterward.) On June 4, Nazimova's forty-sixth birthday, Eva sent forget-me-nots and Ivano arranged for a bouquet of roses to be delivered to her hotel. On July 3, she posed for van Dongen, but the portrait has disappeared, and during June, July, and early August her diary records social engagements with Colleen Moore, the Dolly Sisters, Mistinguett, Prokofiev, Gershwin, Jascha Heifetz, English painter Nina Hamnett, American author Max Eastman, and Baron and Baroness Henri de Rothschild. Still "lashed by extravagances" in spite of having made over half her remaining capital to Bryant, she paid four visits to her favorite couturière, the Russian sculptor-designer Lipska, and her diary records a total expenditure of 11,635 French francs (over $3,000) on Lipska creations.

In July, a letter arrived from Jean Adams. No bids to buy or rent The Garden of Alla, she reported, but an offer from director Lois Weber:

> The only money talk I have had with Miss Weber has been based on your last picture. . . . I have said you would do another picture, however, at thirty thousand. . . . She is the most sound person I have ever talked to and has been stripped of all illusion in this business. AND SHE IS SOLD ON YOU.

In fact, Weber had been stripped of more than illusion. The leading female director in Hollywood from 1915 to the early 1920s believed in making movies "for the Good of the Public Mind," and had a run of successes including *Where Are My Children?* (antiabortion) and *The People vs. John Doe* (anti–capital punishment). Now, after a string of failures, a divorce, and a nervous breakdown, she was desperately trying to reestablish herself. Perhaps Adams, with little experience in the movie business, was unaware of Weber's real situation. But Nazimova evidently knew enough about it, or heard enough about it from Ivano, whom she called every Sunday, to refuse the offer.

Like Eva, who told her friend Anne Kaufman-Schneider, "I don't care to frequent those circles," Nazimova avoided the Paris salons of two famous American lesbian expatriate writers, Gertrude Stein and Natalie Barney. But Mercedes had managed to get invited to one of Barney's afternoons, where she met and became friendly with Dolly Wilde. A witty melancholic, physically voluptuous and emotionally fragile, the twenty-seven-year-old Dolly often arrived at parties dressed as her uncle Oscar. On these occasions she wore a purple swallow-tailed coat, knee breeches, and black stockings, and looked, according to Janet Flanner, "both important and earnest." Since 1921, Dolly had been Barney's lover, but was obliged to share her permanently with the painter Romaine Brooks and temporarily with many others—Barney preached and practiced polygamy. Although Romaine took the situation in her stride, Dolly twice attempted suicide. More often, fortunately, she embarked on a brief affair of her own. One of these, on the authority of George Cukor, was with Nazimova. Since Dolly lived in Paris and never visited America, it almost certainly occurred at this time. Mercedes was there to perform introductions, and Nazimova would have been eager to meet the niece of the author of *Salome*. Temporary consolation for Dolly, of course, and for Nazimova proof that the remedy described in her letter to Eva, "a debauch, a passion," could still relieve the pressure of loneliness. There is no evidence that they saw each other again or stayed in touch after Nazimova left Paris, and according to an unpublished section of Mercedes' autobiography, by 1928 Dolly had become a morphine addict. But she kept a diary throughout the 1920s and '30s, and no doubt recorded her impressions of Nazimova and what they talked about. (Had Dolly seen her in *Salome?*) Unfortunately, the diary has not survived. Dolly left it behind when she fled Paris for London in the spring of 1940. And she died a year later.

"I WANTED to see whether I could really frolic again," Nazimova told reporters when she arrived back in New York on August 20. One of them remarked that she looked as if she'd succeeded, unless another face lift rather than a frolic was responsible. Preliminaries over, the reporters fired questions about her divorce from Bryant, and Nazimova evaded them by changing the subject, listing the people she'd seen in Paris, and repeating, "Here I am back at home—and I'm glad—so glad!" Finally she hurried away with a wave of her new cigarette holder, almost two feet long.

A week later, she was back in Los Angeles for a conference with Jean Adams, who composed a brief press release to the effect that Nazimova had obtained a divorce from Bryant in Paris. It gave no details, and Nazimova refused all interviews on the subject. Not surprisingly, suspicions were aroused, and several newspapers instructed their stringers in France to search for proof. But the gossip columnists paid little attention to the story at first. They had a bigger one on their hands: Rambova's announcement that she was taking a "vacation" from Valentino and leaving for New York to star in a film called *When Love Grows Cold*.

In fact, their marriage was already under strain when Nazimova left for Paris. The Valentino movies supervised by Rambova had cost more and earned less than his earlier successes, and on the domestic front Rambova was no less extravagant. When Valentino was unable to continue the payments on a $175,000 estate that she had persuaded him to buy, he accepted an offer from United Artists to advance him $100,000 on signature of a three-picture contract. But Joseph Schenck, the company chairman, disapproved of Rambova's influence, and added a clause that excluded her from playing any part in future Valentino productions. Rambova felt betrayed; the vacation became a separation, then a divorce; and after her attempt at an acting career failed, she began her journey to The Real.

And by the time Nazimova got back to New York, June Mathis was also out in the cold. Originally a Goldwyn production and inherited by MGM after the merger, *Ben-Hur* had begun shooting in March 1924, but bad weather and labor problems had caused long and costly delays in Rome. Unimpressed by the scenes already shot, Mayer and Irving Thalberg closed down production, then replaced the director and leading man, and fired Mathis from her job as production supervisor as well as ordering a rewrite on her script. Back in Hollywood, Mathis found herself scapegoated for everything that had gone wrong; she never worked in an executive position again. So the reign of an extraordinary triumvirate ended with Mathis back where she started as a free-lance writer, Rambova leaving Hollywood forever, and Nazimova having only one offer when she returned to Los Angeles—a request from De Mille (indignantly refused) to test for a brief supporting role, Mary Magdalene in his forthcoming *The King of Kings.*

In October, she had a phone call from Noël Coward's New York producer, Charles Dillingham. He was sending her a copy of *Easy Virtue,* which he planned to produce on Broadway, and hoped she would like the play and the part. She did, and agreed to return to New York to discuss it. But Nazimova's luck continued to turn: by the time she arrived, another producer had taken over the play and cast Jane Cowl. A few days later, Coward arrived from London. Still hoping to work with Nazimova, he asked her to read *The Queen Was in the Parlour,* which he hoped to sell in New York. This time she didn't like the play, not a comedy but a Ruritanian romance, or the part of a queen who gave up her throne for love, and tactfully explained that it didn't feel "right" for her.

Nazimova's engagement diary for the first two weeks of November 1925 records without comment that she saw Eva in *The Master Builder,* Laurette Taylor in Philip Barry's *In a Garden,* and Nina "for tea." From the 18th to the 24th, when an appointment with "Milliken" is noted, the diary pages are significantly blank. Conrad Milliken was Bryant's attorney, and she saw him again, after three more blank days, on the 28th. A note discovered among Nazimova's posthumous papers fills in the blanks: "For ten days brash headlines had pointed their fingers at me and the incessant telephone shrilled its command to jump through the window."

The first headlines appeared after a local Connecticut newspaper, the New Milford *Gazette,* announced the marriage of Charles Bryant, forty-three, and Marjorie Gilhooley, "a local young woman," twenty-three, on November 16 at the First Congregational Church. The reporter added that neither Bryant nor Gilhooley had been married before. On November 18, the New York papers picked up the story, with headlines ranging from factual—"AUTHORITIES DEMAND PROOF NAZIMOVA WAS NOT FIRST MRS. BRYANT"—to tabloid—"WHAT ABOUT NAZZY?" They also printed statements from the town prosecutor, Frank W. Marsh, and Bryant's attorney. Marsh announced that Bryant had declared himself single when applying for a marriage license, and would be charged with perjury unless he could prove that he told the truth. Milliken announced that his client was prepared to swear under oath that he had never been married before. "When a supposed husband and a supposed wife differ about whether or not they have been married," commented the New York *Daily News,* "Broadway doesn't quite know what to think."

Bryant had always insisted on the need for discretion and promised never to reveal their secret, and Nazimova was stunned by this publicly humiliating betrayal. The increasingly blatant way he bled her for money was humiliating enough, but at least it occurred in private. On that first day, she sat alone in her room at the Buckingham, numb with shock, and when she was finally able to think, thinking suicide. Around six o'clock she was startled by a knock on the door. Paul Bern, one of Irving Thalberg's associate producers at MGM, appeared with a bouquet of yellow roses. They had met a year earlier in New York, and her engagement diary for 1924 records going to the theatre with him. Bern specialized in offering emotional support to actresses in trouble, and insisted on taking Nazimova out on the town that night. "Dinner at the Waldorf," he said. "We will dress. . . ." Seven years later, after he married Jean Harlow and could find only one way out of his own troubles, Nazimova noted in her diary for September 6, 1932: "Paul Bern commits suicide—He of the yellow roses. Remember November 18, 1925."

Evidently Milliken advised Nazimova on how to handle the press, for she refused all interviews until after their second meeting. In her first public statement, to the Los Angeles *Examiner* on December 5, she claimed that she fell in love with Bryant in 1912—"you know how charming and handsome Charles was and is"—and wanted to marry him. But when she was unable "for various reasons" to obtain a divorce from her (unnamed) Russian husband, "the newspapers married me to Bryant, just as last summer they divorced me from him." Nazimova herself had announced both the marriage and the divorce, of course, but the interviewer let it pass. Perhaps her wish "to be decent before man and before my God," a calculated nod to the self-righteous, won him over. And by winning over the *Examiner* she gained a syndicated pardon from all the other Hearst newspapers:

> Now that the world knows all, Nazimova prays that her public will drape the mantle of charity over her past—and forget. She loved much, and she gave much. And even in her despair, she rises to the heights of the thoroughbred when she says, "As for Charles Bryant, may God make him happy."

But in private she cursed him. Milliken had told her that he'd advised Bryant to apply for a marriage license in Mexico or Canada, where no questions about his previous marital status would be asked. Instead he went to New England, which surely proved that he *wanted* to humiliate her.

"Bryant to call," her diary notes on December 16, and "Letter from Bryant" on the 19th. The letter has not survived, nor any comment on the phone call if he made it. But Milliken had revealed a dark, cruel streak in Bryant's nature, and it drove Nazimova to another act of exorcism. Getting Orlenev out of her system had called for screams and rolling about on the floor. To lay Bryant's ghost, she went to Who-Torok for a week and picked out by hand every "alien initial" on her linen. "I am plucking the sting out of the bee," she told her maid as she removed every monogrammed "C" from "sheets, pillowcases, bath towels, tablecloths, napkins and more sheets, pillowcases, bath towels, tablecloths, napkins. . . ." By the time she finished, Bryant had satisfied the town prosecutor that he and Nazimova had never been married, and left for a honeymoon in England with the "local young woman," who in fact came from a moderately wealthy family.

Early in January 1926, Nazimova returned to New York. She had found a play that she liked, *Katerina* by Leonid Andreyev, author of *He Who Gets Slapped,* and hoped to find a producer for it. Several expressed "interest" but left it at that. On January 12, she went with Noël Coward to a performance of Rachmaninoff's opera *Aleko,* with a libretto by Nemirovich, at the Jolson Theatre. It was produced by the Art Theatre Music Studio, which Nemirovich had founded in 1920 and which was now beginning its American tour. After the performance, Nazimova met Nemirovich in the lobby. She hadn't seen him in over twenty years, but hardly drew breath to ask if he would consider staying on in New York to direct her in Andreyev's play. He hesitated, then offered to discuss it next day at his hotel. "We saw it would not be possible to work to-gether—and I cried," Nazimova recorded. Her tears were partly from disappointment, partly because she felt stupid when Nemirovich said that he spoke no English. Wondering why she hadn't asked him about that in the first place, Nazimova attributed it to her being "in a nervous condition, tired, worn out and miserable."

Nazimova was afraid that the Bryant scandal might cause her applica-tion for American citizenship to be denied. She was also obsessed with what she saw as the need to repair her public image. She wrote an auto-biographical piece, *My Own Story,* laundering her past so squeakily clean that no American magazine or newspaper would publish it. She turned down an offer to play Mother Goddam in the first New York production of *The Shanghai Gesture:* "I am sorry. It is a good play. But I could not stand up there on the stage and let them call me Mother Goddam. I would like to, but I could not." At least she was more cogent when Lee Shubert sent an olive branch in the form of an offer to star in a revival of *Becky Sharp.* Take on a role in which Minnie Maddern Fiske had made one of her greatest successes? *Never.*

On January 15, she saw Nina, whose reaction to "WHAT ABOUT NAZZY?" she must have dreaded, but there is no record of what her sister said. Later that month, Nazimova wrote her a letter of which only a frag-ment survives: "He [Bryant] decided to leave when he left. It's been four years since we've had sex and other relations steadily came to an end. It would seem that we are friends—no more—something lukewarm. . . ." But, though keeping up the usual front with her sister, Nazimova was writing a long, bitterly funny, and far from friendly poem about her "neuter relationship" with Bryant (see appendix). "Blahsted burden, sex! Don't talk tommy-rot! / See a doctor? NO!" he exclaims, then advises her, "Have a fling, my deah, with some chappie, but— For our income tax—use tact."

On January 18, Nazimova noted: "No money for K." All "interest" in *Katerina* had evaporated, she hadn't worked in more than a year, and with a bank balance down to less than $25,000, she was committed to spending $1,000 a month on the upkeep of two properties, Who-Torok and The Garden of Alla, as well as $500 a month to support her mother in Odessa, her invalid aunt Lysenka, and the impoverished cousin who had helped her obtain a Russian divorce. For quick money, vaudeville was the only solution. In mid-April, she agreed to revive *That Sort* for two performances a day for two months on the Keith-Albee circuit, opening in Cleveland and closing in Washington.

In Washington she coincided with Edith Luckett, who was on tour with a traveling stock company. Five years earlier, Edith had given birth to a daughter and asked Nazimova to become Nancy's godmother. Nazimova accepted, but saw the baby only once before Edith left Nancy with her sister in Maryland in 1923, and left her husband to go back to the stage. Although only small parts in plays that never reached New York came her way, she was the same rambunctious Edith. "Lucky, you are a darling!" Nazimova wrote a few days later. "I don't know what I would have done without you pm Thursday! I was all gone, no brains, no strength, nothing—you were a godsend, truly."

By June 10, she was back in Los Angeles, where Jean Adams had just rented The Garden of Alla for three months to Beatrice Lillie, who was making her first Hollywood picture, *Exit Smiling*. She also introduced Nazimova to her husband, John, allegedly a partner in a company planning to build a "million dollar hospital" downtown. Business credentials established, Mrs. Adams proceeded to bond. "She said she had been worrying about me frightfully, and because she considered herself the best friend I had on earth, she had given all her thoughts for the past six months only to me. . . ." Then she proposed turning The Garden of Alla into a hotel. In return for a ninety-nine-year lease on the property, including the furniture in 8080 Sunset, Jean Adams guaranteed Nazimova a basic annual payment of $14,500, plus 50 percent of the profits when the hotel opened. Exhausted from the tour and still full of apprehensions, Nazimova saw her new best friend as "a messenger from heaven, and because of this emotional nature of mine . . . I grasped at her proposition without consulting anyone else."

The Garden of Alla had by now come to symbolize Nazimova's "greatest failure" and "the place where I had been so unhappy," the silent-movie career that ended disastrously and her life with Bryant. A few years earlier, she had been earning $13,000 a week, but now she was so desperate for money that $14,500 a year seemed "a very big sum." And she was even "so tired of troubles that I was longing to retire from work altogether." For all these reasons, Nazimova signed an agreement that gave Jean Adams power of attorney over her property, except for the contents of 8080 Sunset: she still felt "a love for my personal things." She even accepted Jean's suggestion to build a new home for herself on Orlando Street, on a lot directly across from the friendly Adams house. Longing for a home somewhere, "because as a child I had been deprived of a real home," knowing that she could soon pay for it with a final vaudeville tour, Nazimova gave Jean Adams another power of attorney and $7,500 to buy the lot.

Paul Ivano was away at the time, on location in Monterey as von Sternberg's cameraman on *Woman of the Sea*, a movie that Chaplin produced and for unexplained reasons decided not to release. But even if Nazimova had consulted him, Ivano would probably have approved both schemes. When he met Jean and John Adams a few months later and began to see them quite often, he was as slow as Nazimova to see through them.

On June 27, she had a moment of doubt, but only a moment, when Jean said she needed $30,000 right away because the mortgage she'd taken out on The Garden of Alla was not sufficient to cover all her initial expenses. Seeing Nazimova waver, Jean began to cry, confessed that she was not legally married since the first Mrs. Adams had refused to divorce her husband, that Mr. Adams owed the IRS back taxes, and his "million dollar hospital" deal had fallen through. For the future of their two children, she had to make the Garden of Alla hotel a success. "But when the woman is more successful than the man," said Jean, "there's always jealousy and friction in the house. I'm sure after your experience with Mr. Bryant you know what I mean."

As Jean was no doubt aware, Nazimova's experience with Mr. Bryant included a demand from the IRS to pay his back taxes. When the IRS first questioned Bryant on all the joint returns that he had filed in Nazimova's name, he produced the 1918 agreement in which she assumed full responsibility for his taxes. Frightened to confess to signing a document she knew to be fake, Nazimova paid up for both of them. Perhaps she had just written the check when Patsy Ruth came over and found her "on her big round bed, crying, truly desolate," and mistook it for a sign that Nazimova still "truly loved" Bryant.

"To bank with Jean Adams," the diary records on June 28. That day she handed Jean $10,000, all she could afford for the moment. The entry for June 30 reads, "Appointment with Joseph Schenck." Now married to her friend and admirer Norma Talmadge, he had called Nazimova to offer her a job as special consultant to United Artists on projects for his wife and other contract stars, including Valentino and Gloria Swanson. Nazimova asked for time to think it over, and decided to talk it over with her new best friend. Jean thought it a wonderful idea, and when Nazimova called Schenck back, he made the appointment for the 30th:

> What happened during the next three days I do not know, but . . . Mr. and Mrs. Adams drove up with me to the studio and waited in their car opposite Mr. Schenck's office. The secretary in the waiting room told me Mr. Schenck would see me

immediately, and I waited for over an hour when a very per-
plexed and embarrassed man (I forget his name) said Mr.
Schenck was very sorry but had to leave with his lawyer on
very important business.

Jean and her husband expressed great indignation when Nazimova
told them what had happened, but she felt "so humbled and yet so
proud" that she never mentioned the subject to Schenck or Norma, who
in their turn "never spoke a word to me about the business again." Later
(too late), she realized that Jean and her husband saw Schenck as a threat.
A regular paycheck from United Artists would lessen Nazimova's depen-
dence on them, and trusty Jean must have sabotaged the deal—most
likely by warning Schenck that Nazimova was in an emotionally unsta-
ble condition, something he would have been too embarrassed to discuss
with her.

Toward the end of July, Nazimova was in fact close to nervous collapse
and running a high fever. Jean sent for a doctor, who diagnosed mumps.
But she still held Nazimova to the terms of their agreement, under which
she had to vacate 1438 Havenhurst by August 1. On July 30, while she lay
in bed, moving men arrived to pack up her belongings and put them in
storage. On July 31, Beatrice Lillie moved out of 8080 Sunset, and the
same moving men emptied the house of its furniture. On the morning
of August 1, Nazimova moved into the guest room at her friend Rose
Dione's Hollywood bungalow, and a demolition crew started to bulldoze
1438 Havenhurst. Jean remained "very solicitous, had a doctor come in
and do everything to put me on my feet so that I should be well and leave
for New York." She was impatient, of course, for Nazimova to get another job in vaudeville and come up with the remaining $20,000 for
"initial expenses."

While Nazimova recovered from mumps in Rose Dione's bungalow,
Rudolph Valentino failed to recover from complications following
surgery for a ruptured gastric ulcer at the Polyclinic Hospital in New
York. He died on August 23 and lay in state for three days, attracting
huge crowds. Although Rambova lived in New York, she did not go to
the funeral service on August 30. Under the influence of Mother
Winifred, she had begun attending séances with a medium who claimed
to be in contact with the spirit of Madame Blavatsky. Valentino, her
spirit assured the medium, who assured Rambova and Mrs. Hudnut, was
now reborn on a higher and happier astral plane. As for his body, after
being transported to Los Angeles for another funeral service, it was
claimed by the third member of the triumvirate, June Mathis, who
placed it in a vault she owned at Hollywood Park Memorial Cemetery.

STILL WEAKENED, still trusting, still dreaming of a new life in a new home, Nazimova arrived in New York on September 10 and retired to bed at the Hotel Buckingham for three days, during which she read two novels by Schnitzler and a biography of Liszt and talked on the phone with Edith Luckett, Nina, and Noël Coward. Out and about again, she went with Mercedes to see Garbo's first MGM movie, *The Torrent,* and met with a vaudeville agent, Jenie Jacobs. On October 7, she noted, "Paul arrives," and on the 16th, "Paul leaves for Rio," presumably on location for a movie. On the 24th, she read a one-act play called *Woman of the Earth,* sent by Jenie Jacobs with an accompanying offer to tour it on the Orpheum circuit. By now more of a draw in vaudeville than on Broadway, Nazimova could demand and get a weekly salary of $2,500, and on November 1 she started rehearsing a drama as lurid as any of her silent movies. A gypsy girl kills her faithless lover, then discovers that she's pregnant with his child and seeks absolution from a priest who just happens to be her dead lover's brother.

Cast in a small role was the young actress Isabel Hill, who "quickly became friends" with Nazimova during rehearsals. For the November 10 opening, "we went by sleeper together to Chicago—shared the drawing room—had fun on the way and so on." Exactly what kind of fun is uncertain. During an interview taped in 1975, a few years before she died, Isabel became skittish at times. "We went everywhere together," she continued. "I still feel very emotional about her." Isabel also remembered that the other performers on the bill "adored Alla," who was particularly fond of a female impersonator named Bobby.

One evening Nazimova told Isabel that she never wanted "possessiveness" in a relationship, but seldom escaped it. "Everybody wanted to be possessive with Alla. That was the trouble. She said to me with a laugh, 'But do you realize what a marvelous relationship *we* have? We don't talk so much—we're just *there.*' At the same time, she never wanted to be alone. Frightened of it."

Nazimova also believed this vaudeville tour would be her last and she would perhaps give up acting forever. She began staying in budget hotels so she could "put every cent she had," according to Isabel, into the hotel that would set her free. By mid-December, she had sent Jean Adams over $15,000. Christmas week, *Woman of the Earth* played three performances a day in Oakland, and a reporter from the *Post Inquirer* who interviewed Nazimova in her dressing room found "a sweet and friendly woman, a little lonely." On the dressing table stood "a tiny tree, all trimmed and weighted with cake-candles," sent by Edith on behalf of five-year-old Nancy. But after six consecutive performances over the holidays, Nazimova almost lost her voice. For the seventh, she asked her stage manager to sit in the last row of the mezzanine. A reporter from the Oakland *Tribune* overheard him assure Nazimova that the audience heard every word. "Fine!" she said. "I tricked them. I used low tones till they cracked, then I changed to middle register, then to falsetto, then back again." After a moment, surely with one eye on the reporter, she added: "The audience must never know I suffer in playing Azah. They must think of her as she is, and not be thinking about Nazimova the actress who has a sore throat."

"Nazimova the actress" sounded far from ready that night to give up the theatre, or the theatre of life. Even though, as she remembered later, "my fantastically inclined mind [was] building castles in the air" because the Garden of Alla hotel was scheduled to open on January 8, 1927. And by a fortunate coincidence, she would be in Los Angeles that week: *Woman of the Earth* was due to open at the Orpheum on January 3.

Traveling with Isabel by overnight train from San Francisco, she was met at Union Station on the morning of January 2 by Jean Adams, and the three of them drove straight to the hotel. As a sign at the entrance proclaimed, The Garden of Alla was now The Garden of Allah. (Jean had a last-minute inspiration when she saw the title of Robert Hichens' bestselling novel, advertising Rex Ingram's forthcoming movie, on billboards all over town.) Although Nazimova detested the new name, everything else pleased her. The house at 8080 Sunset was now the hotel's administration center, its exterior unchanged, its interior remodeled to create a lobby, two "lounging rooms," a "dining room de luxe," and bedroom suites on the second floor. Nearby, the pool had been left intact but was now surrounded by twenty-four guest bungalows, which Jean referred to as "Spanish villas." Much of the original landscaping was also intact, and when Nazimova congratulated her on the total effect, Jean correctly judged it a good moment to ask for a "final" $12,500 to settle some unpaid bills.

Since *Woman of the Earth* ended its engagement at the Orpheum on January 6, and its next booking was in Denver a week later, Nazimova and Isabel moved into Bungalow 24 before the hotel's gala opening. Isabel, who apparently saw no reason to distrust Jean Adams, remembered having "a wonderful time." Among the Hollywood celebrities were Clara Bow and Gilbert Roland; MGM screenwriter Frances Marion and her husband, cowboy star Fred Thomson; and Nazimova's old acquaintance

Lilyan Tashman with (in a marriage of convenience for both of them) her husband, Edmund Lowe. From New York, and in Hollywood for a magazine assignment, was Julia Ross with her ten-year-old son, Robert L. Green. A former Ziegfeld Girl and now a leading model, she had first met Nazimova backstage after a performance of the 1918 *Follies*. According to Robert, "I'd be the first person to tell you my mother wasn't completely straight, but she *was*," and she never realized that Nazimova had a strong crush on her. "Many people were quite hazy about homosexuality then," Robert has stated, and Julia was flattered by the attention of a famous actress. At this time Robert was a child radio star, and not quite precocious enough to realize there was something ambiguous in the way the three of them reclined on his mother's bed with their arms around each other. With a crush of his own, on Fred Thomson, he begged Nazimova for an introduction, which became his most vivid memory of The Garden of Allah.

Among the social celebrities at the party were two of the brightest of England's Bright Young People, Lady Diana Manners and Iris Tree. Iris provided an unexpected link to Nazimova's past, for she was the daughter of Sir Herbert Beerbohm Tree, who had taken part in the benefit matinee for the St. Petersburg Players at the Haymarket Theatre in 1905. And as the link to Nazimova's future, Jean sat up with her the following night for a long heart-to-heart talk. For both of them, she said, the hotel would bring not just "money and income, bricks and mortar, but spiritual freedom and independence." From now on they were partners, fifty-fifty, "two independent women working out their own salvation."

No mean player herself in the theatre of life, Jean Adams left Nazimova with "unlimited faith" in her honesty, and when she boarded the train for Denver, "my head was swimming. I saw a brilliant future, I could live beautifully . . . and perhaps still find personal happiness." After playing Denver, Minneapolis, and Chicago, Nazimova arrived in New York on January 30, was met by Mercedes carrying a Welcome Home sign, and opened *Woman of the Earth* at the Palace on February 1. D. W. Griffith was in the audience, and several newspapers reported next day that he stood up and shouted "Bravo!" According to Nazimova's diary, "After performance came D. W. Griffith in dressing room. (BRAVO 4 times from front, the repeated applause)." A mysterious comment follows: "God took a knife to find my heart. . . ." Although she did not record their conversation, stories appeared in the press that he wanted to make a film of the play with Nazimova. This seems likely, for it was the kind of overheated emotional melodrama Griffith admired, but by 1927 he had lost his movie audience and was considered a commercial risk. The project never materialized.

A few nights later, Noël Coward saw the play. "You were obvious enough to please anybody in the world," he told Nazimova, "but your performance was crammed with subtleties." Perhaps the compliment was intentionally ambiguous. Josephine Hutchinson remembered the performance as "terrible. So broad and cheap. She played to the hilt and beyond it. It harmed her reputation." But twenty-two-year-old Val Lewton, who had just finished his first novel, wrote his aunt: "It was just great. . . . The very first note of your voice offstage got the audience, everyone, it was like a shock, no, more like fear or love, for it put a hollow in one's stomach."

All Nazimova remembered was that she "worked harder than ever in my life before and the nervous strain I was under was telling on me." After three weeks at the Palace, she played Boston, then Buffalo, where on March 10 trusty Jean wired an urgent request for another "final" $10,000, promising to repay it with 6-percent interest. Nazimova's "unlimited faith" remained unshaken, but since she had only around $5,000 left in the bank, she sent $2,500 and told Jean to use the power of attorney to sell her lot on Orlando Street.

Back in New York, she learned that Jenie Jacobs had arranged a four-week booking for *Woman of the Earth* at the Coliseum in London, beginning May 25. Although Nazimova's salary would be much lower, and her bank balance was dwindling fast, she accepted it in default of any other offers and looked forward to taking a vacation in Europe at the end of the run. But the first annual payment of $14,500 on the Garden of Allah lease would become due on June 25, and she wrote Jean Adams to be sure to pay it promptly, for she might need extra money in Europe. Jean wrote back telling Nazimova not to worry—business at the hotel couldn't be better—and wished her "one grand glorious time."

Before leaving for London, Nazimova went alone on April 11 to see *Cradle Song,* one of the productions in the opening season of Eva Le Gallienne's Civic Repertory Theatre. Perhaps Nazimova had told Eva about Stanislavsky's use of drama students as unpaid extras, for she included in the company a few young hopefuls whose "payment" for appearing in crowd scenes was the privilege of watching rehearsals. Among them was nineteen-year-old Glesca Marshall, who had heard that Nazimova would be in the audience that evening and "planned to be at the theatre to catch a glimpse of the great actress." She sat alone in the balcony, and after the final curtain looked down to see Nazimova, in a dark suit and furred

Cossack cap, walking along the aisle toward a door that led backstage: "I thought to myself, *There she goes.*"

On May 2, Nazimova wrote Jenie Jacobs that she feared the press would ask embarrassing personal questions when she arrived in London: "I suppose it was my early training in Russia where I was taught to keep my private life and my work separate—and it is this curiosity about my private life that I resent so." In the past, her letter continued, she never had to worry about business matters or "anything outside of my work. . . . *It is this protection against people and things that I miss so much.*"

Until the "WHAT ABOUT NAZZY?" headlines, it seems never to have occurred to Nazimova that she could become a victim of reality, and until he betrayed her, Bryant supplied the "protection" that she missed. In business matters she believed that she'd found a substitute in Jean Adams, and she now appealed to Jenie Jacobs for help in safeguarding her public image. Although Jacobs did her a service by persuading the London *Sunday Express* to publish *My Own Story,* she also convinced her that it was necessary to make a "star" impression in Britain. In spite of her depleted bank account, Nazimova followed instructions to ship her Rolls-Royce from Hollywood to London, travel with a maid, and stay at the Ritz.

Ada Scobie, her former maid, was lured out of retirement by a free trip to the country of her birth. But Nazimova sailed on May 11 without Isabel; the only other member of the company engaged by the London producer was John Dobbie, who played the priest. Arriving at the Ritz, she was expected to attend a "press tea for fifty guests," but pleaded exhaustion and told the desk clerk not to put through any phone calls. Two days later, when she agreed to face the press, Nazimova's fears proved unjustified. The reporters treated her with great respect, the Coliseum audience gave her a standing ovation on opening night, and the Manchester *Guardian* paid high-flown tribute next day: "She [Nazimova] and Chaplin became, and have remained, the giants of the screen, because they alone created for themselves a distinct medium of mimic impression, moulding themselves to the Kinema and the Kinema to them." Beside the "genius" of Nazimova, the reviewer added, Mary Pickford had only "talent."

On the same bill with Nazimova was Helen Morgan, "not yet famous but just unhappy. I was enchanted by her song Blue Birds, and she cried copiously at each of my performances, because she too dreamed of being an actress on the 'legitimate' stage. (Dear little hands.)" Nazimova's diary also commented tersely, "CB in the air," when Mercedes arrived in her suite at the Ritz one Sunday evening, bringing not only champagne and caviar but J. B. Fagan, author of *Bella Donna,* and his wife, Bryant's sister. But a friendship sprang up, and she went to two dinners at the Fagans' house, one with Mrs. Pat Campbell, Somerset Maugham, and Mercedes, another with Katharine Cornell and Guthrie McClintic. On June 15, Nazimova noted, "Maurice Sterne. Now at Hotel Savoy!!!," without recording whether they saw each other. And with Ada Scobie she took a trip down memory lane, in her chauffeur-driven Rolls, to the dingy Whitechapel hotel where she had stayed with Orlenev "in a dark cubbyhole, starving for an ideal." It was shuttered, and "barring me at the entrance door was a moustached poster of Nazimova in an old movie." The lettering was tattered, but she could make out its title: "*The Redeeming Sin.* Retribution? . . ."

When *Woman of the Earth* closed, Ada went off to visit relatives and Nazimova took herself, Rolls, and chauffeur to Paris by way of the Southampton–Le Havre ferry. The rough crossing made her seasick, and although Paul Ivano was waiting at the quay, "the first look at that droop-shouldered figure made me howl silently with helpless fury and I wished I could turn back and be seasick all over again and drift and drift to

With director J. Stuart Blackton of
The Redeeming Sin, *1924*

nowhere!" On Nazimova's side, at least, the relationship was going sharply downhill. During their week in Paris, three different comments appear in her diary beside Paul's name: "Boring!," "When will it ever end?," and "Same old problem, insoluble. All joy taken out." Her bad humor was probably intensified by the fact that the $14,500 that Jean Adams owed her was now overdue. None of it had been paid into Nazimova's bank account in Los Angeles, and the $2,000 that Nazimova had asked Jean to wire to Paris had not arrived.

"Worried, but still trusting," she cabled Jean to send $2,000 to a bank in Nice, where she arrived with Ivano on July 10. At the Negresco Hotel a reply awaited her: "Money sent to Paris." But there was no trace of it. Preferring to blame the bank rather than believe Jean had never sent the money, Nazimova decided to continue to Montreux. They arrived in a snowstorm, which made a pilgrimage to the lake impossible, and she ordered the disgruntled chauffeur to turn around and drive straight back over the Alps to Nice. "Muddled and bored to distraction by my companion," she wondered if "somewhere along the road I'd missed my love. Like Joseph of Damascus in 'The Brook Kerith' who looked for Jesus fervently and passed the King of Kings because He seemed a ragged wanderer. I may have done the same because I am nearsighted."

Shortly afterward, Ivano left for California. To go to work on a movie, or because she dismissed him? The diary doesn't say, nor does it mention the dramatically sudden death that month of the Metro triumvirate's third member. On July 26, June Mathis went with her mother to see a Broadway play called *The Squall*. Halfway through the last act, according to the *Times*, " 'Oh mother, I'm dying, I'm dying,' cried a woman's voice, and Miss Mathis was seen throwing her arms about her mother and sobbing convulsively. Scores of persons rose from their seats, while the players on the stage paused uncertainly."

Mathis was carried out to an alley alongside the theatre, where two doctors from the audience pronounced her dead, apparently from cardiac arrest. She was only thirty-five, but overweight and suffering from high blood pressure. An ambulance took her body to the nearest funeral parlor: Campbell's, where Valentino had lain in state less than a year earlier.

Although Nazimova had cabled Jean Adams to reroute the $2,000 to Nice, there was still no sign of it by the first week of August. Almost out of cash after she paid the hotel bill, Nazimova sailed for New York on the *Ile de France*, and arrived on August 19 to find a letter from Jean Adams awaiting her at the Hotel Buckingham. "Just chatty," it hoped she was well, made no reference to the overdue payment or the $2,000. For the first time Nazimova's faith had its limits. DONT UNDERSTAND YOUR LETTER, she wired Jean next day, AND UNLESS YOU ARRIVE HERE VERY SOON WILL HAVE TO ASK LAWYER TO ADVISE ME WHEN ARE YOU LEAVING ALLA. Ten days later, Jean had not replied, and Nazimova sent another wire: WHY DONT YOU ANSWER MY WIRE STOP YOU MUST KNOW HOW WORRIED I AM ALLA. This time Jean wired back that she would be arriving in New York shortly. But she had not arrived by September 25, the date on which her payment of $14,500 on the lease officially became delinquent. That same day, Nazimova became a U.S. citizen, and one of her deepest fears vanished. But another deepened when Jean Adams sent a wire postponing her trip to New York.

Still Nazimova postponed consulting her lawyer, as if afraid of what he might discover. Instead, with only a few hundred dollars left in the bank, she begged Jenie Jacobs to find her another vaudeville engagement as soon as possible. On October 19, she was surprised to receive a letter from Nemirovich in Hollywood, where Irving Thalberg had invited him to "observe" production methods at MGM, then make a film for the studio. After learning enough English and observing enough of MGM to decide he didn't want to work there, Nemirovich hoped to direct Nazimova in one of his own plays, *The Price of Life*, in New York. But with no financing yet in place, Nazimova couldn't afford to wait. Unwilling to admit she was almost broke, she replied that "previous contracts" forced her to decline this great honor. Nemirovich wired back to ask if she could possibly rearrange her commitments and ADORN PERFORMANCE WITH YOUR GENIUS AND ART. Her need for money even more desperate than her need for art, Nazimova sent more regrets. By this time, thanks to Jenie Jacobs, a contract for her return to the salt mines of vaudeville had materialized.

Mother India, adapted from Katherine Mayo's best-selling novel, was an exposure of the custom in poor Hindu families of selling their daughters as child brides. Apparently no one, including Nazimova, thought she was too old at forty-eight to play Lotus, the twelve-year-old bride in question. For both actors and audiences, it seems, vaudeville was another country.

On her last American tour, the seventy-two-year-old Sarah Bernhardt, minus one leg and wearing a blond wig, had tremendous success playing a young nurse tending the wounded soldiers of World War I. But when Nazimova opened *Mother India* in Bayonne, New Jersey, on November 10, she barely got through the performance. After she had lived in a state of denial about Jean Adams for almost three months, her nerves gave way; she canceled further bookings and went back to New York, where her doctor prescribed sedation and rest.

A week later, no doubt timing her arrival to find Nazimova in a weakened state, Jean called from the Hotel Commodore to say that she was in New York and on her way over for a bedside visit. Insisting that she'd sent $2,000 to Paris *and* Nice, she soothed, bonded, and went into heart-to-heart gear. Then, getting down to business, she claimed to have secured backing from "a two-million dollar corporation" to enlarge the hotel.

"To my great shame," as Nazimova admitted when she eventually consulted a lawyer and related the whole story, "I let her partly influence me again by the display of marvelous plans which she had brought with her made by an architect in Los Angeles." The other part of the influence was Jean's guarantee that an investment of $25,000 would bring Nazimova a share of the annual profits amounting to over $100,000. In Nazimova's present state, a future without Jean Adams appeared even more uncertain than a future with her. Still clinging to the promise of "spiritual freedom," she not only fell for a preposterous story and agreed to overlook the matter of $14,500 for the moment, but offered to raise the $25,000 right away, since Jean couldn't wait for Nazimova to earn it in vaudeville. To clinch the deal, she had urgent "preliminary expenses" to meet.

Not the least surprising admission in Nazimova's letter to her lawyer is the following: "I knew only one person whom I could approach who had money in the bank and was looking for an investment. That was Miss Jean Acker." How and when did they meet again and mend fences? There is no information. But some years later, Acker told a reporter that, after her career in movies failed to take off, she went back to vaudeville and earned good money. By 1929, she had saved $300,000, all of which she lost in the Wall Street Crash. Nazimova's letter also claimed that Acker was interested but wanted her lawyer to investigate the financial status of the Garden of Allah hotel. Rather than let him discover the company's unpaid debts, Nazimova pretended to have found the money elsewhere. But she told Isabel that Acker "said yes, then slipped a note under the door saying she couldn't manage it after all." This seems more likely: it spared Nazimova having to admit to the lawyer that she'd been rejected as well as duped.

When Jean Adams realized there was no hope of getting her hands on $25,000, she left for Los Angeles. Nazimova never saw her again, although they exchanged numerous telegrams over the next two months, and after several unsuccessful attempts, Nazimova finally contacted her by phone. The connection was bad, and Jean cut their conversation short by saying (as Nazimova heard it), "I shall try to get you out of all this," then hanging up. Next day Nazimova sent her a wire demanding immediate payment of the $14,500. Two days later Jean sent $500.

By now almost broke, Nazimova asked Paul Ivano to sell her Rolls, which had been shipped back to Los Angeles. And since denial was no longer an option, on December 18 she wrote W. I. Gilbert, who had defended Valentino at his trial for bigamy, "I am in trouble. . . ." In the beginning, she explained, "it did not seem trouble, [but] a salvation from all troubles to come." As well as a detailed history, thirteen pages long, of the Garden of Allah hotel, she sent Gilbert a copy of the agreement with Jean Adams and a record of all their transactions. "I think," the letter ended, "that I would prefer to have Mrs. Adams dispossessed but I am rather frightened of all the debts the hotel might have accumulated while she and Mr. Adams were running the place. Also what would become of the $51,500 I had advanced?"

W. I. Gilbert to Alla Nazimova, December 31: "YOUR EQUITY IN THE PROPERTY IS SUBJECT TO A TRUST DEED OF $150,000 IN FAVOR OF AMERICAN MORTGAGE COMPANY . . . UPON WHICH FORECLOSURE PROCEEDINGS HAVE BEEN STARTED AND YOUR PROPERTY WILL BE SOLD BY FEBRUARY 16 UNLESS PARTICULAR DEBT COULD BE LIQUIDATED." A letter followed, explaining that, if Nazimova could raise a bank loan of $9,000 to pay the interest and taxes due on the trust deed, she could take over the lease and once again become the legal owner of The Garden of Allah. But there seemed no chance of recovering the $51,500 from the Adamses. They had disappeared, as they'd previously disappeared from two states in the Midwest, where they were wanted in connection with several fraudulent real-estate deals. A man they had taken to the cleaners in Nebraska wrote Gilbert that "the Madame" was the victim of "a shrewd plan, hatched and manipulated by J. A. [John Adams] and his wife," and probably "the biggest haul they've ever pulled off."

With Gilbert's help, Nazimova obtained the bank loan, and finally opened *Mother India* at the Palace on January 20, 1928. None of the leading critics covered the production. The few critics who did gave it favorable notices, even if acclaim for "the first actress of vaudeville" seems a dubious compliment for someone formerly recognized as the greatest Ibsen actress of her time. But although Katherine Mayo publicly thanked Nazimova for her "service to the cause of humanity," the chairman of the New Orient Society accused Mayo of grossly misrepresenting Indian life. Not that the vaudeville audience cared either way. Agreeing with *Bill-*

board that "they don't come much more dramatic and emotional than the redoubtable Nazimova," it filled the house for two weeks.

THAT SAME month, the Civic Repertory Theatre was failing to fill the house with productions of *Twelfth Night* and *La Locandiera*. According to Josephine Hutchinson, at the time Eva's lover as well as a member of the company, "Le Gallienne felt she needed another star name to launch the next season," and the star name she thought of was Nazimova. In Eva's tactful phrase, it seemed the right moment for "a chance of a talk" with her, and they met for the first time in several years at the Buckingham, after Nazimova had given two performances of *Mother India* in one evening.

Nervous and exhausted, she was unable to express her intense emotion when Eva offered her a contract at the Civic. "Yes, take me on," she said. But then, as she later wrote Eva from Philadelphia, on the first lap of a three-month tour as a Hindu child-bride:

> I could not talk to you about myself. . . . It would all sound like a hard luck story and so hysterical. So I talked and talked about this and that, reminiscences about the Art The-atre . . . and all the time I just wanted to cry and not say any-thing, and was so afraid if I gave myself away and told you what it will mean to me to be in your theatre. Wiping out years of restless and useless wandering, striking out personal unhappiness which had assumed proportions out of sheer dis-satisfaction with the work I was doing—cleansing, resurrect-ing my spirit. . . .

And Eva wrote back, "Alla darling your coming to me has meant so much that it is almost hopeless to try and tell you. It is the most mar-velous thing for the theatre that could happen." So many people, the let-ter continued, "feel that they have been robbed of the real you for so many years, and they long for the real you and what you can give them."

Nazimova replied:

> I can hardly wait to show you what I can do and how proud I am to discover that no matter what I had come into contact with I have not succeeded in "drowning" this earnest sincere love for what I believed in twenty years ago. . . . Eva, these last seven years have been like a nightmare. . . . I can hardly con-nect incidents together. But the feeling remains of something unbelievably horrible.

For Nazimova, the way back to reality and her "real" self was through the theatre, not life. And about the theatre, as opposed to life, she could be shrewd and practical. "The important thing," she told Eva, "is to have me make my first appearance in a good important part." At first she was more enthusiastic about *The Seagull* ("it's so beautiful and it would be so glorious") than *The Cherry Orchard,* both of which Eva had suggested. But when Eva decided to produce *The Cherry Orchard* first, Nazimova persuaded her to follow it with the American premiere of *Katerina* instead of another Chekhov play. Accepting the fact that the Civic was a repertory company like the Moscow Art Theatre, and its policy precluded star billing, she agreed to alternate leading and supporting roles, as Eva did, but "in your new productions only—not parts that have been played during the past two seasons." In every other respect, she assured Eva, "I want to *melt* into the body of this theatre and give it all I have to bring."

Top salary at the Civic was $250 a week, another fact that Nazimova accepted, confident she would soon be able to sell The Garden of Allah and have no more financial worries. On April 16, Gilbert wired her in Kansas City, Missouri, the good news that the hotel had been closed: "OPERATING COMPANY BROKE YOU CAN TAKE POSSESSION ANY TIME." But the rest of the wire was bad news. Apart from the interest and taxes on the trust deed, which the bank loan had taken care of, the company had incurred other debts totaling $55,000. Unless Nazimova guaranteed to settle them in monthly installments of $2,500, "CREDITORS WILL RE-POSSESS FURNITURE AND EQUIPMENT. . . . TO REOPEN HOTEL WILL RE-QUIRE OPERATING FUNDS OF $15000 AND HIRING A MANAGER AT $200 MONTHLY.

She replied the same day: "HAVE BEEN COUNTING ON SALE OF PROP-ERTY ALL MY EARNINGS HAVE BEEN WASTED TO PAY ADAMS DEFAULT IN FEBRUARY SHALL BE IN DESPERATE CIRCUMSTANCES UNLESS MONEY OB-TAINED FROM SALE." In Omaha a few days later, Nazimova heard from Gilbert that he'd succeeded in getting a postponement from the creditors, and would try to find a buyer willing to take over the property and its debts. "*Very bad news* from Calif," Nazimova wrote Eva. "Won't bother you with them, dear, but want you to know that if not the thought of our work next Fall to hold on to, I have more than one cause to be really desperate." In a postscript she added, "Don't tell Isabel. . . . I don't want my sister to know about it yet. Isabel sees her very often and might make a slip."

IN THE LAST week of May, the tour of *Mother India* ended in San Francisco, and Ivano drove up to join Nazimova there. At first she didn't find him boring; or if she did, she forgave him. Depressed because no buyer had yet been found for The Garden, she needed emotional support, and was so grateful for it that she suddenly cast Ivano in the role of ideal husband. "I think I understand about Paul—I love him because he hasn't failed you," Eva wrote in reply to a letter from Nazimova saying they had discussed getting married. "I don't know about marriage—is it necessary? Perhaps it would be more comfortable—I don't know. I don't think it matters in the *least* what people say."

Evidently Nazimova still did, but three weeks later she found that loyalty was not enough. Ivano had once written her, "I am happy when you are happy," and what seemed very loving at the time now struck her as feeble and submissive. According to Nazimova's diary of June 9, Ivano had become so boring that she couldn't bear it any longer. He was driving her back to her hotel after dinner, and just before they reached it she asked him to pull to the side of the road. "Paul," she said, "have you ever been enthusiastic about anything?" Only mildly surprised, he thought it over. Then: "Yes, when I worked for Murnau." (Ivano had recently shot the circus scenes in *Four Devils*.) The insult, the look on Nazimova's face told him, was no less an insult for being unintentional. "Please," he said, "give me another chance." But for Nazimova it was the point of no return. "I have given you another chance for seven years. Now you can go to hell." She got out of the car and walked the short distance back to her hotel.

"Curious about Paul," was Eva's reaction. "I'm sorry if it has made you at all unhappy—or has disillusioned you further." Then, very touchingly: "My Darling I only pray that when you work near me you will not find that distance alone was responsible for your Faith in me. . . ." A clue to what made Nazimova finally explode appears in Kevin Brownlow's TV series on the American silent film, *Hollywood*. Fifty years later, unlike the other survivors of that era interviewed by Brownlow, Ivano seems uninvolved, almost patronizing. Rather shriveled as well as "droop-shouldered," he reminisces like a faintly amused spectator. Perhaps this explains why his career peaked very early, even though he worked with von Sternberg and Murnau. Meeting Ivano again in Hollywood in 1940, Nazimova found him unchanged: "When I think of it, it was this complete disinterest in anything except himself that made me shake him off and how difficult that was God knows!"

Apart from one very brief affair, Ivano was the last Young Man in Nazimova's life. And apart from a brief affair with an actress, her last central relationship was with Glesca Marshall, the Young Woman who stayed the course from 1929 until death parted them sixteen years later.

FIVE WEEKS after the breakup with Ivano, Nazimova managed to sell The Garden of Allah, to the man from whom she had originally bought 8080 Sunset. William Hay, a wealthy real-estate developer who had acquired thousands of acres of land in the San Fernando Valley, became the new owner on July 17 and agreed to pay Nazimova $80,000. But once again she went from high to low. Under the terms of their agreement, Hay would settle all the debts incurred by the Adamses and deduct them from the sale price, and finally all that remained for Nazimova, who had sunk over $250,000 into the place since she first bought it, was $7,500. Some of this she spent (wasted) on hiring private detectives to track down the Adamses, hoping to sue them, until the detectives failed to come up with a lead after two months.

But at the same time, Nazimova's luck did start to return, and the long, disastrous second act of her life in America led indirectly to a third, which proved her greatest. "Oh, my sins!" exclaims Madame Ranevskaya. "Look at the mad way I've always wasted money, spent it like water, and I married a man who could do nothing but run up debts. . . ." At the end of the play, she hears the "sad and lonely" thud of an ax striking a tree, and the parallel between the loss of her orchard and Nazimova's loss of her estate is too close not to have resonated in performance. *The Cherry Orchard* restored her reputation as an artist, and she had just enough time to add to it before her luck turned again.

II

"Life and Happiness"
1928–1935

She [Nazimova] looked old and tired that night,
dressed in an ancient grey sweater and baggy skirt,
with black-rimmed glasses and her hair pulled
back. After a few drinks we all decided to play the
game, "Who am I?" She excused herself, went up
a few steps to her bedroom quarters and returned
in about fifteen minutes, totally transformed. She
had made up, with blue around her eyes, shocking
red lips, hair brushed in a halo around her head, a
long cigarette holder with a brown cigarette alight
and a large Spanish shawl around her. She slithered
sexily down the steps, saying, "Well, who am
I?" . . . I went to her and whispered, "I know. You
are Alla Nazimova twenty years ago." I was right.
It was an incredible impersonation.

— CHERYL CRAWFORD

ALLA WANTED ME TO JOIN THE CIVIC REP
with her," Isabel Hill remembered. " 'Go and see Eva,' she said, 'Make
her like you.' " Then her voice on the tape became skittish again: "But I
just didn't want any part of the Civic Rep." Robert Lewis, the future theatre director and cofounder of the Actors Studio, whose career began as
an apprentice at the Civic, explains what Isabel preferred not to be iden-
tified with: "It was a lesbian theatre. Eva lived upstairs with Jo Hutchinson, and most of the apprentice girls—May Sarton and Glesca Marshall
among them—were lesbian. So was the set designer, Gladys Calthrop. So
was a considerable part of the audience."

And so was a considerable part of the neighborhood, which Eva chose
because it had a theatre, a former burlesque house on 14th Street near
Sixth Avenue, available at a low rent. "Although the auditorium was
shabby," Irene Sharaff remembered, "the seating capacity was around
eleven hundred and it had an exceptionally well proportioned stage."

The location, for most of Eva's company, was a happy coincidence. During the 1920s, Greenwich Village became one of the two major enclaves of gay-and-lesbian life in New York (Harlem was the other), its nightlife sufficiently "notorious" for the Clara Bow movie *Call Her Savage* to feature it in a nightclub scene where the waiters dressed as chambermaids, and the clients—women in mannish tweeds, men in artist's smocks—sat with their arms around each other.

A few blocks away from the Civic, Robert Lewis recalled, was a nightclub called the Cosmic:

> The lesbian singer Spivy performed there to a largely lesbian audience. Many of the Civic girls went there after the show, and the Cosmic stayed open until two in the morning. Some of us then went on to Harlem, and came back to the Cosmic around five, where Spivy cooked us eggs and bacon for breakfast. Then we went on to the theatre for ballet class, fencing, and so on, and rehearsals starting at ten. Sundays we slept late. . . .

"Those were the 'Van Vechten years,' and everything was much freer," Lewis remembered. "You slept with whoever. Whites were closer to blacks. 'Black and white united fight,' was a popular slogan, black militancy was in the future, and we were all leftists—that is to say, against war and fascism." This was an entirely new ambience for Nazimova, but even though she took an apartment on Perry Street, in the center of the Village, she never became a part of it. Neither did Glesca, who lived in a rooming house a few blocks away and, unlike the other apprentices, came from a well-heeled, well-connected family.

Like Nazimova with the Art Theatre, Glesca later exaggerated her importance at the Civic. Although she claimed to have understudied Eva as Varya in *The Cherry Orchard,* she was in fact just one of several apprentices chosen by Eva, who also directed the play, to sub for her during rehearsal. Glesca also claimed to have studied elocution and music for five years in Boston, during which she attended rehearsals of the Boston Symphony Orchestra under Pierre Monteux (a family friend), and to have studied ballet with a former Russian ballerina, and acting at a little theatre in Santa Barbara. All this, commuting from East to West Coast, by the time she was nineteen? The one undeniable fact about Glesca at nineteen is that her imagination had crystallized around a single human being. She had never seen Nazimova onstage, only glimpsed her in the audience for *Cradle Song,* but was obsessed by the legend of "this famous, enigmatic actress."

"Apprentices," Lewis remembered, "never got to know the stars,

As Ranevskaya in The Cherry Orchard, *with*
Eva Le Gallienne as Varya

hardly spoke to them." But Glesca seized her chance after rehearsal one
day when "Nazimova asked if there were someone who could run an er-
rand to Macy's. I could. I did. I returned with whatever it was she
needed, [and] that evening she asked if I would care to have dinner with
her. Remaining calm, I accepted." Glesca doesn't record what they talked
about, only what happened after they walked back to Nazimova's apartment from the restaurant. Almost as soon as they entered the living
room, Nazimova "fainted, blacked out, with hardly a murmur." Panicked, Glesca wondered what to do, and did nothing. Then, just as suddenly, Nazimova revived and began to sob. "It had to be," she said. "It all
had to be. The home-house was gone. . . . Am I asking for a beginning?
I am, for the fourth time in my life." As Glesca stared at "the broken
face," wondering what to say and saying nothing, Nazimova turned
abruptly away, went to her bedroom, and closed the door. Not wanting

The Cherry Orchard. *Wearing the black lace dinner gown, a Worth original discovered by Irene Sharaff*

to leave her alone, since from time to time "short, wild screams" came from the bedroom, Glesca spent the night on the living-room couch and went back to her rooming house at dawn.

At rehearsal a few hours later, Nazimova showed no sign of emotional strain. She invited Glesca to dinner that night, and many following nights, never referred to her collapse, but talked compulsively about Jean Adams and The Garden of Allah. Although Glesca never made the connection, it seems clear that rehearsing *The Cherry Orchard* had aroused an Emotion Memory that led to another "hysterical condition of the heart." After dinner, as Glesca tells it, they walked back to Nazimova's apartment and "sat quietly with a piece of time" for a while; then Glesca returned to her rooming house. And as their relationship developed, "slowly she became my mother and I, in need, became her child."

But this impression of their relationship doesn't seem to have been shared by anyone else. Both Isabel and Irene Sharaff remembered that Glesca moved into Nazimova's apartment before *The Cherry Orchard* opened. "Glesca fell madly in love with Nazimova," said Sharaff, "and devoted her whole life to her." As for the needy child, Jo Hutchinson found no trace of her: "Glesca was always looking out for herself. Hard as a rock. She'd turn up at the end of a rehearsal or a performance and announce in a very uppity manner, 'I'm waiting for Nazimova, I'm taking her home.' "

"People talk against Glesca," said Isabel Hill, "but she was *there*. Gave up her life for Alla." Sharaff agreed, and so did Lewis ("Glesca was totally devoted"), and there was also general agreement on Glesca's physical appearance. It produced a memorable image from Sharaff, "Like a good piece of steak, but needed seasoning," and a thumbnail sketch from Nancy Reagan, "Shortish but sturdy, cropped blondish hair, and *not at all* feminine."

And there can be no doubt that Nazimova loved Glesca deeply to the end. When Glesca went off to visit her mother in February 1944, the star and the star-struck had been together almost sixteen years. "The place where G. sat on couch for her last cup of coffee was left untouched. Pillow crumpled," Nazimova noted in her diary. "Could not write. Walked from room to room until 2 at night. Silly."

THERE WAS considerable advance publicity for *The Cherry Orchard,* part of it a public exchange of compliments between Eva and Nazimova. In an article for *The New York Times,* Eva welcomed an actress "who has touched the highest pinnacles of fame and success, and who has come to us because she felt lonely for the theatre—the plays in which she had been brought up." In *Theatre Magazine,* Nazimova praised Eva for having the courage to launch a genuine repertory theatre, and insisted she was joining it "as a member of the company," not as a star: "If you are the star, your part is the whole thing. You are the great itsky. Thus is created an inflated personality."

For the 1928–29 season, Aline Bernstein replaced Gladys Calthrop as chief designer, and Irene Sharaff's first job in the theatre was as Bernstein's assistant. Because several plays were in rehearsal simultaneously, she remembered, "the schedule was very tight," and *The Cherry Orchard* was rehearsed at night. "I've watched many rehearsals and better directors since then, but for me none of them had the magic of watching Nazimova create a role." The magic also worked on Eva, who allowed Nazimova to direct her own performance. Bernstein had discovered some original Worth dresses, all in perfect condition, among them "a black dinner gown of handmade silk lace over a foundation of chiffon and taffeta . . . typical of Worth's genius." Nazimova was particularly pleased with it, and Jo Hutchinson remembered "finding her in her dressing room on opening night, sewing and repairing a minor tear in it, with her hat on. 'I have to do this myself,' she said. 'I always did.' "

While putting on her makeup, Nazimova liked Irene Sharaff to read aloud to her. "I used to read from Proust. There was a passage about falling leaves she loved and wanted to hear often—it connected with the mood of Chekhov's play." As she read, Sharaff kept glancing up to watch Nazimova create her stage face. Offstage, she still wore the startlingly white makeup that she'd devised almost thirty years earlier. When it came off, Sharaff noted her "slightly pockmarked complexion." After applying a new foundation of subtly blended colors, Nazimova placed a dab of white on the bridge of her nose, whose dilated nostrils always reminded Sharaff of "a frightened horse" but now looked proud and aristocratic. All this took over an hour, with an attention to detail as meticulous as a painter's, and "the final touch was always a flourish of a large swan's-down puff laden with fine rice powder, which sent a cloud of white dust through the air." Then Nazimova fitted her period wig over a strip of gauze wrapped around her head, stepped into her Worth costume, and was transformed into "a Boldini portrait come to life."

When Nazimova read a play aloud all the way through, and took all the roles, it was sometimes (as with Maurice Sterne, Mercedes, and now Glesca) a technique of seduction through talent. But sometimes it was a way of familiarizing herself with the work as a whole, and all its characters. Before *The Cherry Orchard* opened, she read it to her nephew, Val Lewton, who found the experience even more vivid than seeing the play a week or two later. "Without costumes, taking all the parts yourself," he wrote, "without so much as moving from your chair, you created a cross-section of a people's soul. The theatre, with all its physical aids to illusion, couldn't and didn't do that." A few years later, she read *Ghosts* and *Hedda Gabler* to Robert L. Green, the son of Julia Ross, "and talked to me not only about the action of the plays, but the backgrounds of the characters, where they came from, what motivated them. . . . It was the result of her Stanislavsky training, and anticipated the whole approach of what came to be known in New York as the Method."

THE MOSCOW Art Theatre had included *The Cherry Orchard* in its 1923 New York season, the only major production of any play by Chekhov in America until Eva's, which opened at the Civic on October 15, 1928. Aware that she would be measured against Olga Knipper,

who had won high praise as Ranevskaya, and also that she had to reha-
bilitate herself in the eyes of critics like H. L. Mencken, who had written
her off as "a nine days wonder" in *Smart Set*, Nazimova had a bad attack
of stage fright. Fortunately, she was unaware that Mrs. Patrick Campbell,
who had played Ranevskaya in London, was in the audience. Alexander
Woollcott, sitting nearby, heard her talk throughout in "a stage whisper
like the wind in the chimney of a haunted house." But Mrs. Pat failed in
her attempt (not the first) to disrupt a rival's performance. "When I left
the theatre," Robert Garland wrote in the New York *Telegram*, "customers were standing on their seats and lifting their voices in 'Bravo!
Bravo!' and unless my ears deceived me, 'Attaboy, Alla!' " Brooks Atkinson in the *Times* found that Nazimova brought to the part "a flowing
rhythm that catches every evanescent mood and intonation," and Woollcott sent her a note: "I was so enchanted by your playing in *The Cherry
Orchard*. Bless you."

Chekhov had disliked Stanislavsky's production of his play, complaining that he failed to "see the comedy in it," and "dragged out an act that
should have lasted twelve minutes to forty minutes" of social drama.
Nazimova didn't make this mistake. "I didn't know that *The Cherry Orchard* was a comedy," Noël Coward told her after the performance, and
Robert Lewis found her "beautiful, elegant, *witty*—and turn-of-the-
century Russian. I've never seen anyone who could touch her. In fact,
watching other actresses after her, I feel Nazimova pushing them out of
the way, telling them how to do it." George Cukor remembered a particularly original moment when she suddenly switched from comedy to
tragedy:

> A tall young man wearing a blouse comes into the room. Na-
> zimova looked at him, ran over and threw herself on him, sob-
> bing. He was the tutor of her son who'd drowned years before.
> Usually actresses play this moment rather sentimentally, but
> Nazimova gave you the impression the boy had only just been
> drowned. She had this beautiful, rather fragile voice, and she
> sobbed as if he was actually carrying the body of the child. It
> had a terrible stab of immediacy.

Over the years, Nazimova's Ranevskaya, like all legendary performances, became a subject of agreement and disagreement. For Jo
Hutchinson, the scene at the end of the play "when Ranevskaya realizes
she's lost the cherry orchard was extraordinarily poignant. Nazimova
slowly got up from her chair, put on a pair of gloves, and made the moment a gesture of farewell to the home she realized she'd have to leave."

But for Cheryl Crawford, at that time casting director for the Theatre Guild, it was the only moment when Nazimova was less moving than Olga Knipper. Knipper remained in her chair, but "as the truth hit her slowly, her hands fluttered on the table, her face grew immobile." For the rest, Crawford found Nazimova "wayward, sexually attractive, careless of her precarious situation, glamorous," qualities that Knipper was too old and heavy to bring to the part.

And if Nazimova conveyed the quicksilver temperament of Chekhov's heroine so perfectly, it was, according to Sharaff, because she had a similar sense of humor, could move naturally and unexpectedly from drama to comedy, "go onstage for a dramatic scene, then come off and tell a dirty joke." But for Jo Hutchinson this ability reflected not only Nazimova's "mischievous delight in surprise" but her extraordinary technical skill: "She was so masterly in her handling of props that, right after the poignant business with the gloves, she could whisper, 'What are you going to have for supper tonight, Jo?' "

With *The Cherry Orchard* sold out for the season twenty-four hours after opening night, and an average of half a dozen curtain calls followed by demands for a speech greeting every performance, a grateful Nazimova sent Eva several Christmas gifts, including a Schiaparelli hat, with an accompanying note, "I take off my hat to you." And two weeks later she left another note in Eva's dressing room: "Eva, you have given me life and happiness. Alla."

BUT THERE was less happiness in the theatre of life at Who-Torok. In mid-December, Glesca borrowed a car and chauffeur from one of her cousins to take Nazimova to Who-Torok, where Nina was still living in the gatehouse cottage that Nazimova had deeded to her. To Glesca she seemed "truly an older sister with that definite attitude of knowing just a bit more than her famous relative. Her greeting was gracious and cool. Her jealousy was evident." Glesca didn't meet Val, who had moved to New York, but Lucy's jealousy was no less evident, and apparently extended to Glesca as well: "She did not bother to speak to me." On the drive back to New York, Nazimova was clearly enervated. "She put her head in my lap and I covered her with the car robe."

But in spite of her cool welcome, Glesca loved Who-Torok, and drove out with Nazimova every following Sunday. Within a month, the first explosion occurred, set off when Nazimova complained that her sister and niece were unfriendly to Glesca, and added that she found Lucy's voice irritating. "It is strange that the quality of my voice gets on your nerves," Lucy opened fire in reply. "Glesca's laugh in anyone's ear we would not call sober. . . . It is strange that you resent our polite civility to your 'friend.' Her peculiar relationship to you demanded at least that from us, even though her personality never appealed to us." Then Lucy launched the personal attack that caused Nazimova never to speak to her again: "Having been brought up in childhood to regard you as the greatest most admirable character, it came naturally as a disappointment to find that . . . at bottom you have a self-centered, petty character not at all in keeping with your talents."

Nazimova's reaction, on January 24, 1929, was to write her sister a letter explaining that, after bringing Nina and her children to America, and paying for their education, "I don't believe in family any more. . . . I think one should build one's own family around one—of people *that are kin in spirit and tastes.*" As in the past, the bond of "sister-love" remained, but only in Nazimova's letters. In the future, they would see each other very infrequently.

A month later, on February 23, Nazimova opened in her second play at the Civic, but neither critics nor audience shared her admiration for *Katerina*. (Almost no one except Andreyev did. He considered it his best work.) A loving and faithful wife who finally leaves her pathologically jealous husband, Katerina embarks on a series of affairs, but remains faithful in spirit to her husband and finally goes back to him. A tragic heroine for audiences in the tsarist Russia of 1912, she seemed merely foolish and masochistic to New York audiences in 1929. The critics dismissed the play but praised Nazimova's performance, although the review in the New York *Sun* cannot have been entirely pleasing to Eva. It concluded that, after *The Cherry Orchard,* "Mme Nazimova is the star . . . even if she is not officially billed as the star, [and] she deserved the cheers as she had never done better acting."

Because advance bookings for *Katerina* were disappointing, Eva made some changes in the performance schedule, and by the end of the season Nazimova had played *The Cherry Orchard* sixty-four times to *Katerina*'s eighteen. But even for only eighteen performances of Andreyev's play she found it impossible to be "mechanical," and, as in *Hedda,* "needed watching." Isabel, who thought *Katerina* "the finest thing I ever saw her do," watched it several times and remembered complimenting her one night on "that brilliant twisted smile you gave in the last act." Nazimova stared at her in surprise. "What twisted smile?" she asked. "And when?"

A few days before the season closed on April 15, Nazimova was offered a movie contract by Edward Small, a former agent who had just become a producer at Columbia. Since the arrival of sound, the studios had begun to make foreign-language versions of their pictures for the international market, and it occurred to Small that, since Nazimova spoke French and German, she could become a trilingual asset. Unlike many foreign stars of the silent era (Ramon Novarro, Pola Negri, Vilma Banky), who were rightly fearful of their heavy accents, Nazimova welcomed the opportunity to make a voice test at a studio in New York: "The talkies are a remarkable invention and I want to do the very best I can." Her very best was more than good enough for Small, and on April 22 the Los Angeles *Times* announced: "Nazimova will be the first actress in Hollywood to make 'talkies' in any other language than English. This is expected to set a precedent which may force Hollywood to go polylingual." But the rest was silence. Like so many of Small's projects, this one (and his contract with Columbia) evaporated.

At the end of April, the Civic began a four-week tour, playing Philadelphia and Boston, with Glesca taking over the small part of a twelve-year-old boy in *Katerina*. This time the Philadelphia *Inquirer* reviewed the play in terms that may not have pleased Eva: "If Miss Le Gallienne's company has done nothing else, it has restored to us the Nazimova of fifteen years ago, the great, magnetic, flaming Nazimova we used to know." In any case, Isabel remembered that, although "everything was very happy at the beginning of the season," there was some tension between Nazimova and Eva by the start of the tour. And shortly after it ended, a brief official announcement appeared in the press: "It is greatly to be regretted that Mme Nazimova has seen fit to withdraw from the Civic Repertory Theatre. Her playing in Chekhov's *Cherry Orchard* and in *Katerina* will long be remembered."

According to Jo Hutchinson, the trouble began when "advance publicity for the tour announced Eva Le Gallienne's Civic Repertory Theatre, although it had been agreed there would be no personal advertising." According to Glesca, whose brother saw the *The Cherry Orchard* in Boston on the last night of the tour, Eva called the entire company onstage to thank the actors for their great work during the season, but omitted to call or thank Nazimova, who left the theatre "and asked my brother to please inform Miss Le Gallienne she would not be with the company for the next season."

One thing is certain. Although both Nazimova and Eva paid lip service to the ideal of an ensemble company without stars, like the Moscow Art Theatre, in practice they engaged in some old-fashioned Star Wars.

Nazimova earned most of the star notices, but Eva compensated by putting a large photograph of herself on the cover of every program, and inside *The Cherry Orchard* program Nazimova's name appeared only once to Eva's three times—"Eva Le Gallienne Presents," "Directed by Eva Le Gallienne," and in the cast list as Varya. That all was no longer "life and happiness" for Nazimova is made clear by the letter she started to write Eva, then apparently thought better of:

> *Was* it a *miracle,* as you called it, that the third season was so successful? Or was it the fact that the people appreciated that they could see better acting? These are not grievances, but there are such things as gratitude and tact. . . .

Shortly after Nazimova resigned, the Civic's business manager informed Glesca by letter that her services would no longer be required at the theatre. By way of compensation, Nazimova appointed Glesca her official "secretary." They spent the summer together at Who-Torok, although not in the main house, which was now rented. Nazimova claimed she did this to economize, but in fact she spent far more than she saved. Unable to resist designing another "dream-house," she planned to build it with the extra money she earned from appearing in advertisements for Lucky Strikes and Lux Toilet Soap, and the summer rental on the main house. But she ended by using some of her savings as well. To Nina's cottage Nazimova added a two-story wing, with hallway, dining room, kitchen, and servants' quarters on the first floor, bedroom, bath, den, living room, and "sun parlor" on the second. In view of the "family" situation, it was an eccentric move. The four of them now lived at closer quarters, and one morning, as Lucy backed her car out of the garage, she caught sight in the driving mirror of Glesca on the patio outside Nazimova's wing. It incensed her so much that she slammed her foot on the gas pedal and backed into a tree. And when Jo Hutchinson came over for a visit, Nazimova explained that she kept the door separating the wing from the cottage locked and bolted, "because we quarrel so much." One of the fiercest quarrels occurred when Nazimova added an extra bathroom for Glesca, which "really aggravated" Nina and Lucy. But as Christmas approached, Nina felt the need for an expression of seasonal goodwill. Although living next door to each other, the sisters usually communicated by letter, and for once (and once only) Nina went on record that she had reason to be grateful to Nazimova:

> How could I ever forget those first years? Your guidance, your advice . . . which finally landed me in the life of work [at MGM] in which I found myself! Alla, everything I have,

everything I am I owe to you—my sorrow is only that I could never tell you my feelings for you, could never be of use to you when you needed love and sympathy. It is just that—a peculiar embarrassment would overcome me, making me feel awkward, self-conscious, afraid of appearing insincere.

Apart from reading several plays that had been submitted to her, none of which she liked, Nazimova spent much of that summer making notes for her autobiography. Among her posthumous papers is an outline of the years 1910 to 1930, a period in her life that she felt the need to apologize for and headed "Alibis." Most of them are self-explanatory. "A disastrous (for me) love affair (1912)" refers to Bryant, "Lack of good plays (1910–1928)" to her stage career in the years between her last Ibsen tour and *The Cherry Orchard,* "Aestheticism (1920–1925)" to *Camille* and *Salome,* "the movies and neurasthenia (1919–1929)" to her rise and fall as a silent-movie queen, "loss of self-confidence and melancholia (1925–1930)" to being betrayed by Bryant and conned by Jean Adams, "Disillusion in idealistic-communistic art theatres (1929)" to her resignation from the Civic Repertory. But Nazimova also records an "aversion" to publicity from 1905 to 1907, when in fact she was giving a great many interviews, and it's difficult to understand why "love of solitude (1923–?)" should be an "alibi." If Isabel Hill was right, it conflicted with her fear of being alone, and when Nazimova made these notes she was living with Glesca. Another posthumous note confirms the suspicion that Nazimova was mythmaking here, and fearful elsewhere of revealing too much about herself. "I had to learn," she noted, "through hard lessons, to change my speech, its color, tempo, mood, to suit the personality and intellect of a long line of widely different types of interviewers, and now, with this chameleon skin pulled over mine, I fear to show the texture of my own. What if my naked self proved shocking?"

Almost every one of these "Alibis" cast Nazimova in the role of a victim, as if she still clung to the pain of her childhood. But in projecting an image of the lonely star, deeply wounded by her "disastrous" love for Bryant, she passed over her relationships with Mercedes, Eva, and Rambova as well as Ivano. To clothe her shocking naked self? It would seem so, except that, after writing a few pages to develop the part she called "My Life," Nazimova found that she didn't believe in it, and " 'My Life' had not been my life." She tore the pages up and decided not to tackle the adult Nazimova until she'd finished the story of her earlier years. Since it was still incomplete at her death, how much of her later self she might have revealed will never be known. And if Glesca knew, she wasn't telling.

IN THE stock-market crash of October 24, Nazimova was not as unlucky as Jean Acker. She lost about half, as opposed to all, her savings, but had been out of work since the end of May, and by the end of the year still hadn't found a play she liked. Then, in January 1930, Lawrence Langner of the Theatre Guild offered her the leading role in Turgenev's *A Month in the Country.* This came about through Lynn Fontanne, one of the Guild's leading stars, who recommended that Langner see Nazimova's Ranevskaya. It revised his opinion, created by *The Unknown Lady,* that the movies had corrupted her stage acting, and when, a few months later, the Guild decided to produce Turgenev's play, he realized that she would be perfectly cast as the charming, feckless, discontented aristocrat who falls in love with the tutor of her ten-year-old son. Pre-Chekhovian in its ironic approach to dramatic situations, and like *The Cherry Orchard* subtitled "A Comedy," *A Month in the Country* had first been performed in Moscow in 1872, then revived by the Art Theatre in 1909, with Olga Knipper as Natalya Petrovna.

By 1930, after its modest beginnings off-Broadway fifteen years earlier, the Theatre Guild had become the main source of "quality" Broadway theatre. *A Month in the Country* was the latest in a series of American pre-

Before the dress rehearsal of A Month in the Country. *In foreground, Nazimova and Mamoulian. In background, at extreme right, Alexander Kirkland*

mieres that included Pirandello's *Right You Are If You Think You Are,*
Shaw's *Heartbreak House* and *Back to Methuselah,* O'Neill's *Strange Inter-*
lude and *Marco Millions,* and the Lunts as an acting couple in Molnár's
The Guardsman. To direct Turgenev's play, Langner chose Rouben
Mamoulian, who had staged *Marco Millions* and made one of the most
adventurous early sound films, *Applause.* A Russian Armenian, he literally as well as metaphorically spoke Nazimova's language, and sent her a
note at the end of the first week of rehearsals: "If the best American actresses came to see just one of your scenes at rehearsal, they would have
to quit acting and sell stockings. Mamou." She also established a warm
rapport with Alexander Kirkland, who played the young tutor and wrote
an affectionate memoir of Nazimova after she died. Although he accepted some of her self-created myths as fact (the gold medal awarded to
"only one student in five thousand" that she won at the Art Theatre, how
she personally "discovered Valentino as a movie extra"), he created an indelible image of Nazimova at work:

> I remember her making a brilliant hysterical exit in *A Month*
> *in the Country.* As the door slammed behind her, Natalya
> Petrovna dematerialized and Alla Nazimova stood there,
> lighting a long Russian cigarette. She would sit cross-legged
> on a backstage chair, listening to the scene beyond the canvas
> walls, her glowing eyes expressing pleasure or scorn at what
> she heard.

But her first entrance was another matter. In spite of her virtuoso technique, which for Kirkland made her "arrestingly interesting even in
trash," she still succumbed to almost nightly attacks of stage fright. Phyllis Jenkins, who was married to Kirkland at the time, remembers that
Nazimova often said, "I think I'm losing my nerve," and always asked him
to stand in the wings in her sight line when he wasn't onstage. "It gave her
confidence, and it suited him, because he was totally fascinated by her acting." Another spectator in the wings was Katharine Hepburn, who played
the small part of Katya the maid. She never met Nazimova, but "just used
to watch her—she had great concentration—total—fascinating—
couldn't take my eyes off her."

Langner also watched her repeatedly, fascinated but disconcerted by
her refusal to be "mechanical." One night she played Natalya "as a
charming and delightful woman," another as "a sulky and lovable creature," another as "positively mean and disagreeable," and, whatever characterization she chose, it was always "completely consistent from the
beginning to the end." And although the critic of the Washington *Post*

described Nazimova "in a comedy role" as "the quintessence of artistry" when the play previewed in Washington, when it opened in New York on March 17 *Time* magazine found that her "pliant, emotional portrayal" created a "delicate lesson in anguish."

Soon after the New York opening, Nazimova was interviewed in her dressing room at the Guild Theatre by Djuna Barnes, who found her performance "entirely and rightly splendid," without saying which performance she gave that night. The thirty-eight-year-old Barnes had not yet written *Nightwood,* but was famous for wearing a black cape, green eye shadow, and purple lipstick. Almost certainly Nazimova had no idea that she was the anonymous author of *Ladies Almanack,* with its coded portraits of lesbian expatriates in Paris, including Natalie Barney, Romaine Brooks, Radclyffe Hall, and Dolly Wilde, or that she'd had a brief affair with Maurice Sterne. Although the two women never met again, and Barnes never divulged what she knew about Nazimova, she was equally adept in the theatre of life and knew how to look for the person behind the player. She perceived that Nazimova had to be "a very simple woman with a very guileless heart" if she could play "elemental and passionate vampires" so convincingly while at the same time "someone talked her money out of her"; that, when Nazimova's movie career ended in catastrophe, "she took her beating without humor, because she is at heart a child pondering her adult childhood"; and that Nazimova's claim never to have been in love was "a gorgeous lie."

A Month in the Country ran until October, then toured for three months, with Glesca replacing Katharine Hepburn as the maid. "I suppose by then people were wondering why I was with Nazimova so much," she wrote in her memoir. "Some people thought as time went on that I was her illegitimate child. . . . I was simply the surrogate for the child she always wanted. But people were curious or possibly jealous of my closeness to her." This is Glesca at her most disingenuous; nobody "wondered why she was with Nazimova so much," because everybody knew why, and nobody I spoke to who knew Nazimova had ever heard a rumor that Glesca was her illegitimate child.

But as Robert Lewis pointed out, "If Glesca and Nazimova agreed to deny they were lovers, they had to. Especially when Nazimova moved back to Hollywood. Employment depended on keeping your nose clean. And Hollywood, the dirtiest place in America, was the most eager to keep everything clean." And if Glesca later pinpointed 1930 as the year when many people began to speculate about her relationship with Nazimova, her unconscious may have been at work. It was the year Jo

Hutchinson decided to divorce her husband, who told the court that she preferred the company of Eva "morning, noon, and night," a cue for lip-smacking innuendo from the tabloids about "a new angle in the old love triangle." Sixty-five years later, asked her opinion of Glesca for concealing their true relationship after Nazimova died, and of Nazimova for keeping all her affairs with women secret while she was alive, Jo Hutchinson replied with great feeling: "Wouldn't anyone do the same thing?"

One of the very few people to whom Nazimova confided her secrets was Edith Luckett, since May 1929 Mrs. Loyal Davis of Chicago. They met again for the first time in several years during the Chicago run of *A Month in the Country*. At thirty-three, Davis had not yet established himself as a leading neurosurgeon, and Edith, eight years his senior, was at first the couple's major breadwinner, working in a succession of radio soap operas, one of them with another fallen idol of the silent screen, Francis X. Bushman. She kept equally busy on the social scene, and arranged for Nazimova to be the star guest at a Dramatic League luncheon. They sat together, and Nazimova was photographed with "Mrs. Loyal Davis, whose charming little daughter is the godchild of the great actress." One of the speakers at the luncheon recalled having seen Nazimova and Orlenev in *The Chosen People* at the Herald Square Theatre, and the great actress, wearing "a gown of gold cloth trimmed with sable and a matching Russian turban," listened attentively as he described how the play aroused wails and moans from an audience with a firsthand knowledge of pogroms. Later in the afternoon, Nazimova took Glesca to meet Edith, and herself met Loyal Davis for the first time. Although he was conservative and anti-Semitic, Nazimova a Jew and a Democrat (and later a fervent supporter of Franklin Roosevelt), battle lines were never formed. For Davis, who had once hoped to be an actor, she personified theatrical glamour; and for Nazimova, the Davises and Nancy replaced Nina and her children as true "family." From St. Louis, the next stop on the tour, she wrote Edith:

> When I look back it seems that for the first time in many years *I had been home*. What this meant and means to me—you know. I wish Loyal knew. In spite of having had no 5 minutes talk with him alone to know each other—it seemed unnecessary. I do hope he likes me half as much as I do him. He is grand. . . . Enough of this, my dearest friends—just please know you have opened up a corner in my heart I thought had closed for good.

Early in January 1931, Nazimova returned to New York and the Hotel Buckingham, where she shared Apartment 1104 with Glesca. A few

Mourning Becomes Electra.
Alice Brady as Lavinia/Electra,
Nazimova as Christine/
Clytemnestra, Earle Larrimore
as Orin/Orestes

weeks later, Eva called. They hadn't spoken since Nazimova's resignation from the Civic, but at Eva's suggestion they met for a talk and evidently reconciled. "Eva asks me to join CRT again," Nazimova noted in her diary on April 29. Then, on May 6: "Reading Eugene O'Neill's trilogy, *Mourning Becomes Electra*. Disappointed." After rereading it, she changed her mind, but although she accepted the Theatre Guild's offer to play Christine Mannon and turned Eva down, she agreed to appear as a guest artist at the Civic in two performances of *The Cherry Orchard.* She gave them on May 4 and 7, as part of the celebrations of Eva's fifth season, which closed with revivals of the company's other most successful productions, *Cradle Song, Peter Pan, Camille,* and *Romeo and Juliet.*

Just as Nazimova hesitated over *Mourning Becomes Electra,* O'Neill needed convincing that she was right for his New England Clytemnestra, renamed Christine. "She would be grand," he told Langner and Theresa Helburn, not having seen *The Cherry Orchard* or *A Month in the Country,* "if she can be directed to act as she did in her first Ibsen productions and cut out the ham mannerisms acquired later." They assured him that she could and had cut them out, and on June 3 Nazimova noted in her diary: "Lunch with Eugene O'Neill." It was their first meeting, and, twenty-five years after Nazimova's first *Hedda Gabler,* O'Neill told her how often he went to see it and how much he admired it.

What else they discussed is not known, but evidently the meeting went well. On June 7, the New York *Herald* announced that the Guild had signed Nazimova for "one of the two leading feminine roles" in the trilogy. For the other, Christine's daughter, Lavinia, and O'Neill's equivalent of Electra, his first choice was Lillian Gish. Eager to play the part, Gish agreed to be auditioned by the director, Philip Moeller, who thought she seemed "marvelous in type . . . very, very intelligent," and had "marvelous pantomime projection." But since she lacked stage experience and her voice was "monotonous in range," he suggested postponing any decision until Nazimova had coached her for a few weeks. On August 4, Nazimova commented in her diary: "Lillian Gish calls on me to help her with O'Neill play. She is charming." But after two weeks, Gish told Moeller that her voice would never be equal to the role, and he proposed offering it to Judith Anderson. O'Neill (fortunately) rejected the idea and proposed Ann Harding, who was (fortunately) unavailable, and finally everyone agreed on Alice Brady, who had turned down the role of Nina Leeds in *Strange Interlude,* one of the Guild's and Lynn Fontanne's greatest successes.

Promoted from "secretary" to "manager," Glesca had been going to business school and learning fast. She negotiated Nazimova's contract, successfully holding out for $3,500 a week, $1,000 more than her salary for *A Month in the Country.* She also attended rehearsals, like Carlotta Monterey, now Mrs. O'Neill, who noted that Nazimova and Brady loathed each other, "but that was good—it added real feeling to their parts." Both actresses were extremely tense during the seven weeks of rehearsal—Brady slow to get a handle on her part, Nazimova jealous because Christine dies at the end of Part Two and Lavinia dominates the closing scene of Part Three. Both were also physically uncomfortable— Brady because of an injured knee, Nazimova suffering from hot flashes and headaches as she started to experience menopause.

During rehearsals O'Neill made quite a few cuts in his play, reducing its running time from six to five and a half hours, and Nazimova suggested several changes, all of which he agreed to in performance, although he deleted some of them in the final published text. At the end of Part One, as Christine walks toward her husband with a box of poison in her hand, she was supposed to mutter, "Poison, poison." Nazimova objected, joking that it was a line worthy of *The Count of Monte Cristo,* the barnstormer in which O'Neill's father appeared. Earlier in

Part One, when Christine talks about her husband to Lavinia, Nazimova found some of the emotional transitions too abrupt. One speech began, "I loved him once—before I married him," and she expanded this to: "Hatred takes time. A little and a little, day after day, until something inside you . . . I loved him once," etc. In the same scene, Christine tells Lavinia: "I tried to love you. I couldn't. You were always my wedding night to me—and my honeymoon." With O'Neill's agreement, Nazimova gave herself more space in performance: "I tried to love you. I told myself it wasn't human not to love my own child, born of my body—but I never could make myself feel you were born of any body but his. You were always my wedding night," etc. And at the end of Part Two, when the curtain was supposed to fall on Christine in a dead faint on the floor and Lavinia crying out "Father, don't leave me alone!," Nazimova was determined to upstage Brady. She persuaded O'Neill to continue the scene, and the performance text reads: "As if she had heard this appeal even in her faint, Christine stirs and raises herself on one arm, not yet fully conscious, staring before her dazedly." Then, in a whisper, she calls to her lover for help: "Adam! I'm afraid! Adam! . . ."

Tickets for *Mourning Becomes Electra*, which lasted from 5:00 to 11:45 pm, with a seventy-five-minute dinner intermission, were the most expensive in town. The top price was $6.60, $2.20 higher than the next most expensive show, the *Ziegfeld Follies*. After the October 26 opening, Brooks Atkinson of *The New York Times* pronounced it "a universal tragedy of tremendous stature . . . played by Alice Brady and Mme Nazimova with consummate artistry and passion." Most of his colleagues saluted the play in similar terms, but found Nazimova more impressive than Brady; Robert Benchley in *The New Yorker* commented that "the drama lost much when she withdrew into the shades of the House of Mannon never to return."

A few months after the play opened, Nazimova herself reviewed it at the request of *The Modern Thinker and Author's Review*. She wrote mainly about the challenge of acting O'Neill:

> Mr. O'Neill's trilogy is different from any other play, certainly from any play I have been in. . . . In plays by authors equally as famous, the persons of the drama are, however subtle, easily recognized—and acted—as human beings. Mr. O'Neill's characters are mysterious! They are half mask, half character. Take, for instance, my own role—was there ever a mother who had such scenes with her own daughter as I have at the moment they meet in the play? . . . Christine Mannon is completely stylized; and it is the lack of what I call pliability

of character that makes acting in the trilogy, though fascinating to spectators, hard upon the actor.

Early in January 1932, Alexander Sanin arrived in New York. Now the
leading director of opera at the Alexandrinsky in St. Petersburg, he had
been invited by the Met to stage an opera based on O'Neill's *The Em-
peror Jones*. On January 13, when he went to see *Mourning Becomes Electra*, Nazimova was apprehensive. She remembered Sanin as violently
emotional in criticism as well as love, but in her dressing room after the
performance he seemed awed by the actress he had berated in June 1900
for wasting her talent on mediocre summer-stock plays. "I have seen
them all," Nazimova's diary quotes him as saying. "You are the greatest
actress in the world." A few nights later, she received a similar compliment from the German playwright Gerhart Hauptmann. Nazimova had
seen and admired his most famous play, *The Sunken Bell*, in a production
by Stanislavsky, and was overwhelmed when Hauptmann came backstage with a signed photograph inscribed to "the Russian Duse." Her
diary also records high praise from Noël Coward, "Most perfect performance I have seen," and Garbo was presumably another admirer. She
never went backstage but saw *Mourning Becomes Electra* several times,
sneaked in and out of the theatre through a side door by someone from
the Guild's publicity office.

The play closed in April, and after it played three weeks in Philadelphia and another three in Boston, Nazimova decided to spend the summer at Who-Torok. But she soon changed her mind and wrote Glesca,
who was visiting her mother: "I've got to get out, Doodie. . . . I want a
HOME, not an annex with people next door who hate my living there.
I need peace of mind, and with neurotic, over-sensitive and 'temperamental' relatives on the other side of my wall such a thing is impossible.
I just CAN NOT stay there—*not this summer,* Doodie."

As "Doodie" suggests, they now had private nicknames for each other.
In her memoir, apparently unaware that it hardly supports her claim of
a mother-daughter relationship, Glesca explains that her nickname was
inspired by a love scene in a movie they'd recently seen together. When
the hero told his girl, "You are my sacred duty," he pronounced the last
word "doodie." It decided Nazimova to call Glesca "Sacred Doodie,"
which she later shortened to "Doodie." And in return Glesca came up
with "Moosie," after "Madame Moosie-Moosie," as Nazimova had once
heard herself referred to by an extra on location.

Doodie in private as well as manager in public, Glesca strikes a new
note of self-assurance in her account of a trip to Europe with Moosie that

summer. Names are dropped thick and fast: the "Pierre Monteux family," with whom she has been to Europe "several times before"; Fanny Brice and Beatrice Lillie, fellow passengers on the *Ile de France;* "Mary Garden's sister" and "the Prince de Borghese" in Montreux; Fritz Reiner and Maria Chebotari, "the prima donna of the Dresden Opera," in Venice. Glesca found Chebotari particularly charming—unlike Nazimova, who commented in her diary: "Russian stupidity, conceit, lack of manners . . . but what a voice, so gangway."

Diary notes on the trip also include a haikulike poem:

> Montreux—Montreux you beautiful city
> In sunshine
> But oh God how vile
> You manage to be in rain.

And revisiting the lake seems to have stirred childhood memories of Russia as well as Switzerland. "Yalta . . . sea waves splashing, balcony, breeze, cornet from orchestra in park," one entry reads, followed a few days later by another: "Yalta at night. Sea storm. Wind howling through shutters."

BEFORE LEAVING for Europe, Nazimova had signed with the Theatre Guild to play O-Lan in an adaptation of Pearl Buck's 1931 novel *The Good Earth.* Rehearsals began soon after she returned to New York and settled into Apartment 1104 at the Buckingham with Glesca. Philip Moeller was again the director, but this time Nazimova disagreed with his staging, which she found much too slow. As a member of the Guild board ("with a very bureaucratic outlook," according to Robert Lewis), he tended to pull rank when criticized, and there was considerable tension between them. "Moeller is breaking me," she noted on September 9, ten days before the first preview in Philadelphia. Pearl Buck, who attended the dress rehearsal there, was unhappy with the adaptation as well as Moeller's staging. Next evening she wired Nazimova: "You are my only hope."

"Play over at 11.45: BAD," Nazimova recorded after the first preview. Next evening, September 20, "Play over at 11.30, but I am BAD," and on the 21st, "Play over at 11.15: I am Better." Although she received good notices in Philadelphia—unlike Claude Rains, who was unhappy in the role of O-Lan's husband—the critics found Moeller's direction too solemn and sluggish, and after *The Good Earth* opened at the Guild Theatre on October 17, the New York reviews were similar. Brooks Atkinson in the *Times* complained that in the later scenes Nazimova "subsides into torturesome grimaces," but for Stark Young in *The New Republic* they were part of her "Chinese" style. "Madame Nazimova alone in the company achieves any style at all," he wrote, and, in the way she conveyed "the goodness, the homely love and the kind of mute pain or pleasure that O-Lan should have," transcended Moeller's direction:

> Meantime the chic that is natural to this actress appeared, however drab the woman she was playing. In the doorway, for example, when O-Lan enters just before her death, the figure seen there had style and beauty, and this without doing any harm, for it elevated and simplified the scene.

Young also found Nazimova's makeup convincing, although she wore very little, declined to tape her eyes for Chinese effect because she believed it would leave wrinkles around them, and learned to control her eye muscles instead. But his review was only one of several that worsened Moeller's relations with Nazimova, and her diary sketches a typical scene after the October 20 matinee: "Philip Moeller comes to dressing room. Remark: 'Your hand was shaking after you were dead.' (I autograph photos not answering. He leaves in a huff.) Again insomnia."

Playing the small part of a young Chinese revolutionary was Vincent Sherman, the future movie director, for whom the fifty-three-year-old Nazimova, "with her girlish body," was still extraordinarily attractive. "One evening I told a fellow actor that I could have gone for her, and he said, 'But she likes girls.' I was very surprised, very shocked." Sherman also remembered, like Jo Hutchinson, that, although Nazimova "was very serious about her work," she had a great sense of mischief:

> When I played my one scene, haranguing the crowd, the other actors had their backs to the audience. Nazimova was supposed to be holding her baby, and she would invent business to throw me off. Once she pretended the baby had peed in his diapers and shook her hand, pretending it was wet. Other times she would react to my speech by muttering, "Is that so? Well, whaddya know?" Finally it annoyed me. But I "used" the anger.

In January 1933, when *The Good Earth* was on tour in the Midwest after a New York run of less than two months, the movies appeared to be in Nazimova's future again. Alfred Altman of MGM's New York office wired her about the possibility of a role in *Soviet*, a film about the Five-Year Plan to be directed by King Vidor. She wired back asking to see a script, and on January 20 wrote Nina from Milwaukee: "Al Altman wires

The Good Earth, *1932.*
Nazimova as O-Lan, holding
the baby it sometimes amused
her to pretend "had peed in
his diapers"

he cannot send script, so how am I to know what it's all about. . . . So if you could enlighten me please send me a wire describing *just the woman and her actions.*"

Nina was unable to find out anything, and soon after the tour ended, Altman summoned Nazimova to his New York office. Her diary records his opening remark: "Mr. Louis B. Mayer feels kind of lukewarm about you now—since you asked for the script. You ought to know that he knows better than you what you can do, so you should leave it to him. Look at Lunts picture [*The Guardsman*]. The biggest flop we ever had. They thought they knew what they ought to do etc." Nazimova asks, deadpan, "So Mr. Mayer can play the part for me too, can he?" But Altman doesn't get the joke. "N-no," he says, taken aback, "but he can tell you what you ought to play." And when Nazimova insists that she needs to study a part before playing it, he shakes his head. "The Rasputin script was only two hours ahead of the shooting—and it's a knockout! So why should you know the script before you sign the contract?"

Given that *Rasputin and the Empress* had turned out to be as big a flop as *The Guardsman,* MGM decided Russia was not box-office and can-

The Good Earth. *Claude Rains and Nazimova*

celed *Soviet,* but Nazimova returned to the tsarist empire in a new production of *The Cherry Orchard* for the Civic Repertory. Because of the
Depression, its audiences were dwindling, and a principal backer, the fi-
nancier Otto Kahn, had defected. As a way out of the company's serious
financial difficulties, Eva made a gamble. She took a month's lease on a
Broadway theatre, going uptown "to get the money to save her theatre
downtown," as the New York *Sun* commented, "and to make it possible
to reopen it next season with the policy unchanged." And in the hope of
widening her audience, she asked Nazimova to help out by lending her
star name to *The Cherry Orchard,* which would alternate with a revival of
the Civic's other great success, *Alice in Wonderland.*

   Among the apprentices who witnessed Nazimova in rehearsal were
May Sarton and a German Italian actor, Tonio Selwart. As before, Eva
played Varya and was the nominal director, but it seemed to Selwart that
Nazimova created many of the production's best moments. In the play's
last scene, he remembered, when Ranevskaya has lost her orchard, Eva
directed Paul Leyssac, who played Gayev, to put a consoling, brotherly
arm around Nazimova. But when he tried it, Nazimova said: "Paul, I

don't like that. We should put our faces together—like two forlorn horses." The result was an image that demonstrated to Selwart why "Nazimova was the greatest actress I had ever seen. She always made everything so *alive*."

"A great actress, no doubt about it," May Sarton agreed. And noticed, like Selwart, that Eva occasionally resented finding herself in Nazimova's shadow. "Although both women were very small, Nazimova was so much more *visible*." Selwart remembered that Eva's mother, "a very sophisticated woman," came to a few rehearsals and "used to call Nazimova 'my spiritual son.' It made Le Gallienne a bit jealous. And by contrast, you know, she was a rather cold actress." But this time it was Eva who needed Nazimova, and the friction never became serious.

The Cherry Orchard opened at the New Amsterdam Theatre on March 6 to reviews that found the production an improvement on the original and Nazimova's performance even finer than before. "She has obviously worked on it," John Mason Brown wrote in the *Evening Post*, "[and] discovered undiscovered nuances"; for Woollcott in *The New Yorker* she was "the most glamorous experience offered by the present season"; and for Lillian Gish, also in the first-night audience, the fascination of Nazimova was that "you never caught her 'acting.' "

Because of the demand for tickets, Eva added three weeks to the run of the play. When it closed, Nazimova went to Who-Torok with Glesca, who found Nina and Lucy still unfriendly but at least settled into an attitude of "silent enmity." On June 4, Nazimova noted in her diary: "I am 54. The sky. Tall poplar and elm. The sun. The wild candy in the apple tree." And on June 5: "Sultry day—did not keep my word—did not start on the book." She had planned to work on her autobiography again, but was sidetracked by another movie offer. In the first years of the talkies, Hollywood studios imported a number of Broadway stars because of their experience with dialogue, but some of them, like Ruth Chatterton and Ina Claire, were in their forties and didn't photograph well. No doubt Nazimova's age caused RKO to make its offer of two pictures a year contingent on a screen test. It was shot in New York, and according to her diary for July 24: "Everyone said, 'You look indecently young.' I said, 'I feel thirty.' " But two days later she saw the test: "Terrible photography. Sound excellent. Must never try to look conventionally beautiful. I am depressed." Silence from RKO until August 16, when the diary records: "West Coast Studios not satisfied with test. (No wonder!)" And that was the last she heard from RKO on either coast.

Meanwhile, Philip Moeller had patched up his differences with Nazimova, and proposed to star her with Claude Rains in *The Seagull* for the Theatre Guild. But Langner was not a Chekhov enthusiast, and when he vetoed the idea, the Lunts decided to stage the play under their own management. As a result, Nazimova had no immediate prospect of work at a time when the Depression was affecting many actors in movies as well as theatre. Romantic Hollywood icons like Gloria Swanson and John Gilbert seemed suddenly dated, and Valentino, had he lived, would have suffered the same eclipse. Signaling a movement away from the grand style and "into the streets of American life," Cheryl Crawford joined Harold Clurman and Lee Strasberg in founding the Group Theatre. Sympathetic to its aims, Nazimova contributed money to the Group, although there was obviously no place for her in the social-problem melodramas of Paul Green and Sidney Kingsley. There was little place for her on Broadway either, with Kaufman-and-Hart and Kaufman-and-Ferber creating a highly popular and specifically American type of comedy, *Once in a Lifetime* and *Dinner at Eight,* Noël Coward reinventing the British comedy of manners with *Design for Living,* and Katharine Cornell carrying on the old Anglophile tradition in *The Barretts of Wimpole Street.* But although Eva was forced to disband the Civic after one more season, she could go on tour in the same Ibsen repertory that Nazimova had performed twenty years earlier, play *Love for Love, Private Lives,* and even *Hamlet* in summer stock, revive *Camille* in New York. For a foreigner in her fifties there were far fewer options. And O'Neill, the only contemporary American playwright to provide Nazimova with a great role, had to insert a few lines in his text explaining that Christine was of French and Dutch descent, and "furrin-lookin'."

Lack of any other offers was probably the reason she agreed to appear in a three-character play about the love-versus-career problems of three women, for Alexander Kirkland remembered it as completely unworthy of Nazimova's talent. *Doctor Monica,* set in Vienna, was a Bessie Marbury package with two of her clients already attached: Laura Walker, who "adapted" it from a Polish original; and the Russian Dmitri Ostrov, who had recently directed Judith Anderson in *As You Desire Me.* The cast was equally international: Nazimova in the title role, Danish actress Beatrice de Neergaard as a maidservant, and Gale Sondergaard, the only American but distinctly "furrin-lookin'," as an architect.

Advance publicity claimed that *Doctor Monica* had run for two years in Warsaw, but it lasted only two weeks after opening at the New York Playhouse on November 6. The critics dismissed it as a dated entry in the women's-independence sweepstakes, and considered Nazimova's perfor-mance, in the words of Burns Mantle, "art's labor lost." A year later, the play became an almost instantly disposable movie with Kay Francis.

The day *Doctor Monica* closed, Clifford Odets sent Nazimova *I Got the Blues,* the first draft of *Awake and Sing.* Odets had been an admirer since adolescence, when he was "profoundly moved" by the movies of *A Doll's House* and *Salome,* and hoped that Nazimova would play the Jew-ish mother. But as her diary records, she decided against it: "Excellent, but not for me." On November 23 she noted her reaction to O'Neill's *Ah, Wilderness!:* "What tripe. I'm *really discouraged.*" That same week, the Theatre Guild was considering her for a leading role in O'Neill's latest, *Days Without End.* "Gene and I have been doing a lot of thinking as to Nazimova playing Elsa!" Carlotta had written Langner. "There's lots *against* and lots *for.* (So few actresses feel anything under their skins—and are so artificial. [Jane] Cowl I have always loathed.) Nazimova knows what to love and to suffer means—even if her hair did become dis-arranged in the process!" Under pressure from the leading man, Earle Larrimore, his wife got the part. But Nazimova's loss was hardly Selena Royle's gain, and *Days Without End,* one of O'Neill's lesser plays, lasted only fifty-seven performances.

"HAVE YOU a play? Have you heard of a play?" Nazimova asked Ward Morehouse, drama critic of the New York *Sun,* who had written to ask why she wasn't working. The Theatre Guild, Arthur Hop-kins and Herman Shumlin, she explained, were all willing to "produce a play for me—if they or I could find one," and she had hoped that S. N. Behrman would write a play for her about Emma Goldman. When Na-zimova suggested it, he seemed "very enthusiastic, [but] some other idea must have pushed her into oblivion."

This was in August 1934, when she had been out of work for nine months and was spending another summer with Glesca at Who-Torok; another "revolting family row" erupted. Outraged to discover that Nina had secretly taken out a $10,000 mortgage on the gatehouse cottage but still expected her to pay for its upkeep, as well as the heating bills every winter, Nazimova asked Henry Harvitt to intercede. He got Nina to agree that Nazimova should pay off the mortgage and become the legal owner again; Nina decided to leave the cottage and join Lucy, who was working as a lab assistant in Jersey City.

On August 23, Val Lewton left for Hollywood and an assignment to adapt *Taras Bulba* for David Selznick at MGM. (The project was shelved, but he remained on Selznick's payroll as story editor.) "My nephew is 28," Nazimova wrote Leona Scott, a fan with whom she occasionally corresponded, "married 4 years, has a baby. Fell in love at 16 with a schoolfriend and married her. Knows nothing about 'life.' Writes 'hot' books for a living. That's life too, isn't it?" *Yasmine,* a soft-porn novel that sold in a sealed plastic wrapper for $75.00, appeared under the name "Carlos Keith" while Lewton was working for the MGM publicity office in New York, and as Carlos Keith he also wrote a steamy Depression romance, *No Bed of Her Own,* which Paramount filmed under the less steamy title of *No Man of Her Own,* with Carole Lombard and Clark Gable.

At the end of October, Nazimova and Glesca moved back to the Buckingham, leaving a caretaker couple to look after Who-Torok for the winter, and six weeks later Glesca left to spend Christmas with her mother in Cambridge. At this point her memoir becomes very evasive, but it seems the relationship with Nazimova had been under strain, partly no doubt because Nazimova hadn't worked that year and they had spent too much time together. "I felt I needed a vacation," Glesca writes, "[but] Nazimova feared I was going off for ever." No explanation, although Glesca hints rather coyly that "she occasionally got upset at me when I was naughty. . . . But at times Moosie could be naughty, too, in what she said or in her attitude." Again no explanation of the naughtiness on either side, and an apparent *non sequitur* as Doodie then admits asking Moosie "various questions about sex. I enjoyed our discussions because she would tell me anything I asked about. She wanted me to understand everything. I also recall questioning her on how many lovers she'd had, and started counting them on my fingers, for which she promptly scolded me."

This, of course, is too naïve to be true, like another glimpse of "our home life" described by Glesca. Nazimova had always taken care of her living expenses, and now paid her a modest salary as well. "The reason I don't give you more money is I'm afraid you'll leave me," she had recently remarked, which Glesca found "strange" at first. Then she realized that Nazimova "had finally found the 'home' she longed for with me, and was afraid to lose it. She was at ease and happy mothering a borrowed child." And for the borrowed child "it was enough to be fascinated with everything Nazimova represented. . . . If I wanted to have an occasional fling, I did. Nazimova was not always aware of this. But I never made commitments because of work."

The "borrowed child":
Glesca Marshall

By the time she wrote this, Glesca was drinking fairly heavily, and perhaps fuddled by the various masks of denial she chose to wear. It's hard to reconcile the "borrowed child" (now aged twenty-six), who finds it necessary to conceal "an occasional fling" (if she really had one) from her adoptive mother, with the Doodie who grills Moosie about her sex life. And was Glesca betrayed by her unconscious when she segued from "Moosie could be naughty" to wondering "how many lovers she'd had." Vincent Sherman remembered "a young actress with just a bit part in the play hanging around Nazimova's dressing room" during the tour of *The Good Earth,* and whether or not Glesca heard about it, she learned something else two weeks after leaving Who-Torok:

> I received a strange letter from Nazimova saying she had met a young, brilliant playwright with great potential, who had become the love of her life. (She later told me that she had slept with him the night of the day I left.) . . . She told me she had decided to marry him and move with him to Japan because Japan sounded like a wonderful place to her as [Frederick] Schlick had described it. . . . I remember walking to a cafe in Cambridge and rereading the long letter as tears

poured down my cheeks. I was shocked that she should cut
me off so abruptly. What especially hurt was that she had
written that she was going to let him drive the Chrysler convertible she had given me.

Like the list of "many of my faults" that Glesca discovered as she read
on, the business of the Chrysler convertible seems intended to wound.
And rather than a mother writing to her surrogate daughter, the letter
suggests one lover informing another after a quarrel that she's fallen in
love with somebody else. "I became so mad," Glesca writes, "I tore the
letter in small pieces." So her faults as perceived by Nazimova remain un-
recorded, although others have itemized them; and little is known about
the affair, or Frederick Schlick himself, because "the next six months were
torn up, removed or lost [*by whom?*] from Nazimova's diaries."

In fact, several diary notes and an important letter survive from the
period in question. Though the affair continued, Schlick moved to a
hotel across the street from the Buckingham; he never drove the Chrysler
after Glesca called Nazimova from Cambridge, "wished her well," and
asked her "please not to let him drive my car." And by the end of the year,
the Theatre Guild had found a play for Nazimova, Shaw's *The Simpleton
of the Unexpected Isles*. (Shaw had recommended Mrs. Pat for the role,
but the Guild decided she was too old and too temperamental.) Like *The
Apple Cart*, Shaw's other "Political Extravaganza," the play derives its energy from long and argumentative conversations, in this case on the use-
lessness of idealism, especially the Christian variety. The wit is often
brilliant, but the point of view proved unamusing to Broadway audiences and critics when *The Simpleton* opened on February 18, 1935. According to Langner, Nazimova as the Priestess Prola "had difficulty in
mastering a role in which she fluctuated between a *réligieuse,* a seductress,
a sybil and a saint, and she finally settled for the seductress, which came
more naturally." The Guild sent production stills to Shaw in England; he
wrote Mrs. Pat: "Nazimova, in *your* part, appears a slinking sinuous oda-
lisque. She should have been straight as a ramrod: an Egyptian goddess.
When I am not on the spot, the harder they try, the wronger they go."

Soon after the play opened, Nazimova heard from her cousin in
Moscow that her mother had died. Sonya had taken a series of young
lovers, and only a few months earlier the cousin had informed Nazimova
of "my mother's all-night orgies and young man who threatens to expose
it all if she doesn't pay him 14 dollars. All this at 80. My hat's off to her!"
Nazimova at fifty-six had a lover in his twenties, so perhaps she inherited
Sonya's gene for sexual abundance. And although they kept a distance
from each other for forty years, mother and daughter remained, in a cu-

rious way, close. Nazimova never tried to visit Sonya in Odessa; apart from fearing that the Soviet government would refuse her an exit visa, perhaps she was also afraid of repeating the disappointment of their last meeting, in 1895. Instead she made pilgrimages to Montreux and her "laughing, luscious Mama as she was then," and perhaps Sonya also paid memory visits to the child she had once loved. For she bequeathed everything to Alla, including her late husband's scientific equipment and library, which Nazimova gave to the Soviet government at the request of its consulate in New York.

The Simpleton lasted only five weeks, and just before it closed, according to Glesca, she received a letter from Nazimova "inviting me for a visit so I could meet Schlick." Surprised and mystified, she decided to accept. "It was an awkward meeting for me," Glesca wrote in her memoir, and "Nazimova was highly nervous, fidgety in fact, constantly lighting cigarettes. . . . She wasn't one to react like this in a difficult situation. She usually remained amazingly calm." But if Nazimova found the situation "difficult," why did she create it? Or did Glesca in fact invite herself? She admits to intense curiosity about Schlick, who had written a play about Paul Gauguin, and whom she found "young like me, in his twenties, small and short in stature. I knew we were both tied to her, but in different relationships, theirs being physical. He didn't impress me, and strange as it seems, I was looking for what might have attracted her." Once again Glesca seems confused behind her mask of denial. If her relationship to Nazimova was not "physical," why did Nazimova feel she had to break it off on Schlick's account?

"Reading Yellow Christ," Schlick's play about Gauguin, the diary notes on April 21. A few days later, Nazimova wrote him a long letter dated Easter Sunday: "I wish I had read *The Yellow Christ* before you left. But that evening—you remember?—the task seemed too heavy. . . . Perhaps I should not have read it now. . . . And perhaps I should not have written this letter. . . . And perhaps it is *good* I *have* written it. One thing I know clearly—I have written this—my impersonal opinion of *The Yellow Christ* as I would have written it had I not known the author."

In fact, her opinion is too devastating to be impersonal, and the tone of Nazimova's letter makes it clear that she was personally affronted by Schlick's lack of talent. She finds the character of Gauguin "uninspired and uninspiring" and "*absolutely sexless in spite of all his 'sexy' talk*"; finds the character of Van Gogh "a half-wit, a moron," and the scene when he cuts off his ear as unintentionally funny as only a writer without any sense of humor could make it; finds the play as a whole "constructed to a stereotyped and shopworn formula," overladen with "talk, talk, talk," its metaphors "sweated over" and "artificial," and its dialogue apparently "written by an impotent old man who had once been a lusty lover."

After this, it's hardly surprising that Nazimova never wanted to see Frederick Schlick again. He exits from theatrical history only a few months after entering it, remembered by one actress, Erin O'Brien-Moore, as an unsuccessful playwright who never had his work produced and was "heartbroken" when Nazimova rejected him, and in the obituaries of another actress, Isabel Jewell, as her first husband. Soon after Nazimova wrote the letter, her diary notes that Schlick returned several presents she had given him: "Received my books, my silver ring and a typical letter—'Of course you realize I love you and will always love you.' How did it happen?"

"She frequently said to me, 'Some day I'm going to tell you what happened,' " Glesca wrote in her memoir, "but she never got around to it." More probably, Glesca never got around to telling the full story of an obviously humiliating episode. All that survives to tell Nazimova's side of the story are her two brief diary entries and the copy she made of her letter to Schlick, which must have afforded Glesca's only moment of satisfaction. But Schlick's letter to Nazimova is among the "lost" or "removed" documents of this period, and "while I was away," according to Glesca, Nazimova also destroyed "almost every letter concerning her life before 1925." Once again no explanation, but once again it seems likely that Glesca's own selective hand was at work after Nazimova's death.

If Schlick aroused Nazimova sexually, in other ways he was an anticlimax. She believed in his talent as a writer until she read his play, and then no longer desired him as a lover. (Or a husband. She also confided in Henry Harvitt, who remembered that marriage plans were sufficiently advanced for Nazimova to have a premarital checkup.) As for the list of Glesca's faults, no one listed charm or a sense of humor among her virtues. A few of Nazimova's friends disliked Glesca because they agreed with Jo Hutchinson that she was pushy, and because she had an irritating habit of spouting self-important clichés. This habit also irritated Nazimova, who once noted in her diary, "Doodie is off again on LIFE, ETHICS etc etc," but Doodie took pride in her wisdom. "Achievements of value live only in ourselves, and no one can make them less or greater," she told Moosie. An idea, she adds solemnly in her memoir, "which I continue to believe holds true."

BACK IN Cambridge, Glesca heard nothing from Nazimova until May 1, when a letter asked her "to come visit." It made no mention of Schlick, who was not present when she arrived, and although Glesca was "waiting to learn what had happened and what was going to happen," Nazimova never uttered his name. Instead, she announced that she was leaving next day for Milwaukee, where the Ann Arbor Dramatic Festival had invited her to appear in and stage a performance of *Ghosts*. Then Glesca's account dissolves to Grand Central Station, where she's seeing Nazimova off. Still no mention of Schlick. They say goodbye, and "I was turning to walk away when she said, 'Please come back, I did a very foolish thing.'" Since the train is about to leave, Nazimova has no time to say anything more except: "Go to Port Chester and put the house [Who-Torok] in order."

Although Glesca felt "as if it was time to go 'home,'" she was not yet all the way home. "After the Schlick affair I realized that Nazimova closed herself off from me for a long time. There was love and concern for me in an inward way . . . but not much outward expression of her affection." And it was six weeks before they saw each other again. Nazimova didn't invite Glesca to join her in Milwaukee, where her diary for May 12 notes: "*Ghosts* for the first time . . ."

12

Ghosts

1935–1936

> Sometimes I think we are all ghosts. . . . It's not
> only what we have inherited from our parents that
> haunts us, but all kinds of old dead ideas and all
> kinds of old dead beliefs. They are not actually
> alive in us; but they are dormant, all the same, and
> we can never be rid of them.
>
> —MRS. ALVING IN *Ghosts*

WHEN ROBERT HENDERSON FOUNDED THE
Ann Arbor Dramatic Festival in 1929, it was out of "my fantastic admiration of Nazimova as an artist—so that some day I might have a season
distinguished enough to attract her. For five consecutive years I asked her
to play in the festival, and each year I was graciously refused. And when
she finally accepted to appear in *Ghosts*, it was entirely due to Romney
Brent who was appearing with her at the time for the Theatre Guild."

Brent, who spoke perfect unaccented English but was born Romulo
Larralde in Mexico, played the title role of the clergyman in *The Simpleton*. (Two years later, he became a leading man in British films, notably
opposite Elisabeth Bergner in *Dreaming Lips*.) He had hoped to play Oswald to Nazimova's Mrs. Alving in a Broadway production of *Ghosts*, and
when the money fell through the same week that Henderson made his
sixth offer, Brent suggested they try the play out at the Ann Arbor Festival. After *The Simpleton* closed, Nazimova began directing rehearsals

with another member of the cast, McKay Morris, as Pastor Manders, and *Ghosts* opened on May 12 at the Pabst Theatre in Milwaukee. "After the drop of the final curtain, and the subsequent rise for just Madame Nazimova," the Milwaukee *Sentinel* reported, "there broke out a hurrahing and huzzahing such as we read about in the opera houses of Europe."

Since Brent had another commitment, the run was limited to one night in Milwaukee and three in Ann Arbor. By the last performance, Nazimova had developed acute tonsillitis, and on June 17 underwent a tonsillectomy at St. Luke's in New York. Two days later, she "crocheted a beret for D[oodie] of blue wool. Looked terrible and I never laughed more hilariously in my life. Everything that worried me seemed to be taken out and off with my rotten tonsils." The diary doesn't specify her worries, but after the Schlick affair she was no doubt relieved to find Glesca at her bedside and her chief support system back in place.

That summer, which they spent at Who-Torok, Nazimova tried again to set up a Broadway production of *Ghosts* with herself and Romney Brent. The Theatre Guild was interested and offered her a guarantee of $750 a week and 10 percent of the profits, but "I refuse profits and want $1000 guarantee on 15% of gross." Nazimova's diary is rarely concerned with this kind of haggling, and Glesca's hand may be detected here. The Guild refused Nazimova's terms, but a young producer called Luther Greene, who had seen *Ghosts* in Ann Arbor, accepted them. Although his experience was limited to summer stock, he had Broadway ambitions and offered to find the money to present the play in New York.

On September 24, while still waiting for news from Greene, Nazimova was invited by George Gershwin to the dress rehearsal of *Porgy and Bess*. When she arrived, he gave her a welcoming hug and said, "You're gonna love it!" As her diary records, she did: "Terribly thrilling. Stayed until D and I were worn out with excitement." And on September 29, her other nephew, Volodya's son, came out to Who-Torok: "Arrived 2. Until 9. Hitler makes life *unbearable* for non-Aryans." Before leaving Germany, young Volodya Leventon withdrew all his money from the bank, strapped the banknotes to his body underneath his clothes, and crossed the frontier to Holland. But his mother, who was Aryan, had persuaded his father to stay on in Berlin, at least for a while. Nazimova still thought of Volodya as the eternal student, but after hearing young Volodya talk about him, she noted: *My brother is an old man.*

By the first week of October, Luther Greene had found a partner, Sam Levy, who owned a chain of burlesque houses and dreamed of prestige, and the money for *Ghosts* was in place. But since every Broadway theatre

Ona Munson, 1935

was booked until the end of the year, the production would have to tour for at least two months before opening in New York, and Romney Brent bowed out. Nazimova auditioned other actors for three weeks without finding a satisfactory Oswald, but engaged McKay Morris to repeat his performance as Manders, cast thirty-year-old Ona Munson as Regina, and hired Glesca as stage manager.

Dismissing Ona Munson in a short and frosty paragraph as a musical-comedy actress with little dramatic experience, Glesca claimed in her memoir that she was "not as serious about the production as she was ambitious," and had "attitude clashes whenever Nazimova tried to direct her." But although she began her career in musicals, Ona had played dramatic roles in movies as well as theatre, and in fact received excellent notices for her Regina. The reason for Glesca's hostility was explained later by Harry Ellerbe, the actor finally cast as Oswald: Nazimova and Ona became lovers.

Ona Munson was a gifted and troubled actress, remembered today chiefly for her Belle Watling in *Gone with the Wind*. In 1932, she fell deeply in love with Ernst Lubitsch, who was fond but unfaithful, and their affair ended when Lubitsch married Vivian Gaye, a former agent. Ona decided to resume her stage career in New York, and only three months later Nazimova cast her in *Ghosts*. Schlick had been the last

Young Man in Nazimova's life, and Ona would be the last Young Woman, but Glesca couldn't know this. As she wrote in her memoir, "Nazimova closed herself off from me," and it's not surprising that Glesca appeared closed off to Ellerbe and other members of the cast. In 1950, Ellerbe wrote an account, which was never published, of working with Nazimova. As a record of the actress it's perceptive, but Ellerbe kept his perceptions of her private life off the record. Glesca was still alive, and discretion had become second nature in the repressive atmosphere of the time.

At first Ellerbe found Glesca "intimidating . . . but when I discovered that aside from her chores of running the show, she managed Madame Nazimova's business affairs, both professional and private, I understood the mantle of caution, aloofness, assertiveness, even suspicion that enveloped her." To understand Glesca, he came to realize, was to admire her sometimes stoic capacity for endurance. And with only a few degrees of exaggeration, he found it "ironic that an insignificant understudy in a repertory company should guide a celebrated though bankrupt film star back to solvency and a new career surpassing in brilliance anything she'd known before."

Ellerbe saw the former understudy and the solvent star for the first

In 1939, the final production of Ghosts. *Harry Ellerbe, Nazimova, and Helen Beverley as Regina*

time when he came to audition for *Ghosts*. On the bare stage of the Longacre Theatre, Glesca sat alone in shadow near the wings, and in the glare
of a pilot light Nazimova sat center-stage between Ona Munson and
McKay Morris. "Violet-blue eyes embedded in an incredibly beautiful,
masklike face" was Ellerbe's first impression, his second of a voice with a
slight but "beguiling" accent as she asked, "Have you ever seen this play?"

He nodded. "Two years ago I saw Alexander Moissi play Oswald in
Cincinnati."

"Oh good God!" She sounded horrified. "Can you forget it, do you
think?"

"Easily," he said, and explained that he hadn't liked the performance
or the production. Nazimova smiled, asked the others to leave, and for
"perhaps the most enthralling hour of my life" described the St. Petersburg production of *Ghosts* in which she played Regina. Onstage, according to Ellerbe, she spoke "impeccable" English, but in private, especially
when excited, she pronounced the letter "R" as a "soft" "D":

> Orlenev was an egomaniac actor. He distorted the play to suit
> his conceit. He built the role of Oswald by his *own* writing,
> cutting down Mrs. Alving so much it was no longer Ibsen. I
> was veddy angry. . . . I made a solemn oath. Some day, I said
> to myself, I will present this play true to Ibsen and I will play
> Mrs. Alving because then I will be old. And now, you see?
> Here I am—*old!* And that is my Ghosts story.

Nazimova put on a pair of horn-rimmed glasses and handed him a
copy of the script that she had edited from the English translation, making a few cuts and revising some of the dialogue so that it played more
colloquially. "You will read the first act with me." It was a command;
Ellerbe obeyed, and when they finished she took off her glasses and gave
him a long stare. "Are you a quick study, Haddy?" He nodded. "Veddy
good. You will open in *Ghosts* at the McCarter Theatre in Princeton,
New Jersey, on this coming Saturday night."

It was then four o'clock on Monday afternoon.

DURING REHEARSALS of *A Month in the Country,*
Alexander Kirkland became aware of what he called Nazimova's "duality," the way "cumulus of tears and sunspots of humor" in her eyes reflected abrupt and sometimes mysterious changes of mood. Her
subconscious experience, he believed, was always unusually "close to the
surface of her consciousness"; and during the first few days of rehearsing

Ghosts, Ellerbe found Nazimova's habit of making personal remarks, although "never intended to be offensive," sometimes embarrassingly direct. ("What is wrong with you today? Why so namby-pamby?") He also noted another example of duality in the way she combined traditional "feminine" and "masculine" qualities, at one moment seductively fragile, at the next barking orders "with military terseness."

Nazimova began the first day of rehearsal by warning Ellerbe that she expected a high level of energy. "What is this nonsense about *saving* oneself at rehearsal? What do they save themselves for? Rehearsal is for work, and the harder the rehearsing, the easier the performance." She also talked, as Nemirovich had done, of "training in mental and physical alertness," and the importance of correct breathing. "Write in your script when learning lines, *intake* here, *outtake* there. You lose control of breathing, you lose effect of line." But before the November 2 opening in Princeton, there was time only for Nazimova to lead Ellerbe through the blocking of the main scenes, and to criticize his French when Oswald tells Mrs. Alving about the doctor in Paris who described his physical condition as "worm-eaten—*vermoulu.*" As he spoke the last syllable, she interrupted. "Like most Americans your French is veddy poor. Cut *vermoulu,* darling." Although his performance was warmly applauded, Ellerbe felt she had "carried" him through it and achieved "a small miracle" in five days. Presumably Nazimova agreed: the rest of the cast congratulated him, but she said nothing.

Opening night in Philadelphia, the company "received an ovation the likes of which I'd never witnessed before," even though it was election night and the actors had to raise their voices against the sound of car horns and a brass band in the street outside. This time Nazimova's reaction was to send Glesca to Ellerbe's dressing room with a note criticizing one of his scenes. "Just when do you intend to play it as rehearsed?" He exploded with rage, called Nazimova "a fiend of a woman," and Glesca ran out in alarm. Next day the Philadelphia *Inquirer* announced that Nazimova's Mrs. Alving "should live as one of the great performances of our age," and all the other actors "rose to heights which matched her perfection." Nazimova summoned the cast. "We have been praised to the skies, my darlings, but we are only shallow success. When those honorable gentlemen, the critics, take us as we are, they only prove the greatness of Ibsen. Now we must get to work, hang flesh on the skeleton." It was so charmingly said that everyone, even Ellerbe, felt happy.

The nightly ovations in Boston, according to Ellerbe, were "in large measure due to Nazimova's performance. In her infinite theatrical wisdom she knew this and was none too happy about it." Until the New York opening, she rehearsed the company several times a week, concentrating on the scenes with Oswald, and pressuring Ellerbe to make their struggle over the box of morphine capsules more violent. "Don't be afraid to throw me across the room with full strength. Please, darling, I will take care of myself. And do not hesitate, Oswald would *kill* for the drug, so throw me with force, Haddy. And more *anger*. And *scream* at me. Full force—full strength!"

They rehearsed the struggle for an entire afternoon, and "to watch her slight frame take my full strength, hurtle itself across the stage—reeling, almost but never quite falling, was a revelation in technical believability." Finally satisfied, Nazimova lit a cigarette and launched into an energetic monologue while Ellerbe collapsed in a chair. "The theatre is bigger than life, Haddy, make no mistake. Reality, yes! But *real* reality is dull—it has no technique. It belongs in the kitchen, in the laundry. We must give *illusion* of reality by good acting. Otherwise, stay in the kitchen, stay in the laundry. . . . But tell me, why are so many young actors *afraid* to act?" With hardly a pause, she answered her own question. "They are taught— all in the name of Stanislavsky—*real* reality, they are even encouraged to improvize their scenes offstage before making their entrance, and by the time they make it, they are too exhausted to act! Dear God. Such waste." Then, after a moment of thought: "After the collapse on the sofa, Haddy, take a longer pause before you call 'Mother.' It will hold. And call in thinner voice. Like a child. And when you call for the sun, remember the brain is gone. . . . You are unable to speak the S of sun, make more lisp to it, like a child." And after another moment of thought: "I am directing this scene, you know, the way I recall my father before he died."

The play ends with Oswald's mental disintegration as he repeats over and over "The sun . . . the sun," while Mrs. Alving stares at him, unable to decide whether to keep her promise and give him an overdose of morphine. Neither could Nazimova. In performance, as the tour continued, sometimes she moved to give Oswald the overdose, sometimes she remained frozen with uncertainty. And either way she considered "true to Ibsen." Oswald's syphilis, she told an interviewer, was only a "device" that Ibsen invented "as the supreme test of a woman's soul. For that reason, it doesn't matter that the play is all wrong medically. . . . Oswald inherits the disease, while Regina, a child of the same father does not. And why didn't Mrs. Alving catch it?" At the heart of the play, Nazimova believed, was another disease, Mrs. Alving's fear and guilt, her struggle with the inner ghosts of family secrets and betrayals, dead beliefs and ideas: "The world is full of Mrs. Alvings. There are millions of women living today in secondrate narrow-minded towns, who wouldn't dare to get divorces, who would be afraid of damaging their reputations. Oh yes, Mrs. Alving is everywhere. And Pastor Manders you will find everywhere too, unfortunately."

In "the morphine scene," as Nazimova called it, Ellerbe was astounded not only by her subtle technique, but by the fact that "it never failed to achieve its intended reaction from the audience," whether she remained immobile or moved to give Oswald the drug. And in Toronto she finally congratulated Ellerbe on his progress. "The disillusionment at your father's depravity, the fight for the drug, the condemnation of your mother, good!" But then came one of her sudden and "embarrassing" moments of truth. "You are still namby-pamby when you speak of Regina. You need feverish passion. Do you not know passion, Haddy?" He blushed, because the scene with Regina was his "greatest block in the play," but several performances later he felt that he'd overcome it, glanced at Nazimova, and saw "tears streaming down her cheeks."

Luther Greene had raised only enough money to launch the tour of *Ghosts* with sets, costumes, and props rented from stock, and toward the end of November, Nazimova told him she would not take it to New York without a new technical production. Greene agreed, even though he had delayed booking a Broadway theatre until the tour proved a box-office success, and his only option was a guarantee of two weeks at the Empire, beginning December 12. He engaged a young designer, Stewart Cheney, passing on Nazimova's instructions to avoid the traditional clutter and gloom of an Ibsen set, and to light it he chose Abe Feder, who had lit the Virgil Thomson–Gertrude Stein opera, *Four Saints in Three Acts,* and a year later would start working with Orson Welles and the Mercury Theatre. Cheney's set delighted Nazimova, with its pale-gray walls, its muted accents of green in the drapes and upholstery, and "just the kind of sofa Mrs. Alving would have—uncomfortable." Ellerbe admired the "conservatory" in back, "a dramatic expanse of glass looking out upon a backdrop of a Norwegian fjord," and at the dress rehearsal he discovered that Feder's lighting had a "beauty and rightness in its foreboding quality, [which] affected me like incidental music—emotionally." Feder himself was especially pleased with an effect he created as Mrs. Alving described her late husband's corrupt and debauched life. Afternoon light gradually faded, and as she spoke of the "inheritance" that passed to Oswald, Nazimova switched on a table lamp. "Her face was lighted up grotesquely by the lamp shining up into her face. A simple device, but this was contact between actor and audience."

By the time *Ghosts* opened in New York, Nazimova the director was satisfied with what she called the "symphonic beat of the play—a rhythm not only of sound and movement, but of pause and thought, especially thought." In the margin of her script she frequently noted, "Scene begins here, ends here," which had nothing to do with the rise or fall of the curtain, but was a way of breaking down each act into sections, "like musical sentences—*leit motifs* one can trace through the play. They grow and fade." And when Nazimova the actress made her first entrance at the Empire Theatre on December 12, many people in the audience failed to recognize her. In a plain black dress and severe dark wig streaked with gray, shoulders slightly stooped, she spoke at first in a flat, almost timid monotone. This Mrs. Alving was "a woman who had lived long with grief—she had not slipped into it like a coat. Except at one moment close to the end of the play, her emotion was never an outburst; it was just the frayed escaping edge of something she could not quite hold back." The outburst, when it came, was so extreme and violent that it produced a stunned silence for almost a minute after the curtain fell. Accustomed to spontaneous ovations, Nazimova whispered to Ellerbe: "A flop." Then the curtain rose again, and "as if signalled through a cheerleader's megaphone, screams of bravo and applause topped every demonstration we had known before." It continued for twenty-eight curtain calls according to Ellerbe, thirty-eight according to Nazimova, until she was too exhausted to take any more. Then McKay Morris carried her to her dressing room, where she sat receiving congratulations for over an hour. When Arthur Hopkins told her that she had revealed for the first time "the full meaning of that guilty and stricken mother," she threw her arms around him and said: "Now I am satisfied. Now I never want to do anything again." But Ellerbe remembered that, after the last guest left, "the first thing this Total Woman of the Theatre said was: 'What am I going to do next season?' "

"Great is a word for sparing use," Brooks Atkinson wrote in *The New York Times* next day. "But there is no other way to characterize a transcendent performance of a tragic role." Like the other critics, he also singled out Ellerbe, McKay Morris, and Ona Munson for praise, and Alfred Lunt later recalled that the high quality of ensemble acting was essential to the production's success. "Nazimova, a great actress, did not sacrifice play to performance. She acted faultlessly herself, but she also stepped aside and gave their share of the play to the other actors."

Because advance publicity had been insufficient and *Ghosts* was hardly a "Christmas" play, the Empire had been only three-quarters full on opening night. The reviews guaranteed a six-month run, but Luther

Greene was unable to extend the Empire booking, and Ellerbe remembered that "we braced ourselves for an unjust closing." Then the Morosco Theatre became unexpectedly available for an additional two weeks. "They were sold out before the moving vans could deliver the production to the new stage, and rather than close in the face of success, Madame and Mr. Greene decided to take *Ghosts* on the road once more."

In the audience one evening at the Morosco was Charles Bryant. He didn't go backstage but, as Nazimova told Edith, "wrote me a letter re performance. Of course I did not answer it." And at the end of the run, Ona Munson left the company. According to Glesca, "she had signed another contract," and Nazimova was able to replace her with Beatrice de Neergaard from *Doctor Monica,* who had been "her first choice." Ellerbe recorded without comment that Ona "withdrew from the cast," and in private confided that, by the time *Ghosts* opened at the Empire, her affair with Nazimova was over. He didn't know the reason, but it seems the glue that bound Ona to her lovers, although powerful, usually came unstuck before very long. Unlike the parting with Lubitsch, this one was not bitter: soon after returning to Los Angeles, Ona spoke affectionately of Nazimova when she met Mercedes for the first time. Mercedes, who was living at the beach, made a reference to her new conquest in *Here Lies the Heart.* Ona, she wrote, "loved to come down to the sea, she often came to spend the night when she was shooting at Republic Studios." And in a passionate letter, Ona wrote Mercedes, "I have no desire for anyone other than you. Darling, darling, darling." But a few months later, she left her for the painter Eugene Berman.

On January 17, 1936, two days before leaving for Chicago, the first stop on the tour, Nazimova noted in her diary: "Mae Murray MUST have $330.00 to pay for her child's operation. I gave her a check. She gave me IOU." With her career, her bank balance, and her mind equally on the skids, poor Mae occupied herself mainly in wangling invitations to charity balls, where she commanded the orchestra to play the "Merry Widow" waltz and whirled around the floor by herself. But as Nazimova discovered a few months later, she could be cunning as well as pathetic. The next time they met, Mae denied that she'd ever signed the IOU. "It must have been someone pretending to be me," she said. When Nazimova inspected the document, she found it was signed "Mary Murray," and on May 17 her diary noted: "Mae Murray has vanished."

"Lucky and Loyal," the diary records on January 20, when *Ghosts* opened in Chicago. Loyal was particularly impressed by the way Nazimova directed Oswald's final disintegration, which he found "exactly right medically." On the 25th, when Nazimova and Glesca went to dinner with the Davises, Edith alerted the gossip columnist of the *Herald,* who reported that Nazimova's goddaughter Nancy "calls her 'Zim'—the best she could do with Nazimova when she was an infant," and that the actress "made one of her famous salads, and worked Roquefort cheese into a paste with cream to eat with it." Nazimova's diary reported simply: "To the Davises. Family. Peace. Contentment. Happiness? Must be."

A week later, in St. Louis, twenty-four-year-old Tennessee Williams, working as a clerk typist for a shoe company, found the last scene between Mrs. Alving and Oswald "so fabulous, so terrifyingly exciting," that he couldn't bear to go on watching it, "suddenly jumped up and rushed out and began pacing the corridor of the peanut gallery, trying to hear what was being said on the stage." Also in St. Louis, Nazimova spoke with a reporter for the *Post-Dispatch* who had interviewed her on her first Ibsen tour. "We talked of Russia," the reporter recalled, "and you were something of a revolutionist even then." Nazimova replied:

> I was what we call now a parlor Bolshevist. . . . Nobody who had grown up in Russia and really thought about things, nobody except those whose lives were swamped in caviar and champagne, could help seeing that things should be different. . . . Now I am frightfully interested in what has taken place in Russia and looking forward to a visit there next summer.

She never made that visit, and just as well. By the summer of 1937, cultural terrorism had liquidated the "formalist" theatres of Meyerhold and Mikhail Chekhov, canceled Eisenstein's film of *Bezhin Meadow* halfway through shooting, denounced Shostakovich for his opera *Lady Macbeth of the Mtzensk District,* and Stanislavsky for his production of Bulgakov's *Molière,* which was ordered to close a week after it opened. Equally disturbing would have been the Soviet government's refusal to grant Meyerhold, Eisenstein, and Shostakovich permission to leave the country, something that Nazimova always feared might happen to her if she went back to Russia.

"Arrive in Kansas City. Toothache," the diary records on February 9; on February 11, "Dr. Webb pulled out tooth (1st canceled performance for 30 years!)"; and on February 12, "In bed all day. Dr. Webb says the whole mouth must be reconstructed. Rosy prospect for summer." On February 21, after playing three nights in Denver, it notes: "Travel . . . in 2 hours from 12 feet snow to palms, roses, cherry blossoms. California! I love you!"

At the Speckles Theatre in San Diego, the first stop in California, the future founder and director of the Old Globe Theatre found Nazimova "breathtaking." Craig Noel was only sixteen at the time, but, looking back on the performance sixty years later, he remembered: "The agony and perplexity of the part was all there. And it was *not* old-fashioned acting, simply acting of a kind one doesn't see any more. Like Martita Hunt in *The Madwoman of Chaillot*." In late February, the company moved to San Francisco, then had a two-week break before opening at the Biltmore in Los Angeles. Nazimova rested in Santa Barbara for a few days with Glesca, then drove down the Pacific Coast Highway, stopping at The Garden of Allah to note, "Main Street in place of orange groves."

For the Los Angeles opening on March 16 there was considerable advance publicity, spearheaded by Louella Parsons in the *Examiner*. Recalling *Camille*, she informed her readers that "Nazimova's torrid love scenes with Rudy Valentino pioneered sex and glamour and I might say 'incubated' the possibility of censorship on all future movie scenarios." The usual Parsons rubbish, but an interesting example of how a Hollywood outcast could be transformed into a pioneer fifteen years later. And backstage at the Biltmore Theatre on opening night, Ellerbe remembered, "there was such an over-abundance of floral tributes for Madame Nazimova there was barely room to walk." Two uniformed ushers arrived in her dressing room with "a florist's box the size of a child's casket," containing layer upon layer of enormous gardenias. "But I don't even *know* her!" Nazimova exclaimed as she stared at a plain white card signed Joan Crawford.

After the final curtain, in spite of "the most tepid applause" Ellerbe could recall since the tour began, there was an impressive pilgrimage of the famous to Nazimova's dressing room. It included Irving Thalberg and Norma Shearer, William Powell, Ruth Chatterton, George Arliss, D. W. Griffith, and finally Marlene Dietrich. She straddled a chair, gazed into Nazimova's eyes, and commanded her to remove her wig. Nazimova, as she told Ellerbe later, refused: "I'm sorry, I never remove my make-up until I'm alone." But when Dietrich repeated the command, "I was so mesmerized looking into those beautiful eyes—I took my wig off." Marlene merely nodded, paid Nazimova a few compliments on her performance, then got up to leave. "But the lighting was too dark," she said. "You are the star, yet we hardly see your face, we never really see your eyes. That is where we in the cinema have an advantage over the theatre." A pause. "The *close-up*."

During the tour, McKay Morris had discussed with Glesca the possibility of his friend Stuart Walker's giving a party for Nazimova and the company after the Los Angeles opening. Although Glesca vetoed the idea, when Nazimova heard that Walker was a movie director and had recently made a successful version of *Great Expectations,* she agreed to go on condition the party not be a big Hollywood affair. Morris promised a simple buffet supper with no more than a dozen guests, but by the time Nazimova and Glesca arrived at Walker's Beverly Hills house at least eighty people had assembled and a jazz combo was playing. As well as a few oddly assorted star guests—Carole Lombard, Kay Francis, and Edna May Oliver—there were former members of the Cincinnati repertory company that Walker used to run—Beulah Bondi, Elizabeth Patterson, Elliott Nugent—the usual gatecrashers, some of them claiming to have worked with Nazimova in silent movies, and in Ellerbe's words "a colorful group of mannish women and effeminate boys" surrounding Mercedes de Acosta.

Glesca took one look at the crowd and indignantly suggested leaving at once, but Nazimova shook her head. Morris introduced her to Stuart Walker, who introduced her to three overweight men in dark suits, the producers he worked for at Universal. "I'll try to catch your show," one of them said; then the silent-movie contingent zeroed in, strangers passing themselves off as friends or colleagues. She was rescued by Ellerbe, and seated on a chair with a glass of wine, but a moment later Mercedes hurried over. As she knelt at Nazimova's feet, the entourage followed, one of the boys also kneeling and kissing her slipper.

Guests standing nearby were amused, but for Nazimova a boundary of privacy had been crossed. "Madame arose so abruptly it caused a silence to fall, [and] asked for the powder room." Then Glesca informed Walker that "Madame has a severe headache and I'm taking her back to the hotel."

Next day, her diary records, Nazimova was "in bed all day resting." The following day, she had visits from Val Lewton and his wife, Ruth; D. W. Griffith; and Joan Crawford ("her flowered sincerity and shyness") with Franchot Tone. By March 20, Mercedes had been forgiven. They lunched together, and she arranged for Harry Edington, an agent whose clients included Garbo and Dietrich, to come by later and meet Nazimova for "talk re pictures." But for the moment it was only talk.

During April, *Ghosts* played Detroit, Cleveland, Buffalo, and Washington; then came four weeks at the Golden (now the Royale) in New York. It could have run longer, but Nazimova was exhausted and retired to Who-Torok with Glesca. On June 4, they celebrated her fifty-seventh birthday by seeing Lunt and Fontanne in *Idiot's Delight,* and going back-stage to congratulate them. Next day Nazimova sent flowers, which Fontanne acknowledged: "We have been so inspired by your acting and your kind words of praise about ours that we can never begin to tell you what you have done for us." At the end of June, Ellerbe arrived at Who-Torok to spend two weeks working with Nazimova on the part of Tesman in *Hedda Gabler.* She had decided to revive it, after polling audiences during the tour of *Ghosts.* Asked whether they would prefer to see her next season in *The Cherry Orchard, A Month in the Country,* or *Hedda,* they voted overwhelmingly for more Ibsen.

Although Nazimova had once told Ellerbe that she was too old ever to play Hedda again, the challenge appeared to vitalize her, and she saw nothing incongruous in casting a twenty-six-year-old actor as her husband. The day Ellerbe arrived, they sat in the living room and she read the play aloud in its entirety. Behind her on the wall hung a 1906 portrait of Nazimova as Hedda by the Polish society artist Ivanovski. Ellerbe couldn't decide which was more "dramatically stunning," Ivanovski's likeness of Nazimova clutching a pistol or the reading in "that magnificent voice. . . . [I] felt like a selfish pig for not sharing this fantastic experience with others."

In an interview with *Newsweek,* Nazimova explained that Ibsen's Hedda was a "poseur," and although in the 1900s "a woman posed physically, today she poses mentally." Accordingly, she had changed her approach to the role. In 1906, she had "struck attitudes" and "draped myself around the furniture," but her 1936 Hedda would "sit quietly" on a chair or couch, letting the audience know "by her expression, by her very stillness, what she is planning to say—what pose she wishes to create."

But in private Nazimova had her doubts, which she confided to Edith: "Am working on the script now, trying to make a more up-to-date job of it (like I did with *Ghosts*), and it's terribly hard, because no matter what you do, she's just a villain." Her mood was not brightened by visits to the dentist four times a week throughout July and August, or by a sultry, stormy summer that brought back old fears: "I've built myself a *storm closet,* i.e. a place where I lock myself up during storms." The letter ended with news of Bryant: "CB's wife fell in love with another man. She is divorcing him and taking the two children because he can't support them. Such is life!"

Later, Stewart Cheney's design for an elegant and spacious living room set gave Nazimova a lift and an idea. Its dominant feature was a stairway that curved dramatically up to the second floor, and although Ellerbe

thought it too grand, Nazimova exclaimed, "I see a new entrance for Tesman," and proceeded to describe it:

> Remember, he has just returned from his honeymoon in the
> Alps, and you see, Haddy, he has encountered many yodelers.
> He determines to master yodeling himself, and thinks he has.
> So why not have him enter at the top of the stairs, and seeing
> Aunt Julia below, release his conception of the yodel? Aunt
> Julia screams her delight, and he runs down laughing and yo-
> deling again, and falls into her arms.

Ibsen's stage direction reads, "Tesman enters humming and carrying
an empty suitcase," but Ellerbe had to confess that he loved Nazimova's
idea and found it completely "in character." Nazimova also reproduced
an effect from her 1906 performance, which had reproduced one of Orlenev's effects, in the scene when Hedda tells Tesman she's pregnant: "I
will place myself three inches up on the fireplace hearth, and with the
train of my gown trailing off the hearth, it will make the impression I
tower over you." Then she added an idea of her own that "blueprinted"
the pathos of Tesman in Ellerbe's mind: "When I look down at you with
such revulsion and say, 'Tesman, I'm going to have a baby,' you will look
up at me with joy—and when you take off your spectacles there are tears
in your eyes."

Vincent Price remembered that, when he first appeared on Broadway
that year, as Prince Albert in *Victoria Regina,* "there were three separate
factions as to who was the greatest stage actress of the time—Laurette
Taylor, Nazimova, or Le Gallienne." Laurette at the time was struggling
with alcoholism, Le Gallienne had no company of her own, and only
Nazimova, after the acclaim for *Ghosts,* was in a position to exert total
control over her career. The contract for *Hedda* gave her as much power
as she had enjoyed in the silent-movie days, with Luther Greene and Sam
Levy deferring to her on cast, stage personnel, management staff, and
choice of cities for the tour, as well as guaranteeing her a private drawing
room on the train during the tour, and 15 percent of the box-office gross.
But soon after rehearsals began at the Longacre, problems developed
with two actors of her choice. George Gaul, a veteran of many Theatre
Guild productions, was playing Judge Brack, and although he asked for
his release on the grounds of ill health, he told Ellerbe in private, "I adore
that woman, but she's just too overpowering." And with Eliot Cabot,
who had played her husband in *A Month in the Country,* Nazimova never
reached common ground on the character of the writer Eilert Løvborg.

In a long letter to Cabot, she described Løvborg as "healthy, passionate, magnetic" at the start. "He must have been madly in love with Hedda (why not?) . . . but being in turn teased, checked and teased again, had been literally driven to seek relief elsewhere." Then, after Hedda burns his manuscript, Løvborg becomes a changed man, "stunned, dazed, desperate. . . . Someone (let us call it Destiny) had been fooling him, [and] pity for him should fill the audience's heart." Cabot argued that Løvborg had already been destroyed by falling in love with someone as egotistical as Hedda; Nazimova argued back that she wanted a Løvborg who was not obviously defeated from the start; and on October 21, the day after the pre–New York opening in Boston, her diary records: "Cabot's blow-up. So what?" He was in fact more emotionally disturbed than anyone realized. Before the Boston run ended Cabot wrote Nazimova, "I really do not see how we can go on together," and resigned from the cast; not long afterward, he committed suicide.

Fortunately, the pre–New York tour lasted three weeks, enough time to rehearse a satisfactory replacement for Cabot before the play opened at the Longacre Theatre on November 16. But in spite of capacity business in Boston and Philadelphia, Nazimova was dissatisfied with her own performance: "I feel 50 years old! My Hedda a cross between 1906 and 1936. No good." And although Noël Coward saw a matinee in Boston and told her, "You can come to London and play the telephone book," she was not reassured. After recording his comment, she added: "But it is NOT GOOD." Yet Coward was not being evasive. On opening night Lynn Fontanne sent Nazimova a gift and a note: "Darling, Noel says it is one of the truly great performances he has ever seen, so here's a little crown for you and when the clock points to eleven the agony will be over, and this generation's greatest 'Hedda' will be established."

"*31 curtain calls*," Nazimova's diary noted. "But I know it is NOT good." And next day: "Critics. 6 are good for me, all the rest call me everything from an Oriental to a college widow and the part is as unbecoming to me as an old shoe. I am worn out and sick." Although the part was considered "unbecoming" by the critics who considered her too old for it, Joseph Wood Krutch in *The Nation* spoke for those on whom Nazimova's dramatic impact was sufficiently major to make her age seem only a minor drawback: "I have seen Heddas who seemed more credible in retrospect; I have never seen one who imposed herself so inescapably." But for Nazimova her performance remained a failure, and by November 18 she felt "utterly lost. All my work seems useless, futile— meaningless."

Ellerbe also thought Nazimova's 1936 Hedda a failure, but "*not* because of performance." For him the problem was "appearance": Nazimova could create but not sustain the necessary illusion of a woman of twenty-nine. For her first entrance, she descended Cheney's staircase "swathed in a gold material from shoulders to ankles with a train snaking behind her, [and] a tight collar extending up to and under her chin, and long tight sleeves terminating in sharp arrow-like points over the top of her hands." She also wore "an astonishing, albeit becoming wig of copper-color hair," with two curls that formed "satanic horns" above the forehead. Like the high-necked, long-sleeved costume, Abe Feder's low-key lighting was designed to cover some basic tracks of age, although, as Nazimova reached the living room and the lighting dimmed, it was clear how much this Hedda would owe to special effects. But in one scene Ellerbe found that everything came together, and Nazimova reached "a level never equaled by other actresses in the role." As Hedda burned Løvborg's manuscript, crouched by the fireplace and feeding it page by page to the flames, she whispered, "I'm burning your child, I'm burning it, burning your child," with a quiet but chilling simplicity. Then, as she flung the remaining pages into the fire with a sudden laugh, Feder's lighting made the flames cast a glow on Hedda's angry, distorted face, and brought the second act to an "electrifying" climax.

No doubt the moment was extraordinary, but Ellerbe's distinction between "performance" and "appearance" is not convincing. As he describes it, Nazimova's first entrance suggests an Emotion Memory of the night Cheryl Crawford watched as she "slithered sexily down the steps" in the game of "Who am I?"—an "incredible impersonation" not of Ibsen's Hedda but of Alla Nazimova the silent-movie star. Ellerbe admits that he expected to hear "muted strains of Far Eastern music" as she descended the staircase, and if the appearance was wrong, the performance couldn't be right.

With *The Cherry Orchard,* Nazimova knew that her acting style had entered a new phase. After her early success in America, she once said, she became "hard and crusted and dazzling [and] out to win gasps." Then the movies "swept me into a brief and treacherous vogue [until] the years piled up their wisdom. . . . And so I think I have grown simple. It is a virtue that comes late to complex people." But after playing what the Philadelphia *Inquirer* described as "her first gray-haired role" in *Ghosts,* Nazimova was not wise enough to resist the temptation of playing her third Hedda, and trying to recapture the dazzle of lost youth. In 1925, a reviewer of her last-but-one silent movie, *The Redeeming Sin,* had commented that "the trouble with Nazimova is that she has a Peter Pan complex and just won't grow up. Why won't she be her own great self?" Although she had become exactly that, the Peter Pan complex still haunted her, "dormant," something she could never entirely be rid of, like Mrs. Alving's ghosts.

In January 1937, Nazimova took *Hedda Gabler* on tour, playing *Ghosts* on alternate nights. She was confronted with a ghost from her more recent past when she saw MGM's movie of *The Good Earth* in Cincinnati. Unrealistic enough about her age to believe she could have starred in it, Nazimova had asked Pearl Buck to put in a word with Louis B. Mayer, and now she inevitably found nothing to praise in Luise Rainer's remarkable performance: "Not inspiring, nor inspired!" Back in New York after the eight-week tour ended, she turned down an offer from MGM to play the supporting role of Marie Walewska's aunt in the Garbo movie *Conquest*. Ironically, the role went to Maria Ouspenskaya, to whom Nazimova would lose out a year later when they both tested for the Maharani in *The Rains Came*.

Hoping for "a modern play if I can find a suitable one," she had found nothing suitable by the first week of May, when she left for Who-Torok with Glesca. But on the 30th, five days before her fifty-eighth birthday, she discovered a lump in her right armpit. Her local physician sent her to Dr. William MacFee in New York, who advised an immediate biopsy. And since Nina had developed breast cancer three years earlier, Nazimova was fearfully certain what the result of the biopsy would be.

13

Villa 24
1936–1945

> Truth? What is it? There is one truth when you are
> seventeen and another when you are thirty-seven,
> and when a woman is an actress, she is one time
> seventeen and one time a hundred and seven. So
> when you ask me the truth of my life, I can only
> say . . . "Life has been no easy matter for me."
>
> —NAZIMOVA

SHE HAD ALWAYS BEEN SO PROUD OF HER
body," Jo Hutchinson remembered. "And in her late fifties Nazimova's
body was still fantastic, slim and firm like an Arab boy's. The prospect of
a mastectomy distressed her terribly. It seemed like a mutilation."

Jo was apparently the only person, apart from Glesca, in whom Nazimova confided that the biopsy had revealed a cancerous tumor. "She
didn't even want Nina to know," Jo said, and she feared the effect on her
career if the news became public. But it soon did. In a breach of confidence, one of the doctors at St. Luke's Hospital told his wife, stage actress
Helen Menken, that Nazimova's right breast had been removed during a
five-hour operation on June 2. Realizing what had happened when letters of condolence began to arrive, she endured one of the most prolonged and abysmal lows of her life:

> June 25: Every time I go to Dr. I have "depression
> fits"!

> June 27: To know that one's body is carrying the
> death blow and might strike any moment.
>
> July 1: Hysterics at night. This constant fear at a
> blow from nowhere.
>
> July 7: I can do nothing. Nothing *lives* in me. I
> eat, sleep, walk, but I am not alive.
>
> July 11: My arm hurts so it leaves my mind blank
> to everything in the world. I *must* think.
>
> July 15: What can I do to stop remembering ugly,
> filthy incidents? . . . I can't sleep.

Back at Who-Torok on July 16, she broke down during an examination by her local physician with the sinister name of Dr. Coffin: "Went to pieces and yelled will it never end? Pump." (As a result of the operation, fluid began to accumulate in her breast and had to be regularly drained with a syringe pump.) The July 17 entry is the last for a month: "Night-mares. Day-mares!" And on August 19, although Dr. MacFee pronounced the cancer in remission (it never returned), he told Nazimova: "You should not work for 1 year for full recovery. (Shall not be normal for 1 year after operation. This means radio only.) Am terribly depressed."

During August she had visits from Edith and Loyal Davis, Harry Ellerbe, Henry Harvitt, and Hortense Alden, who had played a supporting role in *A Month in the Country* and came with her husband, James T. Farrell, author of *Studs Lonigan*. But there is no evidence that Nina ever got in touch, in person or by letter.

Although everyone found Nazimova very discouraged about her future in the theatre, she had begun to think about a future in movies as the result of a letter from her nephew Val Lewton, still working for David Selznick:

> Dear Alla: Yesterday George Cukor, during a conference [on
> *Gone with the Wind*], suddenly went into a long paean of
> praise about you as a woman and an actress. . . . All this re-
> whetted David Selznick's interest in you and for at least an
> hour they did nothing but discuss how best to bring you back
> to pictures and picture audiences. It is David Selznick's feel-
> ing that you are still a great draw but that it would require ex-
> actly the right type of story and combination of other players
> to bring you back to a pre-eminent position in this business.

Selznick's interest in Nazimova was first whetted because his father produced the movie of *War Brides,* and in 1935 he had offered her the role of Madame Defarge in *A Tale of Two Cities.* But she turned him down. "I couldn't do it, and I knew it," she told the New York *Sun.* "When I learned I had to fight with Edna May Oliver, I gave up [and] told them to get Blanche Yurka." Now, on Selznick's behalf, Val wrote to ask Nazimova if she had any ideas for a "screen vehicle." In reply, she asked him to tell Cukor that she remembered their first meeting and "the little picnic on the lawn at Who-Torok and the chat we had," then suggested the story of Madame Curie. On September 9, Val informed Nazimova that Selznick was interested, but "wanted to know what sort of a deal he could make with you," and whether she would consider the idea of first playing "a strong supporting role in some other picture in order to build you to a pre-eminent place on the screen." Nazimova's reply has not survived, but it seems to have been unsatisfactory. On September 27, Val wrote her that "two factors stand in the way of a deal." One was "David's worry that you may not see the necessity of playing supporting roles," and the other was money. Nazimova had met with Selznick's New York representative and demanded $4,000 a week. The figure was no doubt suggested by Glesca in her capacity as "manager," for Val wrote that it was unacceptable and advised Nazimova "to turn the money question over to some really astute agent."

By mid-October, three factors were standing in the way of a deal. Universal owned the rights to a biography of Marie Curie and refused to sell; Nazimova declined a contract for one picture with an option for a second, because of "the embarrassing possibility of the option not being taken up"; and she agreed to consider a supporting role only "if it is a good part, i.e. indispensable to the picture . . . and if this part were offered me only as an introduction to pictures." According to her cousin Henry Harvitt, the basic problem was that at first Nazimova "believed she must be starred in movies, or else she wouldn't accept." A fight with Edna May Oliver was certainly an alarming prospect, but Madame Defarge "was not the only supporting role she was offered and refused."

But by the time negotiations with Selznick broke down, Nazimova's interest in movies had been "re-whetted," and Eva had phoned to express complete disillusionment with the American theatre. After forming a new company that quickly failed, she was "through with uplift, representing Art, being on a pedestal! . . . Is leaving with G. [Marion Evensen, her current lover, known as "Gun"] for Europe and Russia—terribly drunk. Company told her: You are finished and you are taking it out on us! We had no direction, no tuition, nothing from you . . . (she was crying.)" This was on October 24, when the idea of going back to live in

California and find work in movies was already on Nazimova's mind. A week later, leaving Glesca at Who-Torok "to settle pressing business affairs," she took the train for Los Angeles.

NAZIMOVA HAD first met Morris and Elsa Stoloff in 1928, when Morris was concertmaster for the Los Angeles Philharmonic. Now musical director for Columbia Pictures, he lived with Elsa on Stone Canyon Road in Bel Air, and Nazimova stayed with them during most of November. According to Jo Hutchinson, who had been living in Hollywood since 1934 and was under contract to Warners, "Elsa was very helpful in the period after Nazimova's mastectomy. She knew how to calm her down." Nazimova also trusted her with some intimate confidences, and had written several letters about the affair with Ona Munson, which Elsa later destroyed because she "didn't think them important."

Stone Canyon revived Nazimova's love for California: "At 6 in the morning I hear again the lovely morning [sic] dove! This canyon is so beautiful. Drove through several canyons in Hollywood looking for houses. Too conjested [sic]; like living in Coney Island." Bel Air, of course, was too expensive, and Nazimova finally decided to rent a house on Selby Avenue in Westwood. By this time she had landed her first job, although not as an actress. Cukor arranged for her to coach Edythe Marriner (later Susan Hayward) for her screen test as Scarlett O'Hara. Nazimova's diary also records, "Talk about doing *Ghosts*." A few years previously, Arthur Hopkins had hoped to make a movie of it, and Cukor was no more successful in persuading a studio to back the project.

At the end of November, Glesca arrived with her mother, whom she installed in the house on Selby. This was not a success. Nazimova took such a dislike to Mrs. Marshall that California and her new home began to seem "dull and boring," and she told Jo Hutchinson that she felt "like a prisoner," dependent on Glesca for transportation and trapped in the company of a woman she couldn't abide.

She probably overdramatized the situation, but her relationship with Glesca was changing. Her mastectomy apparently signaled the end of Nazimova's sexual life, and in her own life Glesca would soon find a new romantic focus. As Nazimova's love for Glesca became needier, Glesca began to feel her own power. Jo found her sometimes "cold, like a secretary," and she had grown more demanding. When she learned that Nazimova had contacted Sam Zimbalist, now a producer at MGM, about the possibility of a job as acting coach or production assistant at the studio, Glesca asked Nazimova to ask Zimbalist about a job for herself. Zimbalist arranged an interview with Bill Grady, an executive in the talent department, and according to Glesca's increasingly self-important rewrite of her past, she made such a strong impression that he put her in charge of "directing tests of new talent sent in from all over the world." In fact, the job Grady offered was as assistant to two directors, George Sidney and Fred Wilcox, on tests of actors under consideration for long-term contract.

Meanwhile, Louis B. Mayer, with whom Zimbalist had promised to set up an interview, was too busy to see Nazimova for several weeks. On January 1, 1938, she noted in her diary: "Lunch at Garden of Allah. There's a place for a home." The house on Selby was definitely *not* a home, although more tolerable after Mrs. Marshall left at the end of the month. Finally, on February 8, Nazimova saw Mayer in his office and learned that she would become "Sam Z associate producer until ready for 'producer.' Not to be publicized in case work is not for me and so no harm done."

Then Zimbalist had an attack of insecurity. Only recently appointed a producer after several years of apprenticeship as an associate, he feared the competition might be too great. When Robert Florey saw her again that year, he "suddenly realized that the glamorous Nazimova of *Salome* had become a little old lady," but perhaps, through the lens of memory, Zimbalist saw the autocratic Metro producer-star who brought him to Hollywood. Her diary notes the reason he gave for backing away: "If she was as good as he knew she could be, he might be fired! . . . Wants to put me off on somebody else."

At the end of February, according to Glesca, "Nazimova and I moved to 629 Frontera Road [Drive] in Pacific Palisades, where we rented a charming house, also furnished, for the rest of the year." Jo had the impression that Nazimova "was often lonely there." Although Mercedes lived nearby, on Napoli Drive, Glesca was cool to her and to other of Nazimova's friends—Jo, the Stoloffs, and Paul Ivano, whom she finally met with his wife, Greta. "As I think back about the period of the twenties when she [Nazimova] first knew Paul," Glesca comments, "it seems that the general atmosphere of abandonment of morals as well as economic values in America, along with her personal circumstances, allowed such a relationship."

Such holier-than-thou-ness can be understood, if not forgiven. When she wrote her memoir, Glesca was living with Emily Woodruff in

Columbus, Georgia, and their relationship provoked much local gossip. Expecting her account of life with Nazimova to be published while she and Emily were still alive, Glesca had to keep two masks of denial firmly clamped to her face. And perhaps (especially when drinking) she started to believe in them.

When Jo visited Nazimova at the house on Frontera Drive, "she often played scenes from different plays in different ways for me, to illustrate how many approaches there could be to a single scene." But although Nazimova sometimes longed to act again, just as often she claimed that acting no longer interested her, and she wanted only to work on her autobiography, or perhaps in the kind of job that she had once hoped for with Joseph Schenck and Sam Zimbalist. At a previous low point in her life, touring *Woman of the Earth* to earn the "freedom" that she expected *The Garden of Allah* to provide, she had threatened to give up acting. Now her options were severely limited. The mastectomy was a shock from which she never entirely recovered, and its timing seemed particularly cruel. It struck, after many highs and lows, when she was at the summit of a career that had renewed itself for an extraordinary run of eight years, from *The Cherry Orchard* to *Ghosts*. But Florey was not the only person to remark how suddenly Nazimova had aged, and if she could no longer be a star, did she want to become just another Hollywood character actress, competing for roles with Ouspenskaya and Yurka?

FROM *Salvation Nell* in 1908 to *Romance* (which became a Garbo movie) in 1913, Ned Sheldon was the leading Broadway playwright. In 1915, he began to suffer from what appeared to be severe rheumatoid arthritis, but by ten years later it had developed into a creeping paralysis that no doctor could account for. By 1928, Sheldon could move only his head and neck, and a few years later he went blind. But he kept in touch with the theatre from his bedroom, where Thornton Wilder, Robert Sherwood, and Charles MacArthur read first drafts of their plays and asked for advice, and where John Barrymore, Alexander Woollcott, Katharine Cornell, and Lillian Gish often visited him. Nazimova, whom he had admired since first seeing her in *Zaza* with Orlenev in 1905, was also a visitor when in New York, like Mercedes, who believed Barrymore was "the love of his life" and attributed Sheldon's mysterious illness to "emotional frustration."

Another occasional visitor was George Cukor. On a trip to New York in April, he went to see Sheldon and mentioned that he had just signed a contract to direct *Zaza* at Paramount. Sheldon remarked that of all the famous Zazas he'd seen, from Réjane to Gloria Swanson, none could compare with Nazimova, even if you didn't understand Russian. "Won't you tell me about it?" Nazimova's diary records that Cukor asked on his return. She did, then suggested he give her a job on the movie, "designing, helping with suggestions, helping with script, acting etc. He got excited!" Paramount had planned the movie to launch its new star, Isa Miranda, imported from Italy as a successor to Dietrich, whose popularity had temporarily slumped. The producer, Albert Lewin, agreed with Cukor that Nazimova should look at Isa Miranda's test and give her reactions. "I told him she was Mae Westish and said what to do etc. Then came proposition: 15 weeks at 500 per." And since she couldn't drive, the studio agreed to provide a car and chauffeur.

"ALLA DEAR I HEAR YOU HAVE BECOME DIRECTOR," Sheldon cabled when he heard the news. "AM VERY GLAD BUT THEY WILL NEVER GET ZAZA TO EQUAL YOURS I STILL REMEMBER THAT AFTERNOON AT PARK THEATRE BOSTON AND HOW WONDERFUL YOU WERE." After a few days of shooting, it became clear that Miranda was overwhelmed by the problem of acting in English. The studio closed down production, announced that its new star had been injured in an automobile accident, and replaced her with Claudette Colbert. She gave one of her best performances in a movie of exceptional period charm, although as lamed by censorship as Miranda was by the English language. Credited as "production advisor," Nazimova wrote her fan Leona Scott, "Don't praise me or blame me for *Zaza,* I had too little to do with it." Fanny Brice, who struck up a friendship with Nazimova on the set, had more to do with it. She coached Colbert for the musical numbers.

Interviewed for the Los Angeles *Examiner* on the set, Nazimova told a reporter, who didn't bother to check the facts: "No, I have never been married. I never found anyone I wanted to marry." (Was this another example of her subconscious taking over, and blocking an unwelcome subject from her conscious mind?) Nazimova also announced her decision "to retire permanently as an actress," adding that she now "hated" all her silent movies. "My goodness, how we used to ham. . . . Somebody will probably dig among the ruins of our civilization and find that we existed. Can't you see the scientists shaking their heads over us, as they have over early Greeks, Romans, Egyptians and Babylonians?"

Having dismissed her past as a silent-movie star, a few weeks later she moved to The Garden of Allah. In September, shortly after *Zaza* finished shooting, the villa she shared with Isabel Hill for the gala opening in 1927 became the final home of Nazimova and Glesca. Villa 24, she wrote Nina, "is on the second floor . . . a living room, a dinette transformed into Glesca's room, a kitchenette, my bedroom, a tiny bathroom, and occupies less space than the ground floor of Who-Torok cottage." In one way she was still keeping up appearances with Nina, for Robert Lewis remembered "two beds in the bedroom," and Nazimova's diary mentions several times that she entertained guests for dinner in the "dinette."

Villa 24 overlooked a section of the gardens, and the pool Nazimova had built in 1919. But she claimed not to mind facing her luxurious past every day, or picking up her mail in the lobby of the place where she had once lived as Mrs. Charles Bryant. "In spite of this place having been my own I have absolutely no regrets or bitter feelings about having lost it," she told Nina. This was surely not to keep up appearances, for otherwise how could Nazimova have borne to live there? And Harry Ellerbe found "not a trace of bitterness (there could never be with her), but the enthusiasm of a child showing off her toys," when she took him on a tour of the home she had once owned. "I can live cheaper and better here than anywhere else," the letter to Nina continued. Maid service and utilities were paid for by the hotel, she could walk to the market, drugstore, and bank, "there is no need of clothes except slacks, sweaters and skirts, and in the summer we can swim in the pool."

Another advantage, which Nazimova didn't mention, was the management's respect for individual privacy. With no house detective to check on guests, or guests of guests, The Garden of Allah had become a popular place for extramarital assignations as well as for residential unmarried couples of all kinds. Many of the Algonquin Round Tablers— Dorothy Parker, Robert Sherwood, Charles MacArthur, George Kaufman—had stayed there when they first came to make quick money in Hollywood. By now they had either made enough and gone back to New York, or decided to make more and live in rented Beverly Hills houses. As the place where Scott Fitzgerald first met Sheilah Graham at a party given by Robert Benchley, or where Dolores Del Rio first met Lili Damita (before she married Errol Flynn) in the pool, The Garden had been considered raffishly chic. By the end of 1938, it was just raffish.

And by the end of 1938, Nazimova had changed her mind about retiring as an actress, even though Dr. MacFee had written to congratulate her on the *Zaza* assignment and predicted that "your work in the theatrical world will take a slightly different course from past activities." Her year of recovery up, she decided to go to New York in search of a play. To

*Twenty years on. Nazimova in
1938 at the front door of
Villa 24 at The Garden of Allah*

go with her, Glesca wrote in her memoir, "I quit my job at the studio," but in fact she was fired as a result of what Jo Hutchinson called "the scandal over Hedy Lamarr." As well as assisting on tests, Glesca occasionally worked as "dialogue director," which involved running lines with actors before a take. Cuing Hedy Lamarr in her trailer on the set of *I Take This Woman*, Glesca made what the actress interpreted as a pass. The producer was informed, she lost her job, the studio made sure no one leaked the story, and Nazimova probably never knew about it.

On February 1, 1939, she left for New York, stopping in Chicago to spend a couple of nights with Lucky and Loyal Davis while Glesca went on ahead to alert the caretakers at Who-Torok and see that the cottage was in order. On February 18, she drove Nazimova to meet Theresa Helburn in New Haven and see the Theatre Guild production of *The Philadelphia Story* on its pre–New York tour. "She is attractive," Nazimova commented in her diary about Katharine Hepburn, "but the play . . . We spent an evening getting more depressed about the theatre." Nazimova was irritated, according to Glesca, by what she considered the "snobbishness" of Philip Barry. A meeting the next day with Helburn and Lawrence Langner proved no antidote to depression. "Atmosphere of dead wood," Nazimova noted, and turned down the role of the lion tamer in the Guild's production of Andreyev's *He Who Gets Slapped*. "Good show but—'am not excited,' as Doodie says." Whether Doodie influenced Moosie here is uncertain, but Nazimova would have done better with the Guild and Andreyev than with a pair of novice producers and *The Mother* by Karel Čapek, author of *The Makropoulos Secret*.

The Mother was set in Czechoslovakia, its central character a woman with three sons drafted into the army, and Nazimova believed it could be a success in the vein of *War Brides*. But its climax was radically different. Renouncing pacifism after losing two sons in a war, the mother tells her fourth and youngest son, "There comes a time when one must fight," and hands him a gun. The change of heart disturbed Nazimova, but the producers assured her that the message of the play, which opened in London a week before Hitler invaded Czechoslovakia, had been enthusiastically received. Perhaps, since the role in *He Who Gets Slapped* did not appeal, she chose *The Mother* in default of anything better. On Broadway that season, Nazimova saw and admired Tallulah Bankhead in *The Little Foxes,* Judith Anderson in *Family Portrait,* and Clifford Odets' *Rocket to the Moon*. But as she told the New York *Sun,* she couldn't have been cast in any of these (not even in Robert Morley's part, she jokingly added, in *Oscar Wilde*): "For me it has to be a foreigner or a translation." That was why, Nazimova explained, "I've never done Shaw." Since *The Simpleton,* unlike marriage, had not been a personal disaster, did this fiction emerge from Nazimova's subconscious, on the spur of the moment, to reinforce her point? In any case, once again a reporter failed to check the facts.

Miles Malleson, who had directed *The Mother* in London, was imported for the New York production, and at the first reading, on March 20, Nazimova "startled him. . . . Too different from English conception." By April 1, she had decided: "Malleson is unimaginative as director but nice person." By April 8, she had begun to take over at rehearsals: "Malleson is slipping. I have to advise actors." On April 10, the diary noted: "Rehearsals. Malleson is asleep." And on the 13th, after the dress rehearsal in Richmond: "Malleson's lighting is infantile."

In Richmond as in Washington, the critics reported that audiences were applauding Nazimova rather than the play, and agreed with them. They also praised eighteen-year-old Montgomery Clift, who played the youngest son, and who sent Nazimova a note when *The Mother* opened

In 1939, last appearance on the New York stage, as
mother to eighteen-year-old Montgomery Clift
(on couch) in The Mother

in New York at the Lyceum on April 25: "Mummy darling, being Tony to your Mother has meant more to me than anything in the world— Merci et bonne chance, Monty." Once again the final curtain fell to prolonged applause, the actors took seven or eight curtain calls, and members of the audience began running down the aisles to the footlights, cheering and whistling. Tom Palmer, playing another of the sons, thought that *The Mother* had proved a "sensation" after all:

> But Nazimova was muttering as the curtain was going, "I do not like this, I do not like this." And she was right. Because instead of a straightforward ovation, it was hysteria—a cult audience. They were going wild over her, not the play, and she was aware of it.

Next morning the critics almost unanimously praised Nazimova and Clift but damned the play, which closed two days later. On April 28, back at Who-Torok, Nazimova noted: "Home. Dazed. Stunned." She told Glesca, "This is the end of my career in the theatre," and was almost right. All that remained was a revival of *Ghosts,* with Harry Ellerbe as Oswald, that played one week at Westchester Playhouse and one week at the Brighton Theatre in Brighton Beach. For Helen Beverley, who played Regina, there was no sign that Nazimova had been dazed and stunned only two months earlier:

> She was very careful, very strict, and directed every nuance, every pause. We had only two weeks' rehearsal, but she instilled such a love of the play . . . I found her performance magnificent, and in the final scene, after Oswald said, "Give me the sun," Nazimova fell on the floor at his feet with a wonderful movement—she always moved wonderfully—that was unforgettable.

After Ouspenskaya, with whom Helen had studied, Nazimova's precise and detailed sense of drama was illuminating. "Ouspenskaya used to fix the class with a very stern, rather frightening look, a monocle in one eye, and tell us to imagine we were blades of grass on the ocean bed. And everyone swayed." Also illuminating, in retrospect, was that "I could tell Nazimova liked me very much. I was very young and didn't really know anything then, but later I thought, perhaps she liked me too much." Helen was soon offered a contract at Paramount. But she married Lee J. Cobb, who insisted that she give up her career.

By the summer of 1939, Nazimova's hair had gone almost completely gray, and she wore it "cut schoolboy fashion," according to a reporter from the New York *Post*, who interviewed her in Brighton Beach. In "rust-colored beach pajamas" and carrying "a huge Chinese straw hat," she seemed full of "a vital eagerness" and attributed it to the summer-theatre audiences. "They pay twenty-five and fifty cents, and the place is silent as a temple. It's as though hundreds of hands were pulling from you everything you have to give." And her last weeks in the theatre reminded Nazimova of her first weeks on a New York stage with Orlenev: "I haven't had such an audience since I played in the Bowery, over a saloon, twenty-six years ago."

IN THE AUDIENCE at Brighton Beach was Nazimova's brother, Volodya, who had come to America a few weeks previously with his German wife, Frieda. The couple was now living in Brooklyn with their son, Volodya, and all three came out to Who-Torok soon after *Ghosts* closed. The eternal student seemed very old and diminished. Suffering from stomach cancer, he refused an operation that was then the only hope for a cure. Volodya had forgotten, Nazimova found, many things that she remembered, among them his infatuation in Yalta "with a blind chorus girl whose name was Hildebrandt," how he sang "I am the Gypsy Baron," and how she realized he was "my brother under the skin" after they read Dostoevsky aloud to each other:

> I could hardly keep back my tears . . . and when I kissed his cheek he looked at me and there were tears and he held my hand for a long time, and then he kissed it for the last time. . . . "What is your father writing?" I asked the young Volodya afterwards. "Nothing," he answered. "He sits in Central Park, looks at the people, eats, sleeps."

A few months later he died, and Nazimova noted her thoughts after the funeral:

> What makes one cell among the myriad refuse subordination to the established order and suddenly decide to procreate a world of destruction, a world of Hitler-Aryans, in one's own body? . . . [We] buried the emaciated shrunken body of lovely brother on a small hill in St. Michael's Cemetery in Flatbush, Brooklyn, on a cold snowy day. . . . There were no services, remember? The undertaker, a young man, read the Lord's Prayer. My sister wept. She kissed me and for once clung to me. It was hard going down the hill. The wind was pushing us, the ground was slippery and she was very heavy. I put her in her car. That was the last time I saw my sister, too.

By this time, Nazimova had starred in two radio plays written and directed by Arch Oboler for his NBC radio program, "Everyman's Theatre." *The Ivory Tower*, written specially for her, was the story of a German schoolteacher who grew up during the reign of Kaiser Wilhelm and survived World War I and the fall of the Weimar Republic, only to face life under the Nazis. Nazimova liked the script well enough to accept the Federation of Radio Artists' minimum wage of $21, and Fanny Brice listened to the broadcast on July 8 on her car radio, driving to Santa Barbara. "You were simply marvelous," she wrote. "I was sitting next to the chauffeur, crying like a bastard." But when Nazimova heard the recorded repeat of the broadcast, she had an attack of postperformance depression: "Think it's terrible, too nervous, even hysterical, and oh, so *alien* to the American ear."

A few days later, she tested for the role of Mrs. Danvers in *Rebecca*. Selznick's interest had been "re-rewhetted" with the help of Cukor, who told him of Nazimova's interest in playing the part. "I think that Nazimova is one of the greatest actresses in the world," Selznick wrote his New York representative, Kay Brown, "and, despite her accent, I think she would be magnificent." Nazimova heard a rumor that Hitchcock preferred Judith Anderson, but on July 13 she noted after seeing the test: "I don't care if Hitchcock and Selznick don't like it, because I *DO*." The test has not survived, but although it's hard to understand Nazimova's losing a role to the flat, heavily accented Ouspenskaya (an actress who got by on sheer weirdness), it would be harder to understand Anderson's losing the role of Mrs. Danvers to anyone.

Arch Oboler based his second radio play for Nazimova on a subject that she had suggested, the long-distance relationship between Tchaikovsky and his devoted patron, Nadezhda von Meck, who never met but wrote each other many letters for over twelve years. A recording of *This Lonely Heart* has survived, and gives a good idea of Oboler's style. At the time it seemed adventurous (to Charles Laughton, Walter Huston, Mary Astor, and Ronald Colman as well as Nazimova) but today it sounds very old-fashioned. The dialogue is self-consciously "literary," with Madame von Meck crying, "You up there—whoever You are—listen to me—let him live!" when she hears of Tchaikovsky's final illness, and, when her prayer is not answered, "I walk in the dark—alone. . . ." A battery of sound effects intrudes on almost every scene, echo-chambered voices, crowd murmurs, tolling bells, horses' hooves, and it was probably a mistake for Oboler to tell Nazimova before the broadcast that she had "the most beautiful voice on radio." Her voice sounds self-consciously "beautiful," with as much vibrato as the NBC orchestra's massed strings, playing the title song almost continuously in the background.

This Lonely Heart was broadcast on August 26. Just over a week later, World War II began in Europe, and at MGM Louis B. Mayer took note of the situation by authorizing production of two anti-Nazi movies, *The Mortal Storm* and *Escape*. On February 21, 1940, Nazimova "wired John Hyde [agent] re mother in Mortal Storm because Judith Anderson is out," and heard soon afterward that Ouspenskaya was once again in. But Oboler's radio plays had earned him a screenwriting contract at MGM, where his first assignment was to adapt Ethel Vance's suspense novel *Escape*, about a famous German actress rescued from a concentration camp by her son, who has grown up in America. Both Oboler and George Cukor, assigned to direct the movie, wanted Nazimova to play the actress, and early in March she went to Los Angeles to make a test, which Cukor directed. She returned to the East for the only engagements that her theatre agent had been able to arrange, readings of *A Doll's House* and *Ghosts* at colleges in New York State and Pennsylvania. Lack of work, no word from MGM about the test, and dwindling financial resources brought on another depression. "No sleep last night. Recriminations. What a stupid, cheap, vulgar life I've led."

But since Nazimova still longed to live in California again, and had kept on Villa 24 at The Garden of Allah, she decided to sell Who-Torok, although the real-estate agent warned her that the market was in a slump. In the first week of April, MGM summoned her back to Los Angeles to make another test for *Escape,* and she wondered whether it was good or bad news. Delayed for twenty-four hours in Chicago by a train wreck on the line ahead, she stayed the night with the Davises. The letter she wrote Glesca on the train next day makes it clear not only that their affair had settled into companionship, but that Nazimova knew Glesca at thirty-two was as susceptible as herself to the charms of a Young Woman. In this case her own goddaughter, now nineteen years old. She describes Nancy Davis as "extraordinarily beautiful, Doodie, and the face which has every right to be bold and assertive has instead a soft dreamy quality. And add to this a figure of 'oomph!' You'd go crazy about the child."

In Los Angeles, Cukor phoned Nazimova to say how disappointed he was that Lawrence Weingarten, the producer of *Escape,* had decided to replace him with the more "melodramatic" Mervyn LeRoy. He also warned her that another writer had been hired to develop a subsidiary character as a leading role for Norma Shearer. Playing an American woman married to a German general, Norma would also provide "romantic interest" for Robert Taylor as Emmy Ritter's son. Before Nazimova made the second test, which LeRoy directed, Oboler advised her "to underplay." Her hair was dyed black, and the makeup man confided that Judith Anderson had tested "too sinister . . . and looked too, what you think? Jewish! That tickles me pink, considering she hasn't a drop of it."

"God help me to be good in this test. I've got to be good," Nazimova wrote Glesca, who was in notably high-flown mood when she cabled a reply: "YOU SHOULD BY THIS TIME HAVE FULL CONFIDENCE IN YOUR GREATNESS BUT IT IS MY PRIVILEGE TO REMIND YOU OF YOUR ACHIEVE-MENTS." Fortunately, Weingarten and LeRoy made up their minds within a week, and on May 1 an MGM press release, after comparing the search for Emmy Ritter to the search for Scarlett O'Hara, announced that Nazimova had been cast. Sam Zimbalist sent "5 dozen (yes, Doodie!) yellow roses," and Mercedes invited Nazimova to a celebration lunch, then kept her waiting for an hour while she talked on the phone with her faithless lover, Marlene Dietrich.

Hoping to sell Who-Torok, Glesca remained in the East while *Escape*

*With producer Lawrence Weingarten and director
Mervyn LeRoy, "restyled" by MGM's makeup
department for* Escape

was shooting, but offered "professional" advice based on her supposedly inside knowledge of MGM. "Hitler could learn a few ugly things in Hollywood," she warned Nazimova, and "everyone on the lot is gunning for Shearer, and Norma knows it, and doesn't trust anyone." Untrue, of course, although Norma was unhappy with a thin and poorly developed role. But on one occasion she suggested building up Nazimova's part. Thanking the countess for sheltering her after the rescue, Emmy Ritter says, "You are very kind." Norma found the line very trite, and suggested cutting it, but Nazimova "told her I was going to say it, not thanking her for her kindness to Emmy Ritter, but reading her character. 'You see,' I said, 'this cold exterior of the countess is only an armor which she wears for self-protection. Everybody thinks she is cold. But she isn't, she is sweet and kind and warm. In fact, Emmy Ritter reveals the countess to herself." Norma, as emotional in her way as Nazimova, kissed her and "even asked to rewrite the scene to give me more lines, but I said I had too many as it was—I didn't need so many words. . . ."

Blanche Yurka, who had lobbied for Nazimova's role and settled for the much smaller part of a nurse in the concentration camp, was another matter. On June 13, Nazimova noted, "Blanche Y is sour puss. French evacuate Paris." And on June 14, LeRoy shot a scene (later cut) in which

Emmy Ritter plays the dying Camille for a group of fellow prisoners. " 'God-damn-it!' cried LeRoy when Yurka muffed my best take. 'Tape her line on the soundtrack by itself. You can't spoil a take like this.' "

The scene in which Emmy Ritter was smuggled out of the camp in a coffin, supposedly dead, was scheduled for June 22, but LeRoy didn't get around to the final shot until four the next morning. As the coffin lid shut on Nazimova lying still with her eyes closed, she realized "how fortunate I am to be alive after being ill with cancer three years ago."

On August 5, MGM sneak-previewed *Escape* in Long Beach, and she wrote Glesca: "They want an additional scene with me and Robert Taylor. That's how good I am! Bernie H [Hyman, studio executive] said I was the hit of the show. Now let's see what comes of it." What came of it was that on August 12 Hyman decided "they have to improve N.Sh. part, she is one of their big stars," and brought back Oboler to write two additional scenes for her. A few days later, Norma told Nazimova over lunch that she was going to ask Cukor to direct them. He agreed, but also wanted to retake the scene in which Emmy Ritter thanks the countess, and according to Nazimova's diary she found his direction "illuminating." More important, Cukor had an idea for a new ending. His handling of the confrontation between the countess and the general (Conrad Veidt) provides the only genuine excitement in a mediocre picture.

Reviews for *Escape* were no worse than it deserved, but for Nazimova rather better than she deserved, although it's not entirely her fault if the

The last of Who-Torok, later razed by a developer

performance seems exaggerated. As originally written, Emmy Ritter is a vain, superficial actress whose first request, after being rescued from the concentration camp, is for a makeup kit. All she wants, after experiencing the darkest of realities, is to get back to the theatre. It was the story's ironic edge, lost on the cutting-room floor, that attracted Cukor, and Nazimova cannot be blamed for playing one aspect of a character that was later eliminated. But at times LeRoy allowed her to overreact in silent-movie style, something that Cukor would surely have restrained.

"Horrible. I feel sick," Nazimova noted when she saw *Escape,* but was more concerned with Roosevelt's seeking a third presidential term. "He MUST win," she wrote, and stayed up listening to election results on the radio until she learned, around three in the morning, that he had won.

WITH SOME of her earnings from *Escape,* Nazimova wrote Nina, she created a sundeck on the roof of the apartment below Villa 24, "bought a few plants, even a lemon and a lime tree and 3 Oleanders, put a swinging couch, a couple of chairs there and sit there, read, have tea and even write." But she didn't tell Nina, only her diary, that the sundeck made a good lookout point as well. "From 2–5 a girl in a brassiere and short panties was taking a sunbath on the lawn here."

She also bought Glesca, who returned to Los Angeles on November 11, "a beautiful furcoat." But Who-Torok remained unsold, and Nazimova had no further movie offers until January 27, 1941, when she met with Rouben Mamoulian to discuss playing Tyrone Power's mother in the remake of *Blood and Sand.* "He wants me very much. Gives me script. Read script—part seems too small—don't know what to do." Next day, after "a long talk back and forth with D[oodie]—I decide yes, because just the idea of working is good and because of money."

On February 3, the real-estate agent for Who-Torok wired that he had an offer of $21,000, and at Glesca's suggestion Nazimova wired back asking for $22,000. The buyer agreed, Glesca went east to close the deal, and Nazimova wrote her on February 13, after playing her first scene in *Blood and Sand* for the camera: "The studio [Fox], Mamou, the assistants . . . are crazy about me. Jo Swerling, the script author, thinks I'll steal the picture, but . . . Moosie is sweet and nice, does her work and thinks: let me see the cut version!"

Although her part was not cut, it was never much of a part. As the peasant scrubwoman whose son becomes a famous matador, Nazimova has little to do except look anxious when he forsakes an adoring wife

*With Mamoulian and Tyrone Power on the
set of* Blood and Sand

(Linda Darnell) for a rich and predatory admirer (Rita Hayworth). And apart from Hayworth's performance, and some sumptuous Technicolor, *Blood and Sand* was not much of a picture. Nazimova had no more offers until she met with Josef von Sternberg and producer Arnold Pressburger on June 14, to discuss playing Mother Goddam in *The Shanghai Gesture*. Still unable to come to terms with the role, she turned down the movie as she'd turned down the play years earlier. Ironically, von Sternberg's final choice was Ona Munson (miscast), and another of Nazimova's former lovers, Paul Ivano, photographed the picture.

DURING THE next two years, when the only work Nazimova obtained as an actress was in three more radio plays by Arch Oboler, she wrote several hundred pages of her autobiography in longhand, listened to news of World War II on the radio at least twice a day, saw old friends and made a few new ones, went to the movies, the theatre, and very occasionally a party. Among the social occasions recorded in her diary are "George Cukor's party for Tallulah," "party at Bob

Lewis," and a "very trying" dinner at Jo Swerling's house with Mamoulian, William Wyler, Elisabeth Bergner, and her husband, Paul Czinner. No comment on Tallulah, but an indirect one on Bergner, whom Mamoulian asked at one point in the evening, "When you read a play, do you choose it because of the role or the play?" Bergner answered, "For the role." Then Mamoulian asked Nazimova the same question, and she answered immediately, "For the play, of course."

Her diaries also record the German invasion of Soviet Russia, Roosevelt's declaration of war after the Japanese attack on Pearl Harbor, and concern for her former maid Ada Scobie, now living in London, to whom she regularly sent food packages. In one letter of thanks, Ada wrote, "The butter is lovely," but expressed fear of air raids and wondered "what this terrible war will lead to." And Nazimova wrote Nina:

> What really depresses me is that I can be of no use in this, our present, struggle. Too old for war work, too old for blood donations . . . I have sent 180 old books to the army and navy libraries, a few packages of old clothing, old suitcases etc to the Red Cross, but to be a mere observer and armchair strategist makes me feel like a parasite. . . . If I can not play an active part in this human tragedy, I can at least try to understand the whys and wherefores, and not just wave the flag and shout halleluyahs [sic] when I hear that so many million young Germans were killed by so many million young Russians who later gave their lives to save our useless old veins.

Early in 1942, when the young Frank Sinatra was a singer with the Tommy Dorsey band, he lived in the second-floor apartment of the villa next to Nazimova's. She could hear him rehearse the same song incessantly, which exasperated her when she was working on her autobiography. But she admired his perfectionism. Sitting by an open window to hear better, she commented to Glesca, "What a sexy voice," and "listen to his phrasing," and after Sinatra had rehearsed, recorded, played back, and rerecorded the same song for an hour, "I think he's finally got it." She also listened to Orson Welles when he rented the ground-floor apartment of Villa 24 for a few weeks, and rehearsed his role as narrator for a radio version of Wilde's *The Happy Hypocrite*. An air vent connected the two apartments, and once Jo Hutchinson found her kneeling with her ear to it. "She thought Welles had such a gorgeous voice, but she wouldn't introduce herself, although I'm sure he'd have been thrilled." Nazimova wouldn't introduce herself to Sergey Rachmaninov either when he lived at a nearby villa for a while, even though he'd known and admired Stanislavsky and Chekhov. Or perhaps because. Unlike most exiles in Hollywood, Nazimova avoided the old world, preferring to keep company with the new.

George Cukor had now become a close friend and confidant, with Robert Lewis and James T. Farrell in Nazimova's slightly less intimate second circle. "As an apprentice at the Civic Repertory I never spoke to her," Lewis remembered, "but when I came out to Hollywood, at first playing every conceivable kind of Oriental character, it was different." He took Nazimova to concerts at the Hollywood Bowl, and "she came to see my production of *Noah* [by André Obey] with Lee J. Cobb and Ruth Ford, at the Actors' Lab." Lewis found her "always delightful to be with, 'modern' and forward-looking, a citizen of the world. But she was also from another world—and in terms of career, the problem was what to do with her. She realized this, and never complained."

In Hollywood to write a (never produced) screenplay for Fox, James T. Farrell also found that "the immediacy of her responses" negated the physical impression of age and made him think of Nazimova "as a contemporary, and not as someone older. Her mind and her emotions seemed so much younger than was the case with everyone else I met out there."

Nazimova first met Franklin Pangborn in New York in 1911, when he played a supporting role in *The Marionettes*. In Hollywood since 1927, he had his first major success in *My Man Godfrey*, as Carole Lombard's high-society friend. It established him as one of the supreme "sissified" movie comedians, brother under the skin to Edward Everett Horton and Eric Blore. From 1941 until her death, Nazimova saw a great deal of "Pangy." Together they celebrated a "silly, gay, happy New Year [1942] in spite of WAR," he took her to movies ("Marlene Dietrich in *Flame of New Orleans*. Lousy") and plays ("to *Charley's Aunt* with Pangy. Atrocious bore"), and Nazimova took him and Glesca to a preview of Val Lewton's *Cat People*, his first production at RKO after leaving Selznick.

"Picture good for first half, but could be better. Inconsistent," Nazimova noted in her diary (October 17, 1942), an opinion that she had already expressed to Val after the preview. It didn't improve a sometimes precarious relationship. A few weeks earlier, the screenwriter of *Cat People*, De Witt Bodeen, had come into Val's office and found him "more than merely a little upset." He explained that Nazimova had reduced his wife, Ruth, to tears and near-hysteria by claiming "Val had told her he was seeing his doctor, who had told him he had only a short time to live." And when he accused Nazimova of inventing a gratuitously cruel story, she replied: "But wasn't Ruth happy when she learned you weren't going to die?"

"I wish to God somebody in town would give Alla a job," Val said to Bodeen. "Maybe then she'd stop acting these personal dramas she invents." Perhaps he remembered that at the age of ten he told his mother that he'd seen a black tiger prowling around Who-Torok, and was so convincing that she agreed to accompany him on a "safari." A killer coyote and a trip through the local sewers figured in other childhood fantasies, and as a talented paranoid adult Val channeled them into movies about vampires, zombies, and Satanists.

In the fall of 1942, Nazimova became the third actress, after Blanche Yurka and Flora Robson, to test for the role of Pilar in *For Whom the Bell Tolls*. Lewis Allen, who directed the tests, had told her, "You are the woman. Robson and Yurka did not even give a suggestion of Pilar." But on September 24, she noted: "Bromfield [Louis Bromfield wrote the screenplay] is against me . . . insists on Blanche Yurka!" Then, on October 25: "Yurka is out of Pilar but Sam Wood [now signed to direct the film] is testing somebody else today." And on October 27, doubly impatient for news after being out of work so long: "One whole year plugging and waiting is beginning to wear me down."

Throughout her life, Nazimova seldom recorded her depressions except in her diary. The letters she wrote during 1942 to Mercedes, who had gone back to live in New York, insist that she was "so engrossed in my book that no one can take me away from the desk—writing from breakfast coffee on until the eleven o'clock news at night," and that although Glesca was now working for the Red Cross,

> I don't think that either of us is or can be lonely, we have so much to do, each in her own particular interest and each not interfering with the other. It's been this way for 14 years now and being alone does not mean being lonely, in fact we both love it! . . . Take the advice of an old woman: find happiness and purpose *within yourself,* don't rely on others to bring it you—it does not work in the end.

She used almost the same words in a letter to Eva. Earlier that year, they had met (for the last time, as it turned out) when Eva was on tour in *The Rivals,* and came to tea at The Garden of Allah. "Her spirit old. Very discouraged . . . I feel sorry for her," Nazimova commented in her diary, but gave no hint of feeling sorry for herself when she wrote Eva later: "Engrossed in my book . . . Take the advice of an old-timer. Find happiness and purpose within yourself."

In January 1943, Katina Paxinou, the "somebody else" tested by Sam Wood, was chosen to play Pilar. In April, Pearl Buck recommended Nazimova for Lin Tan in *Dragon Seed,* but the producer opted for an all-

American "Chinese" cast, with Aline Macmahon as wife to Walter Huston and mother to Katharine Hepburn. And that summer the old-timer found it difficult to follow her own advice:

> At 3 in the morning I woke up hearing someone plunge in the pool. There they were in a tight embrace in the shaded corner, the moon lighting the rippling water. I watched them. Jealous. Lonely.

Finally she landed another movie role when Vincent Sherman, now a director at Warner Bros., cast her in *In Our Time* that fall. As he recalls:

> The movie was Jerry Wald's idea—the title an ironic reference to Neville Chamberlain's "Peace in Our Time" speech after meeting Hitler in Munich. He wanted to do a story about a Polish family during the German invasion, but it never really worked out, because of the script. Ellis St. Joseph, who had the idea of creating a parallel to the family in *The Cherry Orchard,* was a talented but rather effete writer. His script was too talky and lacking in action. But I had a great cast—Ida Lupino, Nazimova, Michael Chekhov as her brother, Nancy Coleman, and Victor Francen. Only Paul Henreid didn't interest me. . . .

As Madame Ranevskaya transposed to a country estate outside Warsaw, Nazimova was, to Sherman, "very moving and highly sensitive. In rehearsal I could see the part growing as she explored it. She was very grateful for the work; things hadn't been going too well, and she'd aged a lot." Sherman suspected "personal problems," but the only time Nazimova referred to her private life was "when she made a disparaging remark about Charles Bryant and said he hadn't been fair to her." Bryant, it seems, was still unfinished business, one of the "ugly" and "stupid" episodes of her life that she kept remembering in her diaries. "On the set Nazimova was very creative to work with, and had a wonderful sense of humor," Nancy Coleman remembered, "but when I told her I was getting married and invited her to the wedding, she refused. 'I don't believe in marriage,' she said. Then she sent me a wonderful present."

Nazimova's role in *In Our Time* was relatively small, and she had small hope for the movie, as a letter to her nephew Volodya reveals: "To show how little I cared about the story, I have not even spent my pennies to see the film." But she brought a touchingly fragile quality to the character of an aristocrat living in the past, as well as unexpected flashes of humor. Introduced to the girl her son intends to marry, Nazimova (literally) looks her up and down; then her eyes flicker, and she smiles faintly and con-

In Our Time. *The aristocrat sizes up the
commoner (Ida Lupino).*

In Our Time. *On the
Warner back lot with
Nancy Coleman*

veys without a word of dialogue: "Nice girl, but obviously not one of us."

On October 5, she began work on *The Bridge of San Luis Rey,* also with minimal hope. Other members of the cast included Francis Lederer, Akim Tamiroff, Louis Calhern, and Joan Lorring; but an archetypal B-picture actress, Lynn Bari, starred as a fiery Peruvian dancer, and the director, Rowland V. Lee, was a hack. And in spite of a shoestring budget (presumably responsible for special effects and back projection that would have seemed crude twenty years earlier), money ran out before shooting ended. With two scenes not yet filmed, Nazimova as the unscrupulous Marchesa had little opportunity to do more than establish a strong, magnetic presence. But she was luckier than Blanche Yurka, who had just finished her first day's work as the Mother Superior when production closed down.

BY THE TIME this happened, Selznick had signed Nazimova for a role that he wrote specially for her in *Since You Went Away,* a two-and-a-half-hour tribute to the Ideal American Family during World War II. Her scenes were among the last to be filmed, in February 1944. They add up to only six minutes' screen time, three of them in the background

Two Russian exiles: Michael Chekhov, nephew of
Anton and former member of the Moscow Art
Theatre, with Nazimova on the set of In Our Time

at a Christmas party, but the other three reveal an undeniably great actress. Nazimova plays a working-class immigrant from Eastern Europe employed in a shipyard where Claudette Colbert, the ideal country-club mother, has patriotically enrolled as an apprentice welder. After the elegance of her two previous roles, Nazimova's physical transformation reveals her extraordinary talent for "becoming what the part demands of me." In contrast to the relentless gloss of the rest of the movie, she looks almost unrecognizably drab, as old and worn as the story she tells. It's the story of the underside of the immigrant experience, but Selznick's dialogue is an actor's minefield. Nazimova has to explain how she and her little son (who died, of course) "prayed that God would let us go to the fairyland across the sea," to recite the inscription on the Statue of Liberty, and to tell immaculately photographed Claudette, "You are what I thought America was."

No doubt John Cromwell, a skillful director of actors, helped Nazimova to make the scene ring affectingly true. But as she wrote her

Since You Went Away. *Nazimova as the Polish immigrant at the Christmas party. Others, left to right, include Hattie McDaniel, Joseph Cotten, Jennifer Jones, and Monty Woolley.*

nephew, "The woman has something to say, something very near to all of us 'poor storm-tossed émigrés' (in one way or another.)" Near enough, in one way or another, for her transcendent performance to suggest a long life beyond a brief moment.

OUT OF WORK again for the rest of 1944, Nazimova concentrated on her autobiography. On March 15, she read two chapters to the Davises, who were visiting Edith's Los Angeles friends Spencer Tracy and Walter Huston: "Loyal is really enthusiastic about the writing." On April 20, she wrote Volodya that the first volume was finished and had taken her up to "the important age of ten":

> Seems a long time ago, but everything was so dramatic and of such import to my trend of thought, that every detail had engraved itself in my memory. Unfortunately—or fortunately—each episode (contributed by elders to my childhood) became indelible and had developed weaknesses and fortitude which hindered, or helped, jumping over handicaps and pitfalls that came to me in super-abundance later on. It is not pleasant work to write this book, Volodya, for I re-live each episode. . . .

As well as writing about the pain of childhood, Nazimova read about it in *A Tree Grows in Brooklyn*, which she found "wonderful." But attacks of dizziness made her feel that time was running out, and she wrote Glesca, who had gone to visit her ailing mother:

> Please, darling, speed me on, help me more with typing the stuff. . . . I have about 100 [new] pages done for typing and have simply got to see them typed before going any further. . . . At the rate I am writing now it will take ten more years to finish it. . . . When you come back, then we *shall, will, must* get a maid to do all the work that keeps you from typing.

On April 23, the diary records "2 dizzy spells before getting up," and the next day, "One dizzy spell. It occurs when I stretch. Typed just the same." Her physician, Dr. Larsen, "thinks it's the liver. Maybe the eyes? [They had weakened, and he advised her not to read at night.] Prescribed Panthenol. Typing." A week later, when Glesca returned, the symptoms had disappeared.

In May, Nancy Davis came by for a visit. Many years later, she recalled looking around the apartment and thinking, " 'It was so small, nicely furnished but . . . How terrible it must be for her after all that fame and glamour.' Nazimova had no self-pity, bore her situation very gracefully, but I don't think I could have ended living that way." Nancy had just become engaged to James Platt White, Jr., who was on leave from aircraft-carrier duty. When she brought him to dinner at The Garden of Allah, he made a strong impression on Nazimova: "I think I met one of our great future statesmen, perhaps even a president." The engagement was soon broken off, and White never went into politics, but Nazimova seems to have guessed her goddaughter's "type."

THAT SAME month, according to Glesca, "Emily Woodruff, Nancy Davis, Moosie and I took a trip to the Padua Hills Theatre." But when she described Emily as "a young woman Moosie had met through Bobby Lewis while I was visiting my mother," Glesca was blowing smoke again. She was the first to meet Emily, right after returning from the East. As she came out of the Hollywood post office, Glesca noticed a lady in distress. Pretty, dark-haired, thirtyish, she sat on the steps while tears streamed down her face. "Can I help you?" Glesca asked, and when Emily looked up, she evidently saw in Glesca the kind of help she needed.

Ten years earlier, Hume Cronyn had fallen in love with Emily when they were both students at the American Academy of Dramatic Arts in New York. Although she agreed to marry him, Emily claimed that her family would disapprove, and insisted on keeping the marriage secret. Then she refused to live with him, and Cronyn realized that Emily was suffering from "some deep inner conflict." Divorce ended the marriage but not the conflict. Emily secretly married another actor who hoped to break into movies, they went out to Hollywood together, and she was soon even more desperately unhappy than she'd been with Cronyn. Nancy Reagan remembered her as "gentle, soft-spoken, very Southern, the complete opposite of Glesca," but Emily found in Glesca the opposite who attracted. She left her second husband, and Glesca began the second major relationship of her life. Did it remain secret, like Emily's marriages, or did Glesca tell Nazimova? There is no evidence either way, but either way their longtime companionship remained intact. Nazimova made a new will that spring, naming Glesca her executor and sole heir.

"BEAUTIFUL DAY. Very happy," she noted on June 4, her sixty-fifth birthday, but two months later the attacks of dizziness returned. On November 7, she "voted at 2 o'clock on straight democratic ticket. IT MUST BE F. D. Roosevelt. IT IS. Fuey [sic] to Dewey." But then: "I had that lightening circle in my eyes. It lasted 20 minutes. Left me very weak and nervous." No mention of what Dr. Larsen thought or prescribed. On December 18, her agent reported that Selznick was planning a movie with Ingrid Bergman as Sarah Bernhardt and Nazimova in a supporting role. The next day, he reported that the project had been shelved.

By now Nazimova herself reminded some people of Bernhardt in old age. When she visited Val Lewton at RKO, screenwriter Ardel Wray (*I Walked with a Zombie*) saw someone "very small, very thin, huge eyes in an enameled old face, long cigarette holder for Russian cigarettes, and a marvelous theatricality of voice and manner." But as Nazimova wrote Nina, her foreign accent "eliminates my playing Anglo-Saxons, and, lately, even foreign stories are being done without foreign actors":

> The same goes for radio. As for plays, those that I have turned down have proven to be hopeless failures in New York. Finally, I have stopped worrying about my situation. The money I have received for Who-Torok enables me to live here for two or perhaps three more years (discounting possible illness), and then I shall worry again, but not before.

On February 1, 1945, she went "with Franklin [Pangborn] to see *To Have and Have Not.* [Lauren] Bacall is a 'knockout.' " On April 12, after hearing the news of Roosevelt's sudden death, she felt that "the dearest member of *my* family is gone." Over the next few weeks, the diary is preoccupied with events in Europe: "Mussolini killed"; "Berlin fell. AT LAST." Harry Ellerbe was visiting Nazimova when the news came through on her radio that the Russians had entered Berlin. Earlier in the day, he had been shocked to find The Garden of Allah very run-down, exterior paint chipped and faded, tropical shrubs so overgrown "that they seemed to choke the little villas and obscure the pathways." But Nazimova was "vibrant" as ever when she met him at the entrance to her former home. She showed Ellerbe the hallway transformed to a lobby with registration desk and switchboard, the living room now the hotel dining room. After lunch by the famous pool, they walked to Villa 24. On the way Nazimova pointed to a nearby villa and told him its apartments were occupied by Dorothy Gish and Louis Calhern. "Such dears," she said, and Ellerbe thought of them as "two of the last tenants from the golden days of the Garden," as reluctant to leave it as Nazimova herself, for whom in spite of everything it was still "a place for a home."

After reading from her autobiography, memories of a childhood in

Yalta alternately nostalgic and dark, she switched on the radio for the five o'clock news. When they heard that the Soviet Army had entered Berlin, Ellerbe supposed Nazimova "must be gratified by the success the Russians are having." Although she was, "a meaningful Nazimova pause" followed, and then: "But let me tell you something, Haddy. Don't ever trust the Russians."

Childhood and early sorrows? Stanislavsky, whom by now she had turned against completely, and dismissed to Ellerbe as "a rich amateur"? Orlenev? Nina and Lucy? The old fear of being denied an exit visa if she ever went back? It was getting late; Ellerbe had to leave and said goodbye without asking what was on her mind.

Over the next few days, Nazimova's diary is again preoccupied with public events: "*Britain and USA proclaim end of war with Germany*"; "USSR proclamation of end of war." On May 27, personal history resumes: "No news re work in pictures. D went to see Emily." Next day Nazimova's nephew Volodya and his wife came "to cocktails and dinner. . . . Read [auto]biography to them until 1 o'clock. He was surprised and *impressed* by my characterization of Nina, Volodya," remarking how accurately she had pinpointed "all traits (embryos of traits) developed in them in later years."

ALTHOUGH Nazimova had no wish to leave the little apartment she called "my new home the Garden of Alla with an H," as Glesca became more deeply involved with Emily Woodruff she felt the need for more space. "Looking for a home," the diary noted on June 2. "D is all 'hepped up.' " And on June 4, Nazimova's sixty-sixth birthday, "we drive out with Franklin into the [San Fernando] Valley. Not one house is appealing. The more we looked at the Valley the less we felt like living there. Decided to look only at hills."

Next day her agent phoned: "Am positively to play wife in 'Ethan Fromm' [sic] with Bette Davis when she returns from abroad in September. Oh, please God . . ." On June 14, he phoned again: "May play the 1st wife in 'Anna and the King of Siam.' " The last of "countless hopes held out by various producers, directors, writers," was also the last entry in Nazimova's diary. After dinner on the evening of June 30, according to Glesca, she had "what appeared to be a violent attack of ptomaine, [and] before an hour had passed she was in the Good Samaritan Hospital and under expert care."

But the attack was diagnosed as coronary thrombosis. Another,

*Hollywood, 1944: Glesca,
Nazimova in her favorite
"Chinese coolie" hat, and goddaughter Nancy Davis
(later Reagan)*

painful attack followed on July 2, and the nurse in attendance advised Glesca "to go to the far side of the bed, hold her hand, and talk to her. . . . I began to speak, calling her by endearing names. There was a definite re-action, then the agonized moans. Alla was doing her best to show me she was still with me."

By July 11, Nazimova had suffered two more attacks, and "her cries could be heard down the corridors." She never fully recovered con-sciousness after the last attack, and when Val Lewton paid a visit on the evening of the 12th, she didn't recognize him. At eight-twenty-five the following morning, the nurse checked Nazimova's pulse, then turned to Glesca and said: "She is gone."

THE OBITUARIES created new legends as well as recy-cling old ones:

Theatre Arts Magazine: "Alla Nazimova spent her final years in Holly-wood, living alone on her estate, the Garden of Allah. She played small roles in many recent pictures, even produced a few."

Louella Parsons' syndicated column: "One of Nazimova's great friendships was with Rudolph Valentino. . . . I do not believe nor do I recall that they were ever engaged, for there was a great difference in their ages."

The Los Angeles *Express:* "One of her latest film roles was in *The Song of Bernadette.*"

An uncredited clipping in the files of the Nazimova archive: "During her early movie career she married Charles E. Bryant, a Broadway producer."

ALTHOUGH Glesca knew that Nazimova disliked cemeteries in general and "particularly disliked Forest Lawn," it was at Forest Lawn that she decided to bury her. Presumably she felt it was an act of homage to include Nazimova in the cemetery with the biggest all-star cast. At the funeral service and interment, Val Lewton and his wife and daughter were the only relatives present. Nina, who hadn't answered Nazimova's letters for over two years, remained in Montclair, New Jersey. Cukor, Franklin Pangborn, and Morris and Elsa Stoloff were among the mourners, and many others sent flowers. Glesca wrote a brief and typically high-flown eulogy ("She was no accidental person, born to a life of greatness, but lived and grew and was nourished by experience and by thought"), which was read by John Beal, another friend of Nazimova's last years.

Then Beal read from two books found on her bedside table at Villa 24. Spinoza first interested Nazimova when she learned that he was a Sephardic Jew whose ancestors, like her own, had been expelled from Spain in the Middle Ages. After following "only one law—the law of impulse" all her life and often despising herself for it, she was evidently reassured by Spinoza's attitude to so-called moral choices and values. The passage from his *Ethics* that Beal read had been underlined:

> All such values—good, bad, beautiful, ugly—are human prejudices and therefore, altogether relative. By the same token they are not the cause of desire, but the consequence. We do not desire things because they are good; we call them good because we desire them; and we desire them because we must.

And on a different track to the same kind of peace, Nazimova had also marked a passage from the *Meditations* of Marcus Aurelius:

> For with what art thou discontented? With the badness of men? Recall to thy mind this conclusion, that to endure is a

part of justice, and that men do wrong involuntarily; and consider how many, after mutual enmity, suspicion, hatred and
fighting, have been reduced to nothing; and be quiet at
last. . . . But perhaps the desire of the thing called fame will
torment thee? See how soon everything is forgotten and look
at the chaos of infinite time on either side of the present, and
think on the emptiness of applause; and be quiet at last.

In 1933, a young actress called Peggy Craven saw Nazimova in the revival of *The Cherry Orchard.* (Among the apprentices at the Civic Repertory that year was her husband-to-be, Norman Lloyd.) Sixty years later,
recalling the performance, Peggy described Nazimova as "*the* great actress
of her time. I never saw Laurette Taylor but can't imagine she was better.
Nazimova created a kind of perfume in the air around her. You couldn't
breathe during her silences."

But a few months before her death, Nazimova told an interviewer:
"I've reached the heights but it's been a puny success. I could have done
so much more." Above all she deplored wasting seven years of her life as
a silent-movie star, the period she looked back on as "unbelievably horrible." The personal horror was her offscreen role as Mrs. Charles Bryant,
the professional one an infatuation with her own manufactured onscreen
image; but the real waste was not that Nazimova made movies. She made
the wrong movies, ruling out the right ones by virtually directing herself
in vehicles of her choice, ruling out von Stroheim, von Sternberg, Lubitsch, King Vidor, and other exceptional directors of the time with
whom she might have worked.

Although lost to the theatre during those years, would Nazimova have
"done so much more" by remaining a stage actress? The problem she
found in Hollywood during the last years of her life, that "my foreign accent eliminates my playing Anglo-Saxons," was the problem that had
confronted her earlier on Broadway. Only a repertory theatre could have
provided Nazimova with the great roles she never played, from *Miss Julie,*
the two "Lulu" dramas, and the stepdaughter in *Six Characters in Search
of an Author,* to the wife in *The Dance of Death* and *Mother Courage.*
Then as now, Broadway producers were reluctant to take a chance on
Strindberg, Wedekind, Pirandello, or Brecht, and Nazimova never managed to establish her own company. It was the more practical Eva Le Gallienne, with her Civic Repertory, who was the first in New York to
produce plays cold-shouldered by Broadway, and sell tickets at less than
half the price Broadway charged.

Throughout her career, in fact, Nazimova had the same problem. She came "from another world," as Robert Lewis pointed out, and "what to do with her?" Yet she managed to create five major Ibsen roles, Madame Ranevskaya, Turgenev's Natalya Petrovna, and O'Neill's Christine Mannon, a record equaled by no other foreign actress and few native ones in the American theatre. And for posterity, a greater loss than the roles Nazimova never played is the movie that Cukor was never able to make of *Ghosts*.

There is no description in Glesca's memoir of the look on Nazimova's face as her life slipped away. The last forty-eight hours, when she was drugged and unconscious most of the time, brought a release from physical pain; but did her eyes or her breathing, a flicker, a sigh, or a murmur, suggest thoughts and memories still vaguely alive in the deepest recesses of a failing mind? Nazimova had spent much of her last years reliving her early years as she worked on her autobiography, and it breaks off a few pages after Alla last saw her father at the sanatorium. At the time of writing this final section, Nazimova was reading Spinoza and Marcus Aurelius, and perhaps they helped her to settle the score with a hated father. For she went on to describe how she remembered Yakov frequently saying, "I am above the crowd! I am a lucky man!," then to imagine his despair as the nurse led him away "all drooped and worn out." And then, making a connection with her own descent to the depths, she recognized a "familiar spirit" and added, "God, pity him. . . ."

Perhaps, too, the same bedside authors helped Nazimova again at the very end, helped her to banish the old fear of oblivion, the anger at Bryant, the sense of waste, and by settling the score with herself to become truly "quiet at last."

Epilogue

L IKE THE AEOLIAN HARPS THAT USED TO BE hung in the trees to be played only by the breeze, the actor should be an instrument *played upon* by the character he depicts," Nazimova told an interviewer in 1936. "The actor himself should be a creature of clay, of putty, capable of being molded into another form, another shape." And as Nazimova lay dying, Glesca began molding her into another form, another shape. "Alla has rather confused the staff by telling each nurse and attendant that I am her child," she wrote the Davises, and after "the nurse said, 'She is gone,' from deep within me immediately came the words, 'My mother . . .' The words went throughout the hospital, so that many continued to believe I was her illegitimate daughter." Then, with an even greater leap of faith, Glesca added: "Looking back, I know we both believed she was my mother."

None of Nazimova's friends believed it, of course, and some of them cast doubts on the authenticity of "a Christmas prayer," which Glesca chose for her epitaph. After supposedly discovering it in Nazimova's handwriting among various papers on her desk, Glesca had the words inscribed on a bronze plaque marking her grave:

> Voice of world's conscience
> Christ is thy name,
> Teach us to shun the words of greed,
> Prejudice and strife.
> To earn our bread,
> To share our bread,
> To heed, to follow Thee forever. Amen.

The original, if it ever existed, is not among Nazimova's surviving papers, and its sentiments seem foreign to someone who kept books by two emphatically non-Christian philosophers on her bedside table. But they seem far less foreign to Glesca—especially when "off again on LIFE, ETHICS etc etc."

When Glesca and Emily moved to Columbus, Georgia, their ménage was not welcomed by the Woodruff family. And when Glesca decided to "complete" Nazimova's autobiography, she continued the work of remodeling her, turning her former lover into a mother figure who found Jesus and led a relatively tame private life (for an actress), and by inference sanitizing her current relationship with Emily. It took Glesca until 1982 to add another eight hundred pages to Nazimova's seven hundred, and she died in 1987, aged eighty, without having found a publisher for the work. For her own grave she chose a less exalted inscription: "Here's tae us! Wha's like us? Naebody!" Although Glesca was always proud of her Scots blood, its alcohol content at the time must have been fairly high.

CHARLES BRYANT played a few supporting roles on Broadway during the 1930s. His marriage to Marjorie Gilhooley ended in 1936, and his last appearance on the stage, in 1937, was in *Yes My Darling Daughter.* Eva Le Gallienne saw it and thought him "inexpressibly awful." Bryant died of a heart attack in 1948, aged sixty-seven.

MERCEDES DE ACOSTA lived for a while in Paris after World War II—with a new conquest, Poppy Kirk, who worked for Schiaparelli. In 1961, Mercedes lost the sight in one eye after surgery for removal of a tumor. Stylish to the last, she wore a black eyepatch. And although she had to sell jewelry and private papers (including letters from Garbo and Dietrich) to pay medical expenses, Mercedes drew strength from The Way. She no longer desired to make conquests, and spent her last years learning "just simply and quietly *to be.*" She died in 1966, aged seventy.

MAURICE STERNE became the first American painter to be given a one-man exhibition at the Museum of Modern Art in New York, in 1933. By then he had lived for some while in Bali and Tahiti, which gave his work a mildly exotic flavor. But he turned his back on Picasso and almost every development in painting after Cézanne, and by the late 1940s had been almost completely forgotten. Sterne died in 1957, aged seventy-nine.

EVA LE GALLIENNE had seemed to Nazimova "very discouraged" at their last meeting, in 1942, but by 1957 she had rallied. A notable success in Schiller's *Mary Stuart* was followed by several others, including Ionesco's *Exit the King* and a revival of the Kaufman-Ferber *The Royal Family.* Eva died in 1991, aged ninety-two.

JEAN ACKER played a few bit parts in Hollywood movies during the 1930s, then worked for many years as an extra. In 1957, I came to Hollywood as personal assistant to Nicholas Ray, who was about to start shooting *Bigger than Life.* At the end of one day, he hadn't completely finished a restaurant scene, and two extras, trim gray-haired women in tailored suits, came up to me. One of them asked if they would be needed tomorrow. I inquired her name. "Jean Acker," she said. My facial reaction must have betrayed that I knew who she was, for Acker smiled faintly, surprised and rather pleased. Many years later, when I was researching this book, I learned from Patricia Neal, who had become friendly with Acker during the 1950s, that the other woman was her longtime companion, Chloe Carter. The couple lived together modestly and happily in a Beverly Hills bungalow and went out on extra calls together. Acker died in 1978, aged eighty-five.

DOROTHY ARZNER directed seventeen movies between 1927 and 1937, most of them angled to female stars, including Clara Bow, Katharine Hepburn, Claudette Colbert, Rosalind Russell, and Joan

Crawford. She became a close friend of Crawford in spite of the failure of *The Bride Wore Red* (1937), but not of Maureen O'Hara, who made an expressive face when I asked her opinion of Arzner's work on *Dance, Girl, Dance* (1940). Arzner retired after *First Comes Courage* (1943, with Merle Oberon) was partly reshot by order of Harry Cohn at Columbia. But she directed many Pepsi-Cola commercials after her friend Joan Crawford became a member of the board. When she agreed to be interviewed, which was seldom, Arzner refused to discuss her personal life and insisted it had no connection with her work. She died in 1979, aged seventy-eight.

PAUL IVANO, after *The Shanghai Gesture* (1942), photographed mainly B movies (*Spider Woman Strikes Back,* 1947). Nazimova described his wife, Greta, whom Ivano married in 1935, as "exactly like him. 'Monotony of life,' says Greta . . . and they both sigh." Ivano retired in 1970 and died in 1984, aged eighty-four.

NATACHA RAMBOVA died mad in 1965, aged sixty-eight. At Lenox Hill Hospital she was diagnosed as suffering from malnutrition, brought on by paranoid delusions that any food offered her would be poisoned. In 1935, she had married again, briefly, and, like her aristocratic Spanish husband, she supported Franco, believing he would enable Spain "to reclaim her position of past grandeur." They lived in Mallorca until the island became a battlefield, and Rambova escaped on a freighter with her adored Pekinese. Back in New York, her marriage annulled, Rambova gave lectures on The Real (which Irene Sharaff remembered as "erratically brilliant"). She also collaborated with Mercedes on a play about the Virgin Mary called "The Leader." Although Lillian Gish expressed interest, it was never produced. Rambova willed her extensive collections of Egyptian and Oriental art to, respectively, the Utah Museum of Fine Arts and the Philadelphia Museum of Art.

ONA MUNSON committed suicide in 1953, aged forty-seven. Married to but separated from Eugene Berman, she was living in a mountain cabin near Lake Tahoe. One of the last letters she wrote was to Mercedes, whom she still loved "more than anyone else in the world." Troubled by unemployment and debts, Munson confided that she was now "contacting the Only Power that can help me." But her suicide note read: "This is the only way I know to be free again."

HARRY ELLERBE spent his last few years in a retirement home near Atlanta, where he gradually lapsed into senile depression. When I interviewed him in 1992, Ellerbe sat slumped in a chair, pale and shriveled, gazing ahead at nothing in particular with a terrible sadness. No reaction to the greetings I brought from friends in Columbus, but when I mentioned that I was working on a biography of Nazimova, he grew suddenly, briefly alert. "That should be very interesting." Another long slump, which he finally came out of when I asked what he knew about the affair between Nazimova and Ona Munson. "Oh, *that*." A long pause. I thought I'd lost him, but then: "It didn't last long, just till New York. . . ." The same look of terrible sadness returned to his eyes, and he never came back. Ellerbe died in 1993, aged eighty-three.

ELISABETH MARBURY became a major fund-raiser for the Democratic Party during the 1920s, and campaigned for Roosevelt and against Prohibition. In 1926, Elsie de Wolfe suddenly left her to marry a fifty-five-year-old British diplomat. (Sir Charles Mendl was attracted to Elsie's money, the fifty-six-year-old Elsie to Sir Charles' title and the promise of "respectability" at last.) Bessie found a new close companion in a thirty-six-year-old divorcée whose professional name was Elizabeth Arden, and they acquired neighboring country estates in Maine. After Marbury's death in 1933, aged seventy-seven, Arden bought her estate and combined both properties to create Maine Chance.

NINA LEWTON retired from her job in the New York foreign department of MGM in 1936, and moved to Los Angeles shortly after Nazimova's death. She died in the Motion Picture Country Hospital in 1967, aged ninety-two. Her son, Val Lewton, died of a heart attack in 1951, aged forty-seven.

THE GARDEN OF ALLAH, after several changes of ownership, was sold in 1959 to the Lytton Savings and Loan Association. Dressed as Cecil B. De Mille and Nazimova, the departing owner and his wife gave a fairly grotesque farewell party, with eighty-three-year-old Francis X. Bushman, costumed for the role he played in *Ben-Hur* (1926), as guest of honor. Next day Nazimova's original home was bulldozed along with the villas; the pool was drained and used as a dump for debris. A few years later, Lytton Savings went broke, and today a storage company and a mini–shopping center occupy the three and a half acres of 8080 Sunset.

APPENDIX

Not that it matters . . .

Nazimova described this poem about her "marriage" to Charles Bryant as "one of my sentimental effusions, written in New York in 1926 (I was forty-seven years young), when I stopped drawing home plans for a little while because my imagination proved to be a little 'too expensive.' " Her imagination also encouraged some dramatic (or poetic) license, including the unlikely story of the Negro janitor who assumed that Nazimova and Charles Bryant had just been married when he saw a Russian priest leave her apartment.

> Not that it matters, not that I care;
>> He was stiff and dull, my new leading man,
>> Had no wit for time, tempo, temperament,
>> No sense of drama or humor (none)
>> And no taste for music or literature.
>> But—renowned for slim, lanky, six-feet-three
>> And a profile grand, glossy, dark brown hair,
>> An attractive drawl, a superior air—
>> He, accordingly (as you might have guessed)
>> Was imported to play a keen intellect.
>> A good pipe, roast beef, Scotch with soda, sleep,
>> And quarterly "Scottish Widows' Briefs,"
>> Some peculiar thing which—at fifty brings
>> a "Security"—filled his wants . . . And yet,
>> By some inherent zeal of perversity
>> I contrived to think of this foreigner—
>> A man too frigid to meet or share
>> Any need exceeding mere fellowship—
>> As sole companion till death.
>
> Not that it matters, not that I care:
>> Our first rendezvous? I had prinked myself
>> To look glamorous; he forgot the date.
>> Our second tryst? While I played Chopin
>> He fell asleep. "Don't be cross," he said
>> When I woke him up. "It's these ulcers . . . blahst . . .
>> In my stomach, deah . . . I am weak . . . too weak . . ."

And he wept, forlorn, while I petted him.
"In New Jersey, Madame, you can wed at once,
Do not bother divorcing your Russian spouse,"
Recommended the White Russian Consulate.
But the morning set as our wedding day
Brought frantic calls from the White Russian Consulate:
"Those New Jersey crooks! They enforced the law!
You must divorce or you cannot wed!"
By adversity, on that very day,
An old Russian priest paid a friendly call
And presented me with an ikon. Christ . . .
And at night, when we (would-be newlyweds)
Took our curtain calls, we were met with flares
From the orchestra and old shoes and rice,
For the front page news publicized the fact
Of a wedding done by a Russian priest
In a long black robe and a golden cross—
A "scoop" from a negro janitor . . .

Not that it matters, not that I care:
When we closed the play, publicized at length
Through the lavish land ad nauseam
(As was also my marital happiness),
We embarked for our quasi-honeymoon.
Oh, fair Albion! . . . At the fireside
Chilled by rain and wind, at his feet, I sat
(Shamming blissfulness for his mother dear)
While he . . . he in armchair
Pipe in his mouth, Scotch by his side,
Held forth, content:
On percentage got at a maximum . . .
On income tax, now at a minimum . . .
On his thrift, and stint as "clahrk in a bank" . . .
On his fling and spat with the great Mrs. Pat . . .
When the embers died, he arose and yawned:
"Blah-sted sleepy . . . 'dnight," and betook his love—
His "Scottish Widows"—to bed.

Not that it matters, not that I care:
The World War—he enlisted but was told to wait
And build up his depleted vitality,
(His card also read "leaking heart!")
"What-ho!" He joined me—
And we journeyed West to appear in films.
But the house I bought, marked 8080
On an unpaved road amid orange groves,
Did not fit our neuter relationship,
(Publicized as "super" in Movieland.)
So—between films, while he romped with men

Or hiked the hills with his dogs
(For his leaking heart and vitality)
I drew plans and built a new suite
Apart from my would-be mate,
One more room for his valet, Wilkie,
And an aviary for my doves to coo of love . . .
Hear the hullabaloo in the court below?
He is home. "Down, Mike, down Daisie! *Couche!* Stop!
Blahst this heat! Hey, Wilkie! My tub! Hurry up!
Blahst these blahstedy burrs fouling up my clothes!
It's expensive stuff! Cost two pounds, by Jove!"
("On your left, you see the great movie star's
Gorgeous Garden of Alla without an 'h'.")

Not that it matters, not that I care:
I remember: Once—for publicity—
We were trying out a new "roadster" car,
Dodging palm, pine, oak draped in mistletoe,
Yucca, holly and heather . . . (Ah! God's Own Land!)
But he raced uphill with the brakes full on
Swearing "Blahstedy-blahst!" at the poor machine.
Never laugh at him who is always right.
Never doubt, never speak, never show dissent.
Never dare to hint to a frigid man
That you might feel neglect, or else . . . Or else?
He might shout, aroused from his lethargy:
"Blahsted burden, sex! Don't talk tommy-rot!
See a doctor? NO! A divorce? UNWED!
Not my fault the war and the Bolsheviks
Have held up your case with that bigamist!
Get a lawyer? Haw! Want another 'scoop?'
Front page news: A STAR'S MORAL TURPITUDE!
Have a fling, my deah, with some chappie, but—
For our income tax—use tact."

Not that it matters, not that I care:
To preserve a "front" and accommodate
His developed trend toward manly sport,
I drew plans and built a club's handball court,
Two-bath dressing rooms, a huge swimming pool,
A pool billiard room, a bar dining room,
Changed the name of 8080 from my own
To "the Club What-Ho What-Ho."
And was besieged by sun-kissed, cavorting men
From the early morn till my doves' last coo.
Meanwhile I filmed "Camille," wrote scenarios
Under pseudonyms, with directions
(To be highly followed by my pseudo-mate),
Or "The Doll's House" and Oscar Wilde's "Salome".

"The World's Illusion" by Wasserman was shelved:
I ran out of funds.

Not that it matters, not that I care:
      When he left, I went to his suite and found
      A berated [sic] pipe, a sprung opera hat
      And the negative of our wedding scene
      In a film entitled "The Toys of Fate."
      Funny things one finds after thirteen years
      Of a fiction match to a puppet mate . . .
      But the house seemed void and the doves nearby
      Bill-and-cooed of love and that tommy-rot,
      And the front page news publicized a scoop
      That her "so-called spouse" and a socialite
      Were to wed in New Milford, Connecticut.
      So I sold . . . or leased . . . I've forgotten which,
      But I lost the place at 8080
      And the residue was "his" due, he said,
      Under Common Law. No more plans I drew.
      For—by misapplied domesticity
      And a haunting dread of publicity—
      I contrived to make of my zealous heart
      A blahsted no-man's land.

NOTES ON SOURCES

Chapter 1

O'Neill on Nazimova's *Hedda:* Normand Berlin, *Eugene O'Neill.* This, like all other books cited here, is listed in the bibliography. Background information on early-twentieth-century American theatre: *Broadway* by Brooks Atkinson; *300 Years of American Drama and Theatre* by Garff B. Wilson. On Minnie Maddern Fiske: *Minnie Maddern Fiske* by Alexander Woollcott. The (undated) Don Marquis letter and the (uncredited) clipping that compares Nazimova and Minnie Maddern Fiske: the Nazimova archive in Columbus, Georgia. On *Hedda Gabler:* Ned Rorem to author. The Lunts and Nazimova: Glesca Marshall's unpublished "completion" of Nazimova's autobiography, "Notes from a Borrowed Child." The Lunts' rehearsal methods: *People in a Diary* by S. N. Behrman. Tennessee Williams on *Ghosts:* Alfred Devlin, *Conversations with Tennessee Williams.* Quotes on Nazimova: Patsy Ruth Miller to author; Irene Sharaff to author; Djuna Barnes in *Interviews;* Alexander Kirkland, "The Woman from Yalta," in *Theatre Arts Magazine,* December 1945; Vincent Sherman to author; Mercedes de Acosta, *Here Lies the Heart;* Frances Dee to author; Stanislavsky quoted in *Stanislavsky* by David Magarshack; D. W. Griffith quoted in *Photoplay,* December 1925. All quotes from Nazimova's diaries and her unfinished, unpublished autobiography, "A Mummer's Odyssey": Nazimova archive.

Chapters 2 and 3

All material concerning Nazimova and her family comes from Nazimova's unfinished autobiography. The bibliography lists books consulted on general conditions, and the status of Jews in particular, in late-nineteenth-century Russia. Dagmar Godowsky's comment at the head of Chapter 3 is from John Kobal's *People Will Talk.*

Chapter 4

Material concerning Nazimova at the Moscow Art Theatre and summer stock theatres, her life in Moscow, her relationship with Alexander Sanin, and her marriage to Seryozha Golovin: "Incidents" and other notes and sketches among Nazimova's posthumous papers. Additional material on the Art Theatre is drawn from books and letters (by and on Stanislavsky, Nemirovich-Danchenko, Anton Chekhov, Michael Chekhov, and Richard Boleslawski) listed in the bibliography.

Chapter 5

Orlenev: translated excerpts from his autobiography, published in Russia in 1932, in the Nazimova archive; Marc Slonim, *Russian Theatre from the Empire to the Soviets;* Oliver Sayler, *The Russian Theatre Under the Revolution.* Nazimova and Orlenev: "Incidents" and other posthumous papers in the Nazimova archive; J. T. Grein in *The Il-lustrated London News,* December 1927; Harold Clurman, *All People Are Famous;* Emma Goldman, *Living My Life;* Jerome K. Jerome, *My Life and Times;* taped remi-niscences by Henry Harvitt (Nazimova's cousin) in the Library of Congress collection of Nazimova's papers; Stella Adler, Josephine Hutchinson, and Norman Lloyd to au-thor. Chekhov and Orlenev: biographies of Chekhov, and a collection of his letters, listed in bibliography. Maurice Sterne: his posthumous *Shadow and Light;* James Mel-low's *Charmed Circle.* (Glesca, in "Notes from a Borrowed Child," acknowledges the Nazimova-Sterne affair but mistakenly dates it 1911, when Sterne was in Bali.) Ethnic and mainstream New York theatre 1900–1920: Rebecca Drucker Bernstien to author; Hopkins Hapgood, *A Victorian in the Modern World.*

Chapter 6

The facts of Nazimova's life recorded by Glesca in "Notes from a Borrowed Child" are partly "as told to" and partly as Glesca wished them to be told. They don't always cor-respond with Nazimova's life as seen by others, and this biography is the result of a long process of separating the wheat from the chaff. For Nazimova's career in the American theatre, Glesca drew (sometimes inaccurately) on the diaries, scrapbooks, and letters in the Nazimova archive. In addition, I have drawn on John Seville's ex-tensive collection of Nazimova clippings; the Nazimova collections at the New York Public Library of the Performing Arts at Lincoln Center; and the Nazimova collec-tion at the Library of Congress, which contains all the surviving letters from Na-zimova to Nina, and a letter from Lucy Olga Lewton with important information on Brandon Tynan. Material on Eugene O'Neill and Henry Miller is drawn from the re-spective biographies by Louis Sheaffer and Frank P. Morse. Material on Laurette Tay-lor and Nazimova is from *Laurette* by Marguerite Courtney.

Chapter 7

Djuna Barnes on *Bella Donna: Interviews.* Mercedes de Acosta on Nazimova: *Here Lies the Heart.* Le Gallienne's diary: Helen Sheehy to author. In addition to the sources listed for Chapter 6, information on the Syndicate is drawn from *Broadway* by Brooks Atkinson; on Charles Frohman from the biography by Isaac A. Marcosson and Daniel Frohman; on Arthur Hopkins from *On Cukor* by Gavin Lambert; on Arthur Hopkins and Nazimova from *To a Lonely Boy* by Hopkins. Matthew F. Bern-stein provided information on Walter Wanger. Lester Weinrott provided information on Edith Luckett. Nancy Reagan provided the letters from Nazimova to her mother. Stanislavsky on *Monsieur Beaucaire:* Jean Benedetti, *Stanislavsky.* Anna Rabinovich-Meisel's letter concerning Golovin and divorce: Nazimova archive. Nazimova at Lau-rette Taylor's party: *Laurette.*

Chapter 8

Darryl F. Zanuck quote: Leonard Mosley, *Zanuck.* Evenings at the 8080 Club: Patsy Ruth Miller to author; Robert Florey, *Filmland;* Dagmar Godowsky, *First Person Plural.* Nazimova and Valentino at the Ship Cafe: *First Person Plural,* confirmed by Viola Dana to author in 1987. Nazimova and Metro: Jack Spears, "Nazimova." Ram-bova and Koslov: Michael Morris, *Madam Valentino;* Agnes deMille, *Dance to the*

Piper. Quotes from Paul Ivano and Flower Hujer on Nazimova: Michael Morris, *Madam Valentino.* Djuna Barnes on Nazimova: *Interviews.* Patsy Ruth Miller and Nazimova: Patsy Ruth Miller to author; Miller, *My Hollywood.* Isabel Hill and Nazimova: taped reminiscences by Hill in the Nazimova collection at the Library of Congress. Nazimova's affairs with Dorothy Arzner and Rambova: George Cukor to author in 1972 (when I was taping conversations with him for *On Cukor.* During breaks, I turned off the machine at Cukor's request, and we discussed many people and topics, among them Nazimova. Those interested can look up *On Cukor* and see how his movie *The Marrying Kind* put Cukor in mind of her. Twenty years later, of course, when it was too late, I would have asked Cukor many more questions about Nazimova). Quotes from Irene Sharaff on Nazimova and Rambova: interview with author. The suit for separate maintenance brought by Jean Acker against Valentino, and Valentino's trial for bigamy, were fully reported at the time in the Los Angeles *Times* and the *Herald-Examiner.*

Chapter 9

Abel Gance, Nazimova, and Valentino: Kevin Brownlow, *The Parade's Gone By.* Charles Van Enger and *Salome:* Jack Spears, "Nazimova." Oscar Wilde's *Salome* in Russia: Konstantin Rudnitsky, *Russian and Soviet Theatre, 1905–1922.* Rambova's designs for *Salome:* Glesca's "Notes"; Michael Morris, *Madam Valentino.* Letter from Rambova's mother to Nazimova: Nazimova archive. The Garden of Alla: letters from Bryant to Nazimova in the Nazimova archive. Nazimova and Jean Adams: Glesca's "Notes." Nazimova's finances: Glesca's "Notes." Exchange of telegrams between Nazimova and Nemirovich-Danchenko, between Minnie Maddern Fiske and Nazimova, and Fannie Hurst's invitation to tea: Nazimova archive. Letters from Nazimova to Eva Le Gallienne: courtesy of Helen Sheehy. Letters from Eva Le Gallienne to Nazimova: Nazimova archive.

Chapter 10

Nazimova in Paris: her diaries; Glesca's "Notes." Dolly Wilde: George Cukor to author (see note, Chapter 8); Janet Flanner, *Paris Was Yesterday;* Natalie Barney, *In Memory of Dorothy Ierne Wilde* and *Pensées d'une Amazone.* Le Gallienne and the Natalie Barney–Gertrude Stein circles: Anne Kaufman Schneider to author. Nazimova and Bryant: Patsy Ruth Miller to author. The Garden of Allah: further correspondence between Nazimova, Jean Adams, and W. I. Gilbert in the Nazimova archive. Shaw on Nazimova and *Saint Joan:* Langner, *The Magic Curtain.* Letter to Jenie Jacobs: Nazimova archive. Opening party at Garden of Allah: Robert L. Green to author; Hill's taped reminiscences.

Chapter 11

Cheryl Crawford quote: *One Naked Individual.* Reactions of Nina and Lucy to relationship between Nazimova and Glesca: Glesca's "Notes." Letter from Nina to Nazimova: Nazimova archive. Isabel Hill and Le Gallienne: Hill's taped reminiscences. The Civic as a "lesbian theatre": Robert Lewis to author. The West 14th Street area: George Chauncey, *Gay New York.* Nazimova in *The Cherry Orchard:* Jo Hutchinson, Robert Lewis, Peggy Lloyd, May Sarton, Tonio Selwart, and Irene Sharaff to author;

Cheryl Crawford, *One Naked Individual. A Month in the Country:* Katharine Hepburn and Phyllis Jenkins to author; Alexander Kirkland, *The Woman from Yalta;* Langner, *The Magic Curtain;* George Cukor in *On Cukor;* Mamoulian, quoted in Glesca's "Notes." Nazimova and Alice Brady in *Mourning Becomes Electra:* Carlotta Monterey, quoted in Sheaffer's *O'Neill.* Nazimova and O'Neill: Glesca's "Notes." Philip Moeller on Lillian Gish: Langner's *The Magic Curtain.* Letter from Nazimova to Leona Scott: Joel Siegel's *Val Lewton. The Good Earth:* Vincent Sherman to author. Clifford Odets on *Salome* and *A Doll's House:* Gerald Weales, *Clifford Odets: Playwright. The Simpleton of the Unexpected Isles:* Langner, *The Magic Curtain;* Glesca's "Notes." Nazimova and Frederick Schlick: Glesca's "Notes." Nazimova's letter to Schlick: Nazimova archive.

Chapter 12

Ghosts and the revival of *Hedda Gabler:* Harry Ellerbe's unpublished memoir; Nazimova's diaries; Craig Noel and Abe Feder to author; Alexander Kirkland in *The Woman from Yalta.* Alfred Lunt on *Ghosts:* Morton Eustis, *Players At Work.* Ona Munson: Norman S. Rothschild to author; Gillian Freeman (on Nazimova's letters to Elsa Stoloff) to author; Munson's letters to Mercedes in the de Acosta collection, Rosenbach Library; Scott Eynan, *Ernst Lubitsch: Laughter in Paradise.* McKay Morris's party: Ellerbe's memoir. Lynn Fontanne's note: Nazimova archive. The "three separate factions": Vincent Price to author. Revival of *Ghosts:* Helen Beverley to author.

Chapter 13

Nazimova's mastectomy: Jo Hutchinson to author; Nazimova's diaries; Glesca's "Notes." Nazimova's life at the Garden of Allah: Robert Lewis and Nancy Reagan to author; Ellerbe's memoir; Nazimova's diaries; Nazimova's letters to Nina in the Library of Congress; Nazimova's letters to Mercedes in the de Acosta collection; letter to Eva Le Gallienne, courtesy of Helen Sheehy. Ned Sheldon's cable to Nazimova: Nazimova archive. Ned Sheldon and John Barrymore: Mercedes de Acosta, *Here Lies the Heart.* Opening night of *The Mother:* Robert La Guardia, *Monty.* Montgomery Clift's note: Nazimova archive. Nazimova's letters to Glesca on *Escape:* Nazimova archive. David O. Selznick and *Rebecca:* Rudy Behlmer, *Memo from David O. Selznick;* Nazimova's diaries. Scott Fitzgerald and Robert Benchley at the Garden of Allah: Sheilah Graham, *Beloved Infidel.* Dolores del Rio and Lili Damita in the pool: George Cukor to author. Sinatra and Rachmaninov: Glesca's "Notes." Nazimova and Orson Welles: Jo Hutchinson to author. James T. Farrell on Nazimova: letter to Glesca (July 19, 1945) in Nazimova archive. Fanny Brice's (undated) letter: Nazimova archive. Correspondence between Nazimova and Val Lewton: Nazimova archive. Henry Harvitt on Nazimova and Selznick: Harvitt's taped reminiscences. Ardel Wray on Nazimova: Joel Siegel, *Val Lewton.* Lewton's attitude toward Nazimova: De Witt Bodeen, "Nazimova," *Films in Review* (December 1947). *In Our Time:* Vincent Sherman and Nancy Coleman to author. Glesca and Emily Woodruff: Norman S. Rothschild to author. Emily and Hume Cronyn: Cronyn, *A Terrible Liar.* Nazimova's memorial service: John Beal to author; Glesca's "Notes."

BIBLIOGRAPHY

Acosta, Mercedes de. *Here Lies the Heart.* New York: Morrow, 1960.

Atkinson, Brooks. *Broadway.* New York: Macmillan, 1970.

Barnes, Djuna. *Interviews.* Edited by Alice Barry. Washington, D.C.: Sun & Moon, 1981.

Barney, Natalie. *In Memory of Dorothy Ierne Wilde.* Dijon, France: Darantière, 1951.

———. *Pensées d'une Amazone,* Paris: Emile Paul Frères, 1920.

Beckson, Karl. *London in the 1890s.* New York: Norton, 1992.

Behlmer, Rudy, editor. *Memo from David O. Selznick.* Hollywood: Samuel French, 1989.

Behrman, S. N. *People in a Diary.* Boston: Little, Brown, 1972.

Benedetti, Jean. *Stanislavsky.* London: Methuen, 1988.

———, editor. *The Moscow Art Theatre Letters.* London: Methuen, 1990.

Bentley, Eric. *The Playwright as Thinker.* New York: Reynal & Hitchcock, 1946.

Berlin, Normand. *Eugene O'Neill.* New York: Grove Press, 1982.

Braun, Edward. *The Theatre of Meyerhold.* London: Methuen, 1979.

Brownlow, Kevin. *The Parade's Gone By.* New York: Knopf, 1968.

Chauncey, George. *Gay New York.* New York: Basic Books, 1994.

Chekhov, Anton. *Letters.* Edited by Avrahm Yarmolinsky. New York: Viking, 1973.

Chekhov, Michael. *To the Director and Playwright.* Edited by Charles Leonard. New York: Limelight, 1984.

Clurman, Harold. *All People Are Famous.* New York: Harcourt Brace Jovanovich, 1974.

Courtney, Marguerite. *Laurette.* New York: Atheneum, 1968.

Crawford, Cheryl. *One Naked Individual.* New York: Bobbs Merrill, 1977.

Cronyn, Hume. *A Terrible Liar.* New York: Morrow, 1991.

Curtin, Kaier. *"We Can Always Call Them Bulgarians."* Boston: Alyson Publications, 1987.

Custine, Marquis de. *Empire of the Tsars.* New York: Doubleday, 1981.

Dardis, Tom. *Some Time in the Sun.* New York: Scribner's, 1976.

deMille, Agnes. *Dance to the Piper.* Boston: Little, Brown, 1952.

Devlin, Albert J., editor. *Conversations with Tennessee Williams.* Jackson: University of Mississippi Press, 1991.

Dubnow, Semyen. *History of the Jews in Russia and Poland.* New York: Jewish Publication Society of America, 1920.

Eustis, Morton. *Players At Work.* New York: Theatre Arts Books, 1937.

Eynan, Scott. *Ernst Lubitsch: Laughter in Paradise.* New York: Simon & Schuster, 1993.

Flanner, Janet. *Paris Was Yesterday: 1925–1939.* New York: Viking, 1972.

Florey, Robert. *Filmland.* Paris: Editions de Cinémagazine, 1923.

————. *Hollywood d'Hier et Aujourd'hui.* Paris: Editions Prisma, 1979.

Freud, Sigmund. "Three Essays on the Theory of Sexuality." *Journal of Nervous and Mental Diseases,* 1910.

Godowsky, Dagmar. *First Person Plural.* New York: Viking, 1958.

Goldman, Emma. *Living My Life.* New York: Dover, 1930.

Graham, Sheilah, and Gerold Frank. *Beloved Infidel.* New York: Bantam, 1959.

Hapgood, Hopkins. *A Victorian in the Modern World.* New York: Harcourt, Brace, 1939.

Harrison, Gilbert A. *The Enthusiast: A Life of Thornton Wilder.* New York: Fromm International, 1986.

Hopkins, Arthur. *To a Lonely Boy.* New York: Doubleday Doran, 1957.

Jerome, Jerome K. *My Life and Times.* New York: Harper, 1926.

Karlinsky, Simon. "Russia's Gay Literature and Culture." In *Hidden from History: Reclaiming the Gay & Lesbian Past,* edited by Martin Duberman, Martha Vicinus, and George Chauncey, Jr. New York: Meridian, 1990.

Kobal, John. *People Will Talk.* New York: Knopf, 1985.

La Guardia, Robert. *Monty.* New York: Arbor House, 1977.

Lambert, Gavin. *On Cukor.* New York: Putnam, 1972.

Langner, Lawrence. *The Magic Curtain.* New York: Dutton, 1951.

Lawrence, John. *A History of Russia.* New York: Meridian, 1957.

Le Gallienne, Eva. *At 33.* New York: Longmans Green, 1934.

Magarshack, David. *Stanislavsky.* London: Faber & Faber, 1950.

Marbury, Elisabeth. *My Crystal Ball.* New York: Boni & Liveright, 1925.

Marcosson, Isaac A., and Daniel Frohman. *Charles Frohman, Manager and Man.* New York: Harper & Bros., 1916.

Mellow, James R. *Charmed Circle.* Boston: Houghton Mifflin, 1974.

Miller, Patsy Ruth. *My Hollywood: When Both of Us Were Young.* New York: O'Raghailligh, 1988.

Moore, Colleen. *Silent Star.* New York: Doubleday, 1968.

Morris, Michael. *Madam Valentino.* New York: Abbeville, 1991.

Morse, Frank P. *Backstage with Henry Miller.* New York: Dutton, 1938.

Mosley, Leonard. *Zanuck.* Boston: Little, Brown, 1985.

Nemirovich-Danchenko, Vladimir. *My Life in the Russian Theatre.* New York: Little, Brown, 1936.

Peters, Margot. *The House of Barrymore.* New York: Knopf, 1990.

Rambova, Natacha. *Rudy: An Intimate Portrait of Rudolph Valentino.* London: Hutchinson, 1926.

Roberts, J. W. *Richard Boleslawski.* Ann Arbor, Mich.: UMI Research Press, 1981.

Rudnitsky, Konstantin. *Russian and Soviet Theatre 1905–1932.* New York: Harry N. Abrams, 1988.

Sayler, Oliver. *The Russian Theatre Under the Revolution.* New York: Little, Brown, 1925.

Secrest, Meryle. *Between Me and Life: A Biography of Romaine Brooks.* Garden City, N.Y.: Doubleday, 1974.

Sheaffer, Louis. *O'Neill: Son and Artist.* New York: Little, Brown, 1968.

Showalter, Elaine. *Sexual Anarchy.* New York: Viking, 1990.

Siegel, Joel. *Val Lewton: The Reality of Terror.* New York: Viking, 1984.

Simmons, Ernest J. *Chekhov.* New York: Atlantic Monthly/Little, Brown, 1962.

Slonim, Marc. *Russian Theatre from the Empire to the Soviets.* Cleveland: World Publishing, 1961.

Smith, Jane S. *Elsie de Wolfe.* New York: Atheneum, 1982.

Spears, Jack. "Nazimova." In *The Civil War on the Screen and Other Essays.* New York: A. S. Barnes, 1977.

Stanislavsky, Konstantin. *An Actor Prepares.* New York: Theatre Arts Books, 1936.

Sterne, Maurice. *Shadow and Light.* New York: Harcourt, Brace, 1965.

Toklas, Alice B. *What Is Remembered.* New York: Holt, Rinehart and Winston, 1963.

Troyat, Henri. *Chekhov.* New York: Dutton, 1986.

Weales, Gerald. *Clifford Odets: Playwright.* New York: Pegasus, 1971.

Wilson, Garff B. *300 Years of American Drama and Theatre.* Englewood Cliffs, N.J.: Prentice-Hall, 1973.

Woollcott, Alexander. *Minnie Maddern Fiske.* New York: Century, 1917.

Young, Stark. *Immortal Shadows.* New York: Octagon, 1973.

Yurka, Blanche. *Bohemian Girl.* Athens: Ohio University Press, 1970.

ACKNOWLEDGMENTS

To begin at the beginning: in 1991, my editor, Victoria A. Wilson, alerted me to the existence of the Nazimova archive in Columbus, Georgia, and suggested I pay it a visit with a view to writing Nazimova's biography. The material took, and I am equally grateful for her shrewd support during the years of researching and writing this book.

Many thanks also to the following, who agreed to be interviewed in person or by phone, or who wrote to me about Nazimova:

The late Stella Adler; John Beal; the late Rebecca Drucker Bernstien; Helen Beverley; the late Samson de Brier; Nancy Coleman; Hume Cronyn; Frances Dee; the late Harry Ellerbe; Abe Feder; Robert L. Green; Katharine Hepburn; Josephine Hutchinson; Phyllis Jenkins; Anne Kaufman-Schneider; Richard Lamparski; Robert Lewis; Lucy Olga Lewton; Norman and Peggy Lloyd; Burgess Meredith; the late Patsy Ruth Miller; Craig Noel; the late Vincent Price; Nancy Reagan; Ned Rorem; Norman S. Rothschild; the late May Sarton; Tonio Selwart; the late Irene Sharaff; Vincent Sherman; Lester Weinrott.

And to the following for their valuable help:

Matthew Bernstein, who provided information on Walter Wanger and Nazimova; Kevin Brownlow, who compiled an exceptionally useful list of *Photoplay* references to Nazimova and various silent-movie colleagues, including Capellani; Prudence Crowther, but for whom I would never have known about, and interviewed, Rebecca Drucker Bernstien; Patricia Conolly, ditto for Helen Beverley; Marie Hancock Ellerbe and Clayson Kyle, who arranged for me to read Harry Ellerbe's unpublished memoir; Gillian Freeman, for vital information about her relative Elsa Stoloff; Sam Gill of the Margaret Herrick Library of the Motion Picture Academy of Arts and Sciences, who unearthed several Nazimova references in the library's Special Collections; Hilary Knight, who provided music sheets of "Alla" and "The Red Lantern Song"; Richard May, who arranged a screening of the Turner Library print of *Stronger than Death;* Roddy McDowall, for his introduction to Nancy Reagan; Nancy Reagan, for making available Nazimova's letters to her mother, Edith Luckett; Joseph H. Savage, a major Nazimova buff, for many kindnesses including a video of *Camille;* John Seville, another major Nazimova buff, for sending me copies of his collection of clippings; Helen Sheehy, Eva Le Gallienne's biographer, for copies of Nazimova's letters to Eva, and for putting me in touch with Josephine Hutchinson; David Stenn, for putting me in touch with the late Patsy Ruth Miller; and Gore Vidal for information about Sam Zimbalist and Nazimova.

In Columbus, Georgia, Faye Woodruff was an indispensable guide to the Nazimova archive, and also wonderfully hospitable, as were Clayson Kyle and Norman S. Rothschild.

In Washington, D.C., at the Library of Congress, Alice Birney was another indispensable guide—to the Nazimova collection in the Manuscript Division; and in the Film Division, I am grateful to Rosemary C. Hanes, who arranged for me to view the trailers of *Eye for Eye* and *The Redeeming Sin,* and an out-take from *Madame Peacock.*

In Philadelphia, Elizabeth Fuller at the Rosenbach Library kindly allowed me to consult the Mercedes de Acosta papers.

In New York, the staff of the New York Public Library of the Performing Arts at Lincoln Center kindly granted access to its various Nazimova collections.

In London, at the British Film Institute, the late John Gillett (another indispensable) arranged a viewing of the National Film Archive print of *Putting the Hooray in Cabaret.*

INDEX

Page numbers in *italics* indicate illustrations.

ILLUSTRATION CREDITS

All illustrations not listed here are courtesy of the
Glesca Marshall Library of Theatre Arts.

A Note on the Type

This book was set in Adobe Garamond. Designed for the Adobe Corporation by Robert Slimbach, the fonts are based on types first cut by Claude Garamond (c. 1480–1561). Garamond was a pupil of Geoffroy Tory and is believed to have followed the Venetian models, although he introduced a number of important differences, and it is to him that we owe the letter we now know as "old style." He gave to his letters a certain elegance and feeling of movement that won their creator an immediate reputation and the patronage of Francis I of France.

Composed by North Market Street Graphics,
Lancaster, Pennsylvania

Designed by Anthea Lingeman